**MOBILITY** WITHOUT **MAYHEM**

# MOBILITY WITHOUT MAYHEM

## SAFETY, CARS, AND CITIZENSHIP

JEREMY PACKER

Duke University Press    Durham and London    2008

© 2008 Duke University Press

All rights reserved

Printed in the United States of America on acid-free paper ∞

Designed by Heather Hensley

Typeset in Minion Pro by Tseng Information Systems, Inc.

Library of Congress Cataloging-in-Publication Data appear
on the last printed page of this book.

# CONTENTS

## ACKNOWLEDGMENTS

It is fitting that the process of writing a book about mobility should have featured many journeys. And this has been true in literal and metaphorical ways. Many have shared in these journeys, some for lengthy periods of time, some giving direction when I've been lost; a few could be said to have sent me on the journey in the first place. To all of those whose paths I've crossed and shared, thank you, but the following deserve special consideration.

Before I started writing this book, two professors inspired me to head down this road. Deena Weinstein was an astounding teacher and my first intellectual mentor. She spent countless hours with me as a kid of eighteen discussing social theory and rock music, convincing me there was a way to combine intellectual rigor with personal interests. Through her, I met Michael Weinstein, whose seminar on Michel Foucault and political theory blew my mind and set a standard for me to shoot for. Their vigorous engagement with life still inspires me.

But this book really took off while I was at the University of Illinois surrounded by corn and soy bean fields that engulf Urbana-Champaign in a horizontal expanse that demands motorcycle flight. The mentorship I received and the friendships I built there continue to motivate. In particular, Lawrence Grossberg pushed me to think broadly about mobility and demanded that attention be paid to the political. James Hay was there throughout the process helping to nurture my initial ideas, bring them to fruition, and foster connections I didn't at first see. George Kamberelis pushed me to experiment methodologically and demanded that I not lose sight of the humanity of social actors. Cameron McCarthy provided unbounded encouragement and helped foster a vibrant community of scholars.

Four fellow students at Illinois deserve special thanks: Ted Bailey, Jack Bratich, Mary Coffey, and Craig Robertson. They continue to be a source of intellectual nourishment, and I truly could not have completed this project without their sustained help. Beyond reading early drafts of much of this work, it is the hours of dialogue and debate shared individually and collectively in classes, reading groups, coffee shops, and bars that were most influential and enjoyable. A number of other friends and colleagues have helped in differing and important ways. Thanks to Deborah Vander Ploeg for, among so many other things, helping me find my favorite motorcycle. Thank you to Lynn Fosbender for sharing many a drive in the Bavaria in Illinois, Pennsylvania, and points in between. I wish I could enumerate how each of the following helped me while I was at Illinois and since, but a general thanks will have to suffice. Thanks to Donovan Connelly, Melissa Deem, Greg Dimitriadis, Steve Gilbert, Ronald Greene, Deborah Hawhee, Christopher Kamrath, Samantha King, Tony Kirschner, Robert McCarthy, Robert McClain, Jennifer Mercicia, John Nerone, Michael Palm, Carry Rentschler, Jonothan Sterne, and Preston Wright.

I also want to thank all the people at Penn State who helped me with this book, but especially Chris Russill, who never let a vaguely conceived idea slip by unchallenged and who provided much-needed camaraderie. I benefited greatly from the collegiality, mentorship, and friendship of a number of colleagues at Penn State, but especially John Christman, Kevin Hagopian, Matt Jackson, Matt Jordan, Matt McAllister, and Mary Beth Oliver. Thanks also to Shannon Kahle, Nalova Westbrook, and Miranda Brady for their diligent research and assistance on this book. The exceptional resources and financial support provided by the College of Communications at Penn State were vital to the completion of this project.

Courtney Berger and Ken Wissoker at Duke University Press deserve thanks as they showed great patience and provided moral and intellectual support when it was needed. They also found two exceptional reviewers, who provided insight, located new areas for analysis, and kept me on track when I was going astray.

I would never have headed down this road without the support of my parents, Scott and Susan Packer, and my siblings, Chad and Cassandra. Though my mom has been known to shed a tear when she watches me hop on my motorcycle, it was my dad who gave me my first motorcycle ride and taught me the rules of the road. They provided extensive praise and showed so much pride over the years that it always made me feel like I was doing something worthwhile even if they kept asking when this process would be over and they could see the finished book. Here it is.

Last, I want to thank Sarah Sharma. She sustained me when I was losing steam and encouraged me when I needed it. She takes pride in my successes while giving insightful and demanding criticism. I am excited to start our future projects. But mostly, she makes me proud and happy to be part of her life.

## AUTO-MOBILE AMERICA

All you need to know about American society can be gleaned from an anthropology of its driving behavior. That behavior tells you much more than you could ever learn from its political ideas. Drive ten thousand miles across America and you will know more about the country than all the institutes of sociology and political science put together.

JEAN BAUDRILLARD, *AMERICA*[1]

Being a good driver requires the same qualities that are needed if you are to be a good citizen, a good neighbor, a good son and a good brother. That would mean that *learning to drive must be closely connected with learning to live.* That is exactly so, and accounts for the fact that you cannot teach people to be good drivers without teaching them the same kind of things that make them good citizens, good neighbors, good sons and good brothers. And, as a matter of fact, the converse is true: one very effective way of learning what it takes to live acceptably in the modern world is by discovering these things through learning to drive!

ALBERT WHITNEY, *MAN AND THE MOTORCAR*[2]

Jean Baudrillard and Albert Whitney agree that something profound can be learned from automotive driving. They imagine the automobile as a medium for understanding American society and as a motor for civic education. As an American pioneer in the field of traffic safety, Whitney imagined that driver education would come to be used to teach not only the skills of shifting and steering, but more profoundly how to "live acceptably in the modern world." Thus the automobile was more than a mechanical implement for the advancement of a technology driven modernity; it was also an educational tool fundamental to training good Americans. Automobile use teaches a very different lesson, according to the French social theorist Baudrillard. Its use is the key to understanding American society. As his fellow Frenchman Alexis de Tocqueville had done a century and a half before, Baudrillard used a trip across the United States as a means for investigating American culture and politics in contradistinction to those of Europe.[3] While the horse-drawn carriages and dirt roads of Tocqueville's travels fueled little direct reflection, Baudrillard's station wagon and the highway system he traveled provided the very objects of analysis through which he would come to understand America. Whereas Whitney and his hope that civility would spring forth from proper driver education have long been forgotten, Baudrillard is not alone in affording the automobile such eminence. Numerous historians and social critics have argued that the automobile has long served as the motor driving the contemporary American social system. In simple terms, all economic and social frameworks must to some degree answer to the desires of a population addicted to automobile use. Such organization of society has come to be called automobility.[4] But there are two versions of the automobile's history. On the pessimistic side, the automobile is seen to have torn asunder traditional forms of sociability and civic-mindedness as it fueled individualism, conspicuous consumption, suburban sprawl, environmental destruction, highway carnage, and even oil-related military expansion.[5] In a slightly more optimistic and equally popular version of events, the centrality of the automobile to American society is simply the outcome of a much older desire that is most famously characterized by Frederick Jackson Turner's Frontier Thesis.[6] Near ubiquitous automobile use is claimed to be the offspring of Americans' restlessness and their desire for freedom and wide open spaces, a desire that was conceived during exodus from England and birthed in a boundless continental frontier and that matured through the unifying creation of a national transportation and communication infrastructure, suffered a midlife crisis in a race to the moon, and survives in the quotidian commute.[7] For both stories, the automobile is a vivid means of making sense of American history and society. Surely there is some truth to both of these stories. Yet, it is Whitney's observation that I want to resurrect in order to begin a different history of automotive culture in the United States.

This book is largely founded upon the assumption that Baudrillard's insight is to a great degree correct: driving behavior does provide an object of analysis from which much about contemporary American culture can be gleaned. More precisely, I argue here that the best means for arriving at such an understanding is through an analysis of how driving behavior and the mobility it creates have been dually represented, on the one hand, as having great potential and, on the other, as a serious threat to social order. Unlike Baudrillard, I don't assume that "no one is capable of analyzing it [driving's relation to American society], least of all the American intellectuals shut away on their campuses, dramatically cut off from the fabulous concrete mythology developing all around them."[8] Rather, I suggest that one means of investigating fundamental aspects of American society is through an analysis of how driving has been understood by experts, imagined by citizens, regulated by traffic law, governed through education and propaganda, and represented in mass-mediated popular culture such as film, television, magazines, and newspapers. Whereas Baudrillard's approach called for an archeology of cultural objects—cars, highways, road signs, roadside architecture—the approach taken here provides more of a genealogy of the power/knowledge relationships that determined how to organize and regulate different populations' access to and use of automobility. This book tells a story about the political and cultural battles waged to determine how best to govern automobile-related mobility. Such an investigation asks a number of interrelated questions: Who was granted jurisdiction over determining what type of automotive conduct was correct? According to what forms of knowledge can such determinations be made? and How did these determinations invigorate or deform unequal relations of power? From such a vantage, a long-out-of-print drivers' education manual such as Whitney's is not merely a historical peculiarity, but a good place to start an investigation, as it was the very means by which new drivers were educated in their beliefs and actions. *Man and the Motorcar* understood as such was both an ideological and disciplinary tool for the governance of automobility. It was a "means for correct training."[9] As it turns out, this text also offers insight into how the rhetoric of exclusion began to work in ways that would ultimately lead to unfairly demonizing and stymieing the mobility of women, youth, and racial minorities throughout the automobile age. Before giving too much of the story away, I want to take a closer look at *Man and the Motorcar* as a point of entry into this history.

*Man and the Motorcar* was the most widely used traffic safety manual almost from its inception in 1936 and remained so into the 1960s. Other manuals, for example, *Drive and Live* and *Youth at the Wheel*, similarly written for youths and commissioned by the insurance industry, appeared in the late 1930s. The titles of such books point to the assumed audience for driver education (youth) and to the prevailing concern (self-preservation). Yet Whitney's manual stands out because of its long-standing success and unique, widely influential vision. In fact, it provides several useful starting points for investigating automobility as a form of learned behavior and as a vision of society. *Man and the Motorcar* in one or another of its six editions was used in over two-thirds of states driver education programs. Quite simply, it was instrumental in the education of millions of the first generation of formally trained automobile drivers in the United States. Second, it helped produce the significant shift in driver education's mode of address from mechanical training to civic engagement; a mode of address that increasingly circulated outside the classroom and beyond the orange cone–strewn training courses that proliferated after World War II. Most tellingly, fifty years prior to Baudrillard's observation regarding the automobile's centrality to the organization of society, Whitney formulated a vision of an auto-centric social order. The next thousand years were to be the "Automobile Millennium," an age organized by the automobile from which would sprout a "new race." A brief investigation of Whitney's imagined future race gives insight into how automobility has come to be understood and governed.

*Man and the Motorcar* in combination with the driver education programs in which it was used made citizenship training its ultimate goal. Instead of merely addressing the mechanics of operating an automobile, Whitney emphasized that learning to drive was a means of producing a new safety-conscious society built around his conception of good citizenship. Driver education was an instrument of citizenship training, and by extension proper driving was a sign of being a good citizen. Driving was imagined as a centrifugal force that if properly governed would in its wake reorganize society and citizen alike. Whitney's vision of extending citizenship onto the road opened up a new space for the "development of good attitudes—courtesy, sportsmanship, reliability, responsibility, and those other personal characteristics that make for good citizenship."[10] His definition of citizenship is firmly situated within an American tradition of liberal government. His use of the term in the context of automobiles suggests at least three interrelated modes of liberal citizenship. The first is quite simply that of the economic citizen. Americans' investment in purchasing, insuring, modifying, maintaining, and fueling automobiles was and continues to be second only to the costs of owning or renting a home. Further, Whitney explains, "the automobile has provided more work for more persons than any other single element of American life."[11] Foreshadowing General Motors president Charlie Wilson's infamous dictum "What's good for the country is good for GM, and vice versa," Whitney assumes that the massiveness of economic force exerted by automobility makes it a force for good.[12] Beyond the economic realms of production and consumption, being a good citizen means to be a self-empowered mobile citizen. One aspect of taking part in "American civilization" (as Whitney put it) is to actualize one's potential for mobility. And such mobility "multiplied our power and expanded our horizons. It has given us the freedom to live anywhere. . . . We are a car traveling people—truly 'A Nation on Wheels.'" Modern forms of government as well as industrial and postindustrial economies have become increasingly dependent upon such individualized "power" and "freedom" facilitated by automobility. These capacities have become in the United States both opportunity and obligation. The third means of citizenship implied by Whitney, and reiterated often throughout his book, is that being safe is consonant with being a good citizen. Driving was thus one form of conduct through which one could learn to become a type of individual I will call the safe subject or safe citizen. In fact, according to Whitney the most prominent attribute of this "new race" would be its devotion to safety. A good citizen was to be a safe citizen.

Whitney targeted for change six social and technological elements necessary to better orchestrate and guarantee a safe future for automobility: automobiles, highways, traffic control, speed, motorists, and the public. The future automobile could have "greater speed, but we undoubtedly already have all the speed we should be allowed to use."[13] In fact, "the human organism, both physically and psychologically, is not built for high speeds."[14] Instead, the future automobile should be devoted to "increased safety, comfort, and dependability."[15] After all, "high speeds are for the race track, not for the highway."[16] As to these highways, they will "provide the most spectacular developments in the automobile age of the future."[17] Beyond eliminating collisions, congestion, parking, and pedestrian problems, Whitney's Pan-American highway system will "help break down sectional and national differences"[18] throughout North, Central, and South America. The control of traffic on these roads "will be wise, adequate, and uniform."[19] Surveillance will be greatly increased by future breakthroughs in "radio and electronics and radar."[20] "Punishment will be swift," and offenders will be dealt "with a severity befitting the serious nature of the offense."[21] These are not the most prominent element, however, as "it is the driver who will be in the center of the picture."[22] The future driver will be changed: "He will be a far different creature from the driver of today; he will belong to a new race."[23] This race will have increased mobility and a resultant increased responsibility. Responsibility to what? To safety, for "it is to him that we shall look in making our traffic safe."[24] This new race was to be built on a set of exclusions: "Not only will people with certain physical incapacities not be allowed to drive, but also persons who lack judgment and a social conscience. . . . Another class of drivers will be weeded out, the accident prone . . . [and those] who prove to be incapable of re-education."[25] Ultimately, it is the public's role to demand such a future. Whitney claims such a public "will not be the tolerant, easy-going public of today. . . . It will be a public which sees that the automobile must and can be controlled . . . [to] bring the automobile into its proper place in the world." Calling for an intolerant public to mandate the creation of a new race may have seemed more tolerable in 1936 when eugenics was still widely accepted in the United States and abroad. Such a mandate has at its core a racial logic of exclusion, according to which the impurities of those who don't share the unifying and identifying trait, in this instance a devotion to safety, mark one as an outsider and a threat. For Whitney, the future of American society depended upon weeding out or reprograming the unsafe. Those who remained would constitute a new race; a society of safe subjects.

What evolutionary techniques were going to accomplish this racial metamorphosis? Nothing short of a five-pronged attack, with the bull's-eye painted on the chest of the American driver. How would the automobile, the highway, traffic control, motorists—in particular, their desire for speed—and the public be reoriented, redirected, reprogramed, and reeducated in order to realize the goal of safe automobility? Whitney's answers in many ways proved prescient, as the elements he cited each became targets of much social and governmental concern. Yet such concern did not gain much momentum until after World War II, and it shortly thereafter picked up speed under President Dwight Eisenhower's guidance, as construction of the National Highway System was begun. Coinciding with this oft-gloried program, the all-but-forgotten Crusade for Traffic Safety was initiated. This crusade outlined a strategy for changing public opinion through the power of the mass media, just as they had been used to help fight the recently won war. Although numerous books and documentaries have been devoted to the development of the highway system as well as to the stylistic and technological advances, safety oriented and otherwise, of the automobile, virtually no history exists regarding the American driver or the driving public. One feature of the chapters to follow is a broad cultural history that begins to rectify this omission. Whereas the technological advancement in highways, police surveillance, and automobiles is one means of explaining how the battle for automotive safety has been fought, an understanding of the cultural front lines demands an analysis of what has been disseminated in classrooms, on television, in movie theaters and at the drive-in, on the pages of newspapers, magazines, and novels, in the halls of Congress, and through the airwaves transmitting to car, home, and citizens band (CB) radios. More important, an examination of the cultural and social aspects of this battle proves that accident victims have not been the only casualties. Disenfranchised groups have suffered extensive scrutiny and surveillance, and their mobility has been seriously curtailed by safety-guided legislation and police intervention. Whitney's language of racial exclusion has proven to be more than mere metaphor.

The chapters that follow map some of the key transformations that occurred from about 1946, the year of President Harry Truman's first Highway Safety Conference, to 2005, a year in which the automobile was no longer imagined merely as a safety threat but was described by the Department of Homeland Security (DHS) as a potential threat to national security. The period discussed amounts to little more than the initial 5 percent of Whitney's imagined "Automobile Millennium." Yet it was a period that saw the unfolding of many tactics for governing mobility; some as noted by Whitney have been carried out by police enforcement and through technological means. But the element under greatest scrutiny and surveillance is what could be called the disruptive driver, Whitney's "accident prone."[26] The police, safety advocates, insurance companies, government institutions such as the National Highway Traffic Safety Administration, social scientists, and the automobile industry have all studied the hardest-to-control element in the safe-driving equation, the unruly human element. This ever-changing figure has been represented in film, television, the news, popular periodicals, and government campaigns as a continuous threat to the public and as a sign of social disintegration. The purity of Whitney's safety-conscious "new race" was assailed by the infectious spread of roughneck motorcyclists, hot-rodders, hitchhikers, independent truckers, 1950s housewives, road-ragers, and those who drive while black (DWB). Even under the onslaught of the media and educational campaigns I describe, the public outcry continually fell short of what safety advocates hoped for as one problematic population was replaced by the next. There seems to have been an unending supply of newly dangerous motorists.

According to Whitney, the public generally and individual citizens specifically had to desire safety and see safe driving as a viable and necessary goal. Without such an investment, the engineering and production of safer roads and cars would fail to produce valuable reductions in fatalities. You can build cars with seat belts, but drivers must buckle them. You can lower the speed limit, but only drivers can ease off the accelerator pedal. Even so, for Whitney, overly intrusive traffic control was not the ultimate solution. *Man and the Motorcar* warned that, in the frantic attempt to reduce "death and injury on the highway, any one of dozens of drastic measures may be put into effect that will kill the pleasure and curb the natural liberty of citizens who want to move in motor cars. Under such conditions, the use of automobiles will manifestly decline."[27] Herein lay the real problem facing traffic safety advocates. Driving has been considered and remains synonymous with being a freedom-loving American. The maintenance of American-flavored liberty coupled with the production of an apparatus that sustains increased mobility for American drivers often comes into conflict with the goal of reducing traffic fatalities. There are, then, two intersecting impulses that might often seem in conflict with one another, but each is necessary to the other's current magnitude: safety and automobility. I analyze the discourses that support, invigorate, and legitimate Americans' investments in both safety and automobility. Specifically, I look closely at a number of safety crises that are organized around the seemingly contentious line that separates the safe from the unsafe. It is argued that these crises do not merely consider safe and risky driving behavior. Rather, safe and risky come to be characterized through group or demographic identity. In other words, it is not simply that specific drivers are viewed as unsafe, but rather whole demographic categories, historically disenfranchised, have been described by experts and represented in the mass media as hopelessly dangerous. In these instances claims regarding the unsafe driving or attitudes of a group (women, youth, or African Americans) and the unsafe form of automobility they employ (overstressed commuting, motorcycling, pimping, or hitchhiking) have largely been used to legitimate the monitoring, regulating, and minimizing of access to and use of the automobility system. Furthermore, identifying which activities and what populations are deemed too dangerous and worthy of governmental attention is largely a political, not just a scientific, matter, as the research of the cultural anthropologist Mary Douglas has made evident.[28] This is to say that an explanation of what types of behavior and what types of individuals are considered to be unacceptably risky can be understood only through culturally specific analysis. Rather than beginning with the question of why some groups are riskier than others, I want to begin with the question, Under what circumstances and according to what logics did certain forms of mobile behavior and certain forms of group identity come to be understood as too risky? And in a related sense, How did risky behavior come to be seen as both stupid and immoral? The question, then, is not, *How risky is* motorcycling or hitchhiking? but *Why* have these forms of mobility come to be thought of in terms of risk and safey *at certain moments*, while at other times they have been largely understood in economic or phenomenological terms? I will show that looking merely to the statistical proof will not adequately answer such questions. There has been no necessary correspondence between the statistically determined relative risk of hitchhiking and motorcycle riding and the extent of media coverage, the level of social concern, and the degree of governmental response these activities have received. Rather, it is only through an examination of the cultural, economic, and political context in which such responses arose that one can reach an understanding of why, for instance, there was great concern regarding the safety of hitchhiking in the early 1970s but not during the mid-1960s.

The study of perceived risk and responses to it is fraught with difficulties and has been the object of extensive scientific research and social analysis.

The most prolific and politically dominant approach is that of statistical or insurantial risk analysis. This approach to risk attempts to determine the relative likelihood and the resultant costs of an undesirable outcome occurring in the social, technological, or economic realm. For instance, risk analysis in this form would attempt to determine the likelihood that a Caucasian male motorcycle rider who is aged twenty-two, lives in a state without a helmet law, has accrued three speeding tickets in the past two years, and rides a 2004 Kawasaki Ninja ZX-6R with 125 horsepower will inflict greater economic damage than the cost of their annual insurance premiums. There are, of course, far more variables, economic factors, and state-determined rules and regulations that enter into such equations. But the general premise remains. Such analysis attempts to establish a reliable means for the economic management of risk. Risk analysis of this sort at the level of an individual's insurance and that of the broader social and economic costs of, say, motorcycle use dominates how risk is treated and understood by economics, engineering, and social science. It is a realm of statistical production that has come increasingly to be used to make decisions in every realm of social and economic behavior. Ulrich Beck, in his now-famous book *Risk Society*, argued that the life-world of citizens of a newly forming modernity has come to be organized and regulated according to risk analysis and risk dispersion.[29] The strength of Beck's argument and the far-reaching effects it has had in the academy and upon environmental politics, particularly in Germany, cannot be understated. Beck's work makes apparent not only that decisions have been increasingly made according to such analysis, but more generally that on a global scale such risks, particularly those of an environmental nature, have the potential to affect all populations regardless of class or geography. Furthermore, risk can no longer be assessed, for example, in the fashion that the Ford Motor Company could determine the financial and human costs of the Pinto design flaw. Yet one of his foundational claims regarding risk has come under scrutiny and has been placed in opposition to the more cultural perspective of Douglas, which has to do with the empirical definability of risk.[30] To what degree is risk a culturally constructed means of separating the desirable from the undesirable, whether people, activities, or cultural objects? and to what degree is it a measurable empirical fact of the world? Beck discusses the role of media and the legal structure in constructing risks, while simultaneously claiming that risks exist which not even science can make known. In this sense, risk is neither wholly physically "out there" nor fully produced "in culture." Risk would seem to both pre-exist and escape human perception and has therefore been misunderstood by science, misrepresented by the media, and misapplied by the law. From Beck's perspective, automobile risk would involve a set of concerns that extend beyond traffic fatalities. It would take into account any number of environmental and social risks created by and managed through automobility. Yet it would be not only the possible and established consequences per se, but also "those practices and methods by which the future consequences of individual and institutional decisions are controlled in the present."[31] Such an approach would indeed be fruitful to a set of questions guided by the ways "real" risks do indeed escape simplistic accounts of technologically "manu-factured risks"[32] and how such consequences are managed. My concern here is guided more by the cultural constructionist approach exemplified by Douglas's work. Such an approach investigates the cultural production of risk and its use as a tool in political struggles. It is not only a political struggle over risks and the unequal distribution of their effects as Beck suggests, but more generally it explores how risk, as a rhetorical device, one might say, is used in other political struggles. In this case, struggles over mobility. From such a perspective, automotive safety can be understood as a set of contested procedures and related forms of conduct that are used to govern various populations' automobility. From the perspective of risk aversion, it may indeed be true that outlawing hitchhiking will minimize certain harmful events. When hitchhiking is instead viewed from the perspective of those who depended upon it for their mobility and used it to maintain radical youth solidarity, the use of safety as the rationality for outlawing hitchhiking starts to appear as an attempt to deny these youth their rights of freedom of movement and assembly. One approach might ask how risk has been unfairly dispersed throughout society or how the unforeseen and unseeable risks produced by automobility affect everyone, while the other approach would ask how safety, as a mechanism of governance, has been unfairly dispersed throughout society according to various logics of difference and exclusion. A cultural examination of risk, however, is only one aspect of how automobility will be treated in this book.

A body of work is developing in what some are calling mobility studies. I turn again to Baudrillard, who suggested that, in order to gain insight into

American society, we look more closely not just to the historical significance of the automobile or toward a "sociology or psychology of the car," but also to driving, the highway, billboards, and the rules of the road.[33] In other words, he asked that car culture and its system of signs be taken seriously. And to make its importance clear (as indicated in the epigraph to this introduction), he sideswiped the fields of sociology and political science, in part because they have been remiss in their analysis of the centrality of driving, which, as he says, "creates a new experience of space and, at the same time, a new experience of the whole social system."[34] The British sociologist John Urry is at least partially in agreement. He suggests that it must be seen as a profound failure of sociology that it has yet to adequately account for what he and others are now calling the automobility system. Urry argues that "in general . . . sociology has regarded cars as a neutral technology, permitting social patterns of life that would have more or less occurred anyway. Sociology has ignored the key significance of automobility, which reconfigures civil society, involving distinct ways of dwelling, travelling and socializing in, and through, an automobilised time-space. Civil societies of the west are societies of automobility."[35] Urry further explains that automobility must necessarily be understood as a global system that creates and sustains international dependencies forged by increased automobile use, manufacture, and trade. In the future these interdependencies will grow stronger owing to an expansion of automobility into countries not previously under the automobile's sway.[36] Urry's explanation brings to light sociology's oversight and automobility's expanse, while for Baudrillard it took an outsider's perspective and experience of driving to recognize how central it was to the organization of American culture and society alike. Accordingly, Americans' relationship to the automobile is revealing of an entire worldview. Yet the specific relationships that do exist are not fixed in stone and in fact have been debated and struggled over since the advent of the automobile. In other words, how the automobile has come to be viewed, how it was integrated into and determinative of social relations of power, and what means have been used to understand the role of the automobile have been fought over by several interested parties. Government officials, automobile manufacturers, special interest groups, the insurance industry, social scientists, engineers, and media organizations have struggled with how best to organize and control attitudes and conduct related to the automobile.

In fact it is through these struggles, I argue, that one can best understand the importance of automobility as it exists in America. This route leads to the question of how automobile use has been treated as a problem to be overcome through various governmental initiatives and citizen-led campaigns for driving reform. It is assumed that automobile use and the role it has played in shaping twentieth-century America are of profound importance. But rather than attempting to analyze these social changes and driving behaviors directly, I examine how various automobile-related behaviors have been regarded and represented as dangerous to self and society. This is to suggest that the automobile and the mobility it affords come to organize society in large part according to how they are perceived as disruptions to an idealized social order. From such a perspective, a history of the disruptions said to arise from automobility gives insight into how social order is maintained and reproduced very often according to structures of dominance. Thus an increasingly mobile population is perceived as a set of risks and threats. The means used to manage and control these disruptions tell us much about both the social order and the struggles against it. More specifically, a number of safety scares regarding automobility that feature such fearsome figures as women drivers, hot-rodding teens, homicidal hitchhikers, outlaw motorcyclists, wildcat truck drivers, and even overstressed soccer moms point out not simply the measurable risk each of these figures manifested, but also how their mobility threatened social order. Groups who have been made into an object of scrutiny often find strength and unification through the very struggle they have been forced to take part in. For instance, motorcyclists have produced their own experts, discourse, and policy apparatus in order to fight what they consider overrestrictive safety measures and the unmerited stereotyping seen to be at the root of social ire. As such, a study of how automobility is governed involves taking into account a vast array of forces, cultural, governmental, and economic.

In an earlier work I described the productive tension between safety and automobility. Most generally safety functions "to serve the modern technological monster" that is automobile transport. In this way traffic safety "is a means to an end, not an end in itself." It functions in several ways "to avoid the loss of production" and ensure "the maintenance of efficiency." Safety is "most generally any technique used in the disposition of things and wo/men that avoids loss."[37] Thus safety is not opposed to automobility but works in conjunction with it. Traffic safety is functionally necessary for the very existence of automobility in that it ensures economic profitability and, for the most part, social acceptance. Jorg Beckmann makes a similar argument when he states that "'providing safety' and 'increasing mobility' are seemingly becoming synonymous, rather than being contradictory."[38] Beckmann further argues that the reason the accident is acceptable to automobile drivers is that it is denied. "The risks of driving are denied." he writes, "and the illusion of safety is reconstructed by an accident investigation that aims at preventing the recurrence of the crash. Accident-workers cleanse the road, repair the car, heal the victims and lock up irresponsible drivers—suggesting that afterwards driving has become safe."[39] Beckmann makes this argument on the basis of a particular explanation of an oft-cited claim by Paul Virilio, self-professed "art critic of technology":

> Every time a technology is invented, take shipping for instance, an accident is invented together with it, in this case, the shipwreck, which is exactly contemporaneous with the invention of the ship. The invention of the railway meant, perforce, the invention of the railway disaster. The invention of the aeroplane brought the air crash in its wake. Now, the three I have just mentioned are specific and localized accidents. The *Titanic* sank at a given location. A train de-rails at another location and a plane crashes, again, somewhere else. This is a fundamental point, because people tend to focus on the vehicle, the invention itself, but not on the accident, which is its consequence. As an art critic of technology, I always try to emphasize both the invention and the accident. But the occurrence of the accident is being denied.[40]

What both Beckman and Virilio want to point out is that in order for any technology to flourish users must not be so fearful of impending accidents that they choose not to use the technology. If the accident loomed too large, the argument goes, the specific technology or the system it is a part of would be abandoned, and this is quite obviously so in the case of the automobile. However, the question I would like to answer starts from a slightly different premise. How are the threat of future accidents and the display of accidents past used to legitimate and carry out educational programs to alter driving behavior? From this perspective, I will look not to where representations of the accident have been lacking, but rather to where the accident has been made present to invigorate safety campaigns. I argue that in the United States the accident has been integrated into the automobility system through driver education programs, popular culture fascination, urban legend, and public service campaigns. In particular, driver's education has been littered with the movie images of highway carnage. Some of the most widely circulated and gruesome films produced during the 1950s, 1960s, and 1970s featured frame after frame of decapitated heads, mutilated bodies, and blood-drenched roads. Well before outrage and social concern were generated by slasher films, blood and gore were used for pedagogical purposes and by extension to create, not destroy, civility. The nearly universally used film series by the Highway Safety Foundation, featuring such titles as *Signal 30* (police code for a traffic fatality), *Wheels of Tragedy*, and *Mechanized Death*,[41] was considered the backbone of the national driver education classes that were a mainstay in high school classrooms. In a perverse way, the accident is the very means by which "mobility without mayhem" comes into being. Fear of the accident is the driving force used to legitimate the majority of automotive safety campaigns. At least one entire book has been devoted to depicting Americans' obsession with the car crash, but the spectacular catastrophe didn't begin with the automobile.[42] The train crash was prominently featured on the front pages of newspapers in the nineteenth century in the United States. The prominence of such news stories and the inefficiencies created by train accidents led to the integration of the telegraph into the train system as a means of making it safer via remote tracking and coupling.[43] The *Titanic*, the *Hindenberg*, the 9/11 airplanes crashing into the Twin Towers are all images through fictionalized and more immediate accounts which have been etched into historical memory. The spectacular accident, whether a mistake or purposive, has continually been used to legitimate the safety apparatus and, post-9/11, the security apparatus.[44] These images are used over and over again to verify, legitimate, and provide evidence for analysis as a means of reiterating the importance of safety. To say they are ignored is to argue *not* that they are completely ignored, but rather that *not enough* attention is paid to them and the resultant carnage they produce. It is, in short, to argue that greater attention must be paid to the probability (or certainty) of the accident.

In a related way Urry's description of the criminal side effects created by the automobile help make sense of how automobility has become central to social order and criminality. He states that the automobile "generates massive amounts of crime (theft, speeding, drunk driving, dangerous driving) and disproportionately preoccupies each country's criminal justice system."[45] Taken a bit further, these crimes exist only insofar as traffic safety and risk analysis are themselves a priori to the very system. In simple terms, speeding, drunk driving, and dangerous driving are *made* criminal by the system. They are not criminal activities outside the system. Furthermore, the relative criminality of each of these is wholly contingent. A quick cross-cultural or historical analysis makes this eminently clear. For instance, the speed limit has been lowered and raised at different times and in different states and nations numerous times over the past century. Most important, the institutions which criminalize such actions, namely, the legislative, judicial, and policing apparatuses, have been responsive to the logics of safety and risk analysis in the United States, but only for the most part when economic and cultural capital propel such concern. More generally, a shift has occurred in how criminality itself is understood and governed. Negligently or even purposefully causing someone harm can fairly easily be recognized as socially unacceptable and legitimately punishable. But, for instance, speeding does not necessarily cause harm. It may be imagined that it could or will under certain circumstances cause harm, but unto itself it does not. Rather than criminalizing actions based on their effects, automobile conduct is largely criminalized according to the possibility that it may cause harm. Potentiality is made criminal. If one takes the most vilified form of automotive criminality, drunk driving, as the litmus test, it becomes apparent that risk analysis can be used with great impunity to criminalize some potential dangers while largely ignoring others. Driving with alcohol content in one's blood (BAC) may very well increase the likelihood of one's causing an accident, but it does not in and of itself cause harm, and it does not do so equally in all cases. It is entirely possible that driver *A* with a BAC of .10 percent can drive far better than driver *B* with a BAC of 0 percent.[46] However, such factors are nearly impossible to account for. If statistical evidence were the determining factor used to inform which sorts of automotive conduct were made criminal, talking on a cell phone while driving would be equally or more extensively criminalized than drunk driving.[47] Yet, as of 2007 only five states have outlawed such behavior. I use this example not to call for greater legislative and police action in stamping out driving while cell phoning. Rather, I want to point to the degree to which two equally dangerous forms of conduct are treated in vastly different ways. There are extensive cultural, economic, and political reasons for this difference. Such differences exist for the criminalization of numerous other forms of driving conduct as well, and it takes a careful consideration of their historical specificity to make sense of current concerns regarding automotive safety.

Chapter 1 examines how the concern over traffic safety in the 1950s became a nationwide effort unified in part through Eisenhower's Crusade for Traffic Safety. Drawing upon the successes of the war effort, the crusade attempted to alter public opinion through a massive media campaign aimed at altering personal conduct in the name of the national good. This period also saw the advent of the two-car family that coincided with a growth in suburbanization and expanding consumer wealth. Two dangerous figures came to define the terms of automotive safety during the period, the woman driver and the hot-rodding youth. Both figures expanded the concerns of domesticity beyond the home to include the automobile as a domestic showcase and a vehicle for successful parenting. Women's magazines are surveyed as a primary means of investigating how the automobile was presented as a problem for women to overcome and as a technology necessary to her increasingly mobile life. Furthermore, General Motors (GM) and Ford produced a series of advertising campaigns aimed at inducing desire to be a two-car family and to glamorize a modern domestic mobile lifestyle.

Women's magazines also presented a world in which parenting and marital success were closely interlinked with the dangers of driving. Women were told that their actions inside the home, as enabling wives and diligent mothers, had repercussions on the driving of their spouses and children and by extension the driving public. Sending angry spouses and undisciplined children onto the highways could lead to disaster. Furthermore, special attention needed to be paid to the driving habits of the boys their daughters were dating, and their own sons needed to be saved from the deadly allure of hot-rodding. I analyze numerous B films that warned youth of the dangers of hot-rodding and also some popular adolescent fiction devoted to the same theme. Driver education during the time was widely expanded, and in at least one instance it began in kindergarten. GM produced a film narrated by Jimmy Stewart that publicized this pioneering educational program. The special attention paid to youth and women in the 1950s turns out to be not particularly unique. These two figures and the danger their auto-mobility poses to themselves and others are running themes in most of the chapters that follow. What starts to become readily apparent is that whether uniformly guided or not, the mass mediation of concerns about automotive safety ran across most every media form and, as in most good stories, there tend to be villains and victims.

Women and youth also star in chapter 2, which analyzes the changing dis-course and legislation regarding hitchhiking. While by the late 1970s concern over hitchhiking had largely disappeared, seemingly along with the practice itself, prior to the early 1970s there was widespread acceptance of the prac-tice even though it had been periodically vilified. In this chapter I identify who was responsible for the vilification (primarily automobile insurance companies, but also local police forces, the Parent-Teacher Association, and even the FBI), what media forms conveyed the vilification (film, magazines, newspapers, and popular novels), and what may have been at stake politi-cally. I argue that the terminal campaign against hitchhiking was primarily a reaction against the radical youth movement (in both senses of the term) of the late 1960s and early 1970s. Hitchhiking, as an economic necessity for these and other youth, formed a fundamental part of the ethic of radical youth and functioned as a means for the mobility necessary to activate and maintain mobile community building and political activism. Whereas I ar-gue this was the key political target of antihitchhiking campaigns, it was through the special danger it was said to pose to women and "naïve chil-dren" that hitchhiking was most widely scandalized. Beginning in the 1920s, hitchhiking was sexualized through the dual figures of woman as dangerous temptress or innocent victim. These two possibilities organized women's role in the hitchhiking discourse and explained the danger it posed in general. Hitchhiking served as a metaphor for the freedom of flappers in the 1920s and hippies in the 1960s, the seductive danger of the femme fatale, and the endangered sexuality of trusting young women said to be "asking for it." Thus the freedom provided by hitchhiking was dulled by the danger it posed. Women's sexuality was either under threat or threatening.

This duality of possibilities also carried over into the more general dis-cussions of hitchhiking. Was hitchhiking an economic necessity for some that obligated the more fortunate to lend a Samaritan-like helping hand? Or was it a means for the criminal element to take advantage of unsuspecting and overly trusting motorists? Did hitchhiking lead to Karmic insight à la Kerouac? Or was it a runaway's route to a truly dead end? From the 1930s through the 1970s hitchhiking featured prominently in popular media, which provided some lasting images. In the 1930s and 1940s it was often considered a civic duty to help out those in need of a ride, whether they were job searching, Depression-era migrants, pennant-waving college boys, or military personnel on leave. Following World War II the hitchhiker began to appear as a more ominous figure. In films such as *The Hitch-Hiker*, *Detour*, and *The Devil Thumbs a Ride* hitchhikers appear as cold-blooded murderers. Magazines began running story after story telling of the danger of picking up hitchhikers. The Automobile Association of America (AAA), the largest automotive insurer of the time, started an extensive antihitchhiking campaign. The hitchhiker began to fall out of favor in popular media, and the practice of hitchhiking wouldn't appear as a positive practice until it began to appear as part of the youth movement of the late 1960s. It is glorified for a short time, though its detractors remain, and it starts to be described as a mass movement of sorts. Yet massive police crackdowns across the country, extensive antihitchhiking legislation, and a number of national news scares regarding the rape and murders of young female hitchhikers seem to have put an end to its widespread acceptance. The chapter ends with a discussion of the rise of ride-sharing programs that overlap the demise of hitchhiking. The analysis focuses on how the economic imperatives of middle-class commuters are sanctioned, regularized, and governmentally funded, while the economic and cultural imperatives of radical youth were dismissed and vilified.

Chapter 3 examines how the motorcycle has discursively functioned as a threat to social order and as the dangerous other to the relative safety of the automobile. The motorcycle for some time was generally viewed in terms of its economic viability, not in terms of the danger it posed to self or society. In the 1950s this changed in a hurry largely because of who were seen to be the new motorcycle riders. When *Life* magazine ran a photo of a leather-clad motorcyclist allegedly in the midst of causing a riot in the peaceful town of Hollister, California, in July 1947 the image of the roughneck motorcycle gang achieved national renown. In 1951 this incident was turned into an account in *Harper's* magazine that led in 1953 to the making of the film *The Wild Ones*, in which Marlon Brando rides triumphantly into town on his Triumph while his fellow gang members raised hell on their Harleys. This filmic "riot" further ensconced the biker among the gallery of social undesirables and malcontents. While the outlaw motorcycle gang received growing media attention beginning around 1965, thanks in part to the best-selling popularity of Hunter S. Thompson's *Hell's Angels*, young, middle-class motorcyclists were receiving attention and concern as they bought up inex-pensive Japanese motorcycles. They weren't seen to be a threat to society; rather, their motorcycles were seen as a threat to their health. This differen-tial focus on the danger of the motorcycle continues, though in large part owing to recent campaigns for respectability. The motorcyclist on a Harley is said to be more often than not a law-abiding, middle-class professional devoted to riding his bike for social causes rather than to terrorize.

More broadly, this chapter details how motorcyclists and motorcycling work in discursive opposition to the automobile to validate acceptable levels of risk. Furthermore, motorcycling provides another example of how *who* is involved largely determines *how* risk and safety manifest themselves. There was no concern over the danger posed to roughneck motorcyclists but great alarm once middle-class youth started riding. The chapter also investigates how subjugated populations create solidarity through externally and inter-nally imposed assumptions regarding group affiliation and identity. Beyond examining an array of popular media representations of motorcyclists, the chapter pays special attention to motorcyclists' own descriptions of their relation to risk and safety through an analysis of motorcycle magazines and interviews with motorcyclists. How safety and freedom are interwoven into the primarily phenomenologically framed discourse of motorcyclists pro-vides a counterargument to the prejudiced instrumentalist logic that has structured mainstream discussions about the lack of desirability and even stupidity of riding a motorcycle.

Chapter 4 takes up another iconic figure of the road, the trucker. While the hitchhiker and motorcyclists may have been widely feared, the trucker has most often been represented as a "good buddy," particularly during the 1970s and early 1980s, when a short-lived genre of trucker films was widely popular. The rise of the trucker to iconic status was facilitated and accom-panied by the spread of CB radio. CB radio quickly rose from the relative obscurity of commercial and governmental use for the organization of fleet vehicles to the fastest growing communications technology since television.

By the mid-1970s a CB citizenry was said to be forming, one that, it was claimed, would take back the democratic reins of communications that had been usurped by corporate media conglomerates. The more immediate struggle over which CB was being put to use was the fifty-five-mile-per-hour speed limit imposed to save fuel during the oil crisis of 1973 that was brought on by the Organization of Petroleum Exporting Countries (OPEC). Independent truckers were hard-pressed to deal with the speed limit, which, when coupled with increased fuel costs and fuel rationing, led to economic insolvency.

Truckers responded in two ways, both facilitated by CB. First, owing to the rapid dispersal of information and the wide-flung organization allowed by CB, they were able to quickly organize wildcat strikes across the nation. The strikes created massive traffic jams at key arterial points in the highway system that so slowed the flow of goods that truckers were given the ear of President Richard Nixon to argue their case for economic relief. Second, CB allowed for countersurveillance practices used to monitor the whereabouts of the police so as to negate their ability to enforce the speed limit. This use of CB was not taken up only by truckers: automobile drivers, too, bought CB units and took part in the countersurveillance practices, and they did so to such a degree that the Federal Communications Commission (FCC) held hearings in which new means of regulating the illegal use of CB were called for. Popular culture representations of this battle between police and CB users first gained renown with C. W. McCall's number one crossover song "Convoy," which would later be translated into a film by Sam Peckinpah. Other movies such as the *Smokey and the Bandit* series and television shows like the *Dukes of Hazzard* and *B.J. and the Bear* glorified the everyman struggle against overzealous, corrupt police. Citizens' CB use was also being organized by the police into mobile neighborhood watch programs. Governmental debate and popular representations were thus guided by two inter-related questions: How would the surveillance capabilities of CB be applied? and to what ends? The underlying question had to do with whether "the people" broadly configured would use CB to aid the police in their supposed promotion of safety, or would they side with the antiregulation sentiment of truckers loosely organized around a conception of populist freedom and self-determination. This chapter more than any other interrogates how the communications and transportation technologies increasingly converge in order to govern and monitor mobility while also promoting a sort of self-empowering freedom. I argue that the rise in CB use is a useful historical precedent for understanding the later continued growth of mobile communications.

In chapter 5 I analyze what is often referred to as driving while black (DWB). The chapter looks at the long history of automotive racial profiling and the maintenance of so-called white space. I situate automotive ownership and use within the African American community in terms of what Ralph Ellison characterized as a dual desire and demand to make oneself visible while not drawing too much attention to oneself from those enforcing white power, notably, the police. The automobile has been central to debates within the African American community over the political value of signifying wealth and success in the face of racist oppression and exclusion. The Cadillac has featured prominently in such debates. In 1949 *Ebony* magazine, in an article entitled "Why the Negro Drives a Cadillac," explained that it was the ultimate weapon in the war of racial equality, as it proved the black man could be as successful as any white man. Others within the community argued that the Cadillac should be boycotted rather than desired because GM failed to hire black salespersons or allow black-owned dealerships. This chapter in part presents an analysis of automobile advertising in *Ebony* magazine from the late 1940s to the early 1970s to point out that although black automobile ownership was absolutely vital to the success of Cadillac specifically and the industry more generally, GM worked hard to maintain its distance from black buyers so as to not "cheapen" their brand. Thus the ways in which the economic battles over equality were to be fought and how the Cadillac featured in them were open to debate. Yet this sort of social mobility cannot be separated from spatial automobility.

Much of the chapter outlines how the automobile has been racialized through cultural signifiers related to automotive customization meant to bestow status. Furthermore, partially through the articulation of pimping and criminality, the long history of denigrating or calling into question the legitimacy of Cadillac ownership by blacks is examined. Driving an expensive car while black is not automatically a show of social mobility. It has also historically been a marker of criminality, gangsterism, and even welfare embezzlement. To an even greater degree, signs of black automotive customization like after-market chrome rims; loud, bass-heavy stereo systems;

and even window tinting have been connected to criminality, specifically gang-related drug dealing, through movies and news stories alike. Blaxploitation movies of the 1970s are a prominent example of this process, while the mix of gangsterism and flash exemplified in hip hop culture and videos provides a more recent example. I argue that more attention needs to be paid to how culture becomes a stand-in for race as a means of profiling mobility and the unequal access to social space. Furthermore, DWB can be seen as a protoform of more all-encompassing forms of automobile surveillance that have come to figure prominently in initiatives by the DHS. Keeping the inequities of DWB in mind as these new initiatives are rolled out should be an important element in debates regarding freedom of movement in the face of mounting security concerns.

Road rage is the topic of chapter 7, and in some ways it brings the substantive chapters full circle as we find women drivers reemerging as a social concern. The phenomenon is critically analyzed as a means of looking at how the social control of automobility has been recently reconfigured. In large part road rage is shown to be little more than a well-orchestrated media event originated by the insurance industry as a means of keeping automobile safety on the governmental and media radar. Yet road rage also points to a number of historical changes in how the governance of mobility is imagined and accomplished. What the road rage scare points out is that the risky driver is no longer considered to be confined to any specific demographic but is now thought to be anyone, anywhere, under the right circumstances. Whereas earlier automotive safety initiatives worked through formal governmental institutions to alter the behavior of specific populations (i.e., driver education for youth), responses to road rage were largely imagined to work through neoliberal strategies of privatized entrepreneurial therapies and for-profit grassroots organizations. Furthermore, previous strategies often entailed bifurcating the population along demographic lines into safe and risky.

What the road rage scare again proved is the lack of a correspondent relationship between statistically determined risk and the public exposure and governmental response. While anecdotal data abounded, no matter how the statistics were configured it was nearly impossible to prove something called road rage was actually on the rise. In fact, in some prominent news stories the statistics showed a decline, but the articles still demanded that the public needed to pay more attention. This did not stop psychologists in particular from creating conceptual categories to define one-third of motorists as aggressive drivers. The response was also predominantly led by psychologists, who not only attempted to argue that road rage was a clinical pathology, but offered solutions to the problem organized around self-help and group therapy. Furthermore, these programs called for self-diagnostics, which almost by default would determine that nearly every driver was either a road rager or had tendencies that would lead to being one. By pathologizing the entire driving public and calling upon everyone's memory for anecdotal proof, road rage presented the driving environment as an unwieldy jungle inhabited by danger at every turn. Road rage further stood in as a sign of Americans' increasingly hectic lives. In particular, the dangerous woman driver reappeared. Her station wagon replaced by a sport utility vehicle, she was no longer seen to be docile in her mobile domesticity. Instead, she had managed to achieve automobile equality by becoming as aggressive as her male driving counterparts. The ability of the driving environment to seemingly reprogram women's "natural" proclivity for safety and security became the ultimate sign of the danger of the road.

The concluding chapter contextualizes the cultural history of automobile safety within the newly emergent framework of national security that has, since the events of September 11, 2001, reorganized how automobile threats are assessed. DHS initiatives to create driverless, fully automatic, remotely controllable automobiles are situated within the long history of such futuristic hopes. The discussion sheds light on how the governance of automobility is in part now organized according to national security concerns rather than personal and public safety. While billions of dollars were invested in the creation of what is called the Intelligent Vehicle Highway System (IVHS) during the 1990s, the initiative was seen as a means of increasing efficiency and safety. Since 9/11 the system and the communication, command, and control technologies (C3) necessary for its success are being touted as a tool in the war on terror. A number of initiatives are being experimented with in the United States, including programs for automobile surveillance and control being developed for military theaters. I maintain that this two-pronged attack needs to be understood as part of a larger effort to govern automobility through an all-encompassing surveillance and guidance mechanism that will allow for the monitoring and control of all motorized transport.

Such a system bears obvious threats to privacy rights and guarantees of freedom of movement. It also points out the degree to which earlier safety concerns linked to current national security interests can be used to animate and legitimate attacks on such freedoms. In many instances, as I point out, these attacks occur according to previously created systems of inequity such as race, gender, age, or class. The most recent attacks, however, are not only built upon fear and exclusion, but increasingly organized by a rhetoric of freedom. Most of the c3 technologies being developed, such as the global positioning system (GPS), onboard computers, and integrated surveillance cameras, are marketed and publicized as upscale commercial goods whose only values are those of personal convenience, safety, and freedom. How fitting that, as with the automobile itself, as much of this book hopes to show, Americans' relationship to automobility remains embroiled in a host of commercial and governmental claims regarding freedom, convenience, and safety.

# CHAPTER I

# THE CRUSADE FOR TRAFFIC SAFETY

*Mobilizing the Suburban Dream*

When any particular activity in the United States takes thirty-eight thousand American lives in one year, it becomes a national problem of first
importance. . . . It is one of those problems which by their nature have no
easy solution. . . . [But] in a democracy, public opinion is everything. It is
the force that brings about enforcement of laws; it is the force that keeps
the United States in being, and it runs in all its parts. So, if we can mobilize
public opinion, this problem, like all of those to which free men fall heir,
can be solved.

PRESIDENT DWIGHT D. EISENHOWER, 1954[1]

We Americans resist encroachments on our freedom to drive automobiles
as we please just as we resent restrictions on our freedom to worship
or vote. As a nation we dislike regimentation of any sort. Time and time
again we have demonstrated that we will not readily relinquish what we
regard as our individual rights unless we are convinced that our doing so is
necessary for national welfare.

HARRY DESILVA, *WHY WE HAVE AUTOMOBILE ACCIDENTS*[2]

## Introducing the Crusade for Traffic Safety

The words of President Eisenhower quoted in the epigraph above in
no way mark the beginning of public or even governmental concern
with traffic safety. In fact, traffic laws, highway engineering manuals, academic research, and federal initiatives had all addressed the
issue of traffic safety to some degree starting just a few years after

the advent of the automobile. It wasn't until the 1930s, though, that traffic safety became a subject of organized concern from academics and engineers.[3] This made it a professional discourse, one that featured regularities as to its importance and a bifurcation of its aims and goals. On the one hand was a specifically scientific apparatus that focused on engineering safer cars and roads. On the other was a psychological/sociological current that paid particular attention to drivers, their actions, beliefs, tendencies, and psychological makeup. But there was a sense that both the human and the technological had to be taken into account in order to adequately solve the problems posed by automobile traffic. The DeSilva quotation above, taken from a typical traffic safety book of the era (of which there were many), adequately describes the conceptualization of American sentiment that those involved in traffic regulation were operating under. They viewed freedom as an absolute that could only be diminished through regulation. Thus the desire to alter public opinion in order to erode the public's demand for freedom was at the core of their understanding of the problem. Safety was a hindrance to freedom, but, the regulators argued, an increasingly necessary one. Oddly, by comparing the freedom to drive to religious freedom and voting privileges, the author linked driving to inalienable rights and struggles for social equality. To a degree, Americans treat driving as an inalienable right, and most would gladly give up their voter registration card before their driver's license. But it is neither with these exact concerns nor with the 1930s as the beginning of the safety discourse that I begin this chapter. Rather, it is the first decade after World War II that situates my present concerns. Why this particular period? Because it saw not only numerous changes in the cultural landscape which made automobile driving a necessity in the daily lives of new and growing suburban populations, but also the massive expansion of the highway system. This period witnessed the greatest growth in automobile production and consumption in U.S. history. It was a time when the automobile came to be problematized according to experts' evaluations of specific populations, and governmental and nongovernmental measures were created to address them specifically. As Ike's crusade tried to make clear, it was a time for concerted effort on the part of government and various media organizations to change public opinion regarding traffic safety.

The Crusade for Traffic Safety was initiated in 1954 by "media men to help you, a media man, to save lives in traffic."[4] It was, in effect, an attempt by the

**Crusade for Traffic Safety**

***Here Is My Pledge:***

I personally pledge myself to drive and walk safely and think in terms of safety.

I pledge myself to work through my church, civic, business, and labor groups to carry out the official action program for traffic safety.*

I give this pledge in seriousness and earnestness, having considered fully my obligation to protect my life and the lives of my family and my fellow men.

***Signature***

*Substitute name of your State or local program where applicable.

**FIGURE I. Crusade for Traffic Safety Pledge**
This pledge was an important element in the Crusade for Traffic Safety begun by President Dwight Eisenhower. It asked for the type of commitment and devotion typically reserved for such state institutions as marriage, citizenship, and military service. PRESIDENT DWIGHT D. EISENHOWER, *PRESIDENT'S ACTION COMMITTEE FOR TRAFFIC SAFETY. CRUSADE FOR TRAFFIC SAFETY.* WASHINGTON D.C.: U.S. GOVERNMENT PRINTING OFFICE, 1954.

federal government to organize a concerted effort of media leaders to advocate and spread the gospel of traffic safety. A booklet sent out to every media outlet across the nation outlined the specific ways local media could help in the crusade. The booklet begins by explaining that "traffic safety requires a continuing effort"[5] and that it "will be most effective at the local level."[6] The problem is then compared to the war effort and states that "the basic problem ahead of us now [is]—to make everyone realize that HE and YOU are in the front line of this fight."[7] The "media men" were asked to sign the Crusade for Traffic Safety Pledge, which read, "I personally pledge myself to drive and walk safely and think in terms of safety. I pledge myself to work through my church, civic, business, and labor groups to carry out the official action program for traffic safety. I give this pledge in seriousness and earnestness, having considered fully my obligation to protect my life and the lives of my family and my fellow men."[8] What followed were the specific guidelines for the six media forms deemed necessary to win the crusade.

Daily newspapers were given the tasks of dramatizing coverage of local accidents, pushing the human angle and organizing local safety groups. Weekly newspapers were urged to publish the names of safety offenders, encourage the teaching of safety in schools, push for legislative action, and kick off the program with a "Stay Alive Week."[9] Radio and television stations could "serve no greater need in the public interest than to campaign for highway safety."[10] Specifically, it was suggested they air talks by police, court, hospital, and school officials and insert safety spots into daily programing as well as sponsor safe-driving contests. The moving picture industry was told to produce more locally focused films that dealt with specific regional driving challenges, and theater owners were told to show more safe-driving shorts. Advertising agencies were urged to apply their expertise in "creating desire" for the crusade. Outdoor advertising was "the medium that reaches the motorist at the most important time—when he is at the wheel."[11] They were told to "sell traffic-safety messages . . . keyed to current causes of traffic accidents . . . [to] hammer home the basic theme."[12] Magazines should target "Mr. and Mrs. John Doe" because the "magazine is able to present a more varied, more comprehensive, and more contemplative safety 'sell' than any other medium. Editors have long realized this and have for many years been pushing traffic safety."[13] Their new task was to emphasize success stories and build contacts with existing safety groups in their quest for "facts."[14] Trade journals were to focus on the most specific safety issues of their industry. Trucking and busing firms were given special attention. Last, media trade associations were charged with forging a network for spreading stories and with the creation of outstanding safety awards in the workplace. All of this public relations work was ultimately to "teach Americans everywhere to do things for themselves"[15] when it came to safety, just as the crusade claimed they were learning do-it-yourself home improvement. In fact, "our tool chest is stocked with sound police policies, recognized systems of traffic education, accepted principles of engineering, model laws and proved methods of inspiring public support."[16] The media men and the public at large were said to depend too often on "the official to fight the battle alone."[17] But now, "it is time to Do It Ourselves."[18] One well-traveled advertisement from America Fore Insurance Group provides an example of how advertisers and insurance companies played a part in the campaign. The ad ends with this call: "Yes— safety on our highways is everybody's responsibility! Join the Crusade for Traffic Safety and save a life—maybe your own!"

**FIGURE 2. This Man May Save Your Life**
This was a widely distributed advertisement which made clear that
police enforcement of traffic regulations was for the good of each and
every driver. Yet the determined, almost menacing expression on the
officer's face betrays a somewhat different meaning. AMERICAN FORE
INSURANCE ADVERTISEMENT, 1955.

The crusade is a particularly useful starting point for my analysis because
it directs attention to key conceptual issues present throughout the following
chapters. Reorganizing public opinion is an act of producing a new popular
truth and in this case through a form of problematization. By this I mean
that a phenomenon becomes recognized as a serious public problem through
publicity that identifies it as such and suggests it be dealt with through expert explanation. In essence, it becomes a popular truth insofar as it creates
a sense that reality is adequately represented, that something is amiss and
must be set right, and, most generally, that there is some form of expertise
that can sufficiently come to grips with the situation. Furthermore, in this

instance it was recognized that numerous institutions and organizations must work together to study the problem and orchestrate the crusade. This does not suggest that this specific crusade led to direct changes in behavior owing to its effect on the minds of American citizens. However, it does trace many of the cultural manifestations of this popular truth about automobile safety. The Crusade for Traffic Safety was the focusing, unifying, and publicizing culmination of a preexistent discourse about traffic safety. It was a discourse promoted, spoken, and, to some degree, created by numerous types of experts, including, though not limited to, economists, social and physical scientists, governmental bureaucrats, industrial managers, insurance actuaries, urban planners, and media specialists. The crusade's existence makes clear that these media and government initiatives were imagined to be not only useful, but necessary. It is similar in nature and form to the media's earlier involvement in the war effort. The formation of such a campaign sets the stage for governmental and nongovernmental intervention in ways that are directly and indirectly involved in altering not just minds, but conduct. As will become apparent throughout this book, it begins in nascent form what will, over the next fifty years, become an increasingly neoliberal approach to traffic safety, ultimately arguing for a personal responsibility approach. The pledge itself involves recognition that one is joining the crusade first and foremost to protect his or her own life.[19] The appeal to save the lives of others is secondary. Thus, the crusade ultimately orients itself around personal investment and responsibility through an appeal to the immediate danger posed to the self, as the motivation for joining is said to be a desire to "protect my life." Its emergence in 1954 is important, as it is (1) the culmination of a type of media representation that had been treating traffic safety as dramatic and serious, and (2) it helped shape the media's representation of safety in the following years. This is not to say all media representation that followed toed the party line (though clearly most did), nor is it to say that what followed was vastly different from what had come before (it certainly wasn't). Rather, the crusade represents a unification in form and focus of investments, practices, and goals between government and media regarding traffic safety. By 1954 this unified strategy was said by the Advertising Council to be working, and it claimed victory for reducing traffic fatalities for the first time since World War II.[20]

The crusade treated traffic safety as a problem of national scale and one having great political significance. Eisenhower noted that, like all problems facing "free men" "in a democracy,"[21] this one could be solved through their investment in organizing public opinion. Much like the victory in World War II that propelled him into office, this problem "could be solved,"[22] this victory could be won. It was treated as a front-line battle. The pamphlet itself provides a graph of all the highway deaths in America *since the war*,[23] implying that a war mentality was needed to defeat the next enemy, traffic fatalities. Previous casualties had been soldiers, whereas the new American casualties were "friends, relatives, the neighbor next door."[24] This appeal to one's neighbor offers insight into the kind of person with whom one felt this sense of camaraderie. When it came to traffic safety in the 1950s, it was the idealized imaginary suburb and the neighbors who populated it that served as the benchmark against which all others were to be compared. The media representations of this suburban never-never land were filled with a typological array of malady-laden drivers who were the main culprits against whom the crusade would be aimed. Gender, age, and psychological makeup were the three variables through which these typologies were animated. It is not coincidental that the wide-scale acceptance of psychology, social concern with delinquent youth, and suburban-altered gender expectations over this period played vital roles in how the safety war would be fought and justified. As will be the case in the following chapters, I begin with a set of populations whose problematic mobility helped to justify and orient the crusade. In this case, I begin with the menace of the woman driver.

### Make Room for the Woman Driver

The *Woman's Home Companion* for February 1954 announced the beginning of a new editorial department in the magazine, the House, Garden, and Automobile Workshop, which featured articles intended to "help you [the reader] make better use of your cars."[25] The very first article, "America Discovers the Station Wagon," detailed "the newest development in our mobile living: the discovery of the station wagon as a family car."[26] The increased focus on automobiles was by no means unique to the *Woman's Home Companion* among the plethora of women's magazines of the time. For example, *Good Housekeeping* ran a short weekly feature on women and automobiles, and *Better Homes and Gardens* featured stories explicitly about automobiles and driving in more than half of their issues from 1953 to 1957. Magazines such as *Vogue, Cosmopolitan, Ladies' Home Journal,* and *Independent Woman* also featured their fair share of articles treating the anxiety and excitement surrounding the automobile. This upsurge in coverage corresponded to the sharp increase in women who were driving and families that were moving to the suburbs. Automobiles had been a significant part of life for men and women alike for over forty years. However, with the advent of the suburb and the new ideals it represented, the automobile took a more central role in structuring women's lives. Furthermore, by the mid-fifties, the potential for and the dream of the two-car-family began to take hold.[27] Automobiles thus came to be at the center of women's daily routines. But things were not all rosy. Discourse regarding the introduction of new technologies into everyday lives is often framed by utopian and dystopian logics.[28] On the one hand, there was great excitement surrounding the benefits this new convenience would bring, yet there was also great anxiety regarding how the new technology would alter the stability, patterns, and expectations of everyday life. To further complicate issues, the automobile's introduction into the everyday lives of women came about along with other radical changes, including altered work expectations, new family ideals, expansion of leisure, and movement away from traditional neighborhoods. As Kathleen HcHugh put it, "Automobility threatened nineteenth-century America's preeminent gender distinction—men move and women stay home—the needs of the economy demanded a more mobile female consumer."[29] These changes were intricately linked and in many ways they overlapped and built upon one another to create an idealized version of women's "new mobile lives." As John Hartley makes clear, these lives were dependent upon a confluence of technologies that reorganized domestic labor and expectations. For instance, the refrigerator, a banal and overlooked technology, made possible and practical suburban housing and the new forms of domestic consumption which were replacing domestic production, as food could be stored for lengthy periods of time. The weekly shopping commute to the grocery store replaced the daily walk to local grocers, bakeries, and meat markets.[30] Whereas women's ability to successfully "use the fridge," or the stove for that matter, was not seen as problematic, when it came to the automobile essentialist notions regarding her inability to properly use technology and her supposedly inherent flighty nature made her a potential traffic safety threat.

What were women's lives supposed to look like? and how was their dangerous nature to be tamed? Highlighting and analyzing the links between mobility and changing gender expectations exposes a change in the very conception of what it means to be a good driver and how being a good citizen gets tied to managing one's mobility. This rearticulation depended upon essentialized understandings of gender roles, understandings that were solidified through insurantial practices and legitimated through popular uptakes of psychology. Changes in the relationship between domestic and public space are also examined as the automobile cuts across both, in literal and figurative fashions. In very concrete ways, the construction of a national highway system changed the landscape and cultural spaces that middle-class women in particular traversed. The official rhetoric that authorized such construction informed and responded to the cultural manifestations of suburbanization. Technical manuals such as *Highway Design and Construction*, revised in 1950, accepted and promoted this new sensibility:

> The improvement of roads radiating from the cities made possible the suburban developments, where the land is cheaper and the surroundings are more healthful than in the crowded urban districts. These same roads have made it possible for the city dweller to get into the country and enjoy the woods and the beaches for even one day or to take extended vacation trips through national parks and forests or through scenic and historical regions at long distances from home."[31]

The automobile was more than a means to a "healthier existence." It was both a signifier of domestic success and the means of escaping domestic entrapment. But the family car also became the locus of newfound difficulties for parenting. Adolescent access to mobility was primarily problematized according to safety. This paternalization mirrors the more general problematization of mobility that is the focus of this book. The twofold focus upon gender and age also solidifies popular characterizations of problem populations. In this instance, the teen masculine menace, the hot-rodder, was an especially troubling concern for mothers and potential mother-in-laws. This chapter explores how orientations toward safety changed in the 1950s and how this new orientation presaged most safety scares analyzed in later chapters.

### Suburbs and Station Wagons

In the aforementioned *Woman's Home Companion* article and numerous other magazine articles, the station wagon is presented as the ultimate automotive expression of the new suburban lifestyle. By 1956 it was called the "All-American Automobile."[32] Much like the progression of contemporary middle-class SUV use, the station wagon began as an upscale niche market vehicle for the multiply vehicled affluent outdoorsman or for utilitarian use by those hardy souls who lived in regions that demanded rugged-terrain transport. It wasn't until the early 1950s that the station wagon started to catch on with suburban buyers. This was explained by its so-called all-purpose use value. What were all these uses as reported in the women's magazines of the day? The following excerpt from "America Discovers the Station Wagon" partly answers that question:

> Taylor and Elizabeth Jeffferies are as typical suburbanites as you'll find anywhere in this country. They live in the pleasant community of Greenlawn on the north shore of Long Island, 40 miles from the center of New York City. But Greenlawn could be any one of a thousand residential towns that border our great cities. The Jefferies have three energetic daughters: Lynne, 13; Judith, 10; and Susan, 9. They live in a six-room shingled house, are very friendly with all their neighbors, entertain often but informally and belong to a small beach club. Taylor, who is office manager of a large soap company, commutes to New York daily—as do most of the husbands in town. Liz takes care of the house, the children—and her station wagon. Her life revolves around a series of car pools, in which she takes turns with other wives to do the necessary driving chores.[33]

Following this general description is a set of photos featuring the Jefferieses engaged in everyday suburban activities: dropping off hubby at the train station; Liz shopping for groceries; running errands such as picking up the kids at school; picking up old clothes for charity; taking the aged shopping; going to church; helping out the amateur theater; moving plywood for remodeling; and taking the family to an excursion at the beach. What this and other stories proffer is an ideal model for millions of suburban mothers who are already said to be just like Liz. It also illustrates the ways in which the automobile, if not the station wagon, is a necessity for suburban housewives and, in fact, organizes everyday routines.

Ford articulated its own version of idealized suburban mobility and added one essential element, freedom, in their brilliant short/advertisement *Two-Ford Freedom* (1956). The scene opens in a spacious middle-class kitchen. A

MEET THESE FRIENDLY STATION-WAGON FAMILIES

Join the Kresses on a tour of their farm in the beautiful Pennsylvania hills, page 120.

The Conways will give you a glimpse of city life in and around St. Louis, page 122.

The Jefferies will show you how they enjoy living in a suburb of New York, page 126.

**FIGURE 3. The Family Station Wagon**
These families were featured in the initial installment of a regular feature devoted to the automobile in *Woman's Home Companion* beginning in 1954. They were shown to be typical of suburban, urban, and rural American life; lives which all are said to be increasingly mobile and in need of the perfect family vehicle, the station wagon. R. SCHILLER AND G. HENLE (FEBRUARY 1954). "AMERICA DISCOVERS THE STATION WAGON: ALL-PURPOSE CAR FOR YOUR FAMILY." *WOMAN'S HOME COMPANION*, 117–28.

housewife in a simple floral print dress has a phone to her ear and a smile on her face. "Fine," she says into the receiver, "I'd love to. Thanks, Jean. I'll be there. Two o'clock. Goodbye." She hangs up the phone, looks into the camera, and says, "You know, three weeks ago I couldn't have accepted that invitation. Like so many people these days, we live in the suburbs and Dave needs the car for business." She walks across the kitchen to place a teacup and saucer in the sink. "When he was gone," she continues, "I was practically a prisoner in my own home. I couldn't get out to see my friends, couldn't get out to take part in PTA activities, why, I couldn't even shop when I wanted to. I had to wait 'til Thursday night after Dave brought the car home." She turns to the window above the sink and pulls up the blinds, saying, "But that's all changed now." The scene cuts to the driveway, and a man (Dave) is getting into a sedan. Now the woman is heard in voice-over: "Three weeks ago, we bought another Ford, the low-priced custom line Victoria. Isn't it stunning?" Dave drives down the driveway as the camera follows: "Dave now has it all to himself." The camera reveals a second car in the driveway. "And I now have the Ranch Wagon all to myself." The camera cuts back into the kitchen and, with an even bigger smile, the woman continues, "It's a whole new way of life. Now I'm free to go anywhere, do anything, see anybody anytime I want to." She explains, "It's only good common sense," as she moves across the kitchen to pick up her jacket. "Why be stuck with one expensive car when you can have all the fun and freedom of two fine Fords?" she bewilderingly implores. We fade to a sedan cruising down a country lane and a male voice-over kicks in, "Today, more and more families are finding out how easy it is to become two-Ford families." He then tells us about the great models and options available, adding that "each [has] the extra protection of Ford's life-guard design." As the Ford logo comes into focus he ends with, "So see your Ford dealer soon."

The Ford advertisement evidences a number of claims. First, not only governmental agencies and media companies were engaged in promoting mobile suburban living. Clearly, the automotive industry, along with big oil, had the most to gain from the two-car family ideal. Some conspiratorial explanations go so far as to feature the automotive industry as the key behind-the-scenes promoter of the construction of the national highway system that suburban expansion depended upon. Second, *Two-Ford Freedom* concisely narrates the tension between the suburban domestic ideal and suburban domestic entrapment. The suburban housewife is in fact "a prisoner" who needs to escape. The commercial speaks of the problem as though it is deeply felt and plainly understood by a potential new market faced with a newly organized set of domestic expectations. And further, the advertisement answers any potential objections with the fundamentally ideological reply, "It's only good common sense." Third, as will become much clearer later in this chapter, the final appeal is to safety. "Ford's lifeguard protection" comes to reorient public concerns by articulating a seemingly natural relationship between femininity and automobile safety. Last, the advertisement perfectly summarizes sentiments found in many of the articles published in popular periodicals, down to the necessity of the housewife's car being a station wagon. It makes clear that the connections and expectations of a woman's work in the kitchen, her role as social maintenance worker, her duties to family and husband can be accomplished via the telephone and the automobile. These were, in fact, the two essential domestic tools for the accomplishment of these duties. It is through these communications technologies that she can keep the community intact against the backdrop of the sprawling suburb.

The suburban ideal separated women from the local shopping centers and mass transportation systems historically necessary to negotiate domestic routines and labor. Changing ideals also called for an increase in family size, further making the station wagon appropriate. Furthermore, family travel was at the center of increasing postwar middle-class leisure. The 1950s saw the greatest increase in camping in American history. These changes indicate a reorganization of how public mobility was perceived and managed as well as a corresponding change in the domestic lives of women in particular. The automobile came to be the link between public and domestic and in many ways came to represent the domestic in public. The importance of maintaining a clean home or of being a good provider and the associated insecurities were heightened with the visibility of being on the road, whether around town or cross-country.

An article from *Woman's Home Companion* entitled "Gypsies But Neat" described a method for keeping the car looking good while on a family trip. It assured women that having a clean car was "much better than feeling uneasily that you might be mistaken for a family of Okies."[34] Another entitled "We took the Kitchen with Us" described in detail how to pack a fully functional kitchen in the car trunk in order to provide the family with a hot meal while on a trip.[35] The portable home-cooked meal may seem a bit out of the ordinary in the present age of omnipresent highway exit fast food, but (on a personal note) my father, a baby boomer, often described his mother pulling a portable stove out of the trunk and putting it to use on roadside picnic tables to make a breakfast of eggs, bacon, hotcakes, and coffee. Concerns typically associated with domestic spaces become pronounced when they are transported into the public via the automobile. Women's work and domestic expectations weren't left in the privacy of the home. Rather, the automobile was simply a continuation of the domestic, taking on the status of a traveling household showcase and proving grounds.

Family vacations and camping were on the rise. By 1955 more than 85 percent of all family vacations in the United States were taken in an automobile. This extended mobility demanded that women manage two domestic spaces, the second being fully mobile. In particular, the camping site became an even more visible and thus more problematic space, one which had to be maintained and movable. Camping trailers and motor homes had been gaining popularity since their introduction in 1934, but it was during the 1950s that they became a middle-class necessity for many Americans. The motor home, as the name implies, created a new type of domicile and a new type of mobility for the extended family vacation. Along with it came a new set of domestic concerns and problems. Although the motor home was not central to the automobile literature in women's magazines, many articles did recount methods for dealing with the expectations of domesticity on the road and in the public campgrounds that were sprouting up in the ever-growing number of national and state parks. This alteration in family expectations, mobility, and leisure was regulated through an extension of domestic concerns, as the very form of vacationing in a motor home was simply an extension of the domestic into the natural landscapes of the campground. Nature, the camp, and the great outdoors, traditionally male territory, were domesticated by association and hard work. Women in the wild were expected to domesticate (and in larger campgrounds even suburbanize) nature, to turn the wilderness into a manageable, comfortable, and safe family environment.

Vincent Minnelli's film *The Long, Long Trailer* (1954) provides romantic-comic narrative to just such mobile domestic desires and demands. Starring Lucille Ball and Desi Arnaz during the height of the popularity of their television series *I Love Lucy*, *The Long, Long Trailer* featured the madcap story of Tacy and Nick's attempt to join the roaming existence of others devoted to "Trailer Life."[36] This lot lives out their existence traveling from trailer park to national forest to roadside rest area with "all the amenities of home" and none of the perceived boredom. In one scene the campground functions as a mini-mobile-suburb. All the campers know each other, gossip incessantly, keep up with the Joneses, and turn their small plots into groomed yards. Ultimately, the campers, through a potluck-style impromptu party, instantiate the gendered expectations of domestic care and nurturance as the "neighborhood" women care not only for an injured and bedridden Tacy, but by extension the now-helpless Nick. Yet, as the movie tells it, all boredom-inspiring domestic demands follow the nomadic heroine. In one comic scene after another Tacy struggles and fails throughout to maintain the domestic ideals of the good wife. She first tries to beautify the trailer and pack it with all the necessities of domestic and personal aesthetic maintenance, only to have it all come crashing down upon Nick when he pulls open the door of an overstuffed closet. Later, as Nick drives their specially purchased and outfitted car down the highway, Tacy bears down in the rollicking trailer and tries to cook an elaborate dinner. Needless to say, dinner ends up on Tacy, not on the aesthetically pleasing dinner plates. Foiled, they are forced to eat at a roadside diner. Worse yet, Nick turns the reins of the rig over to Tacy but only after warning her of the absolute necessity of using the specially installed trailer brakes. Near catastrophe is narrowly averted as Tacy proves true to her feminine inability to handle things mechanical, leading to the couple's first marital fight. Finally, Tacy's romantic gesture of collecting a stone at each stop to commemorate their honeymoon, against Nick's warning about the unsafe added weight, proves their undoing. This ultimate breach of the domestic demand for safety nearly leads to a fatal drop off a Rocky Mountain cliff, forcing Nick to literally and figuratively unhitch himself from Tacy and speed off in their car. Ultimately, in a climactic moment of reconciliation, they mutually admit their wrongdoing, decide to give up the nomadic life, and return to their suburban security.

The dangers of leisure travel didn't threaten only marital bliss. In 1954, *Cosmo* explained the particular dangers facing summer vacationers: "A hot-weather rise in highway homicide (and suicide) is inevitable, since normal traffic is swelled by evening rides and vacation trips, but you'll stand a better chance of beating the odds of becoming a vacation statistic if you avoid the most common hot-weather driving hazards."[37] Thus the family vacation was not only a domestic concern, but also another preoccupation with the safety of one's family. No mother worth her salt would want her family to be the victim of "highway homicide." However, this was not the only woman-specific travel worry. An article that appeared in 1955 suggested that women who travel alone should do so with a mannequin sitting in the passenger seat, so as to deter would-be criminals, hitchhikers, and "forward" men.[38]

Women needed to maintain appearances while on vacation. In the article "Good Looks on the Road," *Woman's Home Companion* stated, "This means you as well as your car. Here's how to plan beautywise for a lovely, care-

**FIGURE 4. Mannequin Passenger**
The woman pictured here is securing a life-sized male mannequin
into the passenger seat. She went to such lengths in order to
ensure her holiday travel would be safe. Such gendered visions of
danger on the road have been a mainstay in media coverage. They
continued to animate discussions regarding the reasons women
should have citizens band radios in their car in the 1970s and, more
recently, a mobile phone. K. LANE (OCTOBER 1955). "HOW TO TRAVEL
WITH A BOY FRIEND." *AMERICAN MAGAZINE*, 20–21: 107–9.

free, smooth-running vacation."[39] But the worry ran into everyday lives as
well: "If you've ever heard yourself apologizing for the messy state of your
car—and who hasn't?—you'll agree that it pays to give a good regular wash-
ing, in the interests of family pride alone."[40] Advice of this sort was frequently included in articles describing how to keep the car clean and looking
good. They abounded in detailed photos and descriptions of the products
and methods that worked best, because "driving it clean is like wearing new
shoes or a new hat."[41] But other reasons were cited for an interest in keeping
the car clean. It was said to be safer, to increase resale value, and to uphold

proper public appearance. Thus care for the car was an extension of both caring for oneself and caring for one's home. It was an opportunity and an obligation to expand and make public one's domestic and aesthetic skills.

Furthermore, the automobile became an addendum to the ideals of female beauty. Magazines such as *Vogue* and *Cosmopolitan* ran photo shoots that incorporated the latest in automotive designs and clothing fashions. These spreads glamorized both the automobiles and the women who drove or sat in the passenger seat. This articulation of fashion with the automobile worked well for automobile manufacturers, who were in the midst of the most prolific design revolution in automotive history. Just as new fashions arrived seasonally in the department stores, so too did automobiles arrive on the lots of dealerships. They featured an ever-greater array of features and design accouterments. From the escalating fin to the craze for chrome, these design innovations had little to do with performance. However, specific features like larger doors that allowed women easier access in and out of their cars while attired in bulky skirts or dresses were applauded in *Vogue*. Such features as power brakes, power steering, automatic transmission, and adjustable seats, all of which were responses to the greater number of women drivers, were also lauded. It was assumed that women had limited physical ability to manage such mechanically challenging tasks, and these were considered features aimed at women's desires and needs. This is to say that just as the automobile altered women's lives, women drivers radically altered the automobile. The station wagon seemed to be the perfect vehicle at the perfect time for these changed lives, and advertisements for them claimed that their product surely met these needs. It lived up to the demands of a mobile mother, wife, housekeeper, and community servant. It also fulfilled the role of idealizing a particular type of woman. The corresponding and reciprocal relationships between the automotive industry, suburbanization, women's perceived needs and purchasing habits, and new female ideals came together nicely in the station wagon. The station wagon was, in fact, three times as likely to be a family's second car than all other types of automobiles combined.[42]

In one dreamed-up vision of women's relationship to and desire for automobiles a slightly more glamorous life unfolds. The nine-minute *Design for Dreaming* advertisement produced in 1956 by GM was aimed at women and situated the automobile as a key component in a world dominated by fashionable aesthetics and automated domestic technologies. This magic-realist musical takes a desirous heroine in middream from her bedroom to a fabulous car show in Manhattan. Her clothing is magically transformed from sleeping gown to ball gown as she sings and dances her way through throngs of automobile admirers to get the "low down" on GM's stylishly new and future models. When she sings, "I'll have a Pontiac, tooooooo," her tuxedo-wearing masked dance partner answers, "Okay, we'll have the usual two-car garage." Yet even in this auto-orgasmic dream world, she's never too far from domestic labor. Or is she? As she exits a Cadillac that matches her outfit and unfurling umbrella, her gown sprouts an apron, she starts to faint (the realization of being so out of place seemingly stops her cold), and we hear a voice-over shout, "Better get her into the kitchen quick," as if that might cure her. She wakes in the arms of her masked dance partner and in a Frigidaire kitchen "unlike any she's seen" that features automatic appliances that cook as if "by magic." By its virtue she is magically freed to play tennis or a round of golf or spend a day at the beach; all the while her magic kitchen performs as domestic servant, baking a perfect cake and even applying (while it's still in the oven?) frosting and lit candles. She blows them out, the smoke clears, and she is transformed onstage to perform "the dance of tomorrow" for her adoring audience. This dance is merely the prelude to a series of dual unveilings. Models coordinated by a fashion designer emerge from futuristic automobile models in a sequence that links high fashion with automotive chic. For instance, a male voice-over informs the viewer that the car shown is "a magnificent El Dorado town-car by Cadillac." As the model steps from the convertible, a female voice-over explains that the "ensemble [is] by Christian Dior, Paris." This linking of models (fashion and automotive) further clarifies a long tradition of attention to aesthetics similarly addressed in *Vogue* and *Cosmo*. This was not an entirely new appeal, as the automotive industry, particularly GM and Chrysler in the late 1920s, challenged Ford's "any color as long as it's black" aesthetic through the introduction of multiple color options specifically designed to appeal to women. Automotive advertising played up these features to a female readership.[43] *Design for Dreaming* ends with a ride in the "fabulous turbine-powered Firebird II" on the fully automated highway of tomorrow, where drivers have to check in with the "control tower" before they "take off" into such an aesthetically fine future free of domestic duties (I discuss the highway of tomorrow in detail in the conclusion).

The automobile, in sum, was portrayed much more as a domestic tool than anything else, at least when it came to women. As was true of all the other domestic appliances of the 1950s, the primary concern regarded how well the particular device would enable women to accomplish their domestic obligations. The automobile in general, but the station wagon in particular, is much like the dishwasher, the garbage disposal, and the upright vacuum. It is a mechanical means for accomplishing feminized tasks. How she approached learning to drive was compared to how she approached domestic labor: "A woman attacks the problem of learning to drive much as she attacks the problem of a stack of dirty dishes."[44] But these feminized tasks also take place on the public roads, producing a different set of problems and articulations. The domestic space was historically idealized as a feminized space in which security, safety, privacy, and comfort abounded. It was a refuge from the outside world and a place for nurturing children. The automobile, however, came increasingly to link domestic and public spaces for women, and this linking was accompanied by a homologous linking of feminized domestic ideals with public roads. Like most public spaces, public roads were gendered male and thus were aggressive, production oriented, and competitive. They were properly the space of men, but, with increased suburbanization, affluence, and a female workforce, the number of women driving would absolutely increase. These conflicting conceptions of domestic and public space would collide in the stereotypes regarding women drivers. Women drivers were themselves seemingly concerned with how well they could carry on domestic duties with the aid of the station wagon. However, the jokes aimed at women on the road often made clear the real underlying issue: female drivers threatened to disrupt gendered spaces.

### Battling To Be Better

The psychology of man—his ability to concentrate, his tendency to be distracted, his fears, worries, quarrels, his desire to show off, his many other mental quirks, attitudes and limitations—all have a profound influence upon his skill as a driver. Either they provide him with superior qualifications or they disturb or hinder him. In either case if he is to be a good driver, he must master them.
WHITNEY, MAN AND THE MOTORCAR[45]

A *Brady Bunch* episode in which Marsha dismisses the myth of the woman driver by besting her older male sibling Greg in a driving competition teaches an important lesson about driving: the rules had changed for good. There was much on the line in this battle of the sexes. For Greg there was the obvious need to prove that men were superior to women and that they most certainly were far superior when it came to things mechanical. For Marsha there was the weight of women's liberation and the ongoing battle to prove in every walk of life that women were at least the equal of men and deserved access to all things traditionally thought the privilege of men. But what were the conditions of this battle? What type of competition was it? When men get together to prove who is the better driver, who has the better car, or who is simply more of a man, they race, the understanding being that what automobiles, or most machines for that matter, are truly about is speed and power. That is, technology is intended to speed up a process, in this case getting from point A to point B. But there really aren't any explicitly feminine ways to compete in regards to automobiles. If representations prior to the late 1960s Brady episode taught us anything, it was that when it came to cars and women, the goal was to be seen sitting in a passenger seat in a cool car next to a cool guy. But the Brady battle took place in a parking lot and involved the skills taught in a typical driver's education class. The battle culminated in an event that tested how close the contestants could get to an orange safety cone while backing up without breaking an egg perched atop the cone. The competition measured two things. First, how well Greg and Marsha had mastered the skills taught in their mandatory high school driver's education classes. Second, it tested them on the likelihood they would cause cosmetic damage to their own and others' cars while parking, which might culminate in insurance claims. An unfortunate blow for male pride occurred when Greg knocked the egg off, and when it hit the ground men knew their dreams of mechanical mastery had shattered as well. Nearly twenty years earlier, this same battle of the sexes was being played out in popular periodicals of the mid-1950s. Only this time, it wouldn't just keep male pride in check and add to the mounting representational victories for women: it would reorient the very understanding of what a good driver was and set the stage for the form that the Brady battle took. As Marsha told Greg, "It's not who wins or loses that matters. The most important thing is that we are both good, safe drivers."

An anecdote, a typology of jokes, and a bit of scientific evidence begin to explain how widespread was the belief that women were inferior to men when it came to driving. In 1952 in a Madison, Wisconsin, courtroom, charges against a male defendant for crashing into a woman's car were dropped, even though she had signaled a turn. The defendant's legal loophole? "She was the first woman driver I ever saw who turned the same direction she signaled."[46] Into and beyond the 1950s, jokes about women drivers were popular in nearly all communicative venues, from stand-up routines to *New Yorker* cartoons. In these jokes she was shown to be fearful and naive about technology, automobiles in particular.

The woman driver was more interested in window-shopping as she drove down Main Street than obeying traffic laws. She expected men to always give her the right-of-way out of chivalrous deference. Last, she panicked and overreacted to any surprise. She was, in short, a stereotypically hysterical and frivolous woman. According to Dr. Oscar E. Hirtzberg, head of the Department of Psychological Research at the Buffalo State Teachers College, as of 1934 women very often disregarded the rules of traffic safety. In fact, they generally flouted the traffic regulations regularly obeyed by men. Men, he claimed, were more disciplined and better drivers. This was borne out by "amateur research experts, traffic policemen, and department store executives."[47] (Yes, department store executives. Apparently, in 1934, it was assumed they had special access to women's psychological misgivings.) In 1936 it was more "scientifically proven." The *New York Times* boldly and bluntly explained that "women are consistently lower than men in the physical skill and mental agility needed for driving automobiles." Furthermore, "women drivers are harder to teach."[48] But something strange happened over the next twenty years, something that radically altered not only the status of the woman driver, but also the very notion of what a good driver should be.

Beginning in the 1930s driver manuals discussed the relative importance of safety while driving. It was only one aspect among many that came to characterize a good driver. Of equal or greater importance were such traits as courtesy, efficiency, civility, common sense, navigational competency, and friendliness. In 1955, the American Automobile Association (AAA) posted a study that claimed women were better drivers than men. It made great copy and provided "scientific" evidence that women were superior in their driving abilities. The study not only disproved the claims about how inadequate women were as drivers but went one step further in asserting their dominance over men in this most masculine of enterprises. The AAA also

## Woman Driver's Lament

The lengthy new cars are superbly designed,
But they've added a foot both in front and behind—
Which is just that much more crinkled car to explain,
When a lady has dented the fenders again!

VIRGINIA BRASIER.

Turning left from a right-hand lane is deserving of the epithet, "Woman driver!"

One lady motorist turned around to give her naughty daughter "a long, hard look."

Don't expect a put-upon male driver to be put off by a "helpless li'l ole me" act.

**FIGURES 5A–5D. Woman Driver Jokes**

These cartoons are typical of woman driver jokes that proliferated in newspaper and magazine coverage in the 1930s, 1940s, and 1950s. Women were said to expect chivalrous treatment from men, which would allow them to window-shop while driving and generally disobey the rules of the road. Furthermore, it was imagined that automobiles, like other mechanical implements of modern life not found in the kitchen, were more naturally mastered by men. A. MARBLE (OCTOBER 30, 1955). "PLEA: 'DON'T BE A WOMAN, DRIVER.'" *NEW YORK TIMES,* SM 25; "WOMAN DRIVER'S LAMENT," *NEW YORK TIMES,* AUGUST 25, 1946, 113.

honored "The First Woman Driver," of whom it was said she "never had a dent" in a press-released acknowledgment which coincided perfectly with the association's new standards for good driving.[49]

Actuarial findings told the story of women having accidents less often than men in a typical year of driving. Later counterstatistical gerrymandering would attempt to refute these findings by explaining that men drove four times as many miles while their accident rate was only three times as high. Such figures were deflected through statistics showing that men created more fatal accidents per mile, thus making them more dangerous. Men explained this away as mere coincidence: they drove on highways while women drove in town, where accidents were less likely to end in fatalities. On the debate raged. University psychologists were brought in to explain the psychological makeup of various dangerous driving types, including gender specific types. The National Highway Traffic Safety Department added its statistical two cents. The debate never quite died, at least until Greg's pride cracked along with the egg. What proved even more powerful than the stereotypes that characterized both genders was the chain of articulation that bound insurance claims to being a good driver to safety. The important issue here is not the relative merit of either group's claim upon driving superiority. Rather, of greater interest is the way in which *better* was defined, what so-called science was being used, and how this science was used to rearticulate the popular truth regarding driving.

In order to explain how this change in definitions and stereotypes was accomplished it will help to specify who was invested, first, in, defining what a good driver is and, second, in categorizing populations according to such standards. In his classic studies on social problems Howard Becker describes how and why particular forms of conduct become social problems.[50] In order for something, in this instance automobile fatalities, to become a social problem, two things must happen. First, there must be some objective condition, which then threatens a subjective cherished value. A mounting array of statistical data kept tabs on the death toll of the nation's roads. But this in and of itself did not automatically make automobile fatalities a social problem. The second part of the equation is that these deaths be considered unacceptable and made known to the public as such. Obviously, human life is highly cherished in most instances. There are certain activities in which the loss of life is considered acceptable, and within certain populations lives

The Reward of Modesty—A woman, knowing little of machinery, learns to drive carefully; men get arrogantly confident.

Drawing by Abner Dean.

# Woman Driver: A Myth Exploded

**She learns faster, drives better, has fewer accidents
and won't take nonsense from a car, it says in figures.**

**FIGURE 6. Woman Driver Myth Exploded**
The assumption that women were mechanically inept was once used to denigrate women's driving ability. However, it was also used to explain why she was a better driver than men. She was seen to be more levelheaded and less arrogant on the road. S. BOAL (NOVEMBER 4, 1951). "WOMAN DRIVER: A MYTH EXPLODED." *NEW YORK TIMES MAGAZINE*, 18;46.

are considered more valuable than in others, but automobile accidents were becoming less acceptable. The mounting death toll was being publicized extensively in newspaper articles, magazines, and insurance ads and by the nation's president, who called it "a national problem of first importance"[51] and initiated the aforementioned Crusade for Traffic Safety. As early as 1952, the *Ladies' Home Journal* warned that unless Americans joined together there would be a "Sudden Death for the Second Million,"[52] referring to the fact that over one million Americans had died in automobile accidents during the first fifty years of their use. Furthermore, the cherished values that automobile accidents upset were far more diverse than life itself. Accidents had been problematized as a police problem (police were given the task of enforcing the rules of the road and reacting to accidents), they produced economic problems (particularly for insurance companies), and more generally they disrupted the smooth flow of an increasingly auto-mobile (both autonomously mobile and automobile centered) culture. The police, government agencies (at the federal, state, and municipal levels), and, most important, insurance companies all had a vested interest in getting involved in this social problem.

This makes evident one of Becker's most important insights. The formation of all social problems depends upon what he calls moral entrepreneurs, constituted of those who make the rules, which supposedly will solve the problems, and of those who enforce them.[53] The rule maker "operates with an absolute ethic; what he sees is truly and totally evil with no qualification. Any means is justified to do away with it."[54] The rule enforcer is typically less invested in the ethical dimension and more attuned to accomplishing the specific goals of rule enforcement in a professional fashion and according to guidelines. But in both instances, Becker explains, the moral entrepreneurs have much to gain in *not* eliminating the problem. Typically, numerous institutions (insurance companies), government agencies (Department of Transportation), and special interest groups (MADD) as well as policing forces specifically given the task of dealing with a singular problem (DEA, ATF) are ultimately dependant upon the problem's continued existence. Which is to say that their financial well-being is tied less to to actually eradicating the problem than to the public perception that there is still much to be done and that they are best suited for the task. In this particular instance, though, there is a specific participant whose vested interest works according to two seemingly contradictory logics.

Insurance companies wanted to minimize the number of accidents while creating the perception that there were ever-present and increasingly diverse risks. On the one hand they have a financial interest in decreasing the amount they pay in claims. Through extensive advertisement campaigns, safety crusades, and public awareness programs they worked to minimize the risky behavior of drivers and educate the public of all the dangers present. Yet these attempts to control conduct could not appear to eradicate accidents or diminish their possibility to such a degree that insurance no longer seemed a necessity to motorists.[55] Instead, as Becker points out, they needed to make it appear that the problem was continually at its worst, but that they were doing much to eliminate automobile fatalities and damage. This helps account for the insurance industries' continual crusade to discover and publicize new automotive risks. As I discuss in later chapters, the insurance industry has been involved heavily in antihitchhiking campaigns and almost single-handedly created the furor over road rage. But there is another dimension to automobile insurance which has more far-reaching consequences.

Insurance, as Francois Ewald points out, is much more than a social institution.[56] It is the combination of three factors. First, there is the abstract technology of the actuary. Second, are the actual insurance institutions, which in this case are the outcome of entrepreneurial application of the abstract technology. Third, and most important for my analysis, is what Ewald calls an "insurantial imaginary," which is the particular form that insurance takes because, according to Ewald, in a "given social context, profitable, useful, and necessary uses can be found for insurance technology."[57] This depends upon the creation of risk, not simply an analysis of risk. As Ewalk writes, "Nothing is a risk in itself; there is no risk in reality. But on the other hand, anything can be a risk; it all depends on how one analyzes the danger, considers the event."[58] Risk, in fact, is a neologism of insurance, and it is what makes insurance possible. It comes together with probability to form the notion of the accident. And, "one insures against the accident; the probability of loss of some good."[59] Insurance companies, by always considering an event in terms of their own interests, produce a very risky reality for automobile drivers, one that presents all conduct with a certain type of objectivity that is controllable, whereas previously people had been resigned to "the blows of fortune."[60] Furthermore, as everything can be a risk, this makes everything seem potentially controllable and definitely insurable. Thus the automobile accident is apparently immanent, as everything potentially related to driving is made to seem risky but ideally avoidable because the proper forms of conduct and training can be espoused, learned, and, in theory, practiced. Insurance companies came to lead and invigorate ongoing automotive safety campaigns. Governmental safety commissions were always filled with insurance company representatives, and the statistical data used to legitimate new legislation often came from insurance industry actuaries. The very conceptualization of driving in terms of safety and risk is the outcome of insurantial abstract technologies. This means that governmental initiatives, if not wholly originating in insurance companies' interests, were guided by an insurantial logic. As Ewald explains, liberal governance by the end of the nineteenth century thoroughly came to conceive society in the same terms as those used by insurance—regulation, risk, and responsibility.

One specific outcome of designating risky behavior according to actuarial and demographic data is that certain segments of the population are revealed to be more risky than others. Often these "revelations" coincide with previously held commonsense stereotypes regarding subjugated populations. Becker sees this type of othering as a product of all social problem campaigns. His famous generalized term for these othered deviant groups is *outsiders*. Michel Foucault presents a similar, though slightly less sociological (and more nuanced) analysis of the processes that construct problematic populations. Two key elements of Foucault's understanding, most extensively demonstrated in *Madness and Civilization*, are those of expertise (practitioners of knowledge production) and relations of power (what effects knowledge has on the ability to alter the face of reality). Becker discusses the importance of moral crusades, and explicitly the importance of media saturation, in labeling these others as a particular type of deviant. Foucault doesn't explicitly deal with such issues, but instead focuses upon the importance of positionality (within power relations and as it pertains to changing forms of expertise) for the creation of such categories as the mad or insane. I want to keep in mind the importance of both media exposure and power/knowledge in the creation of these deviant groups, these problem populations.

Most problem populations are compared with the norm and then shown to be lacking in some social nicety or character trait. Women were originally perceived as a problem population when it came to driving automobiles, but in the 1950s, thanks to insurance companies' media campaigns, they came to define and thus reorient the norm. Their acceptance and integration into the driving environment in fact reorients the relationship between mobility and safety and allows for a new formulation, one in which a narrowly defined understanding of safety becomes the measure by which one's driving capabilities are judged and a valorization of safety as the ultimate goal for driving. Whereas other problem populations are generally seen as a danger because of their inability to drive well, women begin in this position but are later seen as safer drivers than men. The new position of women turned the tables and made statistically driven safety standards the measure by which acceptable driving is measured. Thus, the Brady battle needed to take place not on a racetrack, but on an insurance company–friendly driver's education course. Yet it was not only men, via their comparison to women, who were considered a danger.

## Psychologizing Driving

The 1950s seem to bring together the subjects of delinquency, as determined by the social sciences, and bad driving, while also producing a newly understood good driver as the statistically determined least potential offender. This confluence is partially owing to the rise of the social sciences as a legitimate part of the popular culture discourse and, more specifically, to their part in the production of a delinquent youth that was understood as failing to conform and connect with society. In particular, psychology as an explanatory tool and solution for inappropriate social behavior became popularly accepted. Psychology is employed in many of the articles from this period to validate and explain the meaning, importance, causes, and psychological makeup of on-the-road behavior. They demand that we "must look for the psychological factors in the driver."[61] These discussions focus social concern upon male aggression, youth immaturity, and female emotionality. Each speaks to a different, yet "psychologically determined," problem.

Male aggression appears in numerous articles as the cause of a sort of nascent road rage. "The home is feminine and the automobile masculine," asserts a psychological expert in one article. Stereotyping of this form transfers essentialized notions of masculinity and femininity onto the automobile and the public driving environment. Yet it is this very essentialization that the safety experts are attempting to overturn during this time. They are calling, in essence, for a femininization of the road by first assuming that masculine behavior is what leads to accidents and then claiming that women drivers, with all of the essentialist feminine baggage of safety, security, and docility, are the better drivers. This logic both further essentialized assumptions regarding proper gendered behavior and used these assumptions to guide and legitimate new modes of mobility and mobile conduct. The new public spaces occupied and traversed by the mobile suburbanized woman thus needed rearrangement to account for their inherent desire for safety and security.

More general anxieties regarding femininity, masculinity, and mobility can be found in the specific discussions regarding male driving and the ways in which these assumptions guided mobility. The first and most obvious circumstance of these assumptions is the fact that men were the primary drivers in the 1950s, accounting for 80 percent of the miles driven in the United States in 1953.[62] However, the number of women driving was growing; in 1951, 25 percent of women drove, while in 1953 the number had grown to 33 percent.[63] Equally telling is that although women made up 25 percent of the general workforce they made up about 0.5 percent of professional drivers.[64] When it came to the professionalization of this activity the "fact" that driving was masculine was driven home. Truckers, taxi cab drivers, and bus drivers were almost exclusively male. These jobs were naturally given to and desired by men, as driving was seen as a masculine enterprise. Women weren't meant to be professional drivers but could be recipients of their expertise as in the article "You Can Be an Expert Driver" found in the September 1951 issue of *Better Homes and Gardens*. Every expert quoted in the article is male, and their expertise stems from their years behind the wheels of trucks and buses. The article asserts that we all "must drive like a professional or sooner or later . . . well, you've seen them along the road."[65] In "Are *You* Really a Safe Driver?" the *Better Homes and Gardens* reader is given a lesson by a stock car racer, a member of the fastest growing sport in America at the time. Racing, a sport entirely dominated by men in the 1950s, was said to be "the new testing ground of the safety and durability of the family car,"[66] and racers were the ultimate experts at driving safely. These drivers were said to take chances, "but not one fiftieth the chances Mr. Average Motorist takes every day."[67] This type of expert advice situated the road as a dangerous but survivable obstacle course. The fact that an article on automobile racing even appears in *Better Homes and Gardens* speaks volumes, but the successful frame for such a topic was driver's safety education. Like much of this literature, the article assumes that women both need and want more education about driving and that an educated driver is necessarily a safe driver. But the same psychological makeup that supposedly led men into these professions also was said to sow the seeds of their driving destruction.

In "So You Think Women Can't Drive" we find out that according to Professor A. R. Lauer, director of the Driver Research Laboratory at Iowa State University, "women in general are more law abiding than men and have better attitudes toward traffic ordinances."[68] Furthermore, according to the clinic supervisor of Porto-Clinic, a "new testing unit in extensive use by the United States Army," "men have more ease behind the wheel, but women always seem to have the margin of safety in mind."[69] This partly explains why men are naturally more dangerous than women. In general, men's driving habits were attributed to their normal psychological disposition. "It's normal for a young man to be more venturesome than his sister," reminded *Popular Science*. "A boy wants to run faster or hit harder than the next. A girl wants to be more beautiful or dance more gracefully."[70] The assumption regarding who was the better driver, men or women, was being rearticulated here. This change didn't accord with any supposedly causal event; rather, it was attributed to the psychological nature of men and women, which, of course, raises the question of what in man's or woman's nature had changed. In other words, the same nature that earlier was used to explain why men were better drivers was now being used against them. The naturalizing tendency of the psychological discourse can't be underestimated as a legitimating force at this time. It was further used to produce a typology of hazardous, if not criminal, drivers.

It was asserted that 80 percent of accidents were "caused by emotional instability, by hostility, frustration, aggression, finding an expression through an automobile."[71] These psychological factors were seen as the key to unlocking the causes of unacceptable driving behavior. The tendencies are said to manifest themselves in stereotypical ways. Often they allegedly stem from family or domestic frustration, a claim that reintegrates the family ideal into situations where it wouldn't seem to play a part. For example, Dr. Clara Thompson, head of the William Alanson White Institute of Psychiatry, Psychoanalysis, and Psychology, points out,

> Differences of opinion between married people are inevitable. So are violent outbursts now and then. When the hostility is worked through in words and discussion, it is not harmful. When it is kept down, repressed, it may lead to trouble. When the husband drives an automobile after his wife has given him a bad time and he has swallowed his resentment instead of talking back, the chances are good that he will, unconsciously trying to work off his hostility, get into an accident. An automobile is a lethal weapon, an instrument of power—the little man given a hundred and fifty big horses. Under the stress of hostility, he may use this power quite irrationally.[72]

**HE'LL SHOW HER!** He'll leap into his car and go thundering off at seventy miles an hour down a highway crowded with sleepy fellow commuters. The odds are good that his nagging wife will be a widow before supper.

**FIGURE 7. He'll Show Her**
The automobile was described as an aid for completing domestic duties (that is, as if driving were equal to cleaning and shopping) and also as an obligation to extend such duties beyond the home. In this case, the role of being a supportive, loving wife is seen to be responsible for her husband's driving acumen. "Nagging" would not create tension and animosity only at home. M. ZOLOTOW (JANUARY 1955). "YOUR EMOTIONS CAN KILL YOU." COSMOPOLITAN, 14–19.

This assessment, then, reiterates men's aggressive tendencies and their desire to use mechanical objects as weapons—to access power and wield it. It also invigorates a discourse that sees the woman not simply as taking care of her home, but as properly enabling her husband to successfully enter and act in the public world. Thus her domestic arguments may wreak social misfortune. A photo of a bickering husband and wife from this same article is captioned "HE'LL SHOW HER! He'll leap into his car and go thundering off at seventy miles an hour down a highway filled with sleepy fellow commuters. The odds are good that his *nagging wife* will be a widow before supper" (emphasis added).[73] The domestic and public spaces are brought together through the automobile, and the automobile comes to problematize domestic relationships, just as domestic assumptions come to problematize women's relationships to driving. But there was more to this psychologization than marriage counseling.

There was a tendency to typologize driving behavior, and the categories follow more general psychological models of behavior. The new corporate-suburban lifestyle that sociologists of the 1950s decried is said to sometimes lead to aggressive driving behavior, as is indicated in the article described above.[74] More prevalent, according to magazine articles like this, are typological psychological maladies used to diagnose problem drivers. They are the accident prone, whose reckless impulsiveness stems from a desire for immediate pleasures and excitement;[75] the neurotic, who is driven by a masochistic desire to inflict personal harm or is so paranoid that he is as "dangerous as a lunatic with a loaded gun";[76] the dictatorial menace, who must exert his will on the road; and finally, the temporarily emotionally strained, much like the browbeaten husband in the example above. This type of psychologizing leads to a juridical/expert-driven response. A psychiatric clinic was set up in conjunction with traffic court in Detroit to deal with problem offenders by characterizing their psychological makeup and determining whether they were fit to drive, administering therapy where necessary. The article described above demands that "ultimately we must reach the point where psychotherapy will be as compulsory for the emotionally sick driver as glasses are for the myopic driver."[77] Greyhound Bus Company had already created such a program to assure company officials that the drivers were "free from neurotic resentments, fears, and worries and can take the normal irritations of the highway in stride."[78] Such a program is to be expected where bureaucratic professional protocol demands homogeneity and predictability. But Greyhound's manager of safety further contended, "It is high time psychologists and motor-vehicle officials in every state unite to provide a similar screening program for accident prone motorists."[79] This seeming detour into psychologizing is followed for a few reasons. First, it represents the linking of a professional safety regime with personal self-assessment. The growing role of psychology is but one example of other professional/scientific discourses that come to legitimize and orient automobile safety in the 1950s. Psychology, with all of its therapeutic and confessional guidelines, links self-reflection and self-control with automobile safety. Article after article stresses the importance of first recognizing you have a driving problem and then focusing upon learning safe driving techniques. As one *Cosmo* article explained, "With great honesty and the help of your religious adviser or psychoanalyst, you should be able to correct your destructive habits and replace them with a healthier, more realistic outlook. By so doing you should eventually become a safe driver."[80] It makes those tendencies a part of your true self. It provides a psycho-scientific grid of interpretation for the personal will to know the truth of oneself, thus positioning driving actions as signs of psychological maladjustment. Second, as I discuss below, it naturalizes gender expectations regarding mobility and safety. Last, psychology was increasingly used to inform and alter parenting. Problems associated with automobiles and children's access to them formed the theme of numerous articles in women's magazines throughout the 1950s.

According to an article in *Cosmopolitan*, "Women are, by and large, technically inferior to men in handling a car."[81] This lack, however, was said to explain women's heightened investment in learning how to drive properly. A supposed lack becomes an asset. Such an asset that the *Gas Gaskets and Glamour* program was started by mechanics as a weekend course for women to learn not only how to drive their cars properly, but how to tear down an engine and put it back together.[82] An allegedly innate psychological trait is given two very different interpretations. Initially it was proven that women were better (i.e., safer) drivers, and their lack of mechanical ability was a liability. Afterward it became an asset such that, when coupled with education, it provided them with a feeling of accomplishment. The assumption that "women are more law abiding" provides a further assumption, that legal conduct equals safe conduct.

Morality, then, is articulated not only with goodness, but with safety. To be safe is to be moral. Thus, one's moral standing as much as one's psychological character could be read from one's driving. Driving became the sign of character, an attitude which was manifest in many of the articles in women's magazines. While women have historically been described as having difficulties controlling their emotions, it was their ability to put aside emotions like anger that made them different, and better, than men. However, essentialized understandings of women's role as nurturer and caregiver spilled over into another arena of disturbing driving. As noted above in the discussion of male aggressive behavior, it was often the young male who was singled out.

Women's magazines of the day reported that sons presented a specific set of parenting problems when it came to driving.

### The Parent (Speed) Trap

They reach deep into statistics and come up with cold facts. . . . If you know many young people, the likelihood that one of them is a potential highway killer is distressingly real.

"WHO ARE AMERICA'S WORST DRIVERS?"[83]

We must impress on parents and young people the fact that drivers under 25 have the highest accident rate. Our young people must be trained in safety, and this training must start in the home.

ABRAHAM RIBICOFF, GOVERNOR OF CONNECTICUT, 1957[84]

What types of new "truths" were being told about adolescents and, more important, who was doing the telling? As we've seen, this type of expert-produced knowledge was prevalent in the changing attitudes and truths regarding gender and driving. Not surprisingly, similar efforts were focused upon youth. Parents, mothers in particular, were given all varieties of advice regarding how to deal with these dangerous youth. The problem was said to need numerous agents working together in order to educate and refocus youthful conduct. This entailed advice for dealing with one's children at home, mandating high school driver's education classes, and organizing hot-rod clubs for youth.

Giving the car keys over to your teenager was a decision fraught with much anxiety. Mothers and fathers were not only worried about their own decisions; they were intensely invested in the decisions of other parents, particularly when their daughters were to be driven off on dates. The issue of youth driving had gained prominence in the mid-1930s, but it transformed after the war.[85] The 1950s, as numerous authors have noted, was an especially productive period for villainizing youth and specific forms of youth culture.[86] It wasn't just the youths who were obviously troublemakers whom parents were concerned about. As many women's magazine articles made clear, nearly anyone's child could be a potential highway killer. Some of the signifiers were prevalent and conclusive. Hot-rodded cars were an easy giveaway, as were motorcycles (see chapter 4). But how could parents know whether the young man picking up their daughter was going to bring her

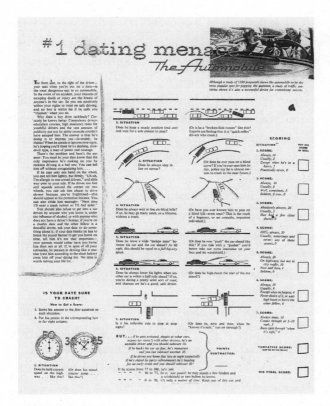

**FIGURE 8. Safety Quiz**
This quiz puts the automobile on center stage in terms of dating and matrimony. Not only is the automobile said to be the most popular place for "popping the question," but it is also the place where a woman can asses the suitability of her potential mate. What becomes especially apparent during the 1950s is that driving behavior was assumed to open a window onto the soul. R. IMLER (NOVEMBER 1955). "#1 DATING MENACE: THE AUTOMOBILE." *LADIES' HOME JOURNAL*, 56.

home safely? After all, as the *Ladies' Home Journal* article "#1 Dating Menace—The Automobile" saw it, there was no greater threat to a daughter's safety on a date than the young man's attitude toward safe driving. In fact, the article provided a "safety test" that proved whether young Romeo was worth dating.

Referring to a young man's dangerous driving, the article states, "He's doing it to impress you—favorably he thinks . . . so you'll think he's dashing."[87] The intelligent safety-conscious girl wouldn't fall for such juvenile behavior. Or would she? According to *The Crash Club, Dragstrip Girl, Road*

*Runners*, and other films and novels of the 1950s, the quickest way to lose your girl was to lose a drag race. One young man stated that reckless driving was the girls' fault, not the boys': "I think the girls are a lot to blame. The guys show off for them — especially the ones with hot rods. If the girls wouldn't pay any attention, all that would stop."[88] In some cases, as in the film *Road Runners*, for instance, hot-rod oriented homosocial bonding trumped any battles over "broads." For the most part, though, dating, with all of its potential peril, had been made even more dangerous by the automobile. Parents had to be even more invested and more vigilant in monitoring the behavior of their children and their daughter's gentlemen callers. Again, though, there was a sense that the automobile, and in particular the way it was driven, provided insight into the general worth and moral rectitude of the driver. A young man's vehicular conduct determined whether he was datable. Young women were given the skills to measure and quantify such conduct so they could objectively make decisions.

The most obvious giveaway of potentially dangerous behavior was hot-rodding. An activity that was dealt with in a most interesting fashion by the police, it is also the youth auto-activity that has taken on the greatest cultural significance as the topic of numerous B movies, Hollywood shorts, novels that might be termed adolescent motor-dramas, and, of course, a number of well-known films. From James Dean's fateful death-defying leap in *Rebel Without a Cause* to Harrison Ford's postcrash ego deflation in *American Graffiti* to James Taylor's and Brian Wilson's epic string of drag victories in *Two-Lane Blacktop*, the drag race has become an often-used male proving ground in youth films. This was no more apparent than throughout the 1950s, when an entire cycle of films made their B-movie mark. The drag race takes on many variations. There is the spontaneous traffic-light drag, the side-by-side back-road form of chicken, the high-noon style race for pride, a girl, or both, and the ultimate: the drag for pinks. Traffic-light dragging is informal, and according to youth film often takes place between a tough-guy sort and an unsuspecting geek who invariably gets shown up. His car's inability is equivalent to his general inability to get the girl, impress the guys, and avoid getting his ass kicked. The feeble car is simply an extension of his general lack of masculinity.[89] The chicken-drag occurs when another vehicle approaches mid-drag in the oncoming lane (*Stand By Me*), the drivers must confront each other driving head-on (*Footloose*), or there is some known danger that is avoided at the last second (*Rebel Without a Cause*). The winner usually forces the other dragger, the oncoming vehicle, or both off the road, thus proving not only the fury of their car, but their fearless ruthlessness.[90] The high-noon showdown actually takes place at night on some back road and usually involves an excited young lady, the object of intense male affection, who is the figurative prize of the competition. This scenario plays out the specific gender stereotypes as explained above. Vehicular showmanship is not simply the act of man versus man. It is also the act of man spurred on by woman, who also serves as the ultimate prize. The beauty of this scenario is that attempts to deter such activities took place in two ways. They dismissed female desire for such men by pointing out how juvenile, immature, and dangerous such men were, yet the men still claimed these women as their victory prize. But even if women's desire was often shown to be at stake, the ultimate form of dragging had to be dragging for pinks. The winner of these drags won not only pride and women's affections, but the pink slip (title), and thus ownership, of the loser's car.

These truths were made most evident in two popular culture forms aimed at youth, hot-rod films and adolescent novels, both of which clearly elaborated for them how they were to understand their own vehicular behavior. The popularity of these forms reigned throughout the 1950s but showed up intermittently in the late 1940s and has never quite died, though their popularity was waning by the early 1960s. The B films that worked in the hot-rod vein could arguably be said to begin with the film *Devil on Wheels* (1947), which, according to *Daily Variety*, was supposed to publicize "the current hot-rod car craze among juv[enile] America which is causing so many thousands of deaths annually. . . . the film accomplishes its goal—namely, to make audiences conscious of the peril of such hopped-up autos."[91] This description typifies what nearly all the movies tried to accomplish. Clearly, though, it wasn't the hopped-up automobiles that were blamed. It was the juveniles who drove them. This said, as was made clear by most of the books and movies, the juvenile was merely part of a car-wrecked social order that was largely responsible for his behavior. In this sense, juveniles were understood in typical 1950s Parsonian discourse as an effect of society's failures that only social programs and better parenting could solve.

The failure on society's part couldn't have been more clearly signaled than in the adolescent novels of Henry Gregor Felsen. Felsen broke into the juve-

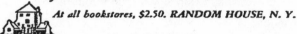

**FIGURE 9. Street Rod Advertisement**
This advertisement from the *New York Times* bears special attention, as it articulates a vision of modern youth as difficult to understand and problem-ridden, a population that parents desperately wanted to understand. As with other "delinquency" literature of the 1950s, youth were envisioned as a confused lot searching for meaning through dangerous activities and associations, in this case a hot rod club. STREET ROD AD. *NEW YORK TIMES*, AUGUST 16, 1957, BR16.

nile market with *Hot Rod* in 1951, which stayed on the juvenile best-seller list for a remarkable twenty-seven years. Unlike his comrades in Hollywood, Felsen was never blacklisted for being (briefly) a member of the Communist Party. His traffic safety novels, after all, spectacularly illustrated and unashamedly preached the gospel of the dangers posed by reckless youth at the wheel. His novels and instructional books on the theme also included *Street Rod* (1953), *Crash Club* (1958), *Boy Gets Car* (1960; released as *Road Rocket* in 1963), *To My Son the Teenage Driver* (1964), *A Teen-Ager's First Car* (1966), and *Living with Your First Motorcycle* (1976). Both genres featured the same concerns relating to the dangers of youth and the danger posed by youth with automobiles. They were also presented as useful reading for parents who wanted to gain "greater understanding of modern youth, its urge for independence, and its problems."[92] The *New York Times* often reviewed these books and in every case saw them as tremendously useful tools. As one reviewer put it, "*Street Rod* should have helped cure this national illness, [but *Crash Club*] has probably won the crown once and for all with this truly frightening book. It should be required reading in every freshman classroom."[93] It's hard to say precisely what made *Crash Club* worthy of the crown, but a précis gives a flavor of the genre.

*Crash Club* is a morality tale set in the small Midwestern town of Raccoon Forks. Two principal protagonists, Mike and Galt, vie for the attention of Donna, the local high school beauty, via their automotive exploits. The principal of the local school acts as the voice of sociological reason and explanation. The story begins with his assessment of the fad of the year, customized drag racing, which he sees as just another passing fancy that will quickly fizzle out and is not initially worthy of direct intervention. The main concern of the principal is the fate of Raccoon Forks. It rests on his shoulders, as there are plans to build a military production factory in the town, which is contingent upon the developer's son, Galt, getting along in his new high school. Thus attempts by Galt to dethrone Mike and take his rightful place as Donna's boyfriend were not the mere passing fancies of youth but may very well have determined the fate of the town. Needless to say, the wealthy Galt showed up in his fancy fuel-injected Chevy and disrupted the pecking order of small-town automotive egos. By a twist of fate, Mike was able to regain prominence as the leader of a new club, one built not on dragging, but on crashing. Galt, whose past as an automotive hothead had led to the deaths of a previous girlfriend and a police officer in auto accidents, was called upon to match the crashing exploits of club members or risk losing face. When he destroyed a car driven by a member of a high school rival, the crosstown conflict escalated into a late-night chase down a country lane. Mike fled in his dad's new Thunderbird while Donna and Galt sat in the rear. Mike ultimately saved Galt's skin (temporarily) by escaping from the posse that wanted to exact revenge on Galt, only to crash into an unseen train, killing Galt and temporarily paralyzing himself. In the end, Donna rejoined Mike, and Galt's father chose to push his plans forward because, even though his son was dead, Mike had risked his life for his son. The ultimate moral: speed kills, no matter who you are or what your intentions may be.

## Trophies Instead of Traffic Tickets

The creation of organized dragging uniquely brought together the desires of youth and police alike. Its outlaw forms had been a key sign of youth rebellion and delinquency, though it represented a great amount of personal investment and presented a much greater threat of financial loss than its formalized version. Draggers were almost exclusively young men who not only liked to drive fast but typically were involved in the customizing of their automobiles. The customizing craze, made nationally popular in the 1950s, is said to have begun in two very different ways and for two different reasons in radically different contexts. One trajectory of the popularity of customization originated in the hills of the Appalachians, where moonshiners were forced to build fast cars in order to outrun police. The mafia-controlled alcohol trade during Prohibition didn't depend on such grassroots technological know-how. Their profitable business allowed them to simply buy faster cars than the police could afford. This led police forces around the United States to upgrade their own automobiles, starting a trend that continues to this day. However, in perpetually downtrodden Appalachia, techniques for at-home hot-rodding came into being in order to keep ahead of the increasingly powerful police cruisers. Bo and Luke Duke of the *Dukes of Hazzard* are the descendants of such grassroots automotive enterprise. Their uncle Jessy, after all, was a moonshiner. Even with the continued success of the *Dukes of Hazzard* through syndication twenty-five years after its inception and the movie update in 2005, this type of hot-rodding is the far less glorified version. It was in California that the popularly acknowledged form erupted.

Postwar auto customizing in California is generally attributed to two factors, both military. The aesthetics are said to be driven by the nose cone painting on World War II fighters and bombers. The desire to hot-rod the engine derives from the need-for-speed created by postwar boredom. The intensity of physical experience the war created, particularly for pilots, was missing in the suburbanized postwar world. Furthermore, the soldiers who returned to California from the Pacific Front had worked on all things mechanical in the military and had the technical skills to hop up engines. Many stayed in southern California and formed a community organized around customizing and hot-rodding.[94] Drag racing, however, had occurred both on the street and in the desert extensively before and even during the war, as H. F. Moorehouse explains in *Driving Ambitions*. The desert races had become increasingly formalized, but it was the street drags that received much media attention. The general popularity spread throughout the nation and was quickly served and fueled by extensive media exposure and hot-rodding magazines. Specific laws and regulations were quickly passed in local municipalities to outlaw not just the activity of drag racing on public roads, which obviously in and of itself amounted to an infraction of speed limits and lane use, but also the very signifier of dragging—customizing. Ordinances that limited changes that could be made to cars were written under the guise of safety concerns. Such limitations as wheel and fender sizes, minimal car heights, light placement, and in some cases color schemes made the hot-rodder in a customized car an easy target of police harassment. By 1950, there was a general furor across the nation over juvenile drag racing, which was thought to be of epidemic proportions, a speed epidemic. As Moorehouse details, this furor over youth dragging was quickly articulated to youth driving in general, and insurance agencies were quick to latch on to the phenomenon in order to raise the rates for all vehicles, even the family sedan that might be driven by eighteen- to twenty-five-year-olds.[95] Like other social problems, drag racing received a fair amount of media attention, which structured criticism in terms of juvenile delinquency. The desert drag organizations attempted to alter public perception and the conduct of drag practitioners. As Moorehead notes, the most popular and influential force in drag circles, *Hot Rod* magazine, attempted to "improve the behaviour of hot rodders by promoting a puritan ethic which warned against frivolity, and urged study, labor, artisanship, improvement, patriotism, and the like."[96] These attempts coincided with the professionalization and commercialization of the sport. Moorehead does not contrast a free, spontaneous, and creative subculture with a formalized, organized, co-opted, and inauthentic activity; he goes to great lengths to argue against such an interpretation. Rather these changes were a response to police pressures and an act of rearticulation in the name of self-preservation, both of the sport and for the drivers who increasingly used safety as the reason for the formalization of race practices. It might also be understood as a part of what Nicholas Rose describes as neoliberal governing through community. There was a concerted effort to regulate the conduct of drag racers through the official timing organizations and clubs that had been around for almost twenty years by 1950. This attempt was also aimed at unifying and expanding the sport by defining more specifically what constituted drag racing and hot-rodding, thus providing an official unity where none had formally existed. This act of capture, in Deleuzean terms, is what leads to struggles over the definition of authentic drag racing as opposed to racing by mere imposters or posers. The very terms *inauthentic/authentic* are thus by-products of the process and don't merely describe two different formations of the act, subculture, or organization. However, self-regulation is integrated with official attempts by exterior forces to reorient and redirect delinquent driving.

Police across the nation created a series of hot rod clubs that promoted safe driving and demanded that all members have absolutely clean traffic records. Their logic was simple, as the inaptly named criminologist Dr. Walter C. Reckless of Ohio State University claimed: "The way to fight juvenile delinquency . . . is to form hot-rod clubs with the help of city officials."[97] The clubs were organized and monitored by police officers who would join youth in their drag racing activities on designated drag strips and racetracks, far from pedestrians and other motorists. *Road Runners* (1952), a short, explained that until a formal drag strip was created with "rules designed for safety and fair play" hot-rodding youth were a serious problem on the streets. One central element was the use of "automatic expulsion" from legitimate drag strips by any member caught dragging on the public streets. The stricture led to a reduction in delinquent dragging by "as much as 90% in some communities." Another Hollywood short from 1954 told the story of a young man whose life was radically altered by just such a club. He began as a wanna-be street-rodder whose pathetic attempts at building and dragging a hot rod led him straight into trouble with the law. He was offered a pardon in exchange for joining a hot rod club, which first demanded that he take a driver's education course. He then slowly learned the rules of safety and true mechanical prowess. After competing in officially sanctioned drag races for a short period, he began to realize what an incompetent loser he had been prior to joining the official club, but now he was full of confidence. His hot rod club experience and knowledge had sent him down the road toward useful and gainful employment as an automotive engineer. He was now poised, the audience was told, to make all of our lives better by adapting the methods of modern engineering to automobiles of the future. This juvenile delinquent to dutiful citizen story epitomizes the magazine articles of the mid-1950s, which sung the successes of such clubs and programs. They found their way into popular culture representations as well. In *Drag Strip Girl*, a dragger is handed an ultimatum by the police: either quit street dragging and start a car club operated under strict safety rules or lose the legal drag strip. He responds, "These lousy legal drags take all the fun out of it." The film also provides a notable exception to these dominant representations, as Fay Spains refuses to be the trophy of the illegal draggers in *Drag Strip Girl*. In this film the female ultimately can't be won by merely exhibiting illegal on-the-street drag proficiency. In fact, her initial desire for the illicit dragging hero is replaced by her desire for a male who competes in a legal drag. The movie further complicates issues of gender and drag as her character becomes enamored not just of draggers, but of dragging itself. Like so many of these films, *Drag Strip Girl* primarily serves as a potboiler that channels antidragging messages through a plot whose ultimate conflict leads to human roadkill; in many cases these films explicitly supported the co-optation by legal club dragging. The clubs represent a mode of reincorporating delinquent youth not just into proper society, but into a safe traffic regime, one that was properly or improperly seen by youth as an infringement if not on their rights, then on their right to fun. *Road Runners* explained the switch in simple terms: "Trophies instead of traffic tickets. He'll never speed on the highway again . . . for through this safe and productive outlet, these boys satisfy their desire for knowledge and speed."

### Tomorrow's Drivers

Two other programs, one — driver's education — a fully integrated part of American youth experience and the other — the High School Safety Institute — little known, played central roles in safety practice. In its initial issue of *Safety Digest*, the Automotive Safety Foundation asked the question, "Should Schools Teach Safety?"[98] Not surprisingly, the answer was a resounding yes. This view was supported in the article by E. W. James, chief of the Division of Highway Transport, United States Public Roads Administration. The following quotation from James was foregrounded in the essay: "If a young person is going to apply for a license to drive an 80-horsepower machine on the open road, it is more important that he be able to do so properly than to sing, to draw, or to acquire a smattering of nature study."[99] Aside from pointing out the lack of relative importance attributed to the arts and nature, the quote clearly presents the school's utilitarian role of producing safe citizens. The article ended by stressing that "the time has come for educators to assume leadership in safety education."[100] By the 1950s they had.

With the aforementioned explosion of automobile use, availability, and necessity in the 1950s, it is no surprise that the automobile had become central to youth's everyday lives. Most high schools were offering driver's education classes, and those that lacked them were under increasing pressure to add them to the curriculum. These were seen as the most important attempts yet to deal with delinquent driving and higher accident rates among youth. However, driver's education in one form or another had been around since the early 1930s, and there were numerous books on the subject. They stressed very similar points and applied similar strategies to the driving environment. As one might expect almost all of the early driver's manuals were underwritten and published by insurance institutions. One of the important links made was that between driving and citizenship:

> Being a good driver requires the same qualities that are needed if you are to be a good citizen, a good neighbor, a good son and a good brother. That would mean that *learning to drive must be closely connected with learning to live*. That is exactly so, and accounts for the fact that you cannot teach people to be good drivers without teaching them the same kind of things that make them good citizens, good neighbors, good sons and good brothers. And, as a matter of fact, the converse is true: one very effective way of learning what it takes to live acceptably in the modern world is by discovering these things through learning to drive![101]

By joining driving to general concepts of good conduct and responsibility, good driving was made into not just a skill, but a moral responsibility and civic duty. Driving was viewed as an extension of and metaphor for being a good citizen. Furthermore, as many authors have noted, following C. Wright Mills's *The Power Elite*, education after the war was increasingly bent on producing a productive citizenry. Driving in general and safety in particular were essential elements of a productive citizenry. Driver's education was often framed in terms of man's (i.e., students') ability to control and manipulate power. There was a sense that drivers were continually at odds with their conflicted desires to unleash that power or control it in a productive fashion. This type of rhetoric achieves ultimate clarity when the power of the automobile is compared to the newfound power of the atom. In *Man and the Motorcar*, beneath a photo of a mushroom cloud wreaking destruction on a remote tropical island, is the caption, "Whether power comes from atomic fission or gasoline combustion, man must be in control."[102]

This sense of responsibility, fear, and potential destruction must have resonated with the bomb-sheltered youth of the day. By placing the atomic weight of the world on each high school driver's shoulders, these textbooks and comprehensive classes insisted that safety and responsibility were the keys to automotive success. On the road and in driving simulators, motor/mental skills were regimented and disciplined, while in the classroom the rules of the road and civic duty were internalized. Finally, exacting testing procedures both in the car and in the classroom were implemented to determine who was capable of being a good mobile citizen. These efforts culminate in the production of a crash course in the precarious balance of personal freedom and civic responsibility. They assume there is an innate desire to speed and drive in an unhindered fashion, and thus education is the way to tame this youthful exuberance. Because of such assumptions, articles explained that "respect for law, fair play, and co-operation should be taught early in the home" to prepare youth for driving.[103] But parents simply weren't doing enough, and driver's education couldn't begin early enough.

In fact, youth, well educated at the High School Safety Institute (a weekend safety seminar for high schoolers), were now "carry[ing] the play it safe message back to their schools and their families."[104] This reversal of concern and transmission, folded back upon the parents, points out the encompassing reach of the safety regime. Such tactics have been used in other government programs and educational/surveillance campaigns. Attempts to integrate recent immigrants through their school-age children at the turn of the century, Hitler Youth strategies of using schoolchildren to monitor their parents' behavior, and, most recently, attempts by the Narco-Carceral Complex[105] to get children to "rat-out" their parents for drug use come to mind. As one father complained, "I have to be careful when I drive now. Charlie [his son] will jump me if I do one thing wrong."[106] This is not to suggest that such campaigns were as nefarious as those mentioned above. It does, however, point to another means of involving parents, and furthermore programs like the High School Safety Institute attempted to create complicity between students and the safety regime, in essence granting them the power to spread knowledge and enforce traffic safety. This type of apparatus gains legitimacy through its articulation with education and truth. Parents and children alike are supposed to be monitoring each other's conduct, thus providing a "caring panopticon."[107] Driver's education and safety programs from the period were concerned not just with traffic fatalities. It was assumed that much more was at stake. In addition, driver's education cannot be understood outside of more general changes in the character of education at the time. Given the scope of my book, it is sufficient to say that driver's education became one of the featured foci of the burgeoning traffic safety apparatus, and its insertion into the vastly expanding public education institution made it a part of nearly every youth's training and experience.

In 1954, General Motors Corporation produced *Tomorrow's Drivers*, a short about a school in Phoenix that began driver's education in kindergarten. The movie does a thorough job of explaining that good driving education is a key element of citizenship training. *Tomorrow's Drivers* depends upon the star power and general all-around Americanness of Jimmy Stewart's voice-over as support for the film's claim that traffic safety is a form of good citizenship. Stewart explains, "What you are witnessing is one of the most interesting and important experiments in driver's education today." The film opens on a driving course of miniature, leg-powered cars and two-foot-tall traffic signs. Six-year-old drivers are shown running stop signs, speeding, passing on corners, failing to indicate turns, etc. Stewart intones that "most of our traffic and motor safety problems are created by a few childishly inconsiderate drivers." Beyond merely learning the rules of the road, the students at this Phoenix school learned a number of other lessons about authority ("Each child learns that the big men in the blue uniforms are their friends"), rights ("Learn an awareness of others and the rules and regulations needed to protect the rights of others and to protect those rights"), and safety's place in the cognitive hierarchy ("Safety consciousness is something that can be learned along with spelling and arithmetic"). This is the exact type of educational experiment that will be called for as a cure for road rage nearly a half century later. It is fitting that an autocentric city such as Phoenix would attempt to implement such a program. It also points out how fundamentally essential to a 1950s worldview the automobile had become. Driving an automobile, at least in some rhetorical circles, was considered equally important to the lessons of math, of greater importance than the arts, and essential to citizenship training. In idealized representations of 1950s suburban living, safe driving had become essential to life, liberty, and happiness. Learning these lessons at a very young age was the natural extension of such a belief.

## Conclusion

I want to end this chapter where I began it, by recalling President Eisenhower's proclamation that public opinion regarding traffic safety must be changed. Why was it at this moment and in this fashion that the alteration had to take place? Numerous partial answers are offered in this chapter. More traditional explanations for the change follow one of two logics. First is the great man theory. In this account, Eisenhower is given credit for recognizing the importance of an interstate highway system, thanks to his firsthand experience of Germany's autobahn, which had given Hitler the means to carry out blitzkrieg warfare. Eisenhower's corresponding duty to address public needs led him to recognize the importance of traffic safety. The second explanation is that of old-fashioned necessity and progress. According to this account, science, government, and concerned citizens, due to a biopolitical obligation to life, have always attempted to overcome the social and technological glitches in the social fabric. Thus, as new technologies for averting disaster have become available and as our increasing concern for leading a more humane existence has evolved, humanity has overcome the limitations of nature and the side effects of technology. Both interpretations are fraught with problems, neither is very compelling, and most certainly no explanation provides the whole picture. In fact, there simply is no whole picture. Instead, I have presented a series of fragmented, corresponding, crisscrossing discursive trajectories.

I hope it is apparent in the preceding sections that key thematic elements cut through these fragments. First, it is impossible to think about safety or mobility without taking into account attempts to govern conduct. This governance came from numerous sources: insurance agencies, government organizations, safety organizations, subcultures, educational institutions, and the home, to name some dealt with here. This governance depended upon organizing concern and directing energy by defining the safety problem in terms of specific problematic populations, among them supposedly inept women, aggressive men, and delinquent youth. These conceptualizations are the outcome of particular knowledge-generating institutions and discourses, including the insurance industry's demographic and actuarial practices, psychology's character typologies and essentialized assumptions regarding gender, sociology's theories of alienation and delinquency among youth, and popular media's prosafety, gore-mongering tendencies and villainizing rhetoric. Last, far-reaching changes in the social, physical, and cultural makeup of the United States were taking place, for example, massive suburbanization, the building of the interstate highway system, an invigorated economy and automobile industry, changing gender expectations, and an increase in two-car families. These trajectories collided most obviously in the Crusade for Traffic Safety.

The model for the crusade can be seen in the war effort, which had ended less than half a decade before. The crusade was able to engage public opinion head-on. The means of verifying the need for traffic safety and for legitimating the tools of the campaign were already in place. It was a question of organizing and orchestrating the specifics. The general tendencies in favor of traffic safety were already present and had been building momentum prior to the war, only to be interrupted and supplanted by the war effort. Whether the crusade had any real effect on the number of traffic fatalities or on specific individual conduct is hard to say. What is obvious is that concern for traffic safety and for safety in general has continued to increase over the past fifty years. The specific means of generating concern, villainizing specific populations, and ultimately monitoring and disciplining those populations have remained largely intact, particularly in regard to hitchhikers and motorcyclists.

One element of the campaign that I briefly mentioned (and that will recur later) is the issue of neoliberal practices that tend to work at the level of personal responsibility, as opposed to government intervention. Driver's education classes were aimed at individual compliance and the production of civic responsibility. The notion that one must have a responsibility to oneself and to the sanctity of one's life appears in the crusade's pledge and in its closing statement. But this notion rarely appears in the other literature. In the mid-1990s, in the face of the road rage crisis, this type of appeal appears with greater regularity and to a degree changes the focus from problem populations to a universal, internally self-monitoring driver. Rather than, as in the past, being psychologically typecast for the role of dangerous driver, we are now all potentially becoming road-ragers.

Last, changes in the very conception of public and private space need to be further elaborated. One of the continuing themes of this book deals with an expansion of mobility for populations that have been othered in various social arenas: women, African Americans, youth, and motorcyclists. This mobility continually comes under fire in the name of safety. This chapter marks out some of that terrain and describes how women's access to automotive mobility was at first a safety concern. Insurance agencies entered the debate, regarding women's supposed driving deficiencies in such a way, through actuarial practices, that the very means by which good driving is measured was altered. This coincided with and legitimated essential gender assumptions which, when articulated to women's access to the public space of the automotive world, in turn demanded what might be called a feminization of public space. Thus the chain of articulation that bound women-domestic-security was rearticulated as women-public-safety. Certainly, it was not traffic safety alone that brought this rearticulation about, but it remains a constant throughout the rest of this book and becomes particularly acute as women begin hitchhiking in the late 1960s.

# CHAPTER 2

# HITCHING THE HIGHWAY TO HELL

*Media Hysterics and the Politics of Youth Mobility*

This is the true story of a man and a gun and a car. The gun belonged to the man. The car might have been yours—or that young couple across the aisle. What you will see in the next seventy minutes could have happened to you. For the facts are actual.

PROLOGUE, WRITTEN AND VOICE-OVER, TO *THE HITCH-HIKER*, RKO, 1953

## Introduction

Maybe it was merely an unfortunate twist of media-induced fate that turned hitchhiking into an almost universally feared form of mobility. Likewise, the hitchhiker became a sinister figure, better left standing in the rain on the side of the road, right thumb aloft while his left, it is assumed, patiently toys with a concealed gun. With the release of *The Hitch-Hiker* in 1953 many of the sensationalist accounts of pathological hitchhikers that had been appearing regularly in newspapers was given cinematic life. The story is fairly straightforward. A hitchhiker is picked up by a newlywed couple, and he kills them. He continues on a killing spree that is finally stopped after a five-hundred-mile murderous trek south into Mexico. Maybe if one of the two working titles of *The Hitch-Hiker*, *The Persuader* or *The Difference*, had stuck we would today fear rhetoric instructors or mathematical equations. Though clearly no single film can be blamed for the fear surrounding hitchhiking, it didn't stop hitchhikers at the time from worrying that the film would dramatically alter their lifestyle. Self-described "highway nomads" in a 1953 *Hobo News* article condemned the movie as a threat to their very existence and pleaded with readers to stop the movie's release.[1] RKO, the film's production company, received protest letters from hitchhikers about their advertisements, one of which read, "Have you ever picked up a hitch-hiker— We guarantee you won't ever after seeing this picture." Not surprisingly, RKO refused to address hitchhikers' concerns. In fact, RKO cited the veracity of the movie as the reason for its release. Ida Lupino's timely *Hitch-Hiker*-inspired fame and her supposed investment in cinematic truth were used to shill Rheingold beer in a 1953 advertisement that read, "'How do I pick a plot?' says Hollywood's famous Ida Lupino, director of *The Hitch-Hiker*. 'Well, above everything else, it has to be true to life. Yes, I'm a girl who *always* chooses perfection. And that's why I choose . . . Rheingold.'"[2] Even given the concern and cultural debate, it is still quite possible the media effects of this sensationalist B film were minimal, and, in fact, it was the cumulative effects of insurance companies' public relations campaigns, an FBI crackdown, widespread antihitchhiking legislation, and news stories decrying the dangers of hitchhiking and of picking up a hitchhiker that over the years conspired to make the practice nearly extinct. What is clearly known to drivers anecdotally, statistically, and experientially is that Americans do not hitchhike as they once did. It is not too strong a claim to say that hitchhiking as an activity and the hitchhiker are widely feared and avoided. This has not always been the case. Prior to the mid-1970s, with some degree of variation, hitchhiking was a widely popular means of transportation in the United States. It was variously perceived as an economic necessity, an invitation to youth to experience America, a travel ticket for the GI on furlough, the only means of commuting in cities that lacked mass transit, and even an underground railroad for runaways trying to escape unlivable conditions. Granted, the discourse and practices pertaining to hitchhiking have changed radically over the past three-quarters of a century, but the issues to be addressed here are how and why the changes occurred, what did hitchhiking allow as a form of mobility, and who benefited from its disappearance and ultimate governmentalization via carpooling. Often a form of mobility is linked to a specific population that is presented as problematic. In other words, an activity takes on a vilified, criminalized, or pathologized identity. In this instance, one who hitchhikes becomes a hitchhiker. It is in this process of characterizing the hitchhiker, as well as the ride-giver, that hitchhiking is made to appear unsafe. Its unsafeness criminalizes hitchhiking and dooms it to pop cultural oversignification, yet actualized obscurity. This chapter wanders the long path that led to the demise of hitchhiking, paying special attention to the political casualties strewn along the roadside of its past.

There were at least four radically different phases of hitchhiking's acceptance or rejection in the United States, phases which can be mapped across the varying treatments of the practice in popular novels, movies, newspapers, hitchhiking guides, periodicals, and academic studies over the past seventy-odd years. The importance of providing the history of these phases is in the recognition of the contingency of hitchhiking's articulation to varying political and cultural movements and agendas. Hitchhiking was not always circumscribed or organized by the logic of danger versus safety. Such a logic limits attempts to consider hitchhiking in political terms. One way of approaching hitchhiking in its political dimensions is to ask, How has the hitchhiker been stereotyped along class divisions, according to changing notions of youth, seen to be a form of gay pickup, or understood in terms of an out-of-control female sexuality? A second approach asks, Which agencies (criminal, insurantial, religious, academic, political, governmental) have been invested in understanding or stopping hitchhiking, and what are their motivations, whether hidden or obvious, for doing so? Last, the issue of a politics of hitchhiking has to do more generally with the governance of mobility. Hitchhiking needs to be understood in terms of what I call throughout the book a disciplined mobility. What is it about hitchhiking that is disruptive of the structures of mobility and that make it into a problem? How might any residual usefulness of hitchhiking to these structures have been appropriated? The brief history that follows refuses to present the story of hitchhiking in a teleological fashion, as if the danger of hitchhiking has steadily increased until ultimately its demise was unavoidable. Rather, a series of chronologically and thematically overlapping moments in context are sketched to foreground the means by which a once vital, politically charged, and useful form of mobility has been written and at times brutally stomped out of existence. These sketches are organized according to varying phases. Each phase is characterized by a dominant truth of what hitchhiking meant during the time as well as a sort of subjugated undercurrent of differing opinions.

## Phase I: The Civic Samaritan

From the Depression days, when millions of jobless men drifted from town to town looking for work, until 1945, when homeward-bound GI's thumbed cross country, many motorists considered the hitchhiker a welcome traveling companion.

"A NEW RULE OF THUMB," *NEWSWEEK*, 16 JUNE 1969: 63

The first phase, what I'm calling the civic Samaritan, ran roughly from the beginning of the widespread use of the automobile in the 1910s through World War II and, to some degree, into the Korean War. The wars are foregrounded because it was often young soldiers who were seen as being highly acceptable and popular hitchhikers. As an upstanding citizen, you could aid in the war effort or at least in general national defense by helping out a GI racing home on furlough to reestablish contact with his lonely fiancé and much-missed family. During the Depression and the vast labor migrations that resulted from it, picking up an out-of-work traveler or family was seen as providing a needed hand to the many who were suffering a worse fate than one's own. John Steinbeck's *The Grapes of Wrath* and his more autobiographical *Travels with Charley* glorify just such national neighborliness as an antidote to corporate and governmental facelessness. Magazine articles from the period took on a distinctly American religious and civic tone when discussing hitchhiking. According to Chapman Milling, "There is much to be said in favor of hitchhiking. It is not so much the principle of *noblesse oblige* as it is simply the neighborly American way of doing things . . . most of us feel a little guilty when we whiz by a hopeful looking man whom we visualize staring regretfully at our vanishing car. . . . It is the fact that the average American motorist still desires, in spite of the well-known risks, to help the man or woman he believes worthy. And, until human nature changes for the worse, rides are going to be given."[3] It was one's duty both as an American helping in the economic and military struggles being waged and as a Samaritan to help those less fortunate.

Besides the GI and those down on their luck, a third category of hitchhiker often referenced during this phase was the college boy. He will return as a problematic character in the 1950s and as part of an entirely different generational division in the late 1960s, but in the 1930s and 1940s the young college freshman, as he was often referred to, found a special place in the heart of road travelers. It was claimed that times were changing, and many of the new college boys were no longer from privileged families; they were paying their own way through college and every little economic break, like a free ride, was helping them make their way in the world.[4] The college boy's tactics for securing a ride as well as his easily replicable costume figured heavily in the discussion. Others began to mimic the university insignia cardigan and pennant-bearing suitcase in order to secure the rides generally the exclusive purview of the college boy. At the time mimicry was considered unfair play, not a threat to safety.[5]

The college boy was not a problematized category. Middle-class American youth did not yet exist as a scrutinized category. Dick Hebdige explains that the youth category came into being in the late 1920s as a result of the Chicago school of social ecology. But these original problem youth were inner-city juveniles seen to be involved in delinquent activity. Organizing youth as an object worthy of study came out of a belief in youth as struggling through a difficult period of maturation, which led to their acting out of aggression in an often violent fashion.[6] These characterizations, however, did not apply to college boys. As Hebdige explains, "Youth becomes the boys, the wild boys, the male working-class adolescent out for blood and giggles: youth-as-trouble, youth-in-trouble."[7] So, although the college boy stereotype prevailed, it was not formulated as a unity for the scrutiny or beneficence of governmental or insurantial institutions. The distinction is important, as the very production of a unified population is itself a necessary part of governmental action aimed at reorganizing conduct.[8] There was little reason to create a problem population like "the hitchhiker" or "nomadic youth" as long as hitchhiking was seen as largely unproblematic and its participants generally well adjusted, despite some stories of crime attributed to hitchhikers. Instead, hitchhiking was considered an activity of college boys. Hitchhiking did not make one a hitchhiker; practice did not lead to identity. Hitchhiking youth began to appear as a generalized problem later, as we will see. Beat and hippie hitchhikers will be described along the youth-as-trouble line, while hitchhiking runaways will appear in the guise of youth-in-trouble.

A *Review of Reviews* article from April 1937 titled "Thumb Fun" considered hitchhiking an adventurous activity not only for young men, but also for girls who were guided by the same impelling force which drives boys and who were as decent as any "homegirl."[9] Equally surprising is the claim that hitchhiking was regarded not only as acceptable, but also as training for professional success. "To the hitchhiker himself," the article advised, "there is one final word. Hold your head high—not arrogantly, but proudly. The road develops characteristics in you which are requisites for entrance into business and professional life. If you are impatient, it teaches you to wait. If you have a temper, it fosters a placid nature. If you are selfish, it teaches you to be generous. If you are impetuous, it forces you to think."[10] The article adds to the notion of hitchhiking as civic good. Not only can one benefit the nation by picking up hitchhikers, but hitchhiking provides a free civic education to those willing to have a little "thumb fun."

The assumed protagonist in most of these accounts is a young man. However, as the abovementioned article indicates, a number of young women were hitching the nation's byways. The popular truth regarding men in this phase is organized by education, civic duty, economic necessity, and adventure. But that presented for women is slightly different. In fact, the earliest treatments of female hitchhiking describe two possibilities, fearful flight or a free-spirited flapper. Girls accounted for 44 percent of runaways, according to an article in *Science News Letter* from July 1941. They were said to be escaping unlivable family situations, and hitchhiking provided a means of escape that was "reasonably safe," according to the psychiatrist employed to legitimate the story's claims.[11] Hitchhiking, young women, and running away continue to be narratively bound, but the efficacy and effects of hitchhiking change in ways that reorganize assumptions about agency and victimization.

Hitchhiking-away for women at this time was seen as a last resort. A different sort of story was told regarding a pair of road-savvy, knickers-clad, guitar-playing flappers in a series of 1928 short stories in the *Saturday Evening Post*.[12] These adventurous young women provide a counterpoint, suggested in other literature of the time as well,[13] to the forced-flight runaways and their active engagement with life on the road. Zula and Elise, the *Post*'s protagonists, play the freedom-devoted foils to the men they encounter, who are trapped in the seemingly fixed places the women effortlessly pass through. These men dream of leaving, but their makeshift plans to join the women on the road invariably come undone owing to their domestic ties and their inability to break free of them. For the women, the power of flight is given precedence over the security of domesticity. In this sense, hitchhiking functions not only as a means to adventure, but also as an escape from the domestic expectations of 1920s womanhood. Much as San Francisco would popularly come to be seen in the 1960s, New York in the 1920s was a hitch-hikable Mecca for many of these freedom-loving young women looking to escape the narrowly defined gender norms of small-town America.[14]

Hitchhiking's relative use-value as a means of escape for women was already being problematized by their "dangerous sexuality." As one article noted, "It is a wise policy to refrain from helping the latter [unmarried women] across State lines," as that practice was made illegal by the Mann Act, which functioned dually as a key part of antiprostitution measures and antimiscegenation laws and mores.[15] In later periods, women's sexuality was problematized in new ways that would mark them as either sexual victims or temptresses. By problematizing mobility through women's sexuality, the liberating possibilities of both were radically altered and limited. Furthermore, because of another supposed weakness women were seen as being potentially problematic drivers as early as 1925. An instructor at the YMCA Automobile School was worried that seeing as women were "more tenderhearted than men," they were "more apt to take these parasitic wanderers aboard" and get themselves into unsavory and unsafe situations.[16] As we'll continue to see, gender and explanations of women's sexuality in particular figure as prominent means by which views regarding hitchhiking were altered.

One aspect of the identification of a problem population is often registration and surveillance. The aforementioned Mann Act was one means by which this could be accomplished in the control of female mobility.[17] In regard to more general mobility, the most obvious example is the driver's license. It legitimates the bearer's conduct within guidelines set out by the state and other governing agents like insurance companies; identifies the individual according to personal and social traits; and provides the police, insurance companies, commercial enterprises, and state institutions a tool for surveillance. A 1938 *Forum* article outlined a policy proposal aimed at balancing three forces: (1) growing concern over hitchhiking related crime; (2) belief in good will toward strangers; (3) American freedoms of personal choice and responsibility.[18] The proposal worked against the grain of a sudden outburst of antihitching laws by acknowledging the desire of citizens to continue giving and taking rides in the face of the new laws while recognizing that a regulatory apparatus was needed to take care of the potential dangers. It simply asked for a licensing system under which hitchhikers would be required to carry a self-identification card that provided personal information. Registration would be granted only after applicants' crime and fingerprint records had been checked. The license, it was claimed, would keep dangerous criminals from registering and equally play a part in the expanding fingerprint surveillance grid.[19] The license would have legitimated the practice of hitchhiking by rationalizing it and integrating it into a larger system of state-organized and -monitored mobility. A similar system will be proposed some thirty years later as a means of addressing the same concerns. An important question is why the policy wasn't put into practice. Although hitchhiking was seen to meet certain social and economic needs and could have been easily integrated into an expanding regime of mobility and surveillance, it was instead made illegal in a growing number of municipalities, on more state roads, and eventually on all federal highways. I categorize these changes in governance as the beginning of Phase II, in which the popular truth and dominant representations of hitchhiking turned rather dire.

### Phase II: Homicidal Hitchhiker

Before summer is over you are sure to see a hitchhiker with his thumb aloft. Is he a college boy? Is he a serviceman trying to get home quickly? Or is he a vicious thug, a gun hidden in his shirt, waiting to get you?

DON WHARTON, "THUMBS DOWN ON THUMBS UP," *READER'S DIGEST*, JUNE 1955: 57

Phase II, the homicidal hitchhiker, may best be summarized by the 1953 AAA antihitchhiking campaign "Thumbs down on thumbers." The campaign focused on the danger posed to motorists by the ill-intentioned hitcher. This radical rearticulation of the American driver from civic Samaritan to potential victim marks one of the early signs of what has become a culture of fear and safety. Part of this fear is marked by an inability to definitively recognize or read the signs of danger; the dangerous other now looks just like us and seems normal enough. Safety, on the other hand, is an increasingly self-dependent freedom from danger. In other words, it has become not only the right, but the responsibility of each American to be safe. Accordingly, the first attempt to stop the threat that hitchhiking was said to pose was a plea to drivers. AAA pamphlets and feature stories in popular magazines informed drivers of the new dangers posed by hitchhikers. The explicit message of insurance companies and governmental agents reaching all the way to the FBI's J. Edgar Hoover was that each driver should avoid hitchhikers at

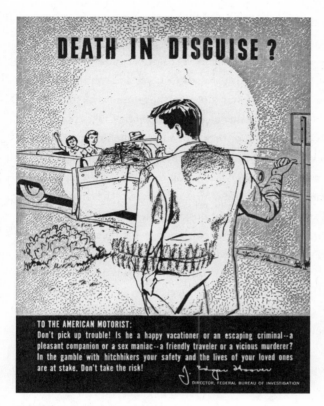

**FIGURE 10. Death in Disguise**
The FBI was one of many organizations that worked to curb
enthusiasm for hitchhiking. This poster, circulated by the FBI, is
representative of the fear tactics used in antihitchhiking campaigns.
Not only could you not trust strangers, but you could not even
trust your own judgment to determine who was a threat and who
was safe. P. DIMAGGIO, *THE HITCHHIKER'S FIELD MANUAL* (NEW YORK:
MACMILLAN, 1973), 11.

all costs. Staying within the comfort of one's family sedan and simply driving past hitchhikers kept one safe from harm, in effect producing a private
mobile quarantine. According to various sources, this was necessitated by
drivers' inability to detect carriers. As was true of many contagions, it is impossible to identify danger from any obvious visible signs. Even the clean-cut
college boy or the serviceman on leave was a potential killer. A typical article
from this period in *Reader's Digest* made this absolutely clear: "No uniform,
however legitimately worn by a hitchhiker, guarantees safe conduct to the
motorist."[20]

Sometimes the signs were not only undetectable, but downright misleading. A supposedly popular con of the 1950s went down like this: A beautiful woman would expose just enough thigh to get a driver's attention while her nefarious accomplice hid in the bushes ready to attack and rob all drivers enticed by the femme fatale.[21] These narratives lay the groundwork for the radical rearticulation of female sexuality and hitchhiking that takes place in the early 1970s. Why was the notion of the femme fatale hitchhiker a recognizable and powerful image at the time? Film scholars have contextualized the femme fatale as a post–World War II reaction to the vast material changes that occurred during the exodus and return of soldiers.[22] The changes forced dynamic material and cultural fluctuations of gender expectations, from an initial increase in the Rosie the Riveter workforce to a radical redirection of women's lives into suburban housewifery. Following the argument that the production of fear in the driver was a central part of 1950s discourse, seizing on the image of the femme fatale makes perfect sense, as she manifested the fears of returning servicemen unable to cope with changed gender norms. Gender representations are thus in line with contemporaneously conventional symbolism as well as the neoliberal agenda of insurance agencies.

Yet the most popular type of representation of the threatening hitchhiker was clearly epitomized by the aforementioned Ida Lupino film *The Hitch-Hiker*. In narratives like this, the hitchhiker was male and pathological. He was often on the lam, would stop at nothing to further his own cause or escape, and was unidentifiable. *Dark Passage*, released in 1947, is an early version of the narrative. Humphrey Bogart plays a con who, while in the process of escaping from San Quentin, hitches a ride and kills the driver when his identity is threatened by a radio report warning citizens of his escape. These representations were also showing up in popular magazines as both fictional and news accounts. In fact, the original *Dark Passage* story was first serialized in *The Saturday Evening Post* in 1946. An even earlier film noir, *Detour* (1946), works the themes of hitchhiking, danger, and the femme fatale via a convoluted plot about unreachable love and random coincidence. To simplify to hitchhiking themes, *Detour* provides narrative grist to the mill of the femme fatale hitchhiker as well as to the danger posed by and to hitchhikers. In simplest terms, *Detour* makes evident the perceived random danger posed by hitchhikers while associating the practice with unsavory characters and motivations. Ultimately, it is the protagonist's choice to pick up separately two hitchhikers related by love, and this leads to his downfall. Film noir makes extensive use of the hitchhiker. Noirs have often been viewed as a critique of America's inability to reintegrate war-formed masculine identities into postwar suburban regimes. The inability was often characterized by an uncontrollable penchant for violence and a generalized presentation of a world beyond a man's control or even understanding. The GI on furlough in need of a lift is replaced by the potentially dangerous, socially ill-fitting veteran.

Phase II provides much of the tenor of the continuing discursive formation around hitchhiking. In it we begin to see four key articulations linking technologies of governing, safety, and mobility. First, drivers can never fully verify the potential for danger. This leads to the second, which is that danger is therefore always imminent. Third, as a result of this imminence, it is always the individual's responsibility to be on the alert. This makes citizens perpetually responsible for their own safety, thus resituating the sovereign individual as the active node of governmental initiatives. Burchell calls this process responsibilization and sees it as a necessary element of neoliberal processes of governing.[23] For instance, it had historically been the responsibility of the police to keep the highways and byways free of undesirable and dangerous elements, but the onus was now on each and every driver. This responsibilization has a fourth effect in that it doesn't simply address the conduct of the self. It is also an attempt to alter the conduct of potential hitchhikers, as they will theoretically have a much more difficult time traveling if no one picks them up, thus decreasing the number who even try. But against these attempts to curtail hitchhiking there arose a differing truth that didn't have danger as its teleological center, but rather adventure.

### Phase III: Romance of the Road

Jack Kerouac set off a time bomb in the Fifties: *On The Road* with Dean Moriarty and Sal Paradise zigzagging across the country in search of the great beatific scene, its people going off like roman candles; *The Dharma Bums* with Japhy Ryder spinning out visions of the great bhikku movement, the rucksack revolution. A mobile population of saints would take over the forests, mountains, and beaches and live on raisins, cracked wheat, and the Buddha-nature.
GWYNETH CRAVENS, "HITCHING NOWHERE: THE AGING YOUNG ON THE ENDLESS ROAD," 1972[24]

Dean Moriarty is the figure who ties the beats and the hippies together; with a singularly driven individualism escaping suburbanization that ends up a generation later in the communal longing to go further, described in *The Electric Kool-Aid Acid Test*, a collectivism of the adventurous spirit. This is the trope that best typifies the romance of the road phase of the hitchhiking discourse. Kerouac's *On the Road* is a hallowed text, standing in as a description of beat and thus hip-youth activity of the 1950s as well as a guide and catalyst for later 1960s youth wandering. Youth and youth mobility have posed disciplinary problems since the inception of youth culture in the 1950s, described in chapter 1. As Lawrence Grossberg states, "Youth exists only as a mobile and flexible alliance or distribution of practices; yet its mobility and flexibility must constantly be disciplined, stabilized or even homogenized."[25] Hitchhiking was one of the very practices used to define and sustain the youth movement. To be part of the radical youth scene was to participate in the hitchhiking enterprise, either offering rides to or taking rides from other youth. The late fifties and sixties also marked a time when hitchhiking became an increasingly popular mode of transport for politically engaged youth; it was a means by which civil rights activists headed south and antiwar demonstrators moved from all points to Washington D.C.[26] Not all youth hitchhikers were engaged in such activities, yet it is one element of how politicized youth and hitchhiking were seen as being connected. More generally, it was the so-called hippie sensibilities of free love, community, drug use, and antiestablishment nomadism that were seen as a threat. Hitchhiking made this threat mobile and difficult to monitor. I argue that it is just as much the fear of this threat as of hitchhiking which leads various government agencies and municipalities to outlaw, crack down upon, and propagandize against hitching. These attacks come from the very top of the U.S. criminalization machinery, the FBI.

In *J. Edgar Hoover on Communism*, Hoover claims the U.S. Communist parties had been "mobilizing young people for civil rights demonstrations, protest activity on college campuses, and demonstrations opposing United States action in Vietnam" for years.[27] Furthermore, according to Hoover it was the New Left, largely consisting of college students from the Students for a Democratic Society (SDS), that were most thoroughly and dangerously involved in Communist activity in the United States: "Here is the danger— that a disciplined organization, like the Communist Party, will be able to reach into the variegated, at times almost chaotic, New Left movement, recruit young people, and then train them into revolutionary cadres."[28] Given the nature of Hoover's scare tactics on hitchhiking, his known animosity toward the beat artists who made the notion of nomadic travel on the road famous, and the explicit connection he made between youth, civil rights, and Communism, it is obvious that, in advocating against hitchhiking, forces like the FBI were not solely invested in the safety of America's driving public. Furthermore, his comments make apparent the assumption that youth were unable to formulate a political agenda of their own. The real threat described by Hoover was the organization and direction of youth by an "exterior" force: the Communists. The political threat was not the nomadic youth so much as the chaos that nomadism produced. The instability and plasticity of this chaos allowed for potential redirection. Thus, it was much better to cut the danger off at the pass. As Hoover states, picking up a hitchhiker was "as reckless as passing on a sharp curve"[29]; according to the paranoid visions of Hoover, something of a Dead Man's Curve. Clearly, this was only one of many fronts on which the FBI fought radical youth, but the attack on hitchhiking is entirely overlooked, suggesting an undertheorization of the importance of mobility as a means and method of politics.

My argument here is not that hitchhiking as an activity unto itself necessarily posed a serious threat to the social order. Rather, it is that at this moment the popular truth of hitchhiking was characterized by the themes of freedom, adventure, escape, discovery, and community. The sense of community most explicitly referenced is, of course, youth. In particular, youth who were tuned in, turned on, and dropping out. One essential part of dropping out was heading out, getting as far away from straight society as possible, a society that was micro-form manifested in the split-levels and ranch styles of every suburban dream community. So off they went, hitching their way as far from home as possible—into the mountains and forests, across the Great Plains, toward every urban or rural hippie Mecca rumored to exist. Or at least that's how the story was told. In account after account, young hitchhikers claimed to have experienced vast spiritual changes and came to recognize the authentic humanity that still existed outside the suburban hell their parents' postwar wealth had created. Such accounts served as a powerful siren song. It was a vision of travel that not only filled a spiritual void, but constituted a uniform rite of passage narrative that allowed young people to organize their experiences according to a legitimated youth narrative and to participate in youth community. Swapping stories of the road served two essential purposes. It established one's credibility among other youth, while simultaneously producing an identity for oneself by situating one's experience within a structure that was identified as truly hip or beat.

While the "romance" lasted, a radical rearticulation occurred. The phase II characterization in which goodwill on the part of drivers was seen as a danger—something faulted rather than exalted—was replaced by an ethic of "gas, grass, or ass." These systems of exchange, although less formal than those of straight society, made sense within the loose-knit hippie community that aspired to be free of middle-class restraints. Regardless of the relative success of such liberationist dreams, the ethic of road solidarity was necessary for youth on the move. Paying for gas, getting someone high, heeding Crosby Stills and Nash's call to "love the one you're with" were seemingly worthwhile forms of payment for the experiences said to accompany life on the road. At times they were both payment and experience. By some accounts, part of the romance was the very denial of the fear mongering that had plagued hitchhiking in the 1950s and would again do so in the early 1970s. It was claimed by Tom Grimm in a 1970 *New York Times* article that, "Because the voices of authority in this society have proclaimed hitchhiking dangerous many young people who believe themselves to be in rebellion feel compelled to embrace that danger to prove it harmless."[30] Thus, while the romance lasted, danger itself was claimed to be part of the appeal. As we will see in chapter 3, this attraction plays a part in the phenomenological discourse of motorcycling as well.

As with any historically founded claims to causality, it is problematic to give *On the Road* such credit, yet it is clearly one of the most-cited sources of this period. More generally, this discourse has its reappearance of statements, and these produce an intelligibility and coherence to the narratives of the open road and the possibilities that it furthers. Many other texts flesh out the romance of the road phase, including films like *Easy Rider* (1968), television shows such as *Route 66*, and such pop songs as Creedence Clearwater Revival's 1971 hit "Sweet Hitchhiker," which asked the sweet hitchhiker, "Won't you ride on my fast machine?," clearly referencing the ass element of the youth economy. The *Boston Globe* "got it" when in 1970 it recognized that Jack Nicholson was a "Hitchhiker to Stardom," commenting on the stardom he achieved as a result of his role in *Easy Rider*, in which he plays a lawyer turned dropout hitchhiker.[31] These pop culture representations all reference the zest, economies, and meanings of the open road and play out the spirit of freedom said to characterize a generation longing to expand the limits of their horizons. This romantic discourse of the road was popping up everywhere, and it was not confined to large-scale popular culture phenomena; nor did it exactly begin with Kerouac.

The romantic vision was not the exclusive property of youth-oriented popular culture texts. As early as 1949 and 1950, articles glorifying overseas hitchhiking appear in *Scholastic* and *Harpers*. But in these narratives hitching was the exclusive terrain of upwardly mobile, college-educated adventurers. The characterization of overseas hitchhiking continued in mainstream texts through the mid-1960s, reaching its apex in a *Sports Illustrated* article that claimed that overseas hitchhikers were "enjoying one of the oldest and gayest sports, the Sport of the Open Road."[32] The general recognition in mainstream magazines of hitchhiking's popularity among hippie youth in the United States begins roughly in 1969. The description of these youth differed greatly from those found in earlier accounts. The Harvard graduate earning his degree in worldly street-smarts has been replaced by the "dark-eyed drifter," "the hippie-haired," and the rest of the "rootless do-your-own-thing generation."[33] There is a recognition that youth hitchhiking is a rejection of a middle-class lifestyle ("I don't want to worry about money or wearing the right clothes or any of that trash.")[34] However, they are represented as naive ("These kids are so trusting," stated Sgt. George Williams).[35] The assumption is that their misguided adventure will only lead to pain and suffering "despite warnings by local police, highway officials, and newspapers."[36] The mainstream media attention, however, is not uniform. Countering such fatalist descriptions are those from articles like "Meditations on a Hitchhiking Ticket," from the *National Review*; proving every bit as romantic as any passage from *On the Road*. One passage reads, "I think every man is, to an extent, a hitchhiker on the highway—a spiritually poor man going on foot, and with little worth bringing to life beyond willingness to accept and increase the common trust."[37] The romantic visions clashed with the degraded representations, helping to dispel the romantic position hitchhiking held as both an adventurous activity and collective dream.

There were more focused discussions and elaborations of hitchhiking as well. A slew of hitchhiking guides appeared in the early 1970s. They describe at length how to successfully hitchhike. Yet this is merely one aspect of these guides. They also dwell extensively on the historical roots of hitchhiking, and through that history provide a meaning for contemporaneous hitchhiking. They also articulate a vision, in some ways a politics, of why one should hitchhike and what forms of community it can build. An inventory of these guides sheds light on their youthful, ideal audience. These are books written by and for a traveling population of young Americans who, it is explained, have a unique vision of what America means and what the youth of America are trying to accomplish through their hitchhiking.

*The Complete Hitchhiker* is quick to point out the long historical ties to the hobo and the hobo ethic.[38] The hitchhiker is a self-proclaimed bindlestiff, invested in connecting to and articulating a vision of American wanderlust. The following excerpts from the introduction to the book make clear the wandering ethic: "We're looking for something when we travel around this crazy country and it's not very different from what the hobo was after on his rides. If I knew exactly what it was, I'd write it down and that would be that."[39] "I don't pretend to be an adventurer and I'm not looking for the soul of America or my own identity."[40] This sort of phenomenological explanation of why one travels in a particular fashion is also prevalent among motorcyclists: see chapter 3. Hitchhiking is a search for something beyond the mere act of hitchhiking itself. For motorcyclists, it is the act of riding which is most often used to justify one's experience and desires. A key question then becomes, can we find discursive evidence of this seemingly indescribable "it"? One explanation is the ubiquitous Turner thesis that the beckoning of the wilderness drew Americans across the continent cleared acre by cleared acre. Paul J. DiMaggio, the author of "The Hitchhiker's Field Manual," echoes this phenomenologically incomprehensible sensibility via an excerpt from *On the Road* that opens his guide:

> "Sal, we gotta go and never stop going till we get there."
> "Where we going, man?"
> "I don't know, but we gotta go."
> (Dean Moriarty to Sal Paradise)[41]

There is a sense once again that there is nothing in particular to search for and no specific place to go, but rather it is the in-the-going which matters. Much like Ken Kesey's Merry Pranksters traveling across the country, as described in *The Electric Kool-Aid Acid Test*, those hitching the open road were simply bound to go FURTHER.

Another question being raised, according to *The Complete Hitchhiker*, was why people feared the hitchhiker. The obvious answer is that the various exploitative media representations of the hitchhiker produced a general fear for one's personal safety. As DiMaggio saw it, the answer was that simple: "Every few years the press rediscovers hitchhiking and seems to think that it has uncovered something new. Feature articles run in *The New York Times* and *Life*, a few more people stick out their thumbs, law enforcement agencies get nervous, the press get bored, and the whole thing dies down for another few years. There are always people hitchhiking, but they are not always noticed."[42] However, we might ask whether a more general social fear exists. As Ken Hicks, writing about hitchhikers, explained, "Bums scare the hell out of people. It's frightening to think a man can carry everything he needs to survive in a little bundle over his shoulder. And it's a little strange to think he can be gone tomorrow. It's irresponsible."[43] Furthermore, the guide explains, "hitchhiking in this country means getting rejected by 99% of everybody. It means putting up with and not taking personally all the millions of vindictive motorists who refuse, absolutely refuse, to stop for you."[44] For the hitchhiker in the early 1970s, it seems the fear of others was a felt commodity, one that demanded that hitchhikers not turn the vindictive attitude back upon the vindictive motorists passing them by the scores.

Sometimes, fear runs in the other direction. It isn't the wandering out-of-towner with the long, unkempt hair and dirty, ragged clothes that is feared; quite the opposite. It is the local population firmly rooted in their communities and neighborhoods who were to be feared. It led to what hitchhikers called the Redneck Heebie Jeebies. The locals were to be feared. These supposedly normal Americans, who pass up the hitchhiker, refuse a ride, and maybe even yell red-baiting slogans or heterosexist jokes, are the problem population for the hitchhiker; especially the hitchhikers of the past, who were easily identified as part of the hippie youth movement. In many cases, hitchhikers were warned against wearing youth styles of the day, as it made getting rides from straights more difficult. Wise advice, it would seem, if the youth of the period believed in the existence of local populations like those portrayed in *Easy Rider*. One guide adds to the legend of southern inhospitality. It reported that long-haired hitchhikers were "molested by cops and local toughs who objected to their hippie-style hair. A few were shaved bald."[45] So who exactly was the safety threat?

Local police forces across the country might include potential rednecks, and they posed problems for hitchhikers. As it became increasingly illegal to hitchhike in the United States, run-ins with Johnny Law became more likely and more problematic. The long-standing distrust and disdain of many police officers for vagabonds and hippies placed the youth hitchhiker in an unpleasant predicament. Nearly all the hitchhiking guides gave extensive advice on how to deal with differing hitchhiking laws and with the police whose job it was to enforce them. Avoiding the police was at the top of the list. This was accomplished by traveling on any road other than the "nastiest of all roads,"[46] the major interstates, where it was wholly illegal to hitchhike. It meant being more discreet and staying well off the roadside in many instances or on roads that fed major highways. One could also look for rides at rest stops and truck stops. Inevitably, it wasn't possible to perpetually escape the gaze of a police force on the lookout for hitchhikers. For the most part, the live-and-let-live ethic of the hitchhiking manuals carried over to their advice regarding side-of-the-road police interrogations. Hitchhikers were told to act relaxed (even if they weren't), to carry plenty of identification (like PTA cards or, more likely, student IDs even if years out of date, but please, by all means, leave that SDS membership card at home), be friendly, "and, under no circumstances whatsoever should you try to explain that you have gone off to look for America in hopes of finding a small corner of it that isn't plagued with the authority, hatred and greed that is the underlying principle of the capitalistic system."[47] They were told to always pretend to have a destination and someone there to see. It was stressed that hitchhikers should never appear to be "just wandering or have a que sera sera attitude."[48] Whether in response to any real threat to the capitalist system or otherwise, it wasn't only the police who were reacting to hitchhiking. By the early 1970s, attempts were made by various governmental agents, media accounts, and special interest groups to rearticulate the defining spectrum of hitchhiking.

### Phase IV: Asking for It

We're not trying to stop them from going places. We're just afraid of what might happen to them on the way.

SGT. GEORGE WILLIAMS OF THE LOS ANGELES JUVENILE DIVISION[49]

Unless there is serious physical injury or homicide involved, hitchhike-rapes are normally given low priority by both police and criminal courts. "Why should we waste our time?" asks one West Coast detective. "Most juries figure that if the kid put out her thumb, she was asking for it."

NATHAN M. ADAMS. "HITCHHIKING — TOO OFTEN THE LAST RIDE," *READER'S DIGEST*, JULY 1973: 61–65

Girls who stick out their thumbs are "just asking for it."

SAN FRANCISCO PATROLMAN, 1971[50]

In the previous three stages described, the themes of youth, female sexuality, and danger emerge and submerge without ever coalescing to form one defining statement. In the fourth phase, the answers to the questions Who's asking for it? and What exactly are they asking for? became crystal clear. The answers revealed the supposed truth that would spell the demise of hitchhiking. Youth were definitely asking strangers for rides, and, according to the somewhat dubious statistics provided by scare accounts that began surfacing as early as 1969 in such magazines as *Newsweek*, *Seventeen*, *Good Housekeeping*, and *The PTA Journal*, they were asking for "it" all over the country and in record numbers. Unfortunately, according to many accounts, what young women were really asking for was trouble, and as far as many people were concerned it was their own fault if they met with such trouble. "Female hitchhikers practically invite rape," claimed *Good Housekeeping*.[51] Blaming the victim is a common trope in the history of rape, but there is much more to be said about the particularities of why rape came to center the discourse of the early 1970s. Women's relation to mobility is often characterized by the dualisms of public/private or domestic/work. The threat posed by the femme fatale was her ability to cross the boundaries between public and private in ways that most women were not allowed. Furthermore, the femme fatale often was the disruptive force that destroyed the domestic lives of the men they were involved with.

The female sexual liberation called for by Second Wave feminists and counterculture gurus was often linked not only with gender and body politics, but also with the very possibilities of mobility. The two were and have continued to be coupled in popular literature and film. This was evidenced in nonyouth representations as well, for instance in *Alice Doesn't Live Here Anymore* (1974), and continued most succinctly, according to film critics, in *Thelma and Louise* (1991). The adolescent girl coming-of-age novel *Truck* by Katherine Dunn describes the exploits of a teen hitching her way down the

Once an almost solely male practice, thumbing a ride is now common among girls. The result: a shocking rise in rape and murder. Here's how to stop these crimes

BY LESTER DAVID

## HITCHHIKING:
## The Deadly New Odds

**FIGURE II. Hitchhiking: The Deadly New Odds**
This menacing photo and caption appeared in *Good Housekeeping* in 1973. It is significant in that it points out a few common associations that were being made at the time regarding hitchhiking and gender. In many instances female hitchhikers were said to be "asking for it," and thus if they were raped it was assumed, even by the police, to be their own fault. L. DAVID (JULY 1973). "HITCHHIKING: THE DEADLY NEW ODDS." *GOOD HOUSEKEEPING*, 38–46.

West Coast, all the while learning about life and love.[52] Tom Robbins's *Even Cowgirls Get the Blues* chronicles monstrously thumbed Sissy Hankshaw's sexual bartering for mobile freedom.[53] Sissy ends up joining ranks with a group of lesbian-ranch revolutionaries, further binding the period's themes of sexual, political, and mobile liberation. Robbins's novel comes too late in that by the time of its publication, scare accounts urging women to quit hitchhiking worked against this liberating mobility and sexuality by producing a new popular truth: hitchhiking is an invitation to rape.

Young women were being raped in the narratives popping up as the Woodstock generation uprooted and headed for the open road. The female hitchhiker was no longer described as the femme fatale, but as the slut. As the previously cited *Newsweek* article so objectively reported, "All you have to do is stick out your thumb and you've got a ride," says one *miniskirted*

Los Angeles girl. "It's really a trip, because people are so nice [emphasis added]."[54] *Newsweek* seems to assume there is a simple reason the hitchhiker is no longer preying upon unwitting men, but being preyed upon. Gone was the hitchhiker as threat; the civic Samaritan had turned bad, upon bad girls. It was as if the first story hadn't proven powerful enough; the characters were too easily dismissed or simply passed by on the road to Topeka. The new story, though, was a little more disturbing to parents, educators, and the police, who were called together to solve this supposedly rampant problem. They attempted to rearticulate the field from adventure, romance, experience, freedom, sexual liberation, and mobility to the simple binaries of risk and safety. And there was a growing amount of ammunition to do so, particularly when it came to women. Between 1972 and 1973, several high-profile rape and murder cases of young women, mostly college students, provided extensive fear-inducing fodder for news outlets across the nation. Several incidents occurrred on University of California campuses, and, worse still, in the Boston-Cambridge area seven college women were murdered, three of whom were known to be hitchhiking. Yet clearly women weren't "asking for it," if *it* meant anything beyond a free ride, a ride that clearly wasn't problematized in the same way for young men. Women were quite cognizant of prevailing blame the victim explanations, though. As one girl put it, "Short skirts, low necklines and see-through clothes will stop cars with the worst kind of male drivers. . . . Avoid such clothing."[55] Rhetorical clues were also used to ferret out potentially problematic ride providers: "Watch out for the driver who addresses you as Baby, Sweetie, Cutie, Honey, or Legs."[56] In response to their greater, or at least seemingly increased, risk, women at the University of California San Diego began the Sisters Share a Ride campaign, which advocated a women-only network of drivers and hitchhikers. It pleaded with women drivers to come to the aid of their hitchhiking sisters. For women at least, what once was the road to romance was fast becoming the road to ruin. And it was unclear if even sister solidarity could keep hitchhiking alive.

The attempts made by the most influential governing agents of youth, namely, educators, police, and parents, were multiple. Parents and educators made explicit calls to raise awareness in children about the inherent dangers of hitchhiking in such varied sources as popular periodicals (*PTA Magazine*, *Seventeen*, *Good Housekeeping*, and *Reader's Digest*), books devoted to

**FIGURE 12.**
**Don't Take Your**
**Life for a Ride**
This poster circulated
on the University of
California at San Diego
campus is an example of
how women responded
to the need for mobility
provided by hitchhiking
while attending to safety
concerns. If women
chose to give and receive
rides with women only,
the problems posed by
predatory males would
be solved. *LOS ANGELES*
*TIMES*, AUGUST 30, 1973,
PART IV, P. 12.

"new rules for safety" (*Family Safety* and *Lady Beware*), and even a special-interest group, the Parents Children Protection League, explicitly dedicated to "hitchhiking awareness." For their part, legislators were attempting across the country to outlaw the practice altogether, particularly in California and in the "radicalized" college towns of the East Coast university establishment, such as Cambridge, Massachusetts.[57] These legislative battles are worthy of more attention, as they point out what the stakes of struggle were for youth and make explicit that the crackdown was very specifically aimed at so-called radical youth hippies.

The discussion over the legality of hitchhiking, as has been shown in earlier periods, was tied to concerns with the safety of drivers and hitchhikers as potential threats to each other. Around 1970, this debate in several communities, mostly college towns, began to change in tenor. To some degree, the safety angle remained, though somewhat changed, as it was described as a potential traffic hazard. It began to become much clearer that the real issue was the existence, not the safety, of hippie youth. In other words, attempts were made to legislate the appearance of these youth out of existence by banning access to their preferred, or only economically viable, form of transportation. Debate over a proposed ban in Santa Cruz was particularly telling, as was a police crackdown in Berkeley. Few schools were more widely recognized for their students' left politics and hippie lifestyles than those on the campuses of these two California universities. In Santa Cruz, local city council members described the hitchhikers as an "undesirable transient element."[58] The sponsor of the bill claimed that the activity was "very dangerous for the many little children I see hitchhiking every day." Furthermore, her primary professed concern was that "drug users are the ones that give the rides to hitchhikers."[59] It was unclear whether the danger posed was due to drug-induced unsafe driving or the pusherman-like threat these drivers posed to the "little children." Unfortunately for the councilwoman, over four hundred of these "young persons" showed up to protest the potential ban, whether high on drugs or not, it is now impossible to say. The youths argued that the ban was discriminatory and that it would eliminate their only mode of transportation. These were common claims by young protesters up and down the California coast, as other municipalities, including Berkeley, Los Angeles, and San Diego, attempted to outlaw hitchhiking.[60] One universal complaint was the lack of adequate transportation for students to, from, and around their respective campuses. Whether owing to youth pressure or to stated doubts about the legality of such a hitchhiking ban, the Santa Cruz council failed to pass the measure. In that the State of California already had a general ban on hitchhiking that took place along the roadside, it was felt that the police should simply enforce the existing law with greater rigor. These municipal laws called for the ban of all hitchhiking, and it was questionable whether such a statute was constitutional. In most cases in California each proposed ban was met with youth resistance, and for the most part the ordinances were not implemented. However, as the police proved most convincingly on Berkeley's famed Telegraph Avenue, a ban was not the only method of cracking down on hitchhiking.

Police began surveilling heavily hitchhiked areas and randomly monitored hitchhiking youth by asking for identification. If found to be minors, they were assumed to be runaways and were quarantined until their parents came to retrieve them. One crackdown was called crashing the crashers by the police, who detained over 450 youths along Telegraph Avenue in a two-week period. Those being crashed, the local hippie youth, called it the big bust and felt its effects not just as they attempted to hitchhike, but in their homes, headshops, and other hangouts where they were barged in upon, sequestered, and arrested. It was hitchhiking, however, that allowed for the easiest point of entry into the scene, according to the Berkeley and San Francisco police.[61] Several police forces were known to target their crackdowns on Friday afternoon in order to keep hitchhikers jailed until the courts opened the following Monday morning.[62] Along with the hitchhiking guides, various youth counterculture publications, notably the *Chicago Seed*, would pass along vital information regarding regional police tactics as an aid in avoiding them. It relayed this message: "If you can't avoid them [cities with particularly aggressive cops], walk or take a bus to the outside of the city limits."[63] A crackdown in Madison, Wisconsin, home of the University of Wisconsin, netted police Dana Bael, one of the leaders of the revolutionary hippie-offshoot group the Yippies. Bael was best known for "Right on Culture Freaks" and "Weather Yippie," in which he called for greater militancy in the youth movement of the early 1970s. It is unfortunately only too fitting that he was nabbed by plainclothes officers as he was hitchhiking.[64]

These debates and protests make clear a few key elements of the struggle over hitchhiking. First, the crackdown on hitchhiking was, if not exclusively, at least primarily a crackdown on a perceived radical element of youth. The locale of such battles is itself telling. It was in the campus towns and spaces where radical youth were seen to be active that the bans were initiated. The rhetoric in nearly all cases characterized hitchhikers as transient youth, hippies, drug users, students, or, more paternally, children. It was over the issue of children that the legalities of hitchhiking became even more pronounced and the rhetoric more fraught. As the Youth Law Center in San Francisco argued, laws being used to detain and transport youth home were designed to crack down on unfit parents. Furthermore, there were serious concerns regarding the freedom of movement. As a *New York Times* article explained, "What the Berkeley police are saying is that kids don't have the right to travel alone in the land of the free. That is a direct violation of Federal constitutional rights, especially since a large portion of these young people have the written consent of their parents."[65] But young people didn't always have the written permission of their parents, to be sure. Other arguments were being made by such youngsters to account for their actions. At the same time, other arguments were being made, with greater public success, to strip these claims of any validity.

Hitchhiking was seen as a boon by Youth Liberation of Ann Arbor, Michigan, an organization composed of anyone under the age of eighteen interested in asserting freedom in the face of adult oppression. In the organization's book *Youth Liberation: News, Politics, and Survival Information* (1972), the chapter titled "Running Away for Fun and Profit" describes the importance of going underground and the key role hitchhiking plays as cheap and undetectable transportation. The motivation that undergirds this politics was a sense of powerlessness associated with growing up in a highly disciplinary school and home environment. Furthermore, youth considered themselves the largest oppressed minority in the world and even made it clear they were operating under different circumstances than the college counterculture. Unlike other minorities, who could at least count on being recognized as full citizens by the state, youth were not guaranteed even the basic rights of representation until the age of eighteen and not full rights until age twenty-one. According to the group, when oppression could no longer be tolerated, it needed to be fought, and if this was not possible, then flight was necessary.

Runaway narratives have always been represented as sad personal tales or as a rampant social problem. This pro-runaway version of youth on the move was declared by the Youth Liberation movement as a necessary political last resort, a form of long overdue liberation. It represented a flight toward new possibilities. Like hitchhiking, running away demanded modes of exchange, often sexual or criminal, which were, of course, brought to bear rhetorically as the very danger that running away was said to pose. Rather than being seen as an economics by other means, in this case the only means, the tactics of survival and escape were criminalized, pathologized, and demonized. The active agent of youth on the move is reduced to the passive victim of a world beyond his or her capabilities. Their naïve forays of fright serve as pitiable fables of mishap and misfortune. The very things they are often escaping, family, home, and school, are proposed as the solution to their problems. Returning the children is the mantra of the problem literature that arose.

This narrative reached its zenith in the film *Hardcore* (1979). It starred George C. Scott as Jake Van Dorn, a dogmatic Calvinist father from the theologically obsessed world of the Dutch community of Grand Rapids, Michigan, and was directed by Paul Schrader, who grew up in said community and at the time was best known as the screenwriter of another lost-girl film, *Taxi Driver*. Ironically, while Van Dorn is on a Christian youth mission in

California, his daughter uses the opportunity to run away, only to fall prey to Los Angeles's drug-infested hardcore porn industry. Van Dorn tracks his daughter through this world by posing as a porn producer, only to fail in the end. The movie summed up and played off of a number of fears resonant in the runaway narratives and portrayals of youth. In particular, the film links the concern over the two moral and physical pitfalls of these wandering youth narratives, sex and drugs. Furthermore, and with more nuance, *Hardcore* articulated a vision of freedom-seeking youth versus disciplinary community expectations, most explicitly, organized religion.

The freedom/discipline dichotomy also appeared in sociological explanations of the period. In *America's Wandering Youth: A Sociological Study of Young Hitchhikers in the United States*, Walter F. Weiss offers an explanation for the societal trauma that has sent America's youth wandering.[66] For Weiss, as expected of classically oriented sociology, youth must be understood as merely a subset of the societal whole and, in nearly all cases, as an outcome or effect rather than a causal agent. Youth mobility is understood as a problem in this literature, much as it had been in the 1950s. In this explanation, youth's wandering ambitions are the effect of breakdowns in religious, familial, and educational institutions, with a little blame reserved for an existentialism that supposedly attracted youth: Jean-Paul Sartre was able to capitalize on its precepts to "give spice to the bedroom scenes of his plays and novels."[67] In any event, Weiss was able to informally interview over five hundred male hitchhikers by picking them up and offering them a ride, most in Indiana. Two major problems emerge in his research, both of which were being addressed at the time in the subcultural work coming out of the Centre for Contemporary Cultural Studies in England. Firstly, he treats these youth merely as an effect of societal forces and not as active agents for whom existentialism, as just one example, isn't merely the outcome of organized religion's failure, but as something which, not just youth, might choose as a means of making sense of their lives in a productive and potentially resistant fashion.[68] Secondly, Weiss's exclusive focus on male hitchhikers, which he never bothers to justify, assumes the experiences of men were adequate to understanding youth as a whole, as if any changes in the lives and experiences of women were merely epiphenomena of male existence.[69] The sociological bias which treats youth as problem and/or effect finds its way into popular narratives as well, and this will be analyzed in more detail shortly.

In addition, this failure to adequately address youth agency is doubly the case when it came to female hitchhikers.

The key to this struggle over hitchhiking ultimately was that those opposing it were able to rearticulate what statements were "in the true" in the Foucauldian sense. This process has two parts. First, the voices of youth were made unintelligible by situating the desire to hitchhike as simple youth rebellion or peer pressure. Psychologists and youth experts were called upon to verify the inability of youth to rationally recognize the dangers inherent in the choice to hitchhike. They were said to be "determinedly fatalistic about risk"[70] and were in fact simply buckling under "peer pressure."[71] Within the parameters of this discourse, youth were rhetorically denied the agency to act rationally as they didn't have the maturity or experience to recognize the truth. This leads to the second part of this process, which is that "authorities have been forced to act to protect students from their own recklessness."[72] This neuters the power of hitchhiking by reorganizing it as an ill-informed negative reaction to peer pressure and parental "I told you so's," rather than as a positive action leading to freedom, adventure, experience, politics, and community. By producing both a truth of hitchhiking as dangerous and providing the schematic in which it could be understood only along the continuum of safety and risk, this antihitchhiking literature helped create three interrelated effects: hitchhiking quickly began to lose its popularity, was further legislated against, and was increasingly monitored to protect youth from themselves.

The road was treated as the space of youth by four institutions; the academy, the press, the church, and government. It was seen, along with the back-to-nature commune and Haight Street (the favorite gathering place of hippies in San Francisco), as the spaces in which youth culture was enacted and transacted. Therefore, it made sense to go on the road to study youth of the day who seemed to be hitchhiking the highway to hell. These sociological, journalistic, and missionary searches further validated and publicized the road as the space of youth. For the evangelical, the road became an opportunity for spreading the word. In typical fashion, missionaries are sent, not unlike anthropologists, into the field wherever their prey are seen to lurk. If that means picking up hitchhikers and using those moments to spread the word to a "needy" group of "lost souls," then clearly that was what was expected. One could become a hitchhiking apostle, as Edwin T. Dahlberg described in *I Pick Up Hitchhikers*.[73] As a roving missionary, the eighty-five-year-old author describes the importance of bringing the word to those on the road as he lived out the role of the Good Samaritan by traveling across the country picking up scores of hitchhikers. He saw his task as that of a modern-day Job. He stated,

> Too often we dismiss hitchhikers from our minds as a lot of "hippies and bums," trash that ought to be kept off the roads. Some of them may not be too desirable. But they are human beings just the same—people for whom Christ died. I have found among them some of the most interesting and intelligent people I have ever known: some young, some old, some students, some runaways from home; many out of work, some despairing, and others looking hopefully for better opportunities beyond the horizon, as did the Amercan homesteaders, gold seekers, and frontiersmen before them."[74]

For Dahlberg, hitchhikers are an opportunity. Their seeking, their pain, their lack of direction are in a sense a good sign; a sign they need Christ. Whereas Weiss's sociological treatment saw organized religion's failure as one cause of hitchhiking, in this narrative it is a source of opportunity for the redirection of belief and conduct. In a sense, we come full circle. I called the first hitchhiking phase the civic Samaritan. In that period it was a civic/Christian duty to help out fellow (assumed Christian) Americans down on their luck. In the age of "Jesus Freaks," when the current rise of evangelical Christianity was just beginning to move beyond the South, hitchhiking, like the prison, the ghetto, or the "jungle," was seen as a place to tame the "savage" soul through the good graces of God. The governmental response to hitchhiking was somewhat different. Rather than simply treating hitchhiking as a youth activity which should be quashed or exploited, they attempted to appropriate it, make it useful and productive, and make it everything it had been opposed to: adult and suburban. Thus at the same time youth hitchhiking was being monitored, curtailed, and vilified a new version of ride sharing was being proposed as a solution to any number of automotive-related problems: carpooling.

### From OPEC to Henpecked

Carpooling as a governmentally directed initiative became widespread beginning in 1970, first in San Francisco and then much more widely throughout the rest of the decade. It is not merely ironic that as hitchhiking was under increased attack, carpooling was being offered as the solution to smog, congestion, energy efficiency, overburdened schedules, and even mass transit workers' strikes. As should be no surprise by now, when it comes to this newly governmentalized form of mobility, it is around the issue of gender expectations that much of the discourse rotates. Government calls for carpooling and the active pursuit of structured means for making it widespread and uniform need to be understood against the youth form of ride sharing, or hitchhiking. In both cases, the fundamental activity is the same. Someone, often a stranger, provides a ride to another person heading toward the same destination. According to what logic could the same governmental agencies be criticizing youth for hitchhiking and encouraging others to carpool? What were the fundamental differences in how the two forms of transportation were perceived and argued for and against? The issue is not so much the activity per se, but rather what the activity stood for, for what purposes was it used, who was in charge of it, and what economic forms it operated within.

I start with a few general observations. Most obviously and problematically is who was perceived to be the ride-sharer and provider. As should by now be quite apparent, hitchhikers were seen as nomadic, dirty, radical, hippie, drug-using youth. Those who picked up hitchhikers were often viewed as these same youth, perverts (at the time often implying queer), potential rapists, murderers, or unsuspecting victims. Carpoolers were most often described as suburban businessmen and housewives. These suburbanites were described as *victims* of a congested highway system, induced fuel rationing thanks to the Organization of Petroleum Exporting Countries (OPEC), price increases, and out-of-control domestic expectations. The fact that white-flight-induced suburbanization was largely to blame for the situation was apparently overlooked by analysts. For the businessmen-carpoolers, ride sharing aided in efficiency and productivity. It was said to reduce lost highway work hours. It was not merely a green solution to an automobile dependency problem, though it was also sometimes described as such; rather, carpooling was situated within the legitimate world of male production and provided, in a roundabout fashion, a further legitimization of auto dependency.

Youth often argued that hitchhiking was an economic necessity or a choice to specifically avoid being involved in the straight economy, to operate in terms other than economic servitude to the capitalist machine or in pretenses to economic self-determination. Rather, hitchhiking was considered to operate as a form of community sharing, good Samaritanism, or economics by other means within the gas, grass, or ass ethic. In this sense, hitchhiking was often seen as a statement against everything of which carpooling was a part. Yet given the economic disparity between youth, particularly those under eighteen, and working adults, in many cases hitchhiking wasn't a statement against, but rather the only means within that economic system by which youth could afford to travel or even commute. In these terms, hitchhiking was a method to offset this discrepancy. It was a sort of transportation handout, a free ride, without the stigma of being a freeloader. Yet, for those even younger, those without the possibility of getting a license, it was potentially the only means by which transportation could be enacted at all. For this doubly disadvantaged population, hitchhiking was excessively perilous, yet, as detailed above, often a last and only resort. Crackdowns on hitchhiking, then, must be understood at least in part in these political economic terms. They were an attack on a mode of transport that maximized the already-in-use automobile when used within nonsanctioned economies and communities. Carpooling, on the other hand, is precisely the opposite. It is used in the name of legitimized economies of public and domestic production.

In terms of economic production, the focus tended to be almost exclusively upon the long-distance male suburban commuter during the 1970s. The primary concern was, of course, getting to work on time. Congestion was a fundamental problem. By the early 1970s, congestion and lack of parking were seen to have reached near epidemic proportions, and a number of books, academic and popular, were decrying the age of the automobile and predicting that there was no end in sight.[75] The environmental movement was gaining recognition; the Clear Air Act, through amendments and related acts, was getting some teeth; and the automobile was beginning to feel its bite. When the energy crisis hit in 1973, the move to carpooling as a solution for automotive ills rapidly accelerated. An understanding of the forms of governmental initiatives that were put in place to facilitate carpooling is a means of understanding how the typical commuter was understood and supposedly motivated.

In many ways rational economics served as the foundation for formulating carpooling initiatives. Cost-benefit analyses and time-use studies were the means of creating the incentive-laden programs. These included a general appeal that carpooling cut fuel, insurance, and maintenance costs. Yet these savings preexisted any government program to advertise them as such. More proactively, toll fees were reduced or waived for multipassenger cars, reduced-cost or free parking was offered to carpool vehicles, and carpool lanes were created which could be used only by automobiles with two and sometimes three or more passengers. To facilitate the actualization of such programs, highway-entrance parking lots were created for the exclusive use of carpoolers, and computer databases were set up that allowed ride-sharers to locate each other and coordinate carpools. Even with these costly and far-reaching efforts, commuter carpooling never reached the levels environmental and traffic agencies hoped for. Yet hitchhiking, which offered many similar benefits, was never suggested in the popular press or by government agencies as a solution to any of the problems carpooling was said to potentially solve. The California Hitchhiker's Lobby, founded and run by the youth activist Richard Vega in the early 1970s, attempted to create a plan very similar to that offered thirty years early during the civic Samaritan phase of hitchhiking: it demanded an ID system and provided ride-givers credits for the miles they logged with hitchhikers. According to Vega, the plan was aimed precisely at meeting the transportation and lifestyle demands of youthful Californians who lacked reasonable mass transit. A bill to implement the plan was put forward but never made it out of the Assembly Transportation Committee.[76] Vega's lobbying efforts do point to a very different way of governmentalizing hitchhiking. His proposed system would have regulated hitchhiking while keeping the primary population of hitchhikers in mind and in theory would have worked for their needs, not those of corporate suburban America. It was also meant to address the series of safety concerns faced by female hitchhikers, which apparently didn't factor into suburban carpooling.

By the early 1980s, carpooling was described as a necessary and efficient tool for the suburban housewife to meet the ever-expanding expectations of domestic servitude and, in some described cases, to balance career and home. School figured prominently in these accounts, and few, if any, fathers were ever mentioned as playing a part in this type of carpooling. The "annual car-pool duties," were described as an organizational nightmare with all the rule-bound trappings of a written contract. Women were told to set clear, definable rules regarding policies concerning tardiness (wait only five minutes), emergencies (always have backup drivers), and space for extra riders ("Tommy's coming over to play Atari").[77] In many ways the discourse regarding women and carpooling harkens back to that of the 1950s detailed in chapter 1. It functioned as a metonymic activity by which gender assumptions and expectations were made apparent. Carpooling had become an assumed part of the landscape as evidenced in the following *New York Times* excerpt: "Car pooling is as indigenous to the suburbs as crab grass, sewer backups, and other small irritations of life. While it can occasionally make you ill-tempered and irritable, its alternative—driving your children everywhere by yourself—is guaranteed to make you hysterical, spiteful and downright pugnacious."[78]

What is also naturalized in the preceding quotation is the potentially hysterical woman in need of carpooling therapy. Carpooling, then, is seen as a solution to the hysteria-provoking duties of suburban child catering. In the 1990s, as we will see in chapter 6, the hysterical suburban mother will reappear. This time, she'll be driving an suv and wreaking havoc on the road. We've come to know her as a road-rager. But, before its therapeutic value was extolled in the early 1980s, carpooling was seen to solve other concerns of women drivers.

During the energy crisis of the mid-1970s, it was pondered over and over how women could afford to drive to and from shopping centers. Numerous articles detailed this female concern. Not surprisingly, carpooling came to the rescue. Stores and customers were seen to be working in conjunction to keep the flow of capital moving through the mall and not through the gas tank, into the carburetor, and out the smog-producing exhaust pipe. As one suburban mother put it, "We have to do more carpooling, even for our groceries."[79] Organized set schedules for trips to the mall were another aspect of carpool shopping. Necessary and leisure/pleasure shopping were thus both taken care of by ride sharing. In either case, the fact that a key effect of the energy crisis is how it made problematic women's ability to shop is telling. It clearly indicates an economic concern of retail businessmen, who were often interviewed to assess the effect of the crisis on their sales. But much more extensive was the discussion of the trouble it was producing for women attempting to maintain their lives as shopper-providers and shopper–pleasure seekers. The fuel crisis made clear the extent to which middle-class suburban

Americans were dependent upon cheap gas and the readily available transportation it provided. In addition, it made evident how deeply gendered this form of mobility remained well into the feminist movement, twenty years after the initial rise of the station wagon and the two-car family. It was as clear as the blame-the-victim rhetoric organizing the discussion of female hitchhikers and their supposed invitation to rape. So, while the good suburban girl used carpooling to tend to her shopping and children, her husband was organizing himself into transportation worker-pods in order to be efficiently conveyed from the Long Island Expressway into his Herman Miller Ergon chair.

## Epitaph?

For Years Ms. Baby Mayer and I picked up hitchhikers nearly always, and always if they appeared to be clean-cut college boys as I'd once appeared. . . . And then, five years or so back, we just stopped doing it. . . . But it isn't because we don't enjoy the chin music that we quit taking them. It's because we're afraid of them. We're afraid of strange men, the way little girls are told by their mothers to be.

MILTON MAYER, "SORE THUMBS." *THE PROGRESSIVE.* AUGUST 1982: 34–35

Hitchhiking died in the mid-seventies. The final popular truth had been proclaimed. This is not to say that some brave souls don't head out on the highway armed with a small backpack and a "Phish Spring Tour" cardboard sign[80] or find their way into the still-prevalent gay hitchhiking/rest stop pickup scene.[81] The virtual disappearance of hitchhiking as a popular culture referent or as a problem worthy of news coverage is telling. It is assumed that no one hitchhikes and that we all know why it is avoided. This speaks to the fact that popular truth often, particularly in regard to personal conduct, plays a more immediate and affective role than legislation aimed at simply outlawing behavior. Laws were on the books for thirty years with little to no effect on the seeming popularity of hitchhiking. In some small towns antihitchhiking laws were passed in order to keep supposed vagrants (hippie youth) from causing trouble (providing local youth with an up-close view of the outside world). Given a zealous sheriff with little else to do, this may have worked to a degree. But even these laws could have little effect on youth looking to leave the small town. Crossing the municipal boundary by foot before sticking out a thumb was all it took. Neoliberal governing depends not simply on legal compliance, but also on the production of subjects whose freedoms and responsibilities necessitate their investment and belief in popular truth. In simple terms, following the law is not necessarily as important as being safe.

It's hard to say if the romance of the road has died or just changed its modes of transportation. The day of *Easy Rider*'s appeal appears to be dead among youth, though the same baby boomers it appealed to in 1968 are now heading down the road on their newly purchased Harley-Davidsons (see chapter 3). In the age of the Internet, the desire to come face to face with America seems not only anachronistic, but incredibly provincial. Has traveling the "blue highways" been replaced by surfing the communications super-highway?[82] Youth and the risk of their engaging in sexual activity has been used as the excuse for limiting access to travel. But certainly it can't be that simple. In many ways today's middle-class youth have much greater access to capital and mobility than the counterparts in the past, and the economic necessity of hitchhiking may be diminished. Yet, in what may be the most far-reaching aspect of the story, through the generation of fear, the application of surveillance, and a governmental appropriation the demise of hitchhiking has been maintained for over a quarter century. Maybe DiMaggio was right in his historical explanation of hitchhiking's fate: always existing but becoming popular only after a news cycle picks it up again. If so, I for one look forward to that news cycle: if for no other reason than that it may, in some small way, help renegotiate the parameters of how to assess travel, mobility, and transportation. It was once the case that a politicized youth community was to some degree dependent upon and organized by a different political economy and a roving form of community that transcended the fixity of space-bound identities.

# CHAPTER 3

# MOTORCYCLE MADNESS
## *The Insane, Profane, and Newly Tame*

We are bombarded daily with pro-cycle propaganda. Films, television series, commercials, and the record industry feed us the glamour image of motorcycling. Children's toys and the backs of cereal boxes indoctrinate the young. But behind this myth lies the reality of human vegetables, ruined careers, and the slow or fast procession to early graves.

ZONKER, *MURDERCYCLES: THE FACTS ABOUT AMERICA'S NUMBER ONE BLOOD SPORT,* INSIDE SLEEVE[1]

There are people who say that motorcycles are so dangerous that motorcycles should be banned from the streets and highways.

PROCEEDINGS: INTERNATIONAL MOTORCYCLE SAFETY CONFERENCE, 1975, 39

But with the throttle screwed on there is only the barest margin, and no room for mistakes. It has to be done right . . . and that's when the strange music starts, when you stretch your luck so far that fear becomes exhilaration and vibrates along your arms. You can barely see at a hundred. . . . The Edge . . . There is no honest way to explain it because the only people who really know where it is are the ones who have gone over.

HUNTER S. THOMPSON, *HELL'S ANGELS*[2]

### Introduction

Motorcycles in the United States, and those who ride them, have over the past one hundred years been uniquely positioned as the other to the automobile and their drivers. The exact nature of that otherness has changed considerably and will, presumably, continue to do so. What has remained somewhat constant over the past fifty years, though, is that safety and fear have been the guiding principles for making these distinctions. Comparisons between motorcycles and automobiles have at times been utilitarian and economic, particularly up to and through World War II. To a slight degree, these concerns still arise in discussions about motorcycle use. However, beginning shortly after the war—specifically, following a *Life* magazine story about rioting and raping motorcyclists invading the small town of Hollister California—motorcycles have been associated with danger, fear, and antisocial behavior. This has changed somewhat over the past decade, and there is no greater testament to this change than the Guggenheim Museum's "Art of the Motorcycle" exhibit in 1999. These changes correspond, to a degree, with changing rider demographics, or at least with the public face of these demographics. Changes in the acceptability of this form of mobility have also coincided with automotive safety initiatives and concerns. The motorcycle is both a signifier of difference on the road and an addendum to road regulations. This conflicted positioning of difference and similarity isn't purely the product of popular culture villainization or glorification.

Motorcyclists demand that they be seen as different yet treated the same as automobile drivers by the law. The Hunter S. Thompson epigraph begins to explain part of this difference. Motorcyclists differ on the proper relationship to risk, whether it is desirable or should be avoided, but there is near unanimity regarding the very personal, phenomenological nature of riding a motorcycle. It is an activity that is seriously and extensively reflected upon, and the reason one rides is said to be a manifestation of one's character. How these differences have been manifested and governed is the topic of this chapter.

Appreciating the scope of how different the motorcycle is from the automobile demands that one understand what it is about motorcycles and those who ride them that places them at the peculiar intersection of being both too American and un-American. They are a sign of American excess; they are too fast, too flashy, too tight-knit, and too freedom loving. At the same time they are not American enough; they are unwashed, unfriendly, ungodly, undependable, and unpredictable. The very same characteristics, desires, and dreams that are said to drive Americans to greatness drive drivers mad. But it is not simply on the road that motorcycles signify. It is within the realm of culture that they have been situated as an other. Their outsider status is not simply signified by a motorcycle. Instead, a host of secondary and tertiary signifiers fill out the entirety of the representation. The specifics of these nonmotorcycle, but motorcyclist traits are where the action is. It is here, in their dress, talk, and actions, that difference is truly manifest. It is this whole way of life that has most consistently been used to inform and spice up movie scripts, television shows, and books. *The Wild One*, *Easy Rider*, *ChiPs*, and *Zen and the Art of Motorcycle Maintenance* are just a few notable examples in this production of difference. But government reports, American Medical Association studies, and suburban myths that always begin with "I had a cousin who rode a motorcycle" and end with "He was only nineteen when he was hit by a semi" have also played a significant part in this process. This latter form of representation works at a different level. It isn't that it is any less powerful or that it is more or less accurate. Rather, it is about the individual danger posed to the rider as opposed to the social danger posed by riders. In both cases, the motorcycle is compared to the (at times unspoken) other, the automobile. The norm to which it is compared is not a socially, statistically, or morally given constant. The motorcycle is considered dangerous, one could argue, only because in most cases it is more dangerous to ride a motorcycle than to drive a car. Furthermore, the normal American with whom the motorcycle rider is compared is the automobile driver. In a sense, it is anyone who isn't on a motorcycle, which is to say, everyone who is in a car. The motorcycle could be considered that which makes the automobile accident rate acceptable. Thankfully, there are more motorcycle accidents per mile than automobile accidents. If there weren't, against what standard could the automobile be made safe?

Although this line of inquiry won't be taken much further here, it is interesting to compare the differing coverage of two Hollywood movie stars who suffered head injuries while riding. One rode a horse, the other an iron horse. One was supposedly invincible, a man of steel, the other a mostly bit part actor who, as we would find out, was not made of steel. At the time of the accidents, Christopher Reeves's career was a quickly fading memory, while Gary Busey's was on the rise. When Reeves fell off a horse and broke his neck, becoming paralyzed, the collective audience of America embraced his tragedy, honored him for lifetime achievements, and paraded him out to give Academy Awards. After Busey sustained a head injury while riding his Harley, he became the butt of late-night jokes. His movie career foundered, and his most memorable role since the accident was a small part in David Lynch's *Lost Highway*, in which he plays—what else?—an aging, middle-class, Harley-riding, pot-smoking loser. Why exactly is this? It could be argued that the horse verses iron horse comparison is not the only determining factor, although this certainly is the case. Reeves was arguably much better looking than Busey, and his hair was never a mess, but the differences between the horse and iron horse need to be made clear. Not only do considerable class differences arise, but falling off a horse is not considered stupid; it is a right of passage. Getting back on after falling off is an act that requires serious willpower and is a sign of strong character. Falling off a horse and sustaining serious physical damage is a real tragedy and an opportunity to prove one's mettle. *National Velvet* and the recent *Horse Whisperer* taught us this. Crashing on a motorcycle is a sign of stupidity. It is, after all, something Busey was really asking for by engaging in an activity like riding a motorcycle, according to this reasoning. He should have known this was how it would end. In fact, getting on the thing is the first sign of idiocy. This line of reasoning made it so easy to make Busey's new brain damage a laughing matter. The statistical danger posed by riding a horse is, of course, much higher than that for riding a motorcycle. This has never, as far as I know, been brought up in any discussion regarding Reeves's tragedy or Busey's idiocy. It never will be, except in the letters pages of motorcycle magazines, where the "dimwitted" riders complain about their media lot. Riding a cycle is not riding a horse, and the comparison, to most, has no merit. It in fact doesn't make sense within representations of safety mindedness. The comparison between horses and motorcycles, however, did made sense a hundred years ago. In fact, the association of the two was quite common, but those days are long gone. There is no current necessary reason to make the comparison, or perhaps at any point, but why this type of comparison has existed and its more precise content will be given more attention later.

More important than understanding what the differences in the conceptions of motorcycle and horseback riding are, or even how they've come about, is how these differences have been reacted to and governed. If the primary concern of each of the chapters in this book is how mobility is produced and regulated through technologies of safety, the motorcycle should in many ways be the litmus test for all such regulations. It is, as Foucault states, at the points of greatest resistance that power asserts itself most severely. This leads to the assumption that motorcyclists, because their mobility is seen as the most dangerous threat to themselves and their collective behavior as a threat to others, should be extensively governed. To a degree this is exactly so. As will be shown, legislative and police action toward motorcyclists have been incredibly prohibitive and at times brutal. At the same time, safety campaigns, often led by rider groups, insurance agencies, and motorcycle magazines, have increasingly stressed self-discipline, self-improvement, and protective gear, all in the name of safety. Thus, the micropractices and networks of power emanate from and encompass motorcyclists, government agencies, and financially invested industries (insurance companies, the motorcycle press, motorcycle manufacturers, and the motorcycle aftermarket). In this way, just as the representation of motorcyclists cannot be blamed simply on Hollywood, so regulation cannot be blamed solely on big government, as it often is in the motorcycle press. What follows is an attempt to articulate the formations of difference with governing initiatives and regimes. They are never wholly dependant nor determinative of each other. They do, though, at critical moments, make apparent the logic of disciplined mobility in one of its most distilled forms.

### The Iron Horse

Writing a history of any technology is fraught with the danger of technological determinism. This brief overview is not so concerned with exactly why motorcycles have or have not been ridden. It is an attempt to explain how the motorcycle's relationship to the automobile has been altered. For the first half of the last century, this relationship was one of utility and economics. Which is to say that motorcycles have served utilitarian purposes throughout their history, as have automobiles, but this wasn't their only use. It is, however, the standard explanation for their popularity before World War II. As long as riders were using motorcycles for utilitarian purposes, there was no need for a difference to exist. Once their use is no longer considered utilitarian, there is a social need to explain why one would ride. If it doesn't make sense within a standard framework of economy and utility, then there must be another answer. It is this desire for an alternative explanation that has occupied much of the academic, journalistic, and autobiographical discourse regarding motorcycles over the past fifty years.

Up until and through World War II in the United States, motorcyclists were not represented as being extensively different from the population at large. The motorcycle was first considered a means to increase speeds and extend the distances covered by a personal transportation device. Technologically, the key was the combustion engine, which, when attached to the frame of a bicycle, vastly altered personal mobility. The automobile became an extension of the wagon and was put to use as a multipurpose transportation device. The motorcycle, on the other hand, had a more limited number of commercial uses and afforded far less protection from the elements. What the motorcycle did have going for it, until World War I, was a significant price advantage over the automobile and a substantially higher top speed. Following the enormous success of the Model T, differences in price diminished along with differences in utility. Quite simply, the motorcycle could serve some mobile functions, but even with a sidecar motorcycles carried a far smaller load and fewer family members around town and country than a similarly priced automobile.

The motorcycle came into its own as a means of reconnaissance and communication during World War I. It was similarly used throughout the twenties and thirties by police departments across the United States. Motorcycles were more nimble than any automobile of the day and still cheaper than cars while capable of traveling the same speeds. This made them ideally suited for surveillance, pursuit, and response. Outside of governmental use, the motorcycle was witnessing a decline in general use and was seen as something of a leisure and sporting vehicle. As Melissa Holbrook Pierson contended, there was only one reason for riding a motorcycle thereafter: "The only possible answer, disturbing as it was to a bourgeois sensibility, was pleasure. It was a pleasure in which the rider straddled a machine that did nothing to disguise its purely propulsive function and that surged powerfully on while generating ungainly sounds."[3]

By the mid-1930s Harley-Davidson and Indian were the only two remaining American manufacturers of motorcycles, a sharp decline from the more than one hundred existing before World War I. Motorcycles at the time stressed increases in speed, and motorcycle racing had become a popular sport. The outbreak of World War II brought a tremendous increase in motorcycle use, as both Indian and Harley were pressed into service to provide the frontline military forces with the eminently useful vehicles, which were able to cover vast distances over many terrains in a relatively short amount of time. But even in war, the motorcycle was beginning to fall out of favor. The Jeep, with its four-wheel drive, greater stability, and larger capacity, proved to be more useful than the motorcycle for U.S. military purposes. There was, however, an unexpected outcome of military motorcycle use.

## Ganging Up

It has been repeatedly claimed that returning soldiers were unwilling to part with the speed and excitement provided by their Harleys. The civilian use looked very different from police and military use of motorcycles, at least as far as *Life* magazine was concerned. Over the Fourth of July weekend in 1947, a marauding conglomeration of a claimed four thousand motorcyclists "roared into Hollister, Calif. . . . They quickly tired of ordinary motorcycle thrills and turned to more exciting stunts. Racing their vehicles down main street and through traffic lights, they rammed into restaurants and bars, breaking furniture and mirrors."[4]

The short story describing the Hollister incident was epitomized in the accompanying photograph. Astride a giant Harley sat an equally large, obviously drunk man. Two-fisting bottles of beer, he is leaning back, his bike standing amidst a collection of empties. The image made great copy. The *Life* magazine story provided a visual accompaniment to the postwar bikers, one that would not die, and in fact, with the help of Hollywood, Thompson, and motorcyclists' self-promotion, would thrive well into the 1970s. The original *Life* story was picked up by other news agencies, and soon a moral panic regarding out-of-control motorcycle gangs had begun. They were said to exhibit every sort of antisocial behavior, and two members were indeed charged with raping a young Hollister girl. Police agencies, particularly in California, began cracking down on any group of motorcyclists who gathered together.

Against the backdrop of postwar changes in the political, cultural, and economic climate of American life, this reaction is not that surprising. Many of these changes have been acknowledged in chapter 1, which helps explain the particularities of the institutionalization of the safety discourse as it relates to motorcycles as well. There is, however, another motorcycle population that was specifically targeted by the safety establishment, youth motorcyclists. Both populations are the outcome of a unique set of circumstances accompanying the return of soldiers from World War II and the subsequent

**FIGURE 13. Cyclist's Holiday**
This now-infamous photo was choreographed and staged by a *Life* magazine photographer in order to exaggerate the menace posed by "motorcycle clubs" taking a holiday ride. The story and accompanying images are said to have inspired the 1953 film *The Wild One*, which helped to solidify the image of motorcyclists as outlaws. "CYCLIST'S HOLIDAY," *LIFE*, JULY 21, 1947, 31.

cultural ideals they found themselves facing. This was a time of great domestic uniformity, if not empirically, then as an ideal. Suburbanization, the baby boom, and economic prosperity all demanded domestic security, economic reliability, and social normalization. Motorcycle gangs, which began to appear shortly after the war, were quite obviously outside the realm of normalcy. The baby boom youth population, on the other hand, was the outcome of the same domestic stability which biker gangs were seemingly opposed to. Both groups, however, would ultimately face restrictions that were specifically aimed at reducing their mobility and keeping them under surveillance. The two populations were problematic in different ways. The bikers represented a danger to society, while youth were endangered by motorcycling. Both threats were dealt with through safety regulations. Furthermore, the motorcycle and what it stood for, for both groups, would come together by the late 1960s in the movie *Easy Rider*. Two highly diverse motorcycle populations came to be recognizably interchangeable as a sign of youthful rebellion, angst, and freedom.

Part of this angst-ridden representation is personified by Marlon Brando in the film *The Wild One* (1953). The film begins by claiming that the events portrayed in the movie are based on a true incident, namely, the aforementioned Hollister holiday run.[5] Furthermore, the movie warned its audience, "It's up to you to prevent this from happening elsewhere." This Hollywood treatment portrays a struggle between the corrupting influence of a gang and the inner morality of Brando's character. The allure of the gang is driven more by his inability to conform to social norms than by any particular drive to not conform. He is quite simply the rebel without a cause. His angst finds an outlet through an already established social formulation, the gang. The gang's place in Brando's world is typical of a post–Chicago School sociological understanding of what gangs provide: a deviant space of acceptance and a differing form of conformity. In this sense, the motorcycle is not integral to the gang, but merely the means through which uniformity is produced and enacted. Paul Willis would, twenty years later in his book *Profane Culture*, provide another understanding of motorcycle gangs. For Willis, the motorbike was integral to the motorcycle gang and the center around which all other homologous elements of their culture revolved.[6] But in *The Wild One* there is no sense that this is the case. The movie was taken up in two very different ways. For motorcyclists, especially future motorcyclists, Brando's character provided a script, a style, and an attitude for being a biker. Brando's character has been, and continues to be, used to promote and explain riders' investments, attitudes, and inspiration for riding. On the other hand, its supposed verisimilitude provided proof that motorcycle gangs should strike fear into the hearts of every small town across the nation. This dual role is typical of motorcycle gang movies, and when they reached the peak of their popularity in the late 1960s this was still the case.

As impossible as it is to locate the absolute cause, or for that matter the meaning or importance of any phenomena, there is a consistency to the understandings of the motorcycle gang that goes back at least to Thompson's best-selling expose *Hell's Angels* (1966). Hunter rode with the Angels for over a year and supplied the type of new journalism ethnography for the Hell's Angels that Tom Wolfe would shortly thereafter provide for the Merry Pranksters in *Electric Kool-Aid Acid Test*.[7] He sums up the discontent of outlaw motorcyclists:

> The whole thing was born, they say, in the late 1940s, when most ex-GIs wanted to get back to an orderly pattern: college, marriage, a job, children—all the peaceful extras that come with a sense of security. But not everybody felt that way. Like the drifters who rode west after Appomattox, there were thousands of veterans in 1945 who flatly rejected the idea of going back to their prewar pattern. They didn't want order, but privacy—and time to figure things out. It was a nervous, downhill feeling, a mean kind of Angst that always comes out of wars . . . a compressed sense of time on the outer limits of fatalism. They wanted more action, and one of the ways to look for it was on a big motorcycle. By 1947 the state was alive with bikes, nearly all of them powerful American-made irons from Harley-Davidson and Indian.[8]

This lengthy description begins to get at some of the key elements of postwar life that motorcycle gang members seemed to reject. It is a bit too easy to simply attribute this to an inner angst, as Thompson does, that "comes out of wars," but the difference between Ward Cleaver and Brando was real, and there is little question who was patterned after whom.

In *Hell's Angels* Thompson relates his experiences with the Angels along with a running commentary of the historical construction of the Angels as the outcome of media hype and a resistance to postwar ideals. Thompson attributes great importance to Brando on his Triumph Thunderbird and to Marvin as the Harley-riding tough-as-nails gang leader. For Thompson they came to epitomize the attitudes of bikers. It isn't until the later 1960s, though, shortly following the publication of Thompson's book, that motorcycle B films flooded the market. Roger Corman's *Wild Angels*, starring Peter Fonda, is said to be the movie that truly spawned the genre. Fonda plays the leader of a motorcycle gang who steal a police motorcycle, kill a cop, rape a nurse, have an orgy in a church, beat a priest, and finally cause a riot in a small California town where they are burying one of their own. Fonda plays the dual role of Brando and Marvin in this film. As Blues, he is both the angst-ridden loner and the gang leader. The film ends with an apocalyptic vision of Fonda's future. As the rest of his gang flees an onslaught of cops, Nancy Sinatra, his motorcycle momma, pleas, "We gotta get out of here Blues . . . Blues . . . Please, let's go." Fonda replies with stoic calm, "There's nowhere to go." With this statement, Fonda sums up one contention of mine. The motorcycle, though it may be seen as a deterritorializing form of mobility, cannot take you anywhere that isn't already territorialized, that isn't always already prefigured, not only by the governmental striation of space, but also by discourse regarding motorcycling itself. It is such an overloaded arena, so heavily dependant upon phenomenological description, that the very dream of riding free is already bound.

Following the relatively huge success of *Wild Angels*, numerous others biker movies followed within the B-market system of costs and distribution: *Angel's as Hard as They Come*, *Angels Die Hard*, *Angels from Hell*, *Devil's Angels*, *Run Angel Run*, *The Rebel Rousers*, *Hell's Angels 1969*, *Hell's Angels on Wheels*, and, starring none other than Broadway Joe Namath, *C. C. and Company*. They all presented fairly straightforward scenes of brutality, group intemperance, wanton sexuality, and clashes with "the man." Small-town denizens were most often the targets of this anarchy.

In *Easy Rider* small townspeople take their revenge. The movie was said to be about much more than earlier biker films. It was "a symbol and even a metaphor for its generation."[9] Unlike most films to reach cultural canonization, *Easy Rider* didn't have to wait.[10] It is the well-known story of two hippy bikers who sell a bag of unidentified drugs to finance a cross-country quest. This story about the characters' search to discover themselves and America was both a critical and financial success, and it is still watched and revered by both youth and motorcyclists. The film covers some of the same ground as *The Wild One* and reunites angst-ridden youth and motorcycles. In each film, an inner struggle to maintain individualism in the face of social norms is played out, and in each the motorcycle is the mode of escape. It offers the mobility to search elsewhere. But the search, in which the road represents freedom and resistance, is always circumscribed by domesticity, according to Steven Cohan and Ina Rae Hark in *The Road Movie Book*. In the two films being discussed here, law-abiding citizens act out violent revenge upon the youthful protagonists; a classic struggle between anarchy and order, youth and adult, is played out. Vital to both is a series of articulations that stretches between youth, mobility, anarchy, and law and order. Ultimately, we know who wins in these stories. There never is any real question. However, in the so-called real world, similar struggles were taking place over the definition of youth and the regulations being placed on their mobility. Motorcycles played a part in this struggle as well. What *Easy Rider* does is link the two populations whose mobility was under such scrutiny: motorcycle gangs and youth. Fonda and Dennis Hopper don't make up a gang, nor is there any reason to believe they are part of a gang. They do, however, have the trappings of the gang member: a chopped bike, a uniform, and a disheveled, if not dirty, appearance. They also display the by-now worn-out signs of their generation: idealism, search for meaning, and wanderlust. By articulating 1960s youth culture and motorcycles, *Easy Rider* allowed the motorcycle to transcend its angst appeal and ultimately, with the advent of *Zen and the Art of Motorcycle Maintenance* in 1974, become a vehicle for philosophical contemplation. Furthermore, it rejuvenated the wanderlust of the beats and invigorated youth desire for mobility.[11] All of this is to say, the motorcycle was still dangerous, but in a different way.

### You Meet the Nicest People

On the supposedly opposite end of the motorcycle-riding spectrum from the Hell's Angels was a booming market of affluent youth. The genetic outcome of normal suburban breeding, the baby boomers comprised the first youth culture. In *We Gotta Get Out of This Place* (1992), Lawrence Grossberg argues that youth signifies change and transition, and the space that opens up between childhood and adulthood is struggled over, usually in ways that involve, "excessiveness, an impulsiveness, a maniacal irresponsibility" on the part of youth.[12] In response to this undisciplined behavior, an attempt is made to construct youth as a more productive population. Grossberg, leaning heavily on Foucault's notion of biopower states, "Youth was a material problem; it was a body—the body of the adolescent and the social body of the baby boom—that had to be properly inserted into the dominant system of economic and social relationships."[13] In other words, each youth had to be disciplined through various apparatuses, like school, church, and home, in order to create a social body that would be economically and socially productive.

Most of the academic work in this area centers itself around rock music and the various attempts to censor or weaken the supposedly sexually ex-

**You meet the nicest people on a Honda.** Always hits the right note. Prices start about $215* Upkeep no strain. The rugged four-stroke engine gets up to 200 miles to a gallon of gas. The whole package is handsomely styled. And that goes for all 14 models in the line. The world's biggest seller. **HONDA**

YOU MEET THE NICEST PEOPLE ON A HONDA

Maybe it's the incredibly low price. $215 (plus a modest set-up charge). Or the fact it doesn't gulp gas. Just ups 8 - 200 miles to the gallon. Or the way the masterful 4-stroke bike OHV engine carries you along at 45 mph without a murmur.

Or it could be the ease of 3-speed transmission, automatic clutch and the extra safety of Honda's cam-type brakes on both wheels. The optional push-button starter makes you feel right at home, too.

But most likely it's the fun. Evidently nothing catches on like the fun of owning a Honda. You see so many around these days. And the nicest people riding them. Merry Christmas. For address of your nearest dealer or other information, write: Dept. AA, American Honda Motor Co., Inc., 100 West Alondra, Gardena, Calif.

**HONDA**—world's biggest seller!

**FIGURES 14 and 15. You Meet the Nicest People** Honda worked hard to change the image of motorcycling in order to sell their inexpensive motorcycles to a much wider population, one that crossed gender and class divisions. Through its "You meet the nicest people on a Honda" campaign, Honda helped to change attitudes regarding motorcycling in order to make it more respectable. *LIFE,* DECEMBER 6, 1963, 105; MARCH 18, 1966, 29.

plicit and socially degenerative beat and lyrics of early rock music.[14] Less importance has been placed on other youth activity of the era. Yet the explosion of motorcycle use among youth in the late 1950s and throughout the 1960s faced similar attacks. Ultimately, highly focused policy initiatives were aimed at curtailing the mobility of youth and were legitimated through the rhetoric of safety. A quotation from *Motorcycles in the United States*, a U.S. Department of Health, Education, and Welfare pamphlet published in 1968, sums up a number of assumptions not only about motorcyclists, but about the danger they represent to the social body as well as youth's personal bodies: "As an Auto Driver . . . Remember, the vast majority of motorcyclists are not the dirty, rough-neck, out-law types that get the bulk of motorcycling publicity. Most motorcyclists are young, between the ages of 17 and 24. Many are college or high school students or people just starting their business careers. Most are very nice young people who are unfortunately not sophisticated, experienced motorcyclists. By recognizing that many motorcyclists may not be fully skilled, you can take extra caution and avoid possible accidents."[15]

The above quotation attempts to ease drivers' fears of motorcyclists, or at least a specific sort of motorcyclist, while at the same time accepting the fact that if they were dirty, smelly outlaw types, then it would be A-OK to ride them off the road or, at least, disregard their well-being. However, we (the normative automobile driver) are trying to make these nice young people experienced, like the dirty, smelly ones, so that they will be safe. But who then is creating the problem? The angered hick in *Easy Rider* who shoots motorcyclists? or the untrained youngsters?

The real enemy here is a form of mobility that functions as the other to automobiles, which is being accessed by two supposedly different, yet equally disruptive populations. The problem that both groups pose is to some extent the same. It is the problem of disciplining an undocile population. The historical model that Foucault proposes for disciplinarity is that of the confined space: the hospital, the school, and ultimately the prison. However, these are populations whose relation to mobility, not their relationship to confinement, is the problem. The key aim of policy initiatives is thus to somehow produce a more docile motorcyclist or, as some would have it, outlaw the practice altogether.

What is unique about biopolitics is that, first, it depends upon the production of knowledge to validate the normative standards by which populations can be measured, and, second, policy initiatives are mandated to bring the population up to snuff. As noted earlier, automobiles were the normative standard by which safety measures were established. Motorcycle deaths should never come close to the per-mile deaths of automobile drivers. But, as long as they are higher, they can be made the object of intense disciplinary regulation. In a general sense, since motorcycling is a less efficient mode of transportation and less useful to commerce, it can be outlawed. It is only when it becomes a highly fetishized object of middle-class consumption in the 1980s that it is granted a semblance of mainstream acceptability. In the scenario described here, the real question is why, during the late 1960s, was extensive attention paid to motorcycling as a dangerous activity?

As discussed in earlier chapters, there is no ground zero against which either safety or risk can be judged. Instead, acceptable limits are created to validate or invalidate various activities. These limits are quite variable from one time period to another and across different activities and different cultural contexts. It is easier to ignore, and in some instances to relish,[16] motorcyclists' deaths when the riders are thought to be "dirty, rough-neck, outlaw types" than when they are thought to be the progeny of postwar suburban bliss. This may help explain why there was a shift from acceptance of 1,103 motorcycle deaths in 1949 to outrage in 1964 when there were 1,118 deaths; in those same years, the number of registered motorcycles rose from 478,851 to 984,760. The number of deaths increased only 1.3 percent while the number of bikes increased 105 percent.[17] What changed was not the actual risk of riding a bike; in fact, it was seemingly only half as risky, judging from the increase in actual bikes on the road in proportion to the slight increase in deaths. What changed was, first, that who was riding seemed to be changing, and these new middle-class youth riders mattered; second, such concern gained momentum following the publication of Ralph Nader's *Unsafe at Any Speed* and the public hearings and safety mandates that quickly followed.[18]

**Technological Fixes**

Two solutions, usually held separately, were offered during the move toward safer transportation in the 1960s. The most well known and documented centered around the question of automobile safety and how to design and construct safer automobiles. From this Nader-inspired vantage, the enemy was clearly Detroit and its supposedly callous attitude toward an unsuspecting population of automobile drivers. This type of argumentation may have reached its epitome in *Safety Last*, published in 1966,[19] a book that laid all the blame for traffic fatalities on the automobile industry. This line of thinking constructed the social problem as a public health issue, and, as such, a direct enemy needed to be located. According to the authors of *Safety Last*, James O'Connell and Allen Myers, the auto industry was maliciously misinforming the public through the sabotage and silencing of research that proved how deadly their designs were. Furthermore, they were said to be hiding behind two claims, first, that safety didn't sell, and, second, that the public was unwilling to cover the requisite costs of safer designs. The relative truth of these two statements has since been negated by two factors. First, as the safety discourse has gained considerable legitimacy over the past four decades, safety in many instances does sell. It can easily be noted that in the automobile industry, safety has been used to sell new technological features for years, first by European manufacturers such as Volvo, Saab, and Mercedes and later by nearly every automobile manufacturer. Second, the question of whether consumers were willing to cover the costs of these features was muted when the Department of Transportation began placing demands on manufacturers to meet safety specifications in hundreds of areas. These mandated changes have affected car costs greatly, but as all manufacturers are subject to them, all car prices are equally affected. Of course, particular makes which did not pass safety standards simply are no longer available, the original Volkswagen Beetle and MGB being notable examples.

The change in focus is important. As I note throughout this book, it is the driver who has been the focus of social methods for advancing safety. However, in the early 1960s the tide began to turn away from social to technological methods. The human element was beginning to be seen as too difficult to master. The mechanical, on the other hand, was the more reliable and predictable half of the equation. What *Unsafe at Any Speed* did was to further the argument and actually blame the automobile manufacturers for traffic fatalities. It made them responsible in a way that simply had not previously existed. This alteration in thinking and approach drastically changed the automobile safety landscape and partially accounts for the lengthy gap between the extensive driver safety campaigns that occurred during the mid-1950s and the early 1980s drunk driving campaign. The move to a technological fix only partially extended to the motorcycle. In this area of safety, there were still problematic culprits. There were still populations that needed disciplining, and indirectly the technological fixes were a means of disciplining these groups. Policies were mostly directed at the motorcycle rider.[20] These policies generally dealt with the area of education, and multiple forms of rider education began at this time. When the policies weren't directed at the biker, they were directed at a particular type of motorcycle, the chopper.

The chopper was, and to a large degree still is, a vital part of motorcycling culture. Much like the hot rod, the chopper was the backyard mechanic's attempt to produce a better bike that was also a statement of the rider's individuality. Chopping originally meant to literally chop off unneeded parts to reduce weight. The motorcycle of choice was a Harley-Davidson or an Indian, both of which had mammoth fenders and were weighted down by large covers, lights, and front-end suspensions. By chopping off weight, higher speeds could be attained. Furthermore, numerous engine modifications were developed that would increase horsepower. Bikers were very attached to their often hand-built machines and were constantly in the process of modifying and chopping.

Although the regulations against chopped bikes were positioned as a technological fix for regulating supposedly unsafe motorcycles, their implementation was a focused attack on the so-called outlaw bikers, who were thought to be the only ones riding chopped bikes. Regulations provided an easy way to monitor the bikers' activities. The laws gave the police an excuse to pull over a rider on a chopped bike at any time and search it thoroughly. In the name of safety, police looked for nonregulation exhaust pipes, handlebars, tires, brakes, mirrors, foot pegs, seats, passenger accommodations, etc., when in reality their real interest was not the well-being of an outlaw population, but the possibility of busting a known offender for other illegal activities like drug possession, driving an unregistered motorcycle (it was often difficult to legally register a chopped bike, as engines, frames, and other parts came from many sources), driving without a license, etc. Thompson described these tactics at length in *Hell's Angels*, and the effect they had on bikers was immense. Many bikers had a hard time keeping up with the constant deluge of fines, not to mention wasted time spent in court and on the side of the road waiting for cops to measure the height of handlebars. Part of the reason Thompson chose to buy a nonchopped BSA 650, which at the time was considered a large bike, was to avoid these kinds of legal trouble. But because of the stereotype regarding large-bike riders in general, he too was often pulled over and issued citations, even though his bike was new, standard, and unmodified. Bogus laws that were obviously aimed at monitoring an outlaw motorcycle population were doubly removed from their stated aim of promoting safety. In some instances, not only did police presence not help motorcyclists, but they were actively discriminated against and in some instances the victims of police brutality simply because they could be identified as members of a motorcycle gang.

Warren La Coste's *Holy Rider: The Priest and the Gang* is an account of a junior priest's struggle to bring the ministry to a motorcycle gang while fighting off the temptation of becoming a full-fledged member himself.[21] The autobiographical narrative discusses at length some of the difficulties that members of the gang had with police brutality. One such incident between cops and gangs is described by Hank, a member of the New Orleans–based motorcycle gang the Rebels:

> I was just standing there leaning against my car, willing to cooperate, when this mother cop sees my colors and goes nuts. He jumped out of his patrol car and pulled his gun on me like I had just robbed a fucking bank. You'd swear he had just caught Al Capone or something. . . . Then he frisked me looking for some kinda weapon, and he looked pissed cause he didn't find any. . . . When we got to the sub-station, he didn't take me to the main lock up. . . . They never charged me with anything. . . . They pulled me down the hall and threw me in a cell. . . . Then he began this speech about the world being a better place without biker bums like me. . . . He told the big guy to grab me, while Ralph swung his billy stick. . . . He kept beating me . . . [until] he got tired. . . . I laid on the floor drowning in my own blood.[22]

The story ends with biker retribution. Hank and his gang ambush the cop later at his home and beat him to within an inch of his life. What interests me is that the cop is driven by a desire to eradicate or at least punish bikers. This animosity is able to take a violent turn owing to the state's monopoly on the legitimate use of violence, but it takes a less violent, yet no less subtle form in other sectors of society.

In *The Perfect Vehicle: What It Is About Motorcycles*, Melissa Holbrook Pierson, describes numerous occasions in which she was discriminated against simply because she was on a motorcycle.[23] For instance, as a graduate student at Yale she had been allowed access to campus everyday but was denied access by the same guard who normally ushered her in because there were "no motorcycles allowed on campus." She tells of another incident in which she was denied a room at a bed-and-breakfast in North Carolina when she showed up on a motorcycle. The list could be lengthened and extended to numerous sources. The primary issue is not how extensive the discrimination and police brutality against bikers are, but that brutality and discrimination are often masked as safety concerns.

It should by now be obvious that safety is put to use for purposes other than simply keeping the streets safe and protecting the nation's driving and riding citizens. But what explanation can be given for the other population supposedly at risk, youth? Before addressing this concern, I will mention a few historical factors. As noted, youth posed a particularly difficult problem in general. Added to this was a level of affluence which had never been seen on such a large scale. In addition, there was an influx of cheap Japanese and British small-engine motorcycles and scooters. These had proven an economic necessity in war-torn Europe and Asia and served to mobilize populations bent on rebuilding. Accompanying this cheap and available transportation was the creation of the largest highway system in the world, which began to take shape during the Eisenhower years and was still expanding rapidly into the 1960s in an attempt to keep up with sprawling suburban growth. Without even figuring in the effect of such stars as Brando, Marvin, and Steve McQueen, performing admirably on a motorcycle in *The Great Escape* and in his personal life, the above factors helped bring about the explosion of motorcycle use among the youth of this time. It should come as little surprise that the first place the alleged problem was responded to was on college campuses. It was on the University of Illinois campus that the Motorcycle Driver Education Workshop was held in August 1967.

### Dreams of Devils

These proceedings were held in response to the "motorcycle problem, "which was blossoming and had "dropped on us like a bomb."[24] The proceedings were responding to two assumptions. The first, quite legitimate, was an increase in the actual number of riders on campus. The second, though, as explained earlier, was a little less accurate, and this was the hysteria surrounding the assumed increases in the number of motorcycle fatalities. What is offered as a whole is a "multi-disciplinary effort amongst academics and professionals,"[25] which asked cost-benefit questions such as How is our industry affected (insurance agents and industry groups)? or what effects has this had on public health (local medical doctors)? or how is the law going to respond to this phenomenon (state police Captain Dwight Pitman, in charge of state motorcycle safety)?

Two things are made clear by the transcripts from this conference. First, there is a severe gap between the seriousness of the motorcycle problem and gut-level reactions toward motorcycles. The following statement made by Captain Pitman may sum this up best: "I've never been on a motorcycle and gentlemen and ladies that's not the half of it. I don't have the faintest intention of ever getting on one of the things. They are a device of the devil as far as I personally am concerned."[26]

The appeal to the devil, besides being a bit melodramatic, is an old standby where youth are concerned. The most obvious parallel is to rock music and the fifty-year history of such attacks. It is, however, reasonable to appeal to the devil inasmuch as the devil has always signified anarchy, chaos, and unlawfulness. These are the same themes that motorcycle gangs articulated with motorcycling. These articulations had first to be made by motorcycle gangs, setting the stage for Captain Pitman's grand proclamation that Jimmy Premed cruising around campus on his Honda Dream was, in fact, doing the work of the devil. Importantly though, there is a constant shift between the rhetoric normally reserved for the dirty outlaw types and that used in referring to those other, inexperienced riders. There is a seeming anxiety that merely by riding a motorcycle Jimmy may eventually become one of those outlaws.

The second matter made clear in the transcripts is that motorcycle riding is considered a problem that can be located and corralled in the category of youth. So these programs—especially, for instance, two that were passed simultaneously, the 150cc highway law and the ban on 150cc bikes for sixteen- to eighteen-year-olds[27]—work to limit and confine both speed and the routes of traffic for youth. Not surprisingly, where youth are explicitly concerned, it is toward education that authorities turn. It is also no surprise that the majority of the workshop attendees were driver's education instructors. It was to them that Captain Pitman appealed when he decreed, "You're the ones who form their driving attitudes and the reactions that govern their behavior. You are the ones who give them the knowledge upon which they base their decisions and their driving habits."[28] The connection between teaching a skill, riding or driving, and influencing attitudes, an entirely different form of education sometimes called propaganda, is closely linked with driver's education.

As I explained in previous chapters, driver's education has been in place, to one degree or another, since the mid-1930s. The general thesis of driver's training was that skill and judgment are inseparable. Certainly, it becomes apparent that much more is occurring during driver's education than teaching young women how to downshift as they approach a stop sign. In fact, if Captain Pitman had his way it would become obvious to all youngsters that motorcycles are in fact the device of the devil and should be avoided at all costs. What more might be going on? Without simply extolling the virtues of being a good neighbor while cruising down the highway, how might attitudes be adjusted? One of the most prevalent strategies, though its effects are arguable, is the scare tactic.[29] If you can't logically explain why particular actions are safe, and often you can't, then showing the horrid outcome of illogical behavior can work well.

Motorcycle education began to flourish in the early 1970s and has continued to gain momentum over the past three decades. Typical classes are taught by experienced motorcyclists who have completed training of their own. Numerous riders' training courses are taught on the racetrack as well. These are typically run by ex-professional motorcycle racers. Motorcycle education, even within magazine articles on the topic, is regularly associated with skill and speed. It is not simply a matter of observing the rules of the road and articulating them to civility, as in driver's education. Instead, motorcycle training binds the presumed innate desire of riders to go fast with the type of training that allows for speed, but within a controlled scenario, like a racetrack, or as a part in the safety gains that are said to accompany all riding skills. The increased focus on motorcycle training courses has been followed through by universities, motorcyclist associations, local municipalities, motorcycle shops, insurance agencies, and the aforementioned private skills courses. So, there is an attempt by various nongovernmental vested parties to make motorcycling less dangerous or at least seem manageable. The very ability to teach a skill makes it seem controllable. It also, however, verifies that something needs to be taught and can be through a regimented practice. It follows its own logic and demands expertise, through the role of a certified and thus qualified instructor. It is further validated and made worthwhile by insurance agencies, who underwrite and sponsor motorcycle training and also offer a 10 percent discount to those who complete the courses. The logic of actuarial profit is treated as true. Thus, it is assumed, insurance companies would offer the discount only if it cut down on accidents and saved them money.

Typical courses last a total of twenty hours spread over a series of evenings or a few weekends. There is both in-class training and riding course practice. Part of the classroom training deals with defensive driving. Defensive driving is also the dominant pedagogical ideology in driver's education classes. This approach assumes that the road is a hostile environment, one in which the rider or driver should continually be prepared for the worst. This sense of ever-present danger is more fully articulated with outright fear, through the scare tactics employed by instructor anecdotes and film footage of horrific crash scenes. This anxiety is reducible only through defensive riding or driving. But you must then always assume the worst of other drivers or riders and accept that you should actively be in a state of fear. The production and actuation of fear play an important part in all safety campaigns. The fear of hitchhiking and hitchhikers is similar insofar as the safe subject is supposed to realize the impossibility of knowing the intentions of the other, but assume the worst, in both cases. This perpetual fear of others, then, is not particularly selective in determining who the other is. Everyone should be treated with equal trepidation. Such equalization of fear on the road transcends racial, ethnic, class, and gender divides. All kinds of people are to be feared. In an entirely different context and for reasons entirely different from those he was speaking to, Sartre's claim that other people are hell proves to be true according to driver's and rider's education.

### Feeling It: Experiencing the Road

Rider's and driver's education thus plays a significant part in the process of producing safe riders. As discussed in earlier chapters, the specific discursive appeals that validate safe practices emanate from multiple sources. Yet from similar sources arises a vision of the risky rider for whom the risk of riding validates the activity. The continual tension between risk and safety is evident in the motorcycle press. Motorcycle magazines are dependant upon motorcycle helmet, clothing, and accessory manufacturers and retailers for their advertising revenue. Magazine editors and writers receive this gear free and have vested interests in validating the importance of such gear in their publications. However, part of the appeal of the motorcycle is, without a doubt, the rebel image that accompanies riding. Some of this image is neutered by wearing a full-faced helmet, which has only one obvious purpose: to protect you from danger.[30] Being protected is something that automobile drivers are concerned about, not tough motorcyclists. Furthermore, being in the protective confines of steel and glass is likened to being a trapped animal in a zoo. Motorcyclists call auto drivers cagers. Cagers are cut off from their environment, trapped by their fear, and unable to fully experience their mobility.

This self-initiated comparison allows motorcyclists to reappropriate risk and motorcycling as something which can't be measured only according to utility and efficiency. Instead, one must take into account the phenomenological benefits of riding a motorcycle. These include, though are not limited to, being in touch with the world around you, particularly the beauty of nature; having a heightened sense of being in the moment—being "more alive"; knowing and understanding one's machinery in a more intense and extensive fashion than the average motorist; constantly testing and extending one's riding ability; looking and feeling tough; being noticed and creating a scene; and certainly not least of all, experiencing the thrill of speed. These phenomenological validations are recurrent themes of almost all the motorcycle literature. Part of the difficulty of establishing safe riding practices is that they often work toward counterpurposes. Speed limits, helmet legislation, and mandatory riders' education classes diminish, for some riders, the appeal of riding a motorcycle. However, these very illegalities, like speeding, provide guidelines against which riders can measure their riskiness. Not wearing a helmet can simultaneously function as a political statement, the means to magnify experience, and a sign of machismo all during the same commute. The law and safety discourse thus acts as deterrent and enabler. But the motorcycle press has more immediate goals. They must maintain the allure of motorcycling and appease as many riders as possible, while also managing to appease helmet manufacturers. This is one place where phenomenological appeal and safety mindedness come together.

To briefly sum up before moving on to some more specific examples of how these discourses play out in the day-to-day lives of motorcyclists, it should be apparent that the safety discourse hinges upon several key articulations. First of all, it should have been made apparent that one of the key features of safety discourse is the appeal to youth. Safety rhetoric is prevalent when discussions of the health of youth are involved. Second, safety is sometimes used to legitimate policies and practices that have little to do with maintaining the health of individuals, and it is often used to regulate the mobility of particular populations. Third, safety is a key link in the chain that binds citizenship, driving, and law enforcement together. Last, safety education is dependant upon scare narratives which describe the horrible repercussions of a bad attitude.

### Epiphanies: Binding Selves to Safety

In the current self-help, self-analysis, self-disciplining cultural landscape, the notion that you can come to know the self in order to improve it is a powerful belief. When this process is institutionalized, it often proves incredibly successful, as both a tool for changing the social acceptance of an activity and for altering individual conduct. Organizations like Alcoholics Anonymous and Tony Robbins's get-rich-quick infomercial empire offer self-analytic programs for personal understanding and change. Personal conduct is regimented, not in a coercive fashion, but according to a set of steps, a key one being the epiphany. The program cannot work until one has a "bottoming-out" experience that illuminates the extent of the problem and initiates a new course of action. The epiphany plays a key role in these regimens. It is the true sign of one's being, both prior and present. It reveals in absolute terms the truth of oneself. The epiphany has also become an object of academic analysis. Somewhere between the academic and the institutional, one can locate a sensibility that experience itself is telling. It manifests itself and, at times, if we're lucky, speaks to us. Norman Denzin's *Interpretive Interactionism* presents a concise explanation of how the epiphany works and what value it has for the researcher. Denzin writes, "Those interactional moments that leave marks on people's lives . . . have the potential for creating transformational experiences for the person. They are 'epiphanies.' In them personal character is manifested and made apparent. By recording these experiences in detail, the researcher is able to illuminate the moments of crisis that occur in a person's life. They are often interpreted, both by the person and by others, as turning point experiences. Having had this experience, the person is never quite the same."[31]

Denzin provides a brief understanding of what roles experience, researchers, subjects, and change are said to play in the formation of an epiphany. What is left vague is the relation between interpretation and experience as it relates to turning-point experiences. Put simply, my question is, to what extent is the interpretation constitutive of the epiphany? Denzin grants that they are often interpreted, which points out that it is the act of explanation that makes the experience matter. But he follows this with the statement that after this experience, the person is never quite the same. This last statement appears to place the causality of the change upon the initial epiphanic experience.

There is no question that experience plays a key role in the way we interpret the world and that this affects the ways in which we interact. Yet the role of the researcher is often paralleled in everyday life as both roles demand reflection of the past to make sense of it. We interpret the past and place a greater or lesser importance upon different events. As with any interpretive enterprise though, we cannot simply uncover the meanings of experiences or attribute causality without some schema that gives structure and coherence to those interpretations. Thus the same must be said for personal experiences. My interest here is to show that when it comes to motorcycle safety there are three operative logics that help motorcyclists relate their own experiences in accordance with safety. The first is the scare narrative. The second, somewhat ironically, is the notion of epiphany itself. As Denzin states, in the operatives "personal character is manifested." This notion that something unique to one's personal character is the site for locating causality is very readily apparent in the epiphany. Third, the fact that so much of the literature about motorcycling deals with the experiential or phenomenalogical leads me to believe that it is a particularly pertinent strategy of governance. There is constant self-reflection in the literature that is used to legitimate why one rides. What I want to look for instead is the way this focus on the personal is an integral part of the safety narratives analyzed below and not simply unmediated description. In these narratives the individual is the point of causality of accidents, and what are taken from these accidental experiences are insights which mirror those already provided by the safety discourse. Ultimately, then, the epiphany serves the safety discourse well and may be a key link between it and the day-to-day practices which it legitimates.

Magazines devoted to motorcycling often feature sections or special features devoted to the issues of street survival, safety, and protective riding gear. Magazines place a greater or lesser importance on such issues, and some, like the British *Classic Bike*, contain articles that feature lighthearted histories of the farcical relation between fashion and safety. For the most part, though, safety is treated as a deadly serious matter.

An example of how the scare narrative informs this discourse can be found in a typical issue of *Cycle World*, a popular monthly American motorcycle magazine. Kevin Cameron, in his monthly editorial column, describes the reaction of his parents when, at the age of eighteen, he told them he had purchased a motorcycle. He recalled that they quickly told him he would have to get rid of it, and this decision was followed by a series of his parents' stories in which "young hapless lads were gored by the long tiller-style handlebars of their giant Indians or Hendersons."[32] Scare tactics survive and still prove powerful in many ways. They help legitimate the safety discourse because of their down-to-earth rhetorical appeal.

Every year in the spring, just before motorcycles are taken out of their winter hibernation, *Motorcyclist* (the most popular American motorcycle magazine) runs a feature called "Motorcyclist Special Survival Section" in which the editors attempt to prepare the rider for the new riding season. In "Survival 1995," five short testimonials called "Motorcyclist Editors' Greatest Hits" narrated accounts of the editors' most educational accidents.[33] First-person accounts all, the narratives operated as moralizing and proselytizing tales in which safe riding techniques were discovered. The narratives were similar in their dependence upon several formal devices, such as first-person testimonial, humor, and the moral ending. Taken as a whole, the stories work as scare narratives that are meant to instill fear in motorcyclists in an attempt to lead riders to partake of several practices, including buying and wearing protective gear.

The testimonials are followed, first, by an article outlining what to look for in crash protection and, second, an article detailing survival strategies for different types of riding. Protective riding gear is one of the most expensive and most advertised items in these magazines. Furthermore, mandatory helmet laws peaked at their highest level of implementation in the early 1990s and were in effect in all but three states in the United States.[34] Thus there is a strong incentive for narratives of this type not only to justify the purchase of such gear, but also to legitimate the regulations placed on such gear. The narrative strategies employed in these five testimonials will be examined in order to articulate the ways in which the stories explicitly link safety to motorcycling. The testimonials serve as epiphanies, in Denzin's sense of the term, and the importance of the epiphanic discourse will be further elaborated.

"Thinking you will never crash, is like thinking that it will never rain on you. If you're out there long enough, it's going to happen to you."[35] Inevitability and unpreparedness: these two terms sum up one of the key elements in these *Motorcyclist* narratives. It is assumed that one will go down and that when it happens, not only should one be prepared, but often being unprepared is what leads to the inevitable, a crash. An odd logic then surfaces. You will go down, but if you're prepared you shouldn't. However, herein lies the hitch: many accidents, it is said, are unavoidable, thus the attribution of luck to the accidents that can't be accounted for by unpreparedness, bad luck at that. I have found no evidence to prove that most riders go down, though I don't doubt the assertion. Yet statistically, at least in the 1960s (*Motorcycle Safety Final Report*), it was shown that most accidents occur when the drivers are beginners, so in theory there is a Darwinian weeding out of the accident prone and those unlucky enough to be faced with a panic situation before they are trained to deal with it. Not to belabor the point, or to dismiss the repercussions of crashing, but there is no real way to measure the chances of having an accident and furthermore, even if there were, much of the fatalistic rebel appeal of riding would be lost to those who desire it. Riding needs to seem incredibly dangerous, not only for the protective clothing manufacturers to survive, but also to legitimate the regulations placed on motorcycling and, most important, for some, in order that those riding can be gratified by their inclusion into the category of risk taker.

There are several key repetitions among the stories, and categorizing them according to their relationship to safety should prove useful. First of all, there is the riding environment, or what Kenneth Burke would call the scene of the narrative, where the riding takes place:

Hey, it's ugly out there. Accidents are a blink of the eye away, close calls a dime a dozen. Drive an L.A. (or any other big city, for that matter) freeway during rush hour it's easy to see why: Drivers touching up their makeup or mousse, chatting on a cell phone, scanning the daily trades for last weekend's gross. . . . Let's face it—it's a zoo most of the time. With airbags and crumple zones, the price most motorists pay for their blunders is usually little more than a bit of whiplash, some bent metal and an insurance deductible. The penalty for making a mistake (or being on the wrong side of someone else's) on a motorcycle, however, carries much graver consequences.[36]

The above passage begins the "Survival Section" and lays the groundwork for what is to come by imaging the scenario which riders are faced with. Most obviously there is a distinction made between rider and driver, car and motorcycle. And, importantly, when it comes to safety, drivers of cars have little to lose and thus drive carelessly. Motorcycle riders, having much to lose, must be on the lookout, always vigilant, for as a rider "you must prepare yourself for combat on the road."[37] This opposition provides two of the three options for the testimonials to come: either riders were unprepared, a careless driver created a panic situation, or the road itself failed to deliver as promised by the Highway Commission in its goal of providing a safe and hospitable surface.

The environment, or scene, is a treacherous one, a zoo, a combat zone, or an urban jungle. In other motorcycle literature there is the sense that the environment is neither built, maintained, nor engineered with the motorcyclist in mind. These assumptions are reinforced through such narratives. It is a hostile scene. Second, unfortunately, there must be others inhabiting this jungle. These four-wheeled animals of the zoo, or cagers, are the greater enemy; in Burkean terms they are the counteragents.[38] They are out of touch with their surroundings, owing to their hard, protective surface and monstrosity. There is the sense that by being caged they have lost their senses, the acuity of vision, and the olfactory ability needed to sense danger. This often leads to serious ramifications for those in touch with the jungle, those for whom steel and glass walls do not stifle sensate activity, motorcyclists.

In testimonial #1 (T1), the author, Kent Kunitsugo, is cruising down a scenic canyon drive when a dual-axle pickup inexplicably backs out of a pull-off directly into his path, ultimately sending Kent's bike headlong into and Kent himself over the bed of the truck. In T2, John Burns must swerve into the oncoming traffic lane on a blind curve because a dump truck has stopped in the middle of the road. In T4, Art Friedman is distracted by a fight taking place in the car next to him, as the car in front of him swerves into Art's lane and slams on the brakes in order to avoid hitting a car backing into the lane to Art's right. It is thus the element of other's, always drivers not riders, idiocy and carelessness that provides the "panic situation" that all but one of the riders (T3) acknowledge: the moment when the shit is about to hit the fan and often the brakes are applied too quickly, thus adding a second element of the crash equation, unpreparedness.[39]

An oft-repeated safety tip is panic braking practice. In Burkean logic this might be called agency. How something is done or, in this case, why a lack of skill, the ability to get something done, is not present and thus accidents, an unwanted act, are unavoidable. Whole articles are often devoted to just this topic. It is said to be part of one's safety training, part of preparing for road combat. Along with this, any number of other riding strategies are examined from swerving, to lane changes, to riding in groups, to staying alert, to not looking at beautiful women walking down the street (a particularly difficult part of preparation if you believe the accounts of John Burns [T2] as well as numerous letters to the editor columns). All of these articles, though, are focused on one specific aspect of safety, discipline. The rider must be trained, educated, regimented, and ultimately outfitted (more on this later). Much like an athlete or a soldier, it is said that in order to succeed and survive one must be disciplined, and much of this discipline is said to come from within. It must be self-imposed (though external regulatory practices like drivers' tests and courses and helmet laws are acknowledged). However, even though in these stories the importance of self-preparation and alertness is ubiquitous, there is no acknowledgment that this may simply be compliance with a discursive structure far more powerful than their personal character.

They all end their testimonials with words of advice, morals, or lessons. In T1 Kunitsugo explains that he tries to always ride with others for tactical support (sighting and signaling potential dangers). In T2 Burns ends with, "Lesson? Expect the unexpected and be mentally ready to deal with things immediately."[40] Tim Carrithers in T3 explains that he "stays a little more focused on the way out of these palatial digs every night. Take a few seconds to get your mind right before rolling into traffic."[41] In T4, Art chips in with, "The standard statement about those kinds of events is 'not my fault,' but I see it differently. When you climb on a motorcycle, you assume extra responsibility because you are so vulnerable if something goes wrong."[42] This statement is particularly interesting in that the agent (motorcyclist) is forced to have greater agency (skills) in their scenes (street) if their purpose (survival/safety) is to avoid certain acts (accidents). Last, Mitch Boehm in T5 tells us, "The Moral? Ride within your limits. And if you do get into a situation that makes you want to pucker and grab the brakes mid-corner, don't panic."[43] It is the testimonial here that seems to serve as a platform for the expression of expertise due to experience. After the telling of the story of the accident, a lesson must be learned, knowledge must be gained, a motive for the accident must be provided. Something must be attributed with causality and, as shown above, it is usually the scene or lack of agency. In this way, the narratives act as stories from the embattled soldiers at the front, who have come back alive and now must fulfill their duty of preparing the new troops. Though scarred and embittered, they will fight on, only this time they will be better prepared. And, as all ex-soldiers know, better protection is always needed.

"Luckily, that editor was wearing his fully padded/back-protected Aerostich suit, and he sustained nary a scratch. Falling on that nasty, rain grooved concrete felt like landing on a Posturpedic Extra Firm thanks to that suit."[44] Medieval horsemen wore metallic armor, troops in the world wars wore steel helmets and drove armored tanks, cops in the drug war wear bullet-proof jackets, and motorcycle road warriors must also be outfitted. Protective gear is given as the primary reason in all of the accounts for the minimal damage sustained. Helmets, of course, are the first line of defense and are dealt with first in the short article "Ideal Gear Designs" following the testimonials. Jackets and pants, gloves, and boots are also all dealt with. The merits of leather, cordura, and kevlar are covered. Extra padding or armor is called for in high-impact areas like knees, shoulders, elbows, ankles, and backs. Ultimately the importance of this information is that gear ends up often being situated as the fulcrum point between safety and risk, health and injury, or ultimately life and death. It becomes a vital element in the discourse of safety and an agent in all narratives about vehicular injury. Think about the way in which questions are instantly asked of automobile narratives: Were safety belts being worn? Was alcohol involved? With motorcycles the question of whether a helmet was worn is always first. To a lesser extent questions about other types of gear are asked. Certainly it is obvious that the official application of motive for an accident, alcohol, or injury, no seat belt or helmet, is then filtered into everyday discussions.

Thus we have simple narrative structures that explain, with little variation, the cause or fault of the accident. In all of the narratives discussed above, the accidents are said to have been avoidable if only the skills of the agent had been up to task. Agency is always attributed to the motorcyclist. Certainly the scene and counteragents come into play, but when the panic situation arises, the narrative invariably shifts its location of causality. The motorcyclist can either assert agency (skill to avoid the accident) or act improperly (crash). If this were not the case, there would be little point to the stories as far as their investment in safety is concerned, at least outside the area of protective gear. If agency wasn't located with the motorcyclists, there would be little point in telling stories that ended with lessons and morals. It must be assumed, possibly for sanity's sake, that with the proper skills you can avoid an accident. Without this assumption, coupled with the general assumption of risk, motorcycling would appear far too risky for many riders.

As a last point, it might be asked to what extent the accident narratives not only serve to reinforce the safety discourse and to invigorate it with verisimilitude, but may also serve as an element of the risk-taking flip side of the safety discourse. May not passing on stories of crashing invigorate the riskiness of motorcycling while infusing the personal teller with machismo and a life-risking persona? Imagine a man who can look death in the eye, stand up, shake off the dust, and get back on his bike; this is a powerful story as well. In *Hell's Angels*, Thompson describes at length two key counterpractices of the safety narrative. First is a lack of safety gear. Angels initially wore leather jackets with their insignia, or colors, on them, but quickly moved to simply wearing denim vests with their colors on the back, denying whatever protection leather offered. "You will never see a Hell's Angel wearing a helmet,"[45] he writes. According to Thompson, the reasoning behind this is that "the Angels want nothing to do with safety" and "they don't want anybody to think they're hedging their bets."[46] There are still mandatory helmet laws in many states. Helmets must meet Department of Transportation (DOT) or Snell standards in order to display the stickers which verify their acceptance.[47] Some riders who oppose this legislation purchase bootleg DOT stickers and attach them to lightweight plastic half-helmets which barely cover their skull and are far less obtrusive than a full-faced, fully certified helmet. The second characteristic of this attitude is the Angels riding style: "The Angels push their luck to the limit. They take drastic risks with no thought at all."[48] The *Motorcyclist* narratives described above in no way service the tough guy mythology of motorcycling, as the moral of every story is that safety and caution are the guiding principles of riding. The Angels' stories instead serve this tough guy myth and depend upon a fate-driven sensibility, where agency is left to chance. Thompson claims that the Angels were the best riders he had ever seen. They could do things on a bike that no one else could. Yet this level of skill doesn't negate fate; it only works to intensify and expand the possibilities for fates intervention. But the telling of near-fatal crash stories is affectively articulated via the safety discourse to real people's lives.

### Manifest Safety

Seeking a way to understand how the safety discourse is taken on by subjects, I conducted interviews with motorcyclists. We discussed such issues as mandatory helmet laws and speed limits and the difficulties of getting motorcycle insurance.[49] This proved interesting, but no subject discussed created as intense a response as that of accidents. It was here, much as in the narratives above, that the crux of the issue of safety for respondents was evoked, mortality. It quickly became apparent that one motorcyclist in particular, Mona, had taken on the discourse of motorcycle safety fully. When riding, she embodies every safe riding practice offered. She discussed the ways in which she practices safe riding, not just as a metaphor, but actually spends hours training, completing an obstacle course over and over again, always trying to improve her safety skills. There is some overlap between her interest in sport riding, its requirement for a high degree of skill, and her interest in safety. They both, in many ways, demand the same types of road awareness. However, her primary concern was her education and the internalization of attitudes and practices which she simply described as "safe." She talked about the way in which she no longer feels "right" if she rides without a helmet, and she alters her riding dramatically if she isn't in "full leathers," a motorcycle term which describes being fully clothed in protective leather jacket, pants, gloves, and boots.

There is a useful moment in the interview when she suddenly realizes that she doesn't want to be written as the hysterical woman regarding her experience of witnessing another rider down on the exact same bike that she rides. It makes evident precisely what is not my point. The particularities of identity, in a traditional sense, are not what are at issue here. In this instance, her gender may have little or nothing to do with her response. What matters is that there is a legitimized and often-repeated narrative of enlightenment following crashes. The safety discourse is ripe with examples, as I have shown. Her acknowledgment that it was this moment that shocked her into recognition needs little validation. In many respects, it doesn't matter what the chronology of events was. For Mona, that moment was the singular cause of her safe riding. She didn't question the effect of reading accounts of others' crashes. Nor did she reflect on the fact that she had already completed the Motorcycle Safety Foundation (MSF) course, which hinges on such accounts.[50] Instead, an epiphanic moment bore all of the causal weight. In her mind, that moment made all the difference and changed her from being, in her terms, an "uneducated" and "unsafe" rider to her current state of being educated and safe.

Mona's continual use of the term *educated* provided a key articulation to the motorcycle safety discourse in which the difference between safe and unsafe is education. Furthermore, it is not only that she has had access to the information and gone through the training, but that it is the act of internalization of belief and practice that separates the educated from the uneducated, safe riders from risky. Safe in this use equals the good, the knowledgeable, the desired. Unsafe not only means at risk, but also stupid, careless, naive, inexperienced, and ultimately, within the epiphanic schema, unenlightened. Furthermore, all of the examples of unsafe riders against which she positioned herself were "that young pack of riders who zip around campus late in the evening." Here we see again the articulation of youth, group riding, and riskiness. Unfortunately for them, no singular event has led them into the realm of sanity. Terence, another rider discussed his own mishap and echoed this sentiment: "But you know it was a needless accident, really, but in another way it wasn't needless because I learned from it." According to this rider's account an accident, while on the one hand needless, which is to say, stupid, in fact has a purpose: to teach. Thus stupidity naturally produces its own intelligence. He then discussed a few other incidents: "I broke an ankle once, while riding. I broke a shoulder. But nothing has happened in the last twenty years. Probably the reasons why I don't conform to everyone's thinking and such is that I pretty much know the statistics and the variables in terms of what kind of person is likely to be involved in a motorcycle accident. You know there are statistics that prove that it could happen at certain hours and on certain days and certain ages. I know when I was younger I didn't learn very fast, but learning took place." For this rider, response is initiated by expert claims, but what he does with that knowledge is quite different. Rather than following Mona's path toward more safety gear, Terence chooses to avoid riding during statistically determined times of increased danger and in places that could also be more dangerous. Furthermore, since most motorcycle accidents involve young riders, and he survived his slow-learning youth, Terence feels he is no longer at risk to the degree he once was. Most important, the logic of learning and altering one's behavior according to expert knowledge is clearly apparent in Terence. He has learned some lessons and gained some knowledge, and this, he feels, helps keep him alive.

Both Mona's and Terence's accounts parallel the narrative structures of the epiphany that are prevalent in accounts of the creation of the Western subject. This structure follows narratives of self-discovery and a simple model of causality so closely that one single event, the epiphany, so radically alters one's life that all other contextual and historical events fall to the wayside in order that the epiphany provide closure and singularity of cause. The problem with any use of the epiphany is that it is the production, after the fact, by either the interpreter or the subject of experience. For instance, Mona's MSF training was full of scare narratives, but she claimed it wasn't until she actually witnessed someone with her own eyes, who rode the exact same bike that she rode, crumpled on the pavement that it became apparent to her that she needed to "ride more safely." Furthermore, there is a pattern in her story similar to that in so many others in motorcycle literature, particularly the ones examined above. In either case, though, a discursive form, the epiphany, is given experiential weight unproblematically. It seems absolutely necessary here to examine the relationship of the discursive with the experiential.

In specific terms, the question is whether the epiphany actually takes place at the experiential moment or whether it is a post hoc way of interpreting past events in order to structure and give purpose to a memory of an experience. One way of approaching this is by comparing it with religious epiphanies, which it seems to mirror. Much of the safety discourse is oriented around death and fatalities. The leading question is, how can fatalities be avoided, and often one of the first answers given is to recognize the risk factor inherent in riding a motorcycle (note here even the title of books like *Safe Riding: Staying Alive on Your Motorcycle*). Bastardizing this a bit, one could read this as an attempt to make riders recognize their mortality, look into the eyes of death, and see what their future no longer holds. Just as in religious conversion stories, it is the recognition of one's ultimate demise, both worldly and spiritually, that often sparks, or is said to initiate, the process of redemption. In this way, the safety discourse is saving one from death and offering redemption—if not immortality, at least some extra riding years. After Saul becomes Paul, on his way to Damascus, he radically alters his life, turns away from the evils of his past, which included the hunting and slaying of Christians, and begins his new role as an apostle, spreading the word and converting others through a retelling of his own miraculous epiphany. This is precisely what the stories in "Motorcycle Editors' Greatest Hits" also do.

The theoretical assumption is that, of course, the discourse of safety and of the epiphanic form come well before these so-called epiphanic experiences. This is not to claim that these aren't powerfully moving experiences. Rather, the epiphany is more an act of memory reconstruction. Epiphanies offer sensible structure for establishing the motorcyclist as the agent of causality and, by extension, the object in need of ultimate repair. Mortality, death, and the staving off of these fears through faith in one discourse or another is a longstanding tradition. So is the establishment of simple causal models of explanation in our personal lives. This doesn't weaken epiphanies' usage as an interpretive tool. It does switch the focus from the specific personal stories to the discursive context from which these epiphanies arise. For instance, it makes perfect sense that Mona would explain her switch from unsafe to safe riding practices as the outcome of an epiphanic moment that involved the witnessing of a motorcycle accident, as shown above, a common narrative.

Near-fatal stories are retold over and over again in the context of MSF courses in which thousands of motorcyclists receive their primary riding education. Safety plays the starring role in this course. An attempt has been made to show the way in which education and narrative have played key roles in the creation of the safety discourse as it pertains to motorcycling. There are multiple discourses at play when examining the practices of motorcycling. However, safety is the one which legitimates current and past governmental policy. Other discourses and their attentive narratives are outside the truth of what can officially be spoken. Mona's stories of riding at 140 miles per hour down the highway, then, can only be interpreted as being unsafe and uneducated, even by herself. Groups of young men and women riding around town without helmets can only be spoken of as a pack, as if they were wolves looking for prey. But what other responses by motorcyclists to the safety discourse might exist?

Lastly, the epiphany is a tool for neoliberal forms of governance. It connects governmentality or mobile efficiency with personal rationality (i.e., safe conduct). What is unique about its use in motorcycling is that because of the phenomenological bias, the motorcyclist is particularly prone to such personal narratives. Furthermore, owing to the need to explain one's reasoning for riding, since it is abnormal, the motorcyclist is continually working through various grids of interpretation for such reasoning. The safe riding epiphany is the dominant discourse for binding personal experience, truth, and safety together. Other discursive trajectories do exist that provide differing relationships between personal safety and experience.

### Ways of Being a Biker

This last section provides directions down two differing roads for a journey that may detour or speed past disciplined mobility and the safety regime that supports and produces it. The first is more of a personal journey. It describes a series of potential and real responses by individual cyclists to scare narratives, the pull of the epiphany, and its link to safety. The second journey involves fellow travelers. Riding in large groups is a hallowed tradition among motorcyclists, and there are in fact entire articles devoted to doing so in a safe fashion. But it is not this orchestrated, Shrineresque type of group riding that is most interesting. Instead, Gilles Deleuze's and Felix Guattari's discussion of the pack will fuel my analysis of the motorcycle gang. What I want to suggest is that there are both individual and collective means for resisting the appeal of safe riding and disciplined mobility. There is a desire here to rethink the very relation between life and death insofar as intellectual, political, and personal conduct are concerned. Although the analogy may seem a bit strained on first sight, Foucault provides an anthem for those who might articulate the relationships between the death-defying motorcyclist and radical thought. He writes, "I dream of the intellectual who destroys evidence and generalities, the one who, in the inertias and constraints of the present time, locates and marks the weak points, the openings, the lines of force, who is incessantly on the move, doesn't know exactly where he is heading nor what he will think tomorrow for he is too attentive to the present; who, wherever he moves, contributes to posing the question of knowing whether the revolution is worth the trouble, and what kind, it being understood that the question can be answered only by those who are willing to risk their lives to bring it about."[51]

The following analysis uses Foucault's insight about thought in order to address how motorcycle practice works as "thought in action" against the dominant discourse of safety through a series of questions regarding death and risk. Clearly, this is not to suggest riding a motorcycle is a truly revolutionary act in the strictly political sense of overthrowing governments. Rather, when safety has come to dominate the governance of mobility and self-reflection, might it not be useful to look to those who strain against such forms of governance in a way that "locates and marks the weak points, the openings, the lines of force"? If not to those subjugated populations who are the object of scrutiny and the populations against which such forms of governance are aimed and who are in fact "willing to risk their lives" in order to sustain a different relationship to governance and self-reflection, where else might we find the micropractices of resistance? To most, this different relationship to safety appears quite retrograde. But this is precisely the reason why it is worth examining, as it points to how thoroughly intractable the articulation has become that binds safety, intelligence, and, as has been shown, even morality. A first question to examine, then, might be, to what extent does it matter in a motorcycle culture and discourse that death and risk operate so freely? It seems that to some extent riding is equated with risk and death and thus riding must be something worth dying for. To the extent that anything worth risking one's life for is worth it. Now we all know, of course, you can die while driving, flying, sitting on a train, or walking across the street. But, certain leisure activities like riding, scuba diving, or sky diving do entail risk or are perceived as risky. Yet is it this very discursive opposition between risk and worthiness that makes the operation of so-called risky behaviors, that which makes them worth doing, desirable? The desire can't simply come from a phenomenological rush. This may be a real experience. But it is desirable only when it is situated in a discourse that values the rush. The question, then, is how safety operates to neuter the rush, make it not worth dying for, because it is less risky, thus less desirable, but more palatable.

Given that it has already been established that motorcycling culture is highly dependant upon appeals to the phenomenological, there are at least four sensibilities regarding riding and risk; how these sensibilities differ, how they link to a more general relation to self, and how they might uncover weak points or openings and represent powerful lines of force are of primary concern. The responses are by no means a full list of the possible relationships. Furthermore, these are not meant as descriptive categories into which all motorcyclists neatly fit. Rather, they are an attempt to offer new possibilities for thinking about how relationships to risk are in many ways relationships to governing, politics, and rationality. In no way is this section meant as a validation of the experiential, nor is its dependence upon phenomenological description an avocation for a reversion to such methods or epistemologies. Instead, it is in the phenomenological discourse that the narrative validations for risky conduct are hidden.

1. Quit riding—This response is the most obvious and, to some, may seem the only sensible reply. Having an accident might be just what the doctor ordered, as it will knock a little sense into the hopefully ex-rider. This type of response is fairly common, and as one ex-rider explained, he was just too dangerous on a motorcycle. He consistently repeated the line that it was just a matter of time before he would go down, and he had better be prepared. After crashing his motorcycle in the rain and suffering a broken arm and leg, he quit riding cold turkey. He refused to get on a motorcycle of any sort for over a dozen years and then only grudgingly and under intense scheduling pressures would accept a mile and a half ride from me on the back of my motorcycle. His response is hard to actually measure or even locate in the motorcycle press because it is a form of self-negation, at least as far as motorcycling is concerned. Once one quits riding, one is no longer a motorcyclist and not a player in the culture. The extreme case of this response is to proselytize against motorcycles altogether after quitting. There are also, of course, cases in which riding a cycle after a crash is no longer an option owing to injury or death.

2. Hyperreflective self-disciplinarity—This response takes the safety rhe-

toric as truth. The experts are provided legitimacy, and in fact, new motorcycle safety experts from both within motorcycling and without enter the discourse to produce a hyper-safety consciousness (riding schools, MSF, Snell, safe riding articles, medical doctors legitimating this form of riding). Riding skills, safety features on bikes, racetrack gear worn for street riding, discursive demarcations separating the good riders from the bad, the enlightened from the unenlightened. This is Mona's response and, to a lesser degree, that of Terence.

This form also can be seen as the overcoming of external regulation through an even more intensely focused self-discipline. "One can never be safe enough," "there is always room for improvement," "every rider can benefit from these skills." These are some of the validating claims that continually appear in the first paragraph of every safety article. This subdiscourse demands the most extreme form of subjectification, coupled with an extreme self-reflexivity in which one's personal practices aren't simply obedient, but rather ascetic, disciplined, and highly motivated by expert facts. There is a sense in which all riders should professionalize themselves, become self-proclaimed experts. The discourse doesn't demand obedience, but rather a mode of subjection which fits perfectly into the neoliberal model of responsibilization, always in the name of rationality. In simplest terms, the only way to be a sane rider, according to this discourse, is to be a self-monitoring safe rider. This means learning not only the rules of the road, but also what equipment is most protective, what strategies for accident avoidance are appropriate, what methods of braking are applicable to each set of circumstances, what types of automobile drivers to stay clear of, etc. This discourse is primarily concerned with overcoming risk through self-management, assessment, education, and conduct.

3. Risk valorization—This response claims that the risks may very well be true, although they have probably been exaggerated in order to fuel the hysteria. However, there are self-guided motivations like freedom, camaraderie, phenomenological being in the world that drive one to choose practices and a lifestyle worthy of risk. Some things simply are worth risking one's life for. Motorcycling is one of those things.

This discourse doesn't eschew safety in absolute terms, but neither does it maintain the validity of safety as the be-all and end-all for riding.

Safety may be a concern of some, but it doesn't validate or invalidate one's riding. Statements that validate the risk of motorcycling include, "Instead of fear, exhilaration spread through my body! This crazy little event was more exciting than anything I had ever experienced before. I was sure this was the morphine that fed many bikers. The realization that you can come close to destruction yet so easily avoid it."[52] Or, "I think, these days, because life has become so comfortable, everything from running water to central heating, the human race, certainly in the West, finds discomfort almost as unacceptable as it finds danger. And, motorcyclists deny both of those, or fly in the face of both anxieties voluntarily. So that provides a unifying force between them."[53]

The statements above only scratch the surface of the type of phenomenological experiences that are said to make the risk worthwhile. Furthermore, as evidenced by the quotations, it is the sense of risk that, at least in part, makes motorcycling worthwhile. There is an important difference between accepting the risks for other rewards and seeing risk itself as a reward.

The third type of response isn't exactly risk management in a neoliberal form. That would entail simply assessing the risks faced by riding and then determining whether the risks are outweighed by potential benefit. This would treat riding a motorcycle as if it were a purely economic decision. That mode of subjection demands a continuously calculating version of the subject driven by rationality. The question is, what type of rationality supports such a conception? This is where the very phenomenological dependency of this discourse alters the terrain of debate. If safety guides the rationality, then to act otherwise is irrational. To enjoy the risk posits a different set of criteria for conduct. It establishes a means for prioritizing experience over rationality. However, the political potential for such an alteration is severely limited. It may provide camaraderie. It may provide for inner peace. It may even create a reason to enter into the politics of representation as they relate to motorcyclists' interests. It doesn't, though, politicize risk, but rather circumscribes it as an experience, a rush.

4. Flaunting risk—The fourth type of response includes riding in an unsafe manner in order to prove one's resistance to the disciplinary regulations and institutions that guide current motorcycle programs.

Thompson's description of the Hell's Angels, previously discussed, comes closest to this potential. However, before it is assumed that this is being offered up unproblematically as a positive move against governance, it must be recognized that there are serious consequences to disregarding safety altogether.

Hunter's explanation follows the heroic narrative. It is similar to the "rebel without a cause"/Jim Morrison/beats/howling at the moon sort of resistance. One man (at least in nearly all of this literature) stands alone and rages against the machine. To simply ride in a fashion that demands to be read as unsafe (without a helmet, at a high speed, passing on blind curves, while drinking a beer) may appear rebellious, but it certainly isn't productive. However, disregard for safety could prove politically useful and, more important, flaunting a disregard for personal well-being can disrupt the articulations that bind safety, truth, and governing.

A statement of this sort would demand a reorganization of political drives and rationalities which no longer worked along the risk-safety dichotomy. Instead, as Foucault suggests above, the course of political action should be guided only by those willing to risk their lives to bring about change. Bastardizing this a bit and treating the cycle rider as both a political participant in the game of safety and as a metaphor for other politics would mean that flaunting one's disregard for safety, the safe decision, the safe action, the safe theory, the safe tactic is itself a political act that signifies a motivating intensity. It demands attention, much needed, if a course of action is to be determined and carried out. Thus, the safety of any particular action would be relegated to the sidelines. It would not be allowed to determine the parameters of thought and action.

This too is somewhat problematic, and I want to turn to the epigraph from Thompson to elaborate: "But with the throttle screwed on there is only the barest margin, and no room for mistakes. It has to be done right . . . and that's when the strange music starts, when you stretch your luck so far that fear becomes exhilaration and vibrates along your arms. You can barely see at a hundred . . . The Edge . . . There is no honest way to explain it because the only people who really know where it is are the ones who have gone over."[54]

Thompson is describing the pursuit of "the Edge," that mythical place where one has gone as far as possible without going over. He begins to acknowledge the impossibility of this pursuit by letting us in on the secret that the only people who know where the Edge is have gone over it. Which is to say; they are now dead. This makes the Edge a phenomenological potential but a practical impossibility. It is an endless search for that which is not attainable, because in attaining it, you lose it. Furthermore, it is a point that is always approachable only in seemingly infinite half-the-distance increments. You keep getting closer, but you can never get there because if you were there, you would be dead. Since you are alive, the Edge, by definition, must be further out there. Thompson's description of the pursuit, coupled with Foucault's sense that only those willing to risk life for politics should make decisions, raises the possibility that a politics of risk affirmation leads toward an ever-approaching impossibility. It is relentless in its attempt to push the boundaries of what is possible, without ever exhausting the production of new possibilities. In this sense, the exhilaration of risk is a requisite part of politics. It isn't enough to simply ask for risk assessment in determining what course of action is proper, for this predetermines the limits of possibility by operating within the logic of acceptable losses. Instead, there is a need to be exhilarated by the pursuit, pulled forward by "the strange music." I don't believe this is a politics of limited gains and predetermined outcomes, neither as a telos, nor as an imagined possibility. Instead, it depends upon a relation to self and others that is never satisfied and always searching for the cracks and fissures that open up to reveal lines of thought and action previously unknown, unacceptable, or unbelievable.

## Shining the Chrome

I'm afraid that motorcycling has taken a rather different turn than the one just described. Over the past twenty years motorcyclists and manufacturers have made a serious effort to clean up their act as a way of easing police crackdowns and safety advocates' anxiety while popularizing a historically defined fringe activity. Rather than trace out this fall from disgrace, I will briefly discuss two recent historical representations of the motorcycle and bikers. The less well known is the two-hour A&E documentary that has aired several times called *The Wild Ride of Outlaw Bikers*. The other was the spectacularly popular "Art of the Motorcycle" exhibit, shown first at the Guggenheim in New York and then at the Field Museum of Natural History in Chicago. These two all-encompassing histories go a long way in taming the image of the motorcycle and those who ride them.

The moral of *The Wild Ride of Outlaw Bikers* and "The Art of the Motorcycle," particularly as it was presented in Chicago, is that bikers, though once a dangerous element, are now a useful and even valuable part of society. This is accomplished in slightly different ways. The A&E documentary provides a narrative history that traces much of the same ground covered earlier in this chapter. It does so according to a logic of progress. Motorcyclists have always been misunderstood, according to this story. Recently, however, through their own efforts and the social reduction of prejudice, bikers have been able to be viewed as just another consumer fetish group. A group that has made a difference by organizing various fund-raising rallies and runs for such causes as multiple sclerosis, breast cancer research, Toys for Tots, and AIDS. This radical rearticulation of what it means to be a biker has gone the route of family values. The documentary continually informs us that bikers are really a great big happy family and are just like any other normal Americans. This rearticulation has a lot to do with the reemergence of Harley-Davidson (HD) in the 1980s and the tremendous success of their horizontal marketing strategies. By extending the range of goods well beyond that of actual motorcycle gear, Harley-Davidson was able to create one of the most recognizable brands of the past twenty years. From the ubiquitous Harley T-shirts to the nostalgia drenched Harley Cafés, HD has cleaned up its image along with the image of Harley riders. At the same time, the rider demographics have shifted up on the socioeconomic scale, and the typical Harley buyer of the new millennium is as likely to be a professor, lawyer, doctor, or investment banker as a factory worker who listens to classic rock. Truth be told, these days the cost of a used Harley, let alone a new one, is higher than most working-class riders can afford. The Japanese motorcycle manufacturers have helped provide this economic niche with less expensive HD look-alikes. But even this, according to motorcycle purists, has weakened the articulation that once bound HD and the modified cruiser with its rebel image.

*The Wild Ride of Outlaw Bikers* may have missed the boat when it comes to the newest outlaw bikers by dealing almost exclusively with HD and its riders. Other elements of the biker crowd are left out of the picture. In the most recent biker gang scares, the cruiser and HD have been unceremoniously absent. These gangs have instead chosen the sport bike, or "crotch rocket," as their steed. Racing around in large groups at high speeds, these roving youth have been spotted in large cities and small towns alike. They are not gangs in a traditional sense, but rather are loosely affiliated and come together mostly to ride. They chase each other through city streets and play elaborate games of tag and follow the leader, continually pushing each other to ride harder. By limiting its scope, *Outlaw Bikers* helped promote HD while also promoting a type of motorcycle affiliation that is palatable, family friendly, and highly marketable.

The "Art of the Motorcycle" exhibit was criticized by motorcyclists and art critics alike for its link to the market. BMW sponsored this aesthetic and cultural showcase, and some doubted the relevance of some of the BMW motorcycles that were included. The exhibition had the highest attendance of any show ever at the Guggenheim Museum of Art. It attracted half a million visitors during its three-month run (a statistic that rivals the yearly attendance figures for most museums, worldwide). Not only was the attendance unprecedented in the sixty-one-year history of the Guggenheim, but reports implied that of the almost eight hundred thousand attendees, the vast majority were first-timers: first-time visitors to the Guggenheim in particular and, perhaps more significantly, first-time patrons of any art museum at all. The spectacular popularity of the Guggenheim show led to an ad hoc second venue, the Chicago Field Museum of Natural History. When the Field Museum took the exhibit, the motorcycle as art was transformed into the motorcycle as artifact, as motorcycle culture was invoked to legitimate the object for display in this decidedly different cultural space. The construction of the object for two different venues revealed the particular problems of the motorcycle for museum display and exposed the fissures of rationalities of exhibition. More important for my argument, the motorcycle's inclusion in these spaces solidified its place as a legitimate, and thus tamed, cultural practice and fetish.

We can look to Raymond Williams's three definitions of culture in order to illuminate how the motorcycle, understood as culture, was put to various uses and abuses. In the first instance, culture is defined as the best and brightest that society has to offer. Through this appeal, the motorcycle is produced as an aesthetic object, an assertion not without its detractors. Second, culture is defined in its anthropological sense as the meaningful activities of daily lives. Thus, the motorcycle serves as the site for communal identity. This too proves problematic, as it produces an impossible act of capture that unifies, simplifies, and historicizes various practices through the display of an artifact. Finally, culture is understood as a technology of government, and, following Tony Bennett, the public museum has, since its inception, been an important disciplinary apparatus.[55] The exhibit was doing double duty in this regard in that it was organizing the thought of motorcyclists and nonmotorcyclists, while having to discipline an onslaught of first-time museum goers who were, of all things, uncultured bikers. By examining the exhibition in its two manifestations, I want to briefly explain how the exhibit went through three reiterations.

First, the motorcycle's status as unworthy object of beauty but acceptable object of fetish consumerism was invoked. The wild success of the exhibit prompted a variety of predictable responses within the art press. While bike enthusiasts and cultural populists hailed it as evidence that statistics show the people know, cultural elitists cite the same phenomenon as further evidence of the decline of Western civilization. In the case of the latter, the enormous popularity, configured not just as attendance but as a particular kind of attendance, was presented as evidence of everything from the loss of cultural values to the American obsession with speed to the unholy alliance between corporate culture and the fine arts. These critiques are unified by the sense that aesthetic criteria have been despoiled by the motorcycle. For instance, Rick Woodward concluded his review for *ARTnews* with these observations: "The lasting impression from this survey is the tinge of covetousness. One can't help wanting to own one of these babies. The design of the machines seems to have taken a backseat—or at least sidecar—to the designs on the consumer. When an exhibition label can tout one of the sponsor's latest items, in this case the 1997 BMW R1200C, as 'typically environmentally friendly, high-tech, and safe,' the leakage of advertising copy into the curatorial process is unnerving."[56]

With even greater disdain, Peter Schedjahl's review for the *Village Voice* had this to say: "Like guns, motorcycles are innately insane devices—anxiety generators, disasters in waiting, just asking for grief—and objects of unwholesome worship. Oozing displays of Eros, they are fetish machines and religious substitutes, traducing the spirit, while mortifying the flesh."[57] What we get, then, is a dismissal of motorcycles as art. They are instead fetish objects for the spiritually poor, oversexed, and insane. They are, in short, not worthy of true cultural status, but that of the denigrated market. This rearguard line of defense depends upon ad hominen attacks on the biker and exhibits a discomfort with allowing the undeserving and unwashed masses into the temples of art.

Second, the exhibit established the notion that there is a unified motorcycle culture, rather than numerous relationships to motorcycles. As I tried to argue earlier, there are numerous relationships to motorcycling, and they are neither unified nor ahistorical. Rather, they have been varied and continually changing. At the Field Museum the exhibition was legitimated through an appeal to an expanded definition of anthropological culture. The promotional material elaborates: "The exhibition sheds light on the motorcycle not only as an achievement in design and technology but as a cultural icon, influencing and influenced by popular culture. In keeping with the Field's mission to explore the Earth and its people, the Museum's installation supplements the Guggenheim's exhibit with new material, focusing on the diverse individuals and groups who have used the motorcycle to shape their identities. . . . As a cultural exhibit, 'The Art of the Motorcycle' explores the bike's important role in defining community and identity."[58]

The "multiplicity of meanings" were elicited though the classic exhibitionary techniques of any natural history museum. The bikes were arranged chronologically by decade, each introduced by a text panel with a string of terms meant to cue a broader historical moment or context. For example, under the subtitle "The Consumer Years: 1980–99" the text read, "CNN-Dallas-MTV-Chicago Bears-Mt. Saint Helens-Greenpeace-nutri-sweet-Salman Rushdie-rap music-AIDS-etc." The "communities and identities" treated ranged from the "Capitalist Tools"—the motorcycle club organized by Malcolm Forbes Sr., whose members are shown seated triumphantly on their hogs in Tiananmen Square—to the motor-cross racing circuit, to the RUBS (Rich Urban Bikers), who had increased motorcycle sales 43 percent in the preceding years.[59] This buzzword approach to context forces the viewer to fill in the blanks, and it also reveals the extent to which the rationality of the museum display is predicated upon the assertion of a naturalized link between essentialized culture and the artifacts that are said to emanate from it. The progressivist and developmentalist logic was underpinned by the chronological ordering and ultimately the museum exhibit itself, which through its clean-image ending awarded motorcycling an acceptability not granted by the art press. But here, within the contradiction of acceptability and unacceptability, is where the third logic of culture, as a technology for governing, enters the picture.

The exhibit produces two audiences, each of which is governed differently through its relationship to the motorcycle. First, we have those who don't ride. For them, the death-defying exotic other serves to reify the logic of their safe automobiles. Thus their conduct is shown to be rational, as the exhibit is partially guided by the achievement and goal of increased speed and the risky attitude that this represents. Those who drive can gawk at the "primitive natives" who live in their visceral glory. The moto-nut is provided a sanitized, essentialized, and homogenized version of his culture; providing an acceptable unity that makes the biker an active member in civil society. The creation of this imagined community works to situate the biker within, first, a collective culture, and second, the inclusion of this formerly marginalized culture into the legitimating space of the museum instantiates all bikers into a broader civic enterprise. There was much pride in the motorcycle press regarding this inclusion, and bikers were determined to show up in droves to represent themselves in a civil fashion and prove that they were worthy of cultural acceptance. Bennett reminds us that "going to museums is not simply about looking and learning"; the museum is also a place of structured conduct in which behavior is targeted for ethical modification. This behavior was pointed out in a *New York Times* piece about the exhibit titled "Look Ma, No Hands," in which Ali Subotnick claims that to the "surprise of everyone, from security officers to curators and administrators," the code of honor motorcycle aficionados displayed while circulating within the spaces of high culture constrained them from touching the motorcycles.[60] This praise for the well-disciplined patron speaks volumes about the governmental logic of the museum, as a space in which subjects and objects are tamed and managed toward particular ends. When you are both the object and the subject of such governance, the museum is a place fraught with articulatory and disciplinary danger.

## Conclusion

These recent representations of motorcycling bring us back to several key issues that have been the concern of this chapter. The relative acceptability of motorcycling, it has been shown, is not simply determined by its relative safety. There have been moments of great scrutiny about motorcyclists' behavior and even abusive responses to it, but this has in no way accorded to any real threat either to them or to the society they were said to be menacing. Rather, the various attacks on motorcycling have come from differing sources for disparate reasons. The romantic appeal of the motorcycle has drawn anomic, affluent, and adventurous male youth through the past five decades to its fumes and flames like insects naturally drawn to fire. Like insects, these youth are attracted to that which could kill them. It is said to be a natural attraction, as if young men always and everywhere desire danger, speed, and male camaraderie. Yet recently women riders have been on the rise, and two books written by women, *The Perfect Vehicle* and *Flaming Iguanas*, are autobiographical accounts of the authors' fascination with motorcycles and the way that riding has altered their relationship to mobility and life. This relationship between the two is a well-discussed topic among motorcyclists. The various positions regarding this relationship are potentially the most productive lesson to be learned from the motorcyclists' positions pertaining to safety. Because motorcyclists have, over the past fifty years, continually been forced to justify riding a motorcycle, they have spent extensive energy theorizing, describing, and experiencing multiple understandings of the relationship between risk, desire, politics, and governing. This experience constitutes a useful discourse for searching out critical new approaches to safety. Unfortunately, as motorcycle gangs disappear, as motorcycle magazines increase the amount of space given over to safety concerns, and as manufacturers work to clean up the image of motorcycling and increase appeal to an older and more affluent market, I'm afraid that motorcycles and the discourse surrounding them will no longer provide the fertile thought regarding risk and its potential benefits. Although the motorcycle press was wildly supportive of the "Art of the Motorcycle" exhibit and in a sense motorcyclists were able to flex their economic muscle, this validation, via high culture and market capitalism, surely can't be the ultimate sign of societal acceptance. Furthermore, if it is, then just what was it that made motorcyclists appear to be so dangerous for so long? Clearly, market and demographic forces have worked to alter what it means to be a motorcyclist, and just as surely they have made it more acceptable. Just as in the 1960s, when middle-class youth began to ride in growing numbers, a series of initiatives were brought to bear to ensure their safety and to some degree alter the image of what it meant to be a motorcyclist. As motorcycling is increasingly described as a leisure and lifestyle market, rather than a whole way of life, the chrome may shine brightly, but the world it reflects is dulled in large part by the homogenizing force of capital.

# CHAPTER 4

## COMMUNICATIONS CONVOY

*The* CB *and Truckers*

CB is used for many important and helpful social activities, but also for illegal activities. In our complex society, any development has the potential for great good and for harm. It is our responsibility to use the enormous potential of CB to improve our lives and the lives of others.

SCHLOSSBERG AND BROCKMAN, *THE ALL NEW FACT-PACKED 1977/78 CB GUIDE*[1]

The general public's many legitimate uses of CB would be impeded if stringent licensing rules were established. If, on the other hand, widespread abuse of CB cannot be abated in the face of its rapidly increasing use, CB's value for law-abiding users will be undermined and a portion of a valuable national resource—the radio frequency spectrum—wasted.

FEDERAL COMMUNICATION COMMISSION, 1975[2]

### Introduction

What was citizens band (CB) radio and just what exactly were imagined to be the enormous potentials of this national resource? How could it have been imagined that such a thing could be used for both great good and great harm? What sorts of abuses and illegalities were taking place? And who is the collective signified above by "our"? Typically, communications resources are valorized in terms of their ability to transfer messages across greater distances and with greater speed in the hope of democratically expanding free speech. To a degree this is exactly the type of rhetoric that was in wide circulation during the 1970s and accompanied the rapid growth of CB, a two-way radio system open to personal use that could be installed in the home as well as in semitrailers, cars, boats, motorcycles, etc. In many ways the rhetoric was the same as that used to describe new communications technologies over the past decade. In fact, VH1 claimed the Internet was simply the CB of the 1990s. But there are far more telling similarities between the explosion of CB use that occurred in the 1970s and the expanded use of new communications technologies such as the Internet, cellular telephones, Palm Pilots, pagers, and the like throughout the 1990s and into the new century. Much like current debates regarding the perils, pleasures, and possibilities inherent in these new technologies, the midseventies question was, "Nuisance—or a Boon? The Spread of Citizens' Radios."[3] This chapter is not simply interested in following this comparative line of inquiry. Rather, it is an attempt both to understand how a mobile-communications technology became a resource for authorities to "govern at a distance" and to investigate tactics employed to circumvent such governance via the same communications technology.

A second concern is providing an approach toward new communications technologies that foregrounds the long history of mobility as it relates to communications and the goals to which such mobile technologies have been put to use. This assumes that old models for the study of communications technologies are lacking in their ability to help explain the importance of communications technologies as they are utilized for governance. Specifically, that means working against models that "sacrifice too much to the media sphere" and "the tide of pragmatism influenced by expertise."[4] It also means taking into account communications' complicity with liberal modes of governance[5] and the importance that freedom, a long-standing unexamined good within communications, plays in governing. Last, it investigates "how the population knows itself and its duties"[6] in alignment with "popular truths"[7] that in this case are the didactic outcome of a country music, television, and film genre specific to the 1970s: the anticop road genre. This genre will be investigated as one of many discourses which organized thinking and conduct related to CB radio use. Some of these discourses emanate from governmental sources, such as the Federal Communications Commission (FCC), which are explicitly directed at the governance of communications use. Yet the FCC doesn't exist in a vacuum. As will become evident, the FCC itself was responding to other discourses about and uses of CB that weren't originally imagined by early proponents of CB. Due to its mobility, its rapid growth in popularity, and the multiple-point to multiple-point nature of its informative and cultural flow, CB was very difficult to control via a top-down set of regulations and enforcement. Yet these sorts of governmental concerns get at only a fraction of what is meant by governance. The focus here is on how CB allows for new formations of the governance of mobility and how it is utilized in struggles against such governance. In other words, the question of communications policy and governance shouldn't be so narrowly focused as to take into account merely the content of such a medium or who might be able to own it. The more elaborate question is, what types of governance of the population does it conform and allow? This type of approach emphasizes the essential place that communications plays in governance and related thought.

The specific arenas emphasized in this chapter are the ways in which mobile conduct must always be acknowledged as both an actual and virtual field of governance. The notion of governing at a distance can be understood in two different, yet interconnected fashions. First, it is through transportation and communications that the state is able to maintain its hold over the population and in some cases its empire, which James Carey, following Harold Innis, points out quite clearly in several instances.[8] Innis explained that the imperial dependencies produced through communications and transportation infrastructures and their political economic ramifications made them very explicit and effective technologies of power; technologies for governing at a distance. This use of communication to govern remotely is not necessarily built upon any pretense of upholding democratic or communitarian principles, in opposition to the rhetoric which many have claimed is foundational to European and North American liberalism. Yet the second notion of governing at a distance depends precisely upon using communications to activate subjects without being overly intrusive or coercive; which is to say, act according to the most basic tenet of liberal government. It is through a combination of the press, freedom of speech, and the telegraph, Andrew Barry argues, that governing at a distance, in this second sense, was initially ensured.[9] It is a form of governance built upon allowing and encouraging—one might even say fostering—very particular forms of freedom that lead to, and are derived by, the maxim that government rules best when ruling least. For Barry, it is the realm primarily of communications through which this takes place. Much of the debate regarding CB use will fall into either one or the other of these two ways of thinking about governing at a distance. In some instances, CB is used specifically to organize and control how bodies are policed as they move through space. In other instances, CB is a means by which deliberation and the dissemination of information occur. But part of what these notions fail to recognize is that citizens can also act at a distance through mobile technologies.

The distance of one's potential effects and the range of incoming affect become increasingly relative as individuals are able to actively use communications technologies with expanded range. The space of governance is thus not only greater, but of greater immediacy. That is, when a vast population is linked into vastly expansive relations of power (i.e., communications networks) the state's need to effectively monitor, control, regulate, and productively guide such communications conduct is magnified. Conversely, the importance of citizens to reflect upon and resist unwanted effects of such governmental initiative is also magnified. Struggles over how and to what purposes communications technologies can be used are struggles over the very networks of power, including spatial and temporal, in which we conduct our increasingly mobile lives. The emergence of new communications technologies reorients those networks and thus reorients the relations of power in which individuals are imbricated. Certainly CB is not a new technology, and in fact its use has declined dramatically since its 1970s heyday. Owing to the proliferation of cellular telephone technology and changes in speed limits, fuel costs, and police-citizen relations, the CB has become something of an anachronism. But, the initial explosion of CB use has much to offer as an example of how new communication technology is integrated into the power relations of everyday conduct. These relations often accord with governmental initiatives, but as users of CB in the 1970s attest, there is no necessary reason that they must.

The key figures in the discussion about whether CB would be used for "good or harm" were clearly marked in the press, movies, songs, and television shows of the period: truckers, police, and a blossoming CB citizenry. For each of the three groups involved, the stakes were said to be high. Truckers were feeling the economic pinch of OPEC's oil embargo, subsequent fuel rationing, and reduced speed limits. Together these factors pushed independent truckers to the brink of financial ruin. CBs provided the lone weapon in their struggle to maintain profitable delivery schedules by allowing them to keep abreast of fuel availability and, more important, radar-toting police. The growing CB citizenry[10] were expanding the network of mobile communication that, according to the FCC, police, government agencies, and most every popular contemporaneous news account, promised to be the greatest safety device since the seat belt. Information regarding accidents, potential road hazards, drunk drivers, inclement weather, and roadside breakdowns would be relayed quickly and efficiently to an ever greater number of concerned citizens and rescue and response teams.

Personalized anecdotes, often gendered, were used as evidence of how such road dangers might be dealt with (see figure 16). These ever-greater numbers were also, though, getting involved in the countersurveillance network previously composed only of truckers. Police were almost contradictorily positioned, as they were under increased pressure to implement the new fifty-five-mile-per-hour (mph) federal directive, which made them wary and at times hostile toward CB users, yet under their mandate to serve and protect they had to participate in all highway safety campaigns. Somewhat reluctantly, they joined the CB network, and channel 9 became the official emergency channel on which distressed motorists could call for police help or information.[11] Keeping these players in mind, I want to explore a number of questions regarding the various surveillance and communication practices that the CB allowed and the part the device played in the wildcat truckers' rebellion that took place in December 1973. The spirit of the event assumed mythic popular culture status, first on the nightly news, then in 1975 in C. W. McCall's hit song "Convoy," and finally in Sam Peckinpah's filmic adaptation of the song in 1977.

### Citizens Banding Together over Radio

Citizens band radio had a fairly innocuous existence in the United States until it gained prominence in the early- to mid-1970s as a result of three factors. First, widespread use among truckers in their battle to maintain speeds above the newly posted fifty-five mph speed limit was glorified by popular culture and news outlets, and for a short time the trucker became something of an American populist icon whom Americans seemed eager to join. Second, an expansion of mobile communications, directly related to developments in military-driven transistor technology as well as inexpensive Japa-

What begins as a joyful afternoon doesn't always end that way. Safety in times of emergency is only one of the more useful facets of Citizens Band radio. Stranded on the highway, this young lady uses her CB unit to summon aid from home.

**FIGURE 16. Girl in Trouble**

These photographs and accompanying text come from a citizens band user's guide, of which there were dozens. The recurrent image of a woman in trouble on the road is a seeming constant in all automobile safety campaigns. The claim that she summons "aid from home" may be a slight misrepresentation, as the typical range of an automotive-based CB unit was less than five miles in the 1970s. It is far more likely that she would have received aid from a fellow motorist. Given the fear mongering accompanying media coverage of hitchhiking during the same period, it is not surprising such a likelihood was overlooked. This imagery feeds on the same fears resonant in 1970s antihitchhiking campaigns discussed in chapter 2. Not only is the young woman's afternoon at risk, but we are clearly supposed to infer that she and her sexual innocence are at risk. This type of gendering of safety and fear is a recurrent theme throughout other chapters. Advertisement campaigns for cellular telephones fed on this exact vision and asked that parents protect their daughters in case of just such roadside car trouble. F. H. BELT (1973). *EASI-GUIDE TO CITIZENS BAND RADIO* (INDIANAPOLIS: HOWARD W. SAMS), 15.

nese electronics production, reduced the cost of the average CB from $1,500 in the mid-1960s to under $150 dollars by the mid-1970s. Finally, the size of CBs decreased with changes from tube to transistor technology. Whereas police two-way radios had taken up substantial space in the trunk of a car, the CBs that emerged in the early 1970s could fit beneath the dashboard or in a glove box. This led to an explosion of sales and use. By 1976 there were over ten million CBs in use, and the growth of CB was a staggering four hundred thousand to five hundred thousand per month. Even though CB was both a huge cultural and commercial phenomenon of the 1970s, its history as an object of communications research is nearly nonexistent. It never appears as a viable subject on course syllabi, there is virtually no scholarly literature,[12] and it doesn't make an appearance in any widely used communication textbook. The CB absence speaks to a number of biases within a field that tends to focus either on communications technologies whose content can be quantified or textually interpreted or on the ownership and distribution networks of corporate industry giants said to dominate media production, reception, and meaning creation. Even communication research that addresses the uses of communication technologies and texts by so-called subcultures tends to organize studies along identity lines, whether class, age, race, sexuality, or gender. Citizens band may or may not offer much along any of these lines. Which isn't to say one couldn't address issues of identity. Rather, to organize the investments and uses of CB according to taken-for-granted modes of affiliation (class, race, gender, sexuality, nationality, occupation) would seriously limit an understanding of both the power relations—within particular and changing modes of governance—and the specific form of affiliation that for a brief moment seems to bind *nonorganized* truckers. By starting with essentialist notions of identity formation, even if it is simply that of the trucker, we lose sight of the specificity of the sorts of power relations against which resistant identities are formulated and through what cultural and technological mechanisms. This issue will be dealt with in detail in the concluding section, but it is useful to keep in mind that through the CB and because of changing political economic and cultural conditions, the responses of truckers and other drivers was of a different sort from what had come before, and they remain in many ways unique. I am not convinced that other models for approaching communications, mobility, or mobile communications allow for an understanding of this uniqueness.

Prior to 1958 and the advent of class-D citizens radio, two-way radio was limited to amateurs who qualified for stationary radio system licenses, better known as ham operators, and to explicitly commercial and government users. CB was seen as a useful two-way communications tool for businesses dependent upon intracity transportation, such as local trucking firms and cab companies, and it was deployed by large police and fire departments, which were able to coordinate operations in a fashion originally perfected by the military.[13] But in 1958 a new set of frequencies was opened up to the public for general use. This use was still strictly limited in form, if not heavily monitored. Beyond purchasing an operator's license and being allocated a call sign—used to initiate and end all transmissions—there were a series of guidelines that restricted the formal content of transmissions. Three main restrictions applied. First, of the twenty-three stations only channels ten to fifteen and twenty-three were open to communications between stations not under the same license. Second, conversations were not allowed to last more than five minutes, after which time operators had to wait five minutes to begin further communication. Third, idle talk was forbidden; only "necessary communications" were allowed. In short, for the general public CB was not an open system that allowed for the free transmission of ideas and information. Rather, it was to be a utilitarian tool for executing vital commercial and governmental orders and acknowledgments.

Like other communications technologies, CB came to be used for very different purposes, if not in entirely different ways from those imagined and sanctioned. Yet, the claims regarding CB's potential equal any of the utopian scenarios that supported other communications technologies.[14] The democratic appeal seems ridiculous in hindsight, but it uniquely foreshadows two major communications phenomena of the future: talk radio and the Internet. In 1977, when CB was expanded to eighty channels, it was proposed that each be devoted (like 1990s chatrooms) to a particular topic, including politics, film, CB culture, and, with a nod to the 1970s, astrology. These potential uses establish a communications sensibility that promotes niche channeling for a more fragmented, yet supposedly more engaged audience; an audience said to feel shut out and left out by mainstream communications programming, but not out of touch with their fellow Americans.

Joining the anticorporate, anti–big media feelings exemplified in movies like *Network* and *The China Syndrome*, pro-CB rhetoric glorified the CB as the communications medium of the silent majority, who were now given the opportunity to speak their mind. Descriptions of the new possibilities compared CB to television and radio, which were seen as monolithic one-way communications technologies that have "homogenized us . . . at the same time isolating us and silencing us."[15] A fairly informed critique of old media modeled on propaganda accompanied most of the CB guides that were prevalent in the mid-1970s.[16] These critiques focused on the helpless state of old media audiences to participate in their new culture. Rather than being talked to, they were talked at. This led to a situation in which the collective "we" had lost its "ability to create, respond to, and initiate our own cultural life."[17] These criticisms mirrored many of the 1970s populist critiques found within intellectual circles as well as popular film and television. What they generally share is a distrust of multinational corporate control, shown to guide everything from entertainment to the news. They also exhibit a hope for the people to stand up and declare, "We're mad as hell and we're not going to take it anymore."[18] This sort of antimedia populism found its new solution in CB. All of the problems associated with old media were going to be solved, according to the CB proponents.

The following quotation provides insight into the intensity and scope of belief in CB as a communications panacea for prevailing social and economic ills:

> CB gives us back the ability to create an individually oriented culture. . . . CB does not cost anything to operate once you have purchased the set. It is truly FREE SPEECH. There is no CBS in CB. There are no authorities to consult about how to talk or what to say. It is decentralized. . . . We want to have the control we need over our lives; by having our own communications system we can create and participate in local culture and events that are impossible with one-way communications systems. . . . CB is the door to a new world of communications that has no experts and no authorities, and that promises to become a more and more important part of the culture of the last quarter of our 20th century. On CB there is no Big Brother . . . there is only Good Buddy (so far).[19]

Even in the midst of such rousing rhetoric there remains the specter of "Big Brother," on his way to spoil the freedom and potential supposedly inherent in the technology. What wasn't acknowledged was that there was already a struggle over how CB was being used. What follows is an examination of that very struggle—a struggle centered on issues of freedom, community, and Big Brother in his most prevalent guise, the all-seeing eye, or, in this case, the all-hearing ear.

### Surveillance: Seeing Is Believing, but Hearing Is Helpful

Police have been at the forefront of implementing electric/onic communications technologies into forms of governance since 1845, when the description and whereabouts of a train-bound murderer were transmitted by telegraph to police eighteen miles away in London. The man was apprehended as he disembarked from the train. Quite simply, the telegraph is a faster means of communication than the train. Thus began an ever-expanding electronic police communications network. Numerous communications technologies followed the telegraph, but they shared a few key elements. Each allowed for the transmission of greater amounts of information across greater spaces to an increasingly mobile and more organized police force. What began with the use of whistles indicating the need for help, by the early 1900s included telegraph booths with flashing lights controlled at headquarters, and by 1973 had grown into a vast surveillance network that included two-way radio, belt and pocket transmitters, mobile-relay radio systems, radio-linked helicopter and airplane patrols, and nearly ubiquitous automobile patrols. By 1940 most police departments in the United States had implemented the most vital of these communications devices—the two-way radio—which connected automobile patrolmen to state and local police headquarters. This followed a ten- to twelve-year period of one-way radio in which central transmissions were sent out across the frequency modulation, or FM, band to police cars with special radio receivers. These communications technologies were used almost exclusively by police, fire departments, and the military. In this way the state had a virtual monopoly on mobile communications. The state's ability to orchestrate its own movements and monitor the movements of citizens was vastly increased.[20] This control changed radically when citizens began to outfit their automobiles with CBs.

Andrew Barry argues in "Lines of Communication and Spaces of Rule" that electronic communications technologies have been an integral part of liberal governance. As he points out, Foucault laid the groundwork for thinking about how communications worked to expand the facility of the state and reoriented the model for organizing and governing away from the architecture of fixed places. Barry concludes by arguing that communications have ultimately not functioned to increase state surveillance or allow for a "super-panopticon," but rather have become technologies of freedom.[21] To a degree, his argument is dependent upon assumptions regarding what forms of conduct are under surveillance. As many historians of communications have pointed out, communications was long thought of as what we currently consider transportation. It was envisioned as any technology that expanded the spread of information as well as increased the mobility of goods and people. How these goods and people are directed and mobilized is not only a vast project for governments, but being able to govern at a distance, as mentioned earlier, by mobilizing individuals is of paramount importance. However, this doesn't necessarily ensure freedom in any essential sense. As a slew of political theorists following from Foucault have noted, the production, implementation, and organization of freedom are a necessary part of liberal governing strategies.[22] By producing a set of circumscribed and discursively legitimated forms of conduct and then allowing citizens to freely roam within those parameters, governing at a distance is ensured. Truckers, for instance, are free to drive anywhere in the United States, but always within very specific parameters: at specified speeds, on particular roads, when sober, at certain ages, with proper licenses, and carrying certain commodities. This freedom of movement is an essential part of the free flow of goods, peoples, and information in a liberal capitalist state. In certain instances, however, the regulation of one form of communication, automotive mobility, is governed or regulated through the use of another, two-way radio. Furthermore, as will be discussed below, citizens are given the freedom to use CB as a means to expand and intensify the very network used to survey and regulate their own conduct. Thus it cannot so easily be stated that communications technologies should not in some cases be considered a part of a superpanopticon. In this instance, the panopticon is dependent upon the integration of both state and citizens actions, through an electronic communications network. By taking part in CB communication, citizens were given the freedom to ensure their own participation in the surveillance network used to monitor their own activity and communication.

The widespread use of the CB allowed for vast new surveillance and countersurveillance techniques on the highways and byways of America circa 1973. The line between being seen and going unseen was redrawn according to new forms of conspicuity. According to Deleuze's explanation of Foucault's model of surveillance, something must be both conspicuous and situated to warrant surveillance.[23] In this case, two changes regarding the status of truckers were necessary. First, something made truckers conspicuous, worth viewing. Second, ways of situating truckers within surveillance apparatuses became a primary goal of the police. Whereas truckers were not particularly conspicuous before the advent of the fifty-five mph speed limit, once it was implemented they were the segment of the driving public most affected and least likely to comply; thus they became worthy of police surveillance. Truckers were hard hit by the fifty-five, or "double nickel," limit in three ways. First, regulations placed on the trucking industry fixed the number of hours they could drive per day. Second, they were paid by the mile. Third, increased fuel costs and limited availability owing to the OPEC embargo further increased costs and decreased miles as truckers had to make multiple stops at stations that rationed fuel. Given these material constraints, truckers turned to CB technology as a way to counteract the surveillance mechanism of the police and thus continue to drive at profitable speeds.

To understand police surveillance tactics it is useful to return to Foucault's panopticon, which depends upon a stationary, continuously viewable subject. The subject is not always under surveillance, but owing to an architectural solution potentially could be. This produces an internalization of the gaze, which in turn produces a self-monitoring subject. Speed limits and police traffic patrol are said to operate along the same guidelines.[25] Furthermore, a prevalent safety discourse legitimates the speed limit and articulates personal conduct to pastoral governmental initiatives, thus ensuring a concern beyond fear of coercion: fear for life. The trick for the police is to produce a sense that their presence is always imminent. Around each bend, over every hill, under all overpasses may lurk a "Kojak with a Kodak." Like a provident god, the "bear in the air" is watching over us for our own safety. But what happens when surveillance is turned back upon the surveyor? What happens when imminence is made present?

Armed with CBs and driven by a need for speed, truckers produced their own surveillance network: a visual/audio cognitive map of the highway system. Truckers had to map their trajectories against those of sighted smokeys, situating them according to crossroads, highway markers, speeds, and reputations. The "eye of power" was blinded in practical terms by those who could shine the light of surveillance back upon the surveillance tower. Lt. James Jeatran of the Wisconsin State Patrol complained, "I couldn't get in a cruiser without every truck driver within 40 miles knowing where I am."[25]

These countersurveillance practices obviously worked best in groups. Speeding convoys were formed in order to create a roving countersurveillance machine. More "road jockeys" increased the cast of the network and made present all but the most clever of cops. An anecdote from "One lap of America," a 1975 *Car and Driver* article that chronicled an attempt to "put the hammer down and go looking for the 55-mph speed limit," is an account of how the convoy worked:[26]

> A 75-mph convoy has been formed. Up front is a green cab-over Peterbilt known as the "World-Famous Dipstick." Directly behind is the Montana Six-Pack, an immense, long-nose Kenworth hauling cattle, while the Silver Bullet brings up the rear. In this situation, we are watching the "back door," World-Famous Dipstick is in charge of the "front door" and the Montana Six-Pack has the "rockin' chair."
>
> A Smokey Bear appears on the entrance ramp behind us and we shout a warning. The convoy immediately slows to 55-mph and the Bear . . . eases past. . . . The Silver Bullet volunteers to scout ahead and accelerates away . . . we sight Smokey on the roadside with his radar aimed at us . . . we yell into the radio, "Smokey's taking pictures! Back her down! Back her down!"
>
> Responses of "ten-four" and "sure do appreciate that, good buddy" . . . is overriden by a sharper transmission . . . "I got you at 54. You better stay there!"[27]

### Smokey's Got Ears and the Citizen Surveyors

What happens when Smokey's got ears? Not only can he listen in, but he can chime in; inaugurate anti-countersurveillance by disrupting the network with false sightings and readings. Once police began using CBs, which for the most part occurred after truckers began using them en masse, a new space opened up for surveillance. The question of what happens in the prison at night is never adequately answered by Foucault. One answer is the production of silence is demanded, making sound, not sight, conspicuous. It is through the monitoring of noise that guards were able to determine whether prisoners were conducting themselves properly. The movie *A Man Escaped* perfectly represents the importance of noise as the object of nighttime surveillance in the prison. It chronicles the nighttime escape of two French Resistance prisoners of war. Silence is observed to prevent observation. The near-exclusive use of diegetic sound during the escape attempt makes sound's importance clear. The resultant sound of each and every movement is magnified and marks the potential downfall or death of the protagonists. At night, the eye of power becomes the ear of power. At first truckers became conspicuous, as described earlier; now it was their CB conversations which reoriented and refocused police attention, creating an aural space for surveillance.[28]

Truckers attempted to hide through a number of linguistic and technical practices. But CB is an open communication system. This fact made CB seem like an unlikely threat to the U.S. government. As Dean Burch, chairman of the FCC, stated in 1970, "Let me mention briefly the question of security. . . . Amateur radio operators share frequencies with other licenses or authorized operators; thus there is little, if any secrecy. . . . It seems doubtful that anyone would attempt to use these shared frequencies to breach national security."[29] Anyone within range can pick up a truck driver's transmission regarding their speed, location, and destination. Truckers recognized this characteristic and communicated in ways that demanded a special linguistic competency. The truckers' language was full of specialized jargon and slang that was continually changing. Like the truckers, their dialogue was mobile and fluid, yet different geographic dialects existed. Truckers also changed channels according to coded directions and attempted to keep communication open to other potentially helpful and needful truckers, yet closed to the police. The anonymity of their handles, their CB moniker, also helped to disguise their conduct as it wasn't necessarily clear how to connect handles with rigs.

Two scenes from *Convoy* make these points clear. In the first, Sugar Bear, the small-town sheriff antagonist of the film's populist hero, Rubber Duck (played by Kris Kristoferson), eavesdrops on the conversation of an emerging convoy's plan to "lay the pedal to the metal." He gives the truckers the "all clear ahead" and waits for them with his "X-ray machine" aimed at the oncoming truckers. Sugar Bear's linguistic competence allows him to circumvent the countersurveillance measures of the truckers, and it is later contrasted with a group of federal officers' linguistic incompetence as they fail in their attempt to communicate with the now mile-long convoy using all of the "latest quartz multi-channel monitoring technology." The ability to code transmissions, much like radio signals used during World War II, makes the game of cultural competency of key importance. The scene beautifully illustrates the fact that communication and the ability to monitor it are not simply acts of technological sophistication but methods of interpretation and linguistic competency. The technocrats were unable to keep up with the fluidity of the ever-changing language. They had technical competence but not cultural competence. This scene points out the very nature of the bureaucratic-minded governmental official. This technique of governing demands rationality, efficiency, and most importantly, technical proficiency. Thus, it is slow changing and works through normalizing the other, rather than adapting to change. In essence, this type of governing works to create uniform modes of conduct. Thus the FCC called for very structured and limited forms of transmissions. In *Convoy* the incompetent bureaucrats have all of the latest equipment, but they don't speak the language of the people. They are technically in touch, their radios work, but culturally they are from another planet.

This type of populist representation of battles between citizens and government technocrats was made famous in several movies, hit songs, and television shows of the 1970s and early 1980s. *Smokey and the Bandit I* and *II*, *Movin' On*, *BJ and the Bear*, and *Convoy* chronicled the lives of truckers and showcased their fight to maintain profitable speeds. Movies like *The Gumball Rally*, *Cannonball*, *Cannonball Run I* and *II*, and *Gone in 60 Seconds*, as well as the hugely popular television show *Dukes of Hazzard*, demonstrated CB strategies and techniques for counterpolicing. For a short period the trucker became an American icon: a noble solitary figure personifying the open road, existential angst, and freedom, and at other times a mobile community of the road. The truck driver was considered a modern-day cowboy,[30] and the movies about truckers seemed to fill a niche that had been vacated with the death of the western.[31] Just as the CB has been ignored by communications scholars these movies have likewise been overlooked by film scholars. The purpose of their inclusion here is not to prove they are representatives of great art; according to most forms of aesthetic judgment they are not.[32] Instead, what these films provide are exemplary tales of how CB was meant to be used: not according to any inherent technological determinism or FCC guidelines, but according to the contemporaneous popular truths and populist notions of resistance.

Songs glorifying trucking and truckers were a staple of country music, and a number of country music artists played up this very articulation. Red Sovine epitomized the early trucking troubadours. But there were a host of other artists and bands, such as Hank Snow, The Land Rovers, Dave Dudley, and Red Simpson. Their songs dealt with a number of thematics, including amorous exploits with female hitchhikers, battles with the police, the loneliness of the road, families left behind, truckers' vast driving acumen, the nobility of the profession as an extension of the cowboy existence, the love shared between trucker and rig, the call of the road, and even, surprisingly, the safety lessons truckers could teach the rest of the drivers on the road. One of the fundamental characteristics of these pre-1973 themes is the singular and existential nature of the trucker's calling. In many ways, the independent trucker, as a lonely loner entrepreneur, is the paramount exemplar of such themes. He (truck drivers were almost exclusively male) is not glorified for his union membership or for joining the teamsters. Part of what these songs glorify is the notion of the everyman entrepreneur. Yet trucking is described as more of a calling than a means to riches. Thus the ideology of entrepreneurialism isn't so much about economics as about freedom, not that economic freedom isn't a subset of the general discourse of entrepreneurship. Following the wildcat truckers' strike in 1973, this thematic was somewhat overturned. Suddenly it was collective action, through the figure of the convoy, that began to animate the songs and led to the filmic and televisual representations discussed above. Furthermore, how safety was configured in these two periods was radically different.

Red Sovine's *Truck Driver's Prayer* is certainly the most explicit song in this regard. The song begins with Sovine playing the praises of truck drivers, followed by a prayer passed on to him by an Oklahoman trucker:

> Like me an' just about everyone in Country Music who travel a lot,
> Have nothin' but the highest respect for you the truck driver.
> 'Cause it's a fact that some of the best drivers are truck drivers:
> And the most safety minded, the most courteous,
> And the first to stop and help when there's trouble.
> And little things like blinkin' signal lights to help someone pass.
>
> So you just gotta be good people, like some I've had the pleasure to
>     meet:
> Down to earth, hard-working family men . . .

'Cause it boils down to this:
If everyone would drive like you guys do,
There'd be a lot less accidents and deaths on the highway.[33]

Red is attempting to point out a natural articulation and mutual admiration between truckers and country musicians. They both are said to share the road, family values, and a commitment to safety. Red's prayer echoes these sentiments:

Dear God above,
Bless this truck I drive,
An' help me keep someone alive.
Be my mortal sight, this day,
On streets where little children play.
Bless my helper, fast asleep,
When the night is long and deep.
An' keep my cargo safe and sound,
Through the hours, big and round.
Make my judgment sound as steel,
Be my hands upon the wheel.
Bless the traveler goin' past,
An' teach him not to go so fast.
Give me strength for every trip,
So I may care for what they ship.
And make me mindful, every mile.
That life is just a little while.
Amen.[34]

These lyrics bear little resemblance to the glorification of speed and the flaunted attempts of police to regulate it that were the narrative string pulling audiences into the post-1973 trucker subculture. In fact, safety is not reserved for humans but is also manifestly focused upon cargo, the payload. The *Prayer* functions as a lesson to the general driving populace to take note of the professionalized driver and their care of self and cargo; trucker as technique of normalization.

By the time C. W. McCall's "Convoy" hit the airwaves in late 1975, reaching number one on both the pop and country music charts in January 1976, the popular vision of the trucker had been radically altered. Widespread media coverage of the wildcat truckers' strike fixated not so much on independent truckers' plight, but rather on their rather exotic use of CB and the accompanying linguistic practices. Truckers weren't treated as existentially driven loners, but as part of a new "good buddy" subculture that was in part dedicated to breaking the fifty-five mph speed limit.[35] The economic necessity for truckers to do so was not shared by the burgeoning CB citizenry that would soon follow suit, yet follow they would. The desire to share in this subculture and in the antisurveillance knowledge produced by it were clearly essential elements spurring on the amazing growth of CB. A comparison of McCall's song to Sovine's makes acutely apparent how much the image, and what made it attractive, had changed. Whereas Sovine's trucker enacts the most personal of communicative acts, the prayer, McCall's Rubber Duck initiates through a network of CB users a rambling interconnected network of "a thousand screamin' trucks" and "eleven long-haired Friends a' Jesus. In a chartreuse micro-bus." Their goal of getting across country as fast as possible, smashing through police blockades and the tank brigades of the Illinois National Guard on the way, could be facilitated only through collective pedal to the metal power. In the song sequel, *Rubber Duck*, the truckers use the spiritual goodwill of the Jesus freaks to drive across oceans on their way around the world. This "Convoy" mythology of McCall's songs became the blueprint for Peckinpah's movie, which gave faces to these characters and tended to mix in a bit more of the existentialism of previous trucker incarnations. The immense popularity and cultural capital of this song cannot be overestimated. It is almost unheard of to base a movie upon not just the popularity of a hit song, but its very narrative structure. Very few examples come to mind, *Coal Miner's Daughter* and the made-for-television movie *The Gambler* being two, and country music is the obvious common thread of the two.

Toby Miller argues that genre is a key element in current formations of governing. Genre, with all of its structurally and formally organized production and reading demands, helps create popular truths and shows citizens how they should properly conduct themselves.[36] Typically, these reading strategies seem in tune with governmental initiatives. However, during a period of antistate and antipolice populism, these particular songs, films, and television shows provided a lowbrow how-to manual for beating the police at their own game. When everyone from safety advocates to environmentalists to the state was arguing for safer technologies, these narratives provided strategies for escaping the panopticon and increasing, not reducing, speed. They also articulated this act to a formulation of politics that was fairly straightforward and populist. This politics is manifested most explicitly in *Convoy*, in which the enemy of the people is multiple (big business, the media, big brother) but the specific initiatives of the truckers are left vague, and, when pressed, Rubber Duck refuses to voice them during a television interview. But this formulation of how CB should be used by citizens was countered by government-led attempts which were not meant to foil surveillance, but instead used CB to increase it. Furthermore, as the following excerpt from a *Reader's Digest* article reveals, there was at least nominal sentiment that truckers' acts of rebellion should not be viewed favorably: "Let's hope the public rebels at having its highways dominated by trucks that operate all too often outside the law, that present special safety problems and that raise their industrial hell at the general taxpayer's expense. The romance of trucking comes at *too* high a price."[37] The battle lines were not clearly defined, nor was it obvious for which side the public should fight.

Through police-citizen outreach programs the CB citizenry was hailed as the key element in a new program to more efficiently monitor U.S. streets, highways, and neighborhoods. The police encouraged citizens to "help them aid stranded or injured motorists and to spot drunken and reckless drivers."[38] Nationwide organizations like Community Radio Watch, REACT (Radio Emergency Associated Communication Teams), ALERT (Affiliated League of Emergency Radio Teams), and REST (Radio Emergency Service Team) were "on the alert for trouble on the streets and highways and suspicious activity in residential areas."[39] Citizen watch groups certainly were not new, but the added element of mobility vastly expanded the reach and sped up the rate of response for such networks. The success of such citizen involvement was said to be extensive, and various statistics regarding the number of arrests that were aided by citizens were carted out in discussion at the time as verification that it was working.[40] Yet even these citizen uses were not always used in conjunction with police. Neither, however, was CB, when used in opposition to the state, necessarily used for progressive politics, as this excerpt attests: "Using coded numbers referring to prearranged assembly points, a good many of the car-borne rioters cruising the streets when school busing began in Louisville area a week ago brought a new weapon

**FIGURES 17 and 18.**
These songs, inspired by country music and the singers most famous for performing them, were used to promote CB use and sales. Here the image of C. W. McCall and his song "Convoy" are used to shill for Midland CB manufacturers. While Radio Shack, the nationwide chain of electronics stores which still stocks plenty of CBs, produced and sold a Radio Shack exclusive, *all ears*, an LP with "10 new and original song hits with a CB theme." The album was given away with a CB purchase. The songs were "sung and told in the vernacular around which Good Buddies have built a cult of togetherness." By purchasing a CB it was understood that you too could join this expanding cult.

**FIGURE 17. C. W. McCall**
Much as CB users chose a handle, or nickname for use during CB conversations, the advertising executive William Fries chose C. W. McCall as the stage name for the country music singer who would become most famous for his song "Convoy." McCall became the most recognizable figure of the "CB craze," and as such it is only fitting that he was the spokesperson for Midland Radio's request to buy their CBs in order to "Join the Midland Convoy." MIDLAND CB CONVOY BUDDY USERS' MANUAL. FROM HTTP://WWW.CW-MCCALL.COM/MUSEUM/CONVOYBUDDY.SHTML. RETRIEVED MAY 30, 2006.

to the arsenal of the urban demonstrator: the citizens' band radio. Cops . . . struck back in kind . . . with a powerful transmitter of their own used to jam CB."[41] CB remained a problem in that it allowed for surveillance to be turned against the police, thus negating their typical advantage in controlling mobility and space. It further allowed the orchestration of force in space against the police. What becomes very clear is that the technology itself became both a means for battle and the battleground itself.

**FIGURE 18. All Ears**

With the advent of the popularity of CB use among the general public and the rise of the trucker as the "new American cowboy" in the 1970s, CB manufacturers and retail outlets played up these cultural connections. The populist appeal of and for the mythical everyman was plainly on offer in the liner notes for this record given away by Radio Shack with the purchase of any new CB unit. *ALL EARS: 10 NEW AND ORIGINAL SONG HITS WITH A CB THEME.* TANDY CORPORATION: FORT WORTH, TEXAS.

Even with the help of citizens using CB "for good," the FCC, in its report to Congress on October 14, 1975, outlined a new program for "actions taken or needed to curb widespread abuse of the citizens band radio service."[42] At this point the primary concerns were truckers and CB congestion, when in fact the largest boom of CB sales and use had yet to arrive. The major abuse, beyond small talk and lengthy transmissions, was the use of CB to circumvent law enforcement efforts, as noted above. The FCC had requested information from state officials to uncover the extent of abuse and found that in nearly every state this type of police circumvention and countersurveillance was occurring. The solutions offered for curbing such abuses were threefold. The first was to raise fines. This was difficult because of the nearly impossible task of tracking down offenders when they failed to identify themselves according to FCC regulations. This led to part two of the strategy: the increase of mobile surveillance teams who could monitor and track signals with higher-tech receiving devices. This, of course, was a stopgap measure and was not cost-effective. Thus, part three of the initiative called for an automatic transmitter identification system, or ATIS. This system would send out a signal identifying the sender of each transmission, thus allowing the FCC to know where all transmissions originated from and who owned the transmitter. Like all state-licensed activities, driving being the most notable, CB identification systems would be tied to licensing and the manner of enforcing, and assuring proper citizen conduct was to be through the fear of fines and imminent monitoring. The problem the FCC faced was that not everyone was licensed to use CB; thus the frequency of fines levied on licensed users far outweighed that of unlicensed users. Being unlicensed was an advantage, as it increased your invisibility. The FCC therefore continually attempted to create an easier and cheaper licensing process, not necessarily to increase the number of users, who were already causing congestion, but rather to increase the effectiveness of surveillance. In essence, the "law-abiding users" cited in the epigraph above from the FCC exposed themselves to surveillance by following the law, rather than by breaking it.

### The Wildcat Truckers

The Great White Fathers back in Washington don't give a damn about truck drivers. We're classified as the lowest form of life. We've got to shut down this country to show 'em what this is doing to us.

ROBERT LINDSAY, "THE ANGRY TRUCK DRIVER: 'WE'VE GOT TO SHOW 'EM,'" 1973[43]

In December 1973 and January 1974 the infamous wildcat truckers' strike took place on the highways of America. As noted earlier, independent truckers (those not affiliated with the Teamsters or other large trucking companies or concerns) faced serious economic hardship with the onset of the fifty-five-mph speed limit and OPEC-induced fuel rationing. During late 1973 truckers were attempting to voice their concerns through acceptable political channels. They were paid little attention, and in fact the American Truckers Association (ATA) and the Teamsters, both of which had strong lobbying groups and extensive political clout, refused to bring the specific concerns of the independent truckers to light. As a result, independent truckers began shutting down major transportation arteries by organizing massive traffic jams with the aid of CBs. In response, Teamster president Frank Fitzimmons pronounced that the Teamsters were "in no way associated" with and did not support the protest.[44] William Bresnahan, president of the ATA, stated rather boldly, "We do not condone it, in fact we deplore it."[45] Before the advent of CB use, it would have been impossible to quickly organize and mobilize independent truckers. There was a long history of wildcat strikes within the ranks of the Teamsters, but they already had an internal organizational structure with lines of communication in place and a hierarchical structure that could disseminate orders to strike quickly and efficiently.[46] Independent truckers, as their name implies, were not affiliated with other truckers and had no extensive communication network. Furthermore, they had no hierarchy or traditional leadership to organize strikes and shutdowns. The CB not only served as a means of quickly transmitting and spreading the word of a shutdown, but also provided the original space for truckers to discuss and debate their plight.

Across the nation, in small towns and at key interstate interchanges, independent truckers were able to shut down general traffic in a show of force and more specifically the transportation of goods, thereby crippling the economy. Congress convened, and, according to the congressional summation of the hearings, they were meant to alleviate the problems facing independent truckers: "The Subcommittee on Transportation and Aeronautics held hearings on January 30, 1974, to gather information on the problems independent truckers were having in regard to the energy crisis. The full Committee on Interstate and Foreign Commerce held hearings on February 6 on a specific legislative proposal to alleviate the problems of high fuel costs for independent carriers."[47]

This said, much of the hearings dealt not with independent truckers' needs, but with how various governmental agencies could stop the strikes. The following brief exchange points out quite clearly what the committee was trying to accomplish:

> Mr. Jaffe. We have the same problem Mr. Clearwaters alluded to with respect to anything along those lines that was set forth in the Noerr doctrine as to whether this is a protest protected by the first amendment, a protest that is to the legislative branch or executive branch of the Government.
>
> Mr. Kuykendall. May I ask a question?

Mr. Dingell. Certainly.

Mr. Kuykendall. May I suggest that we stop telling what it isn't and start talking about what it is. Are there any laws that apply?

Mr. Jaffe. No; I was trying to explain.

Mr. Kuykendall. I don't think this committee cares why you can't act. If you can act, do you need help from us?

Any number of potential criminal charges were discussed in order to strong-arm independent truckers into giving up their ongoing and seemingly random and impossible to shut down strikes. CB violations were one of the means by which Congress members hoped the FBI, in conjunction with the FCC, might be able to act at the federal level and thereby have nationwide jurisdiction. But the FBI made it clear how difficult it is to actually use FCC violations successfully to confiscate truckers' CBs, allowable by FCC rules and powers. As pointed out earlier, partially through the *Convoy* discussion, it was nearly impossible for the FCC to successfully track down specific violators even given their surveillance equipment. The hope was that the confiscation of CBs would cut off their lines of communication, thus destroying the movement's ability to carry out more strikes. This was also discussed in regard to the most popular truckers' magazine, *Overdrive*, which in November 1973 proposed the sorts of strikes that began to occur in the next month, as is indicated below:[48]

Mr. McCollister. Do you gentlemen have any knowledge of certain magazines, publications, whose readers or subscribers are members of independent truckers, in any way encouraging the kinds of actions that we are talking about this afternoon?

Mr. Baise. Are you speaking of *Overdrive* magazine and suggestions? I will label that "suggestions," which have been made in that magazine, to engage in certain types of actions?

Mr. McCollister. I am not referring to any in particular, but generally, and I am about to ask the question, can that be construed as inciting to riot or in any way encouraging the kind of activities — as I view what I have heard here and the difficulties you have had, one is finding somebody to sue or somebody to enjoin. Does that offer you some opportunity?

Mr. Maroney. Well, I am not familiar with the particular magazine you are talking about.

Mr. McCollister. I am not talking of a particular one.

Mr. Maroney. If there were a magazine put out by a group which advocated violation of these statutes and pursuant to such advocacy or an agreement, a concert of action, steps were taken in furtherance of such an agreement, yes, that would violate the statute.[49]

Such rhetorical circumlocution doesn't hide the attempt to reduce the truckers' strike as politically viable by denoting it a riot. Nor does it specifically emphasize, again, the focus upon the lines of communication necessary for such a movement that didn't have normalized channels of command. The fact that independent truckers didn't have a formalized union or a formalized workspace made this particularly easy. Yet it was precisely the fact that they weren't unionized which also made it impossible to collectively force them back to work, as the following excerpt makes clear: "The negotiations are continuing, and that is our best solution because we are dealing with independent contractors who cannot be forced to work. They may be in violation of their contracts; they may be losing money, facing bankruptcy; but we can't move in on that if they want to face the risk."[50]

The roads, though their workplace, were for public use, yet the number of laws governing their use, particularly as they relate to trucking and commerce, is immense. Hence, a number of other attempts were made to read the strikes as a violation of various laws against disrupting commercial trade across state borders. The most bizarre turn of events regards using anti–Ku Klux Klan legislation as a means to prosecute the strikes as a civil rights violation. It was argued that the truckers were violating other motorists' right to freedom of movement.

## Concluding Remarks

What I want to call for, then, is a renewed importance placed upon the function of transportation as a cultural and communicative practice that defines relationships between the two as complicit. The two need to be thought of in the same terms, especially with the increasingly mobile capabilities of nearly all communications technologies. At the same time, transportation and the forms of mobility produced by its various modes need to be analyzed as key sites of culture and communication. Struggles over mobility and access thus need to be examined in both the virtual and the material realms. Many of the debates over the control of these networks of mobility follow the same logic. Struggles over minority, youth, and gender access to mobility in the material world are of the same forms as those associated with access to various media sites. The CB radio provides a unique site in that it was an early mobile communications technology. It played a part in the expansion of a communications network as well as in providing a new way to map transportation networks. It is literally a technology of both communication and transportation in the classical senses. Struggles over its use and distribution played a key role in redistributing relations of power between state regulatory agents and citizen mobility. Being more mobile became increasingly dependent upon becoming culturally competent with a new communications technology. By investigating how the police and truckers (with the varying affiliation of the CB citizenry) struggled over not simply communication, but mobile conduct, we see the further establishment of an expanding regime of power whose object and *mode* of governance is the mobile citizen.

A second important issue is the creation of new forms of politics that are made possible through new communications technologies and new mobile alliances. I mean mobile in both the sense that those allied are mobile and that the affiliations are not stable but are transformed according to shifts in the cultural landscape. At times these shifts are economic; at others they depend on the signifier of affiliation, and they may coincide with differing definitions of freedom and the possibility for enacting it. This politics of mobility is not invested purely in terms of freedom and control. Freedom is always circumscribed; it is itself a set of limits, an optimal space of possibility. The limits and forms of this space are struggled over as if they are not limits but freedom itself. This does not diminish the worth of struggles for freedom, but it should dismiss the possibility of thinking in terms of absolute freedom versus full control. Thus the wildcat truckers' rebellion was established in order to contest new regulations placed on truckers that were mostly governmental but weren't necessarily aimed at reducing the freedom of truckers, nor at their ability to earn a living wage. But their collective action challenged traditional notions of affiliation and official channels of protest. Whereas the Professional Drivers Council asked "truckers to refrain at once from all obstructionist tactics," and instead "leave their trucks behind and to come here [to Washington, D.C.] to picket,"[51] independent truckers instead decided that a show of real force, stopping the flow of people and commerce, was far more powerful in making their voice heard than traditional representational politics. In relation to communication, obstructing the circuits through which it is enacted may be a far more successful tactic than participating in a so-called public sphere discussion. Previous forms of truckers' political affiliation followed the logic of the mass, while the wildcat truckers utilized what Deleuze and Guattari call pack affiliation.[52] This leads to political activity that works outside the bounds of representational politics and instead (dis)orients itself according to multiple trajectories and desires; in this instance, a distrust of those in power and a desire to operate free of financially debilitating constraints.

Most important, the wildcat truckers' rebellion proved that taking over and disrupting flows and routes is a powerful and effective political activity. The strength of the Internet and mobile communications technologies is their ability to increase flows and expand networks exponentially as the number of users increases. The growth of use in theory should make it more efficient rather than congested, which is the weakness of most forms of material communication (the highways or postal service). But attempts to create virtual traffic jams may prove effective as a means of resistance and protest. However, as mobile communications becomes an increasingly prominent part of everyday life, new strategies for organizing protest and resistance will be needed. Communications may provide the strategies or they may be utilized against such resistance. CBs were obviously used for both, and that struggle more than any other seems to parallel current struggles over emergent mobile communication technologies.

# CHAPTER 5

# OF CADILLACS AND "COON CAGES"

*The Racing of Automobility*

> The fact is that basically a Cadillac is an instrument of aggression, a solid and substantial symbol for many a Negro that he is as good as any white man. To be able to buy the most expensive car made in America is as graphic a demonstration of that equality as can be found.
>
> EBONY MAGAZINE, SEPTEMBER 1949[1]

> "Son, the man's done made it mean something differently. All you wanted was to have a pretty automobile, but fool, he done changed the rules on you!"
>
> RALPH ELLISON, *CADILLAC FLAMBÉ*, 1973, 261[2]

## Invisible Men No More

In 1973 Ralph Ellison broke his two-decade literary silence with the publication of the short story *Cadillac Flambé*.[3] Ellison had fallen out of fashion with many black intellectuals and activists, and his less-than-radical politics were out of step with the political and cultural mood resonating in African American communities across the United States. However, with *Cadillac Flambé* he fictionalized a political act—albeit a personal and some might say impractical one—which spoke to the strategic and metaphoric importance of the automobile in struggles over geographic mobility and upward mobility. In it, the protagonist LeeWillie, while traveling north after a gig in the South, basks in the freedom he feels while driving his Cadillac. But when the southern senator Sunraider refers to Cadillacs as "coon cages" in a radio address LeeWillie had tuned into, the Cadillac no longer signified freedom and upward mobility, but rather entrapment. LeeWillie is now forced to view his Cadillac in different terms. The cage implied criminality and incarceration and by extension the Cadillac did as well. For him, the Cadillac broke the code of white display and success. LeeWillie ultimately realizes his Cadillac could also be a means of trapping the black man into believing he was free; free of economic exploitation, free of white power, and mistakenly—according to Alan Nadel—free to move about in white space. He decides to use the signifying power of the Cadillac in a different way: he drives it onto Sunraider's front lawn and, while playing its swan song on his fiddle, sets it ablaze. This refusal to signify according to Sunraider's lexicon may or may not be a potent form of resistance, but it most definitely gestures toward the importance of the automobile as a site of cultural and material struggle for African Americans. This sign of economic upward mobility could be turned against black motorists, as it signified to police and others the mobile threat of blackness crossing into white space. The Cadillac, or any automobile for that matter, could be both a ticket to freedom and a mobile cage.

*Cadillac Flambé* didn't only make evident the multiple ways that the meaning of the Cadillac could be altered. More important, Sunraider called into question the very legitimacy of Cadillac ownership by blacks. From at least the 1940s onward, this legitimacy was called into question, debated, and culturally represented in numerous and varied spheres. Blaxploitation films, not Cadillacs, had caught fire by 1973, when *Cadillac Flambé* appeared, and in them the Cadillac was not only the ultimate sign of success, but also, in its pimped-out form, of criminality, gangsterism, and excess. These pimp-mobiles had grown out of a flash style that refused to be silenced or hidden away. Yet these myriad forms of Cadillac signification in black culture surely don't begin with Ellison, nor are they first popularized by blaxploitation. An in-depth analysis of *Ebony* magazine from its beginning in 1945 through the 1970s makes startlingly clear that the Cadillac was a cultural fixture in the African American community and conceptions of success therein well before it was riffed on in 1970s films. The blaxploitation genre on its own terms was hugely successful and is claimed to have saved more than one Hollywood studio.[4] How odd that the urban black gangster Mr. Big was deemed a worthy adversary of James Bond in *Live and Let Die* (1973).[5] Unlike Mr. Big,

**FIGURE 19. Whisper's Caddy**
This is the deadly, dart-dealing Caddy driven by one of Bond's nemeses in *Live and Let Die*. At this point in the film Bond has successfully tracked the Caddy to Harlem, where a game of surveillance/countersurveillance is about to take place. Contra all the examples provided in the rest of this chapter, these scenes work to show how, when space is raced black, whiteness becomes an easy-to-monitor signifier.

previous Bond film villains tended to threaten the world's precarious balance of free market global capitalism and Soviet internationalism via elaborate plots to start World War III or cause a global economic crisis. Who would have thought that by administering free heroin on the streets of America's ghettos Mr. Big could wreak enough global havoc to warrant the ire of the British agent Bond? Yet this level of popular recognition and articulation made Mr. Big and his cronies understandable and identifiable threats. Black men in low, long, decked-out Cadillacs were clearly marked as criminal. The most elaborate, pimped-out, and insidiously criminal Cadillac ever may be the one driven by Whisper, Mr. Big's nearly inaudible assassin.

Not only does this Cadillac signify his gangsterism, but it is a weapon for it. Whisper's Caddy has, among other deceptive devices, a fully sighted poison-dart-dealing sideview mirror that he uses in an attempt to kill Bond. 007 escapes, but not without a harrowing chase leading him to Harlem, where his whiteness makes him an easy target for the gangsters' surveillance while the FBI tries desperately to use hi-tech devices to survey black space. Ultimately, though, Bond will restore the white order cinematically disrupted by the Shafts and Mr. Coffees of blaxploitation. I use this anecdote to point out to what extent the Cadillac had, by the 1970s, come to signify criminality. Yet

**FIGURES 20 and 2I. Surveillance in Harlem**
Here we see two henchmen armed with CBs who keep track of Bond as he travels through
Harlem in the back of a taxi. The man in the automobile is following Bond at a safe distance,
knowing that others will keep him updated as to Bond's whereabouts. The second features a
henchman posing as a shoeshine man. He hides his CB in his shoeshine box and discreetly
pulls it out as Bond passes. The henchman bemusedly notes that in Harlem Bond sticks out
like a "cue ball," making him eminently easy to keep under surveillance.

this chapter is about much more than simply how black Cadillac ownership
signifies. Through the figure of the Cadillac a number of key issues regarding
the regulation of mobility and social space are investigated. Furthermore, the
Cadillac is merely one form of automotive culture and signification that has
come to "race" the automobile, that is, mark a particular car's driver as black
or brown. In this other type of racing, the automobile functions as a positive

**FIGURE 22. Surveillance in Harlem**
Whereas the local drug cartel is able to keep Bond under surveillance through a network of strategically placed lookouts who can easily spot his out-of-place whiteness, Bond has to depend upon the hi-tech gadgetry put in use by his American allies in the CIA, who with the help of a well-placed homing device allow Bond to maintain the surveillance of his black nemesis even in Harlem. *LIVE AND LET DIE,* UNITED ARTISTS, 1973.

means of black empowerment while also providing a sight line for police and citizen indignation.

What is so disruptive about black men driving Cadillacs? Possibly these films and cultural representations invoked the flamboyance of the heavyweight boxing champion Jack Johnson, whose shows of economic excess, not the least of which were his multiple automobiles, were legendary.[6] Johnson actually proves a useful historical precursor to the rest of this chapter, as it was precisely through his mobility, via the Mann Act, that his life, sex life, and lifestyle were criminalized. When he crossed the state line with his white girlfriend he was jailed for playing a part in the "white slavery" trade that prohibited unmarried couples from crossing state borders together. The Mann Act was a law that responded to concerns regarding sexual morality and miscegenation, in addition to the increased social and literal mobility of African Americans, and it became a means for criminalizing and monitoring such mobility.[7] Johnson continues to be celebrated as a sign of the empowerment of the flamboyant black masculinity that threatens white sensibilities. His story of defiance, retold in the movies *The Great White Hope* (1970) and *Unforgivable Blackness: The Rise and Fall of Jack Johnson* (2005), articulates a vision in which the enactment of black empowerment is accomplished through economic display and unflinching physical presence. Both of these realities make a statement regarding how to occupy and move through space. In combination they make the statement, "I'm here, I belong, and I dare you to do something about it." Clearly, the Cadillac signified in all sorts of ways for different populations. Yet as a sign of success it has connoted much within the black community, and these very forms of signification and the effects that follow are hotly debated and differentially felt within the black community. But the Caddy is more. There is a duality, if not a plurality, of how the Cadillac signifies and how it mirrors more general concerns regarding black social presence. Ellison, quoted in Alan Nadel's essay on the writings of Ellison, helps situate this duality of signification within a broader history of black signifying practices:

> Negroes suffered discrimination and were penalized not because of their individual infractions of the rules which give order to American society, but because they, like flies in the milk, were just naturally more visible than white folk. . . . In this dark light "high visibility" and "in-visibility" were, in effect, one and the same. And, since black folk did not look at themselves out of the same eyes with which they were viewed by whites, their condition and fate rested within the eye of the beholder. If this were true, the obligation of making oneself seen and heard was an imperative of American democratic individualism.[8]

It is this sentiment which seems to drive Nadel's own proclamation regarding white space. He writes, "It is virtually a cliché that in Western discourse domestic space has been treated as feminine and public space as masculine. Less highlighted and more tacitly accepted is the fact that these spaces are not only gendered but also racialized . . . much of public policy, legal sanction, dominant cultural narrative and popular discourse rely on the unspoken assumption that the public space is white."[9] If we take Ellison's point to heart, two equally productive notions can be highlighted. First, as elaborated in Nadel's quote, we need to account for how white space is traversed by black bodies and, I would argue, black automobiles. But equally important to Ellison's assessment is "an imperative of American democratic individualism" to *be seen*. These dueling imperatives of being seen and the monitoring and maintenance of segregated social space come together noticeably in black automobile ownership.

This chapter examines a number of competing discourses regarding the Cadillac and other automobiles that are used as a means of signifying success. It is the Cadillac that has been at the heart of debates within the African American community regarding a politics of social mobility, while the automobile more generally has been seen as a form for racial mobility. These two forms of mobility cannot be understood separate from each other. As we saw in previous chapters, access to mobility and space operates according to a series of normalizations, such as age, gender, and class. These means of determining who is allowed to drive and where can work against each other, and in many ways it is through class distinction that the Cadillac was envisioned as a means of overcoming the limiting force of racial bias. One means of denying the benefits typically associated with class advancement is to call into question the legitimacy of that advancement. Via a series of historical critiques of black consumption patterns, specifically Cadillac ownership, the white monopoly over class prestige was maintained. A number of explanations were popularized to explain away black success. A black man driving a Cadillac was either a criminal (in approximate chronological order a pimp, a thief, a drug dealer, a car jacker, and then a gangsta), a childlike consumer spending beyond his means, or, in later explanations, an embezzler of the welfare system. This series of explanations not only soothed the bruised egos of insufficiently signifying whites and fueled the conservative fires that consumed social welfare throughout the 1980s and 1990s, but also became one of many means of legitimating racial profiling. This chapter is an attempt to trace the ways in which the automobile has figured as a site of struggle in relation to race. One method of doing so is to look at the prominent cultural representations of black automobile ownership. A second approach is to investigate discussions regarding race and economic display. Last, the chapter examines how forms of African American automobile culture are criminalized. Attempts to "race" the automobile are cultural expressions leading from the imperative to be seen, but also function as a means to enforce the racial segregation of space.

### *Ebony* and the Pursuit of the African American Dream

*Ebony* magazine was one of the most influential national publications for African Americans in the postwar period. In many ways it was as if *Life*, the *Saturday Evening Post*, and *Reader's Digest* were wrapped into one package for a black audience. Its generally integrationist and nonconfrontational politics were mirrored in its representation of black middle- and upper-class success. *Ebony* thrived on and abounded with feature articles describing in great detail the striving for and enjoyment of the spoils of economic success in America. The economic exploits of sports figures, entertainers, entrepreneurs, professionals, and other African Americans who enjoyed economic good fortune were prominently displayed as signs of past and future advancement for African Americans. Yet a vision of success, how it comes about, what advantages it produces, and what it looks like are context specific. Success comes in many forms, and a prominent feature of African American success, according to *Ebony*, was automobile ownership. More specifically, real and true success was indicated by the Cadillac. The Cadillac had been one of the key signs of economic success in the United States for decades prior to the launching of *Ebony* in 1945. The articulation of African Americans and the Cadillac is just another one of the clichéd, if not stereotypical, representations of blackness. But is there something significant and unique to the use of the Cadillac as the premier sign of African American success during the 1950s? *Ebony* answered that question in an article from 1949, "Why the Negro Drives a Cadillac,"[10] and academics even got into the game in 1959 with an article titled "The Stereotype of the Negro and His High-Priced Car."[11] For Paul Gilroy the answer is clear. The automobile is the quintessential sign of American success, and for African Americans this was especially the case, as it also signified freedom from the restrictions on mobility blacks had suffered since their arrival in the Americas centuries before.[12] I want to approach this question from a slightly different angle. How was it made clear in *Ebony* magazine that the Cadillac and the automobile in general were the key sign of success in America? And, to give that question a bit more contextual weight, given that Cadillac seemingly refused to sell their automobiles to African Americans directly, let alone even acknowledge their buying power by placing an advertisement in *Ebony*, why was this snub ignored? The answer to this seemingly simple question will take us in a few distinct directions. For one, the status of the automobile was significant in *Ebony*'s coverage of African American life in many ways, not the least of which has been its use in photo spreads. Second, the history of automobile advertising in *Ebony* reveals a contradictory pattern of recognition and revulsion toward African American consumers. Third, the importance of mobility in general and automobility in particular plays a telling role in *Ebony*'s coverage of African American life in the 1950s.

The driving mantra of *Ebony* was mobility—upward social mobility. It was and still is largely a magazine devoted to the middle-class value of achievement via economic and often social integration. *Ebony* summed up such a vision in its inaugural issue: "As you can gather, we're rather jolly folks, we *Ebony* editors. We like to look at the zesty side of life. Sure, you can get all hot and bothered about the race question (and don't think we don't) but not enough is said about all the swell things we Negroes can do and will accomplish."[13] Such a zesty, mildly bothered attitude appears in a "Photo Editorial" entitled "Why Negroes Buy Cadillacs."[14] The magazine argued that Cadillac ownership by African Americans was important for several reasons. Foremost, the Cadillac was a "weapon in the war for racial equality."[15] It was an "instrument of aggression" in that war, and it proved "for many a Negro that he is as good as any white man." Second, the assumption among whites that African American expenditure on "flashy" clothing and Cadillacs was "proof of a childlike nature, a lack of good judgment, and a tendency to the bizarre and ostentatious"[16] was unfounded, and in fact these expenditures were the outcome of Jim Crow. African Americans were not allowed to live in the best neighborhoods, vacation at most resorts, gain membership in exclusive social clubs, or "join in fashion parades at exclusive women's clubs."[17] Thus the Cadillac was one of the few ways African Americans could compete in their attempts to signify social success.[18] But there was an anxiety that even such signification as this was restricted: "Rumors are floating around to the effect that General Motors is trying to curb sales to colored customers lest their prize species of the automobile trade be labeled as a Negro car."[19] Everyone seemed to realize the stakes of signification. The grounds of this battle were very much cultural, and *Ebony* performed a key role as both active player and a site of struggles over African American automobility.

A different use of the Cadillac as a weapon in the war for racial equality was called for in 1959 by the *New York Age*, New York's oldest black newspaper. The challenge was economic, but it was not aimed at urging people to buy more Cadillacs; on the contrary, it called for the boycott of Cadillac and GM because they refused to hire African American salespeople. Furthermore, the author argued that African Americans should alter their frame of interpretation when they saw a black-owned Cadillac: "No longer should you or anyone else look with envy at the Negro who drives an expensive Cadillac—the epitome of class distinction in the eyes of too many negro 'leaders'—for each Cadillac purchased by a Negro was sold by a white sales-man!"[20] This attempt to rearticulate the meaning of the Cadillac provides a productive means for rethinking just what economic battles were being waged through consumption. Whereas *Ebony* was quick to glorify the eco-nomic successes of these leaders, the *Age* shamed them for not thinking in broader economic terms. While acknowledging the war being waged for racial equality, the newspaper's recommended strategy for winning this war should be economic representation on the sales floor, not representational consumption, as *Ebony* clearly promoted.

One of the most popular genres of *Ebony* magazine has been the suc-cess story, which featured tales of the economic rise of African Americans. The most prominent dealt with celebrities, whether from film, sports, or the music industry, though these were hardly the only successful African Ameri-cans featured. There were also features on doctors, business owners, engi-neers, farmers, oil tycoons, developers, and Dame Fortune's other benefac-tors. They related the trials overcome to achieve success and were invariably accompanied—in fact dominated—by photos that displayed the specific and general signs of their success. Actors were shown on stage or in movie stills, doctors with patients, blues singers in Parisian clubs, and ballplayers hitting home runs. More generally, they were shown with their cars or homes. These highly prominent photographs are particularly telling. In many cases the automobile dominates the photos, and in more cases than not it is a Cadillac doing the dominating. Often it is featured more prominently than homes or the successes themselves.

The Cadillac is also often described in the story in terms of its cost and the number owned. Its value is quantified and objectified by dollars, but its sig-nifying value is often described in terms of its color, size, or flash appeal. The Cadillac is also very often articulated with other characteristics of success, most often dress or style—again being described in terms of flashiness and excess. According to *Ebony*, signifying is an important element of Cadillac ownership, and when this signification is examined from the viewpoint of automobile manufacturers, in particular GM, there is an attempt to distance their brand image from African Americans rather than embrace their in-creased economic success.

**FIGURE 23. Cadillac Success**
This image from 1952 is emblematic of how the Cadillac functioned
visually as a sign of success in the photo-pictorials that were the
staple of *Ebony* magazine. *EBONY, JUNE 1952, 117.*

Automobile manufacturers were not simply answering to the dictates of
market economics in their choice of advertising in *Ebony*. Nor were individual dealerships, particularly throughout the South, that were known to
deny African Americans the right to purchase new cars for decades acting
according to purely economic incentive.[21] The automobile, as a marker of
and a means to freedom, again especially in the South, was a site for struggles
over freedom. To many African Americans, the automobile created the very
possibility of escaping the South, just as it had been vital to farmers escaping
the dust bowl.[22] More to the point in terms of the *Ebony* readership, the
magazine represented a financially viable market for the auto industry's advertising well before 1953, when the first automobile advertisement appears.
In the case of the Cadillac, corporate legend would have us believe that GM

Apache red Cadillac convertible is eighth since 1941. Moore rooms with wife Willa Mae and youngest of four children, Arnelle Deborah, in home of Mrs. Emma Monk, whose house was bombed last year by whites.

**FIGURE 24. Cadillac Colors**
This image is another example of how the Cadillac embodied a sign of success. The Cadillac was often featured more prominently than homes, and descriptions of the specific details of color, cost, and quantity were often provided. EBONY, JULY 1952, 98.

survived the Depression only because of its African American customers.[23] The year before one of *Ebony*'s photo-editorials argued that it was high time American businesses started recognizing this "15-billion dollar market, a merchandising bonanza larger by 19 per cent than the Dominion of Canada."[24] And how might white corporate America have recognized the buying power of their own Dominion? *Ebony* suggested that "they should have suspected it when those fin-tailed Cadillacs and custom-built Buicks began zooming past them on Highway 66."[25] Furthermore, a year earlier *Ebony* had observed that "in recent years, Cadillac car ownership has emerged as an abnormal obsession, especially in Harlem."[26] There was little doubt that by the 1950s the Cadillac was not only a desirable commodity for an aspiring black middle class, but a widely owned commodity, one that demanded, *Ebony* seemed to argue, economic recognition. Other high-priced consumer items of the day were well represented in the advertisements of *Ebony*. Televisions and major kitchen appliances, the other two staples of 1950s middle-class consumption, were found in ad after ad. Even more telling, these ads also featured black families in various states of consumer appreciation. Clearly, consumption, or lack of it, wasn't the problem. Appliances were items of the home, and in an age of intense segregation they were not likely to be racialized because few whites entered the homes of African Americans. The automobile, on the other hand, was an exceptionally public signifier; maybe the most power-ful public signifier in America. One starts to wonder if *Ebony*'s suggestion of a GM conspiracy had some merit. Would the automobile industry forgo the potential profit to be had for fear that their marquee vehicle might be thought of as a "Negro car"? This argument is pretty well supported through an analysis of the advertising in *Ebony* throughout the 1950s, 1960s, and early 1970s.

In September 1953, when the first automobile advertisement appeared in *Ebony*, it had been eight years since the magazine had been launched. The advertisement is vague and the company doing the advertising almost imperceptible. Other *Ebony* advertisements from the period are similar in form and content. This attempt to not connect audience and brand can be explained only if we assume that this was precisely the manufacturers' pur-pose. As seen in the first Chrysler Corporation advertisement, the focus is on the technological benefits of the car, and almost nothing suggests a con-nection between the potential owner and the brand. The second automobile ad appeared in February 1954 and asked, "How'd you like to drive one of these?"[27]

Unbelievably, what *these* were is not answered. The ad simply offers the idea of buying a new car as a means of accessing the technologies of tomor-row today. There is absolutely no way to connect new car ownership with a specific brand, as the ad is sponsored by the Brand Names Foundation, a self-titled Non-Profit Educational Foundation. Apparently teaching the readers of *Ebony* that "auto-makers test experimental models today before putting their insignia on your car of tomorrow" was supposed to get them to not notice the lack of automobile insignias found in the very advertisement they were reading. Ironically, the advertisement itself explains the importance of insignias and brand loyalty. "Because the automobile manufacturer—like the maker of bobby pins, breakfast food or toasters—knows that if his brand name doesn't satisfy you, some other trademark will! So whenever you shop,

**FIGURE 25. Brand Names Foundation**
This *Ebony* advertisement is notable for the absence of any automotive company's name or emblem. Before any automotive company would publicly associate its brand with African American buyers, the American automotive industry, veiled behind the mysterious Brand Names Foundation, ran this advertisement. EBONY, FEBRUARY 1954, 46.

name your brand—and better your brand of living." Apparently the readers of *Ebony* weren't seen to be brand conscious enough. Yet this advertisement purposefully fails to create specific brand identification, while it demands that the reader identify the power of that which it lacks.

The approach explained above is odd indeed, as so much of advertising, and particularly automobile advertising, works according to brand recognition. Yet automobile manufacturers were refusing to articulate the brand advertised in their own ads. The form of this advertisement follows that of an earlier age of advertising, which for the most part had been replaced by the 1920s, when what was sold was not satisfactions, but rather the utilitarian value of the product.[28] The selling of satisfactions, which became the dominant and most successful form, depends upon an empathetic relationship between the advertised product and the potential consumer. The satisfaction of owning the product, not the product's inherent or use value, is what is sold. Cars were no longer advertised for their ability to transport the buyer from home to work and back in an efficient manner; rather, they were said to provide freedom, status, and luxury.[29] Specific brands ask for and often produce a sense of loyalty. An association between a type of person and a particular brand is often formed. Advertisements of this nature draw upon a network of articulations regarding consumers, the product, and the relationship between the two. Hence, the Cadillac bestows status upon its owner, just as celebrity ownership or a row of them parked at the country club bestows status back upon the brand. The imaginary, real, and popularly presented connections between the country club, the elite, Cadillacs, and leisure remained strong throughout the 1950s, and the association of prestige with make had a long-standing history in automobile advertisements.[30] What happens when corporations do not want to be affiliated with particular customers? In the case of Cadillac, they were reported to have refused to sell their cars directly to African Americans. By extension, of course, they also refused to advertise in *Ebony*. But it is clearly not only Cadillac that denies this articulation between African Americans and a particular brand of automobiles. The history of which manufacturers were willing to advertise in *Ebony* and how they did so offers verification of this denial.

Cadillac had not a single advertisement in *Ebony* throughout the first twenty-seven years of publication. GM refused to partake in any public articulation of their premier marquee with black buyers. Instead, a series of ads for midlevel and economy models appeared from Ford, GM, Chrysler, and Studebaker. These ads were fairly typical of most automobile ads from the 1950s. Surprisingly, they were absolutely typical of ads in one conspicuous way: the individuals, couples, and families featured in the ads were all white. They tended to focus on fairly traditional aspects of automobile ownership. Contradicting the notion that African American drivers chose automobiles to stand out, is the "More People Named Jones" ad from Chevrolet. This ad is typical in its representation of race as if it doesn't matter—or at least blackness doesn't—and thus it acts as if this representation is wholly unproblematic. The scene evokes a Norman Rockwellesque Americanism in

which a happy, white middle-class family's consumption is celebrated. The family couldn't be more stereotypically white, and the joyful adoration the wife is bestowing upon the car is matched by the artisan care given the personalized stenciling being applied to the driver's side door. It took another decade before the first African American was featured in an automobile advertisement in *Ebony*. Prior to this all drivers and admirers featured in the ads were white.

The lack of representation of blacks resulted from a bind in which automobile manufacturers found themselves. They clearly wanted the black dollar, but they also didn't want to lose sales to whites who, it was thought, would avoid buying a car associated with African Americans. This lack of representation in the advertisements was never discussed in *Ebony*, in part as it would have conflicted with their economic interests. The magazine did feature numerous stories about automotive entrepreneurs who were either successful automotive salesmen or were among the very first African Americans allowed to purchase dealerships. Even in this instance we can see the troubled relationship between race and automotive signification. Studebaker, whose economic solvency was seriously in doubt (the company came to an abrupt end in 1966), granted a dealership to mild fanfare to a black Detroit business-man, making him the first African American owner of an auto dealership, though the success didn't last long. Studebaker was eager to find new mar-kets and, unlike other manufacturers, was willing to risk whatever negative associations this would create in white buyers. Studebaker also advertised prominently in *Ebony*. This is not to say Studebaker was a more progressive company, only that the dictates of capital responded to concerns regarding race and the perceived effects of being associated with African American drivers. Still, in 1963, even before the demise of Studebaker, there were, as the *Chicago Defender* pointed out, no black-owned automobile dealerships.[31] The *Defender* argued that African Americans, who were purchasing five mil-lion cars a year, should boycott the entire industry until dealerships were granted to at least one black entrepreneur in every major city. The *Defender* asked that "the next time you are admiring the sparkling new car which you cherish so much, ponder on these things:" (1) none of the money spent on new cars trickles back to African Americans, (2) no black distributors means no movement into corporate management, (3) African American de-sires aren't acknowledged by the automotive industry if there are no blacks in management positions. Again we see an argument to unleash the power of consumption to help reach political economic goals, rather than those of signification.

Keeping these economic relations in mind, one should not be surprised that once the Cadillac had been so fully instantiated as an undeniable sign of African American excess owing to the popularity of blaxploitation films in the early 1970s, GM would finally run its first Cadillac advertisement in the October 1972 issue of *Ebony*. There is nothing unusual about the advertise-ment. As one might expect, there are no African Americans happily driving these vehicles. Rather, the luxury cars, at the pinnacle of their pre–oil crisis, pre–Clean Air Act length, grace a double-page spread. The text ends with what might have come as a surprise to an *Ebony* readership so long told not to bother visiting white dealerships, an invitation: "Clearly, you never had so many good reasons to visit your authorized Cadillac dealer." Previously, the purchasing of new Cadillacs often had to be accomplished through a practice

**FIGURE 27.**
*Ebony* **Cadillac Advertisement**
This Cadillac advertisement from 1975 is the second ever to appear in *Ebony*. As in so many automobile advertisements, it seems as if there is no thought given to how whiteness would signify in *Ebony*.
*EBONY*, JUNE 1975, 18.

called bird dogging, in which an independent go-between connected black buyers and white dealerships; the alternative was to buy used.[32] Cadillac's survival had depended and continued to depend on the black dollar, and, like much of the auto industry, GM rose to prominence in great part on the backs of black labor. Yet only in 1972 did Cadillac begin to finally acknowledge its long-hidden family of owners. But surely this didn't mean concerns over how the Cadillac, or any other car for that matter, signified in terms of race. Ellison's Senator Sunraider made this very point, as noted above in regard to the Cadillac. Ironic only in relationship to the project of this book is the stated reason for the senator's outburst: to defend the American auto industry from safety minded critics. The ultimate challenge to the industry, however, according to Sunraider, was that blacks had cheapened the value of the ultimate sign of American success—the Cadillac. To the extent that he, a senator no less, felt cheapened when driving one. The racing of the automobile was a concern for African Americans, senators, corporations, and sociologists.

In 1959, a sociologist at the University of Arizona, I. Roger Yoshino, published a study entitled "The Stereotype of the Negro and His High-priced Car" in the journal *Sociology and Social Research*.[33] He attempted to bring the weight of social science to this troubling concern. What he found in many ways reiterated what *Ebony* had argued ten years before, with a few statistics that discounted the stereotype of the overindulgent African American consumer. What makes this article interesting is not so much its findings, but that the study was done in the first place. Its existence points to the prevalence of the stereotype, but, more important, it recognizes the social and political importance of such a stereotype. Clearly, just as *Ebony* pointed out a decade earlier, the supposed childlike desire to indulge beyond one's means was said to be an indicator of an inherent weakness of African Americans. It allowed for a blame-the-victim logic in which economic lack was the outcome not of institutionalized racism, but of personal mismanagement of finances. Ironically, black Cadillac ownership could be and has been used as justification for cutting various public services program. Once again, we find that Ellison's *Cadillac Flambé* staked out the key concerns and means by which meaning was attributed to Cadillac ownership. In this instance, Senator Sunraider's harangue prefigures the rhetorical means of Ronald Reagan's attack on public services. Sunraider claimed that the proliferation of the Cadillac in Harlem was proof that there was no truth to the claims of African American poverty in the ghettoes of the United States. Cadillac ownership was not only an individual sign of African American success, but also proof that racism didn't factor into the potential for economic success. The Cadillac became a sign of the overabundance of unwarranted welfare payments. Reagan made this eminently clear in his fictional account of a Chicago "welfare queen" who had "ripped off" $150,000 from the government by using eighty aliases, thirty addresses, a dozen Social Security cards, and four fictional dead husbands, using the money to buy a fancy new Cadillac. This welfare Cadillac queen is employed to sum up not only the supposedly bloated and corrupt welfare system, but also the inherently lazy, greedy, and duplicitous nature of the "clearly" undeserving black Cadillac driver. These two examples are further evidence that the legitimacy of Cadillac ownership has been a means of normalizing white consumption and status, while devaluing or dismissing black Cadillac ownership as pathological, criminal, or some combination thereof. Thus, African American Cadillac drivers are signifiers that are always open to interpretation.

In May 1952, the singer Ruth Brown was featured in one of *Ebony*'s success stories. A subarticle, "Ruth's Cadillacs Cause Unpleasantness in the South," points out some of the travails of the road for traveling African Americans.[34] For Brown, driving a Cadillac had proven problematic in at least two ways with two different groups—policing authorities and southern whites. Two anecdotes shed light on these unpleasantries. In the first, an FBI agent stopped Ruth as she was driving her Cadillac into Atlanta. "Is this car yours?" he asked. He was supposedly investigating the matter of a shipment of stolen Cadillacs. Upon providing an ownership certificate for the car, Brown is said to have "brusquely" stated, "Well, I paid for this one" and drove off. The anecdote speaks to a number of key concerns of this chapter. First, the articulation of Cadillac and Ruth's race signifies potential criminality. This articulation becomes more prevalent in later decades. Second, police traffic surveillance and stops are part of a larger concern with the organization and control of public space and mobility, as argued throughout the other chapters. In this instance, it is the mobility of race and the maintenance of white space that is under detection. Within the "us versus them" spatial stratification, traffic stops of African Americans are a clear way to tell "them" where and in what vehicle they should and shouldn't be mobile. This is neither a new nor a defunct practice, as will be discussed later. Third, it makes apparent that readers of *Ebony* were assumed to understand this interpretation of events. On the face of it, a (white) reader of such an account could easily side with authority and assume the FBI agent was conducting a legitimate investigation. However, beginning with the use of the word "unpleasantness" in the title and ending with her defiant reply and exit, the article makes clear the traffic stop should be understood as unwarranted and racist.

The second "unpleasantness" points to deep-seated southern racism faced by African Americans, but with a Cadillac twist. An attendant at a roadside fruit juice establishment, upon seeing Ruth's New York–licensed Cadillac parked next to his stand, shouted, "We don't allow niggers to park that close to us down here, particularly Yankee niggers in expensive cars." Here the double sense of being out of one's place is articulated in terms of space—North vs. South and too "close to us"—and social economics—Cadillac as sign of rising above one's station. Dick Gregory articulates this in terms of jealousy in *From the Back of the Bus*: "Sometimes I think the only one who doesn't resent us owning a Cadillac is General Motors. . . . This car could be

6,000 skipped lunches, but you can hear the teeth gritting a block away."[35] Surprisingly, Gregory seems not to buy into the GM conspiracy, or maybe he points out that GM doesn't resent black ownership but, as argued above, can't publicly admit it. In either case, the unpleasant reception of Ruth and her Cadillac animates the continued means by which the automobile functions as part of police surveillance of race and the question of what the luxury automobile means as a form of signification for African Americans. It is both these considerations which continue to manifest in the driving while black (DWB) phenomenon.

### Low Riding and the Signification of Pimping

The 1990s witnessed the reemergence of the 1970s. It is passé to theorize the various "posts" that might explain such reiterations of cultures past. Rather than do so here, I want to instead examine how the image of the pimpmobile functioned in both eras; in the 1970s via a number of blaxploitation films, and in the 1990s in hip hop and more specifically within news discourse regarding hip hop culture. In both cases the Cadillac and then more generally a pimped-out automobile get clearly associated with criminality and gangsterism. Such an association is not surprising given several factors. First, the notion of "the life" is very often evoked by African Americans to express a type of black masculinity that encompasses consumption on a grand scale and displays of flash and flamboyance in all facets of life, not the least of which is the purchase of an automobile. Second, the general law and order climate stretching from Richard Nixon to George W. Bush has marked black masculinity in general as a sign of criminality, most notably violent drug-related criminality. Third, the very notion of "keeping it real" legitimates or testifies to the truth value of such representations. The validity of hip hop artists' credibility often depended upon their ability to cultivate not just a gangster image but a real gangster past. Whereas the heroes of blaxploitation films were often played off as caricatures and were rather obviously played by actors, hip hop depended upon verisimilitude, and the line between real gangsterism and its fictional and lived mimicry was not particularly clear. In both instances the pimpmobile played a crucial role in the life. Yet the power of the truth claim that bound hip hop to keeping it real added, at least in news accounts, to the legitimacy of cracking down on drivers of flash cars that signified gangsterism and criminality.

Given that public space has been coded and regulated according to white preference, how might we think about struggles related to black mobility—social and otherwise? One key concern must be the maintenance of codes of recognition, if in fact one exists. In other words, race must be recognizable. Segregation and surveillance are both dependent upon knowing how to delineate difference and how and where to observe it. There has been a long tradition of technologies of racial recognition. We can look to all the scientific attempts to define the physically observable characteristics which differentiate white from black, Caucasian from Negro. We can also look to forms of definition which are used when physiognomy fails. The so-called purity of whiteness based on blood, marriage, language use, or political affiliation has been used in legal and scientific discourse from Jim Crow to the Third Reich. What interests me about this long search is this very need to know who and under what conditions nonwhiteness can and should be recognized. In other words, when and where does knowing someone is white or black matter? And what interests does that mattering serve?

Keeping two of the aforementioned historical traditions in mind, we would be well served to examine racial profiling, or DWB, as a recent example of this problem of recognition. How can the police know the race of drivers and why is such knowledge useful? Answering the first question will take up a good portion of the rest of this chapter. The answers to the second question may fall into two categories. First, there have been specific historical, political, and geographical contexts in which the race of automobile drivers has very explicitly mattered to the police and white citizens as well. These include, though certainly are not limited to, brute spatial segregation, for instance, during the expansion of the black middle class in the 1950s, which accords with white flight, as a part of Reagan's and Bush's war on drugs in the 1980s and early 1990s, and as a part of Mayor Rudolph Giuliani's New York cleanup campaign during the 1990s. These are fairly clearcut examples, and some of them will be dealt with below. However, there is a more general way in which knowing the race of automobile drivers is part of a much longer tradition in the United States, which can be traced directly to slavery and the introduction of travel documents that originate as a result of the destabilizing practice of independent black mobility in the South—and under certain conditions in the North as well. Put simply, even if the race of mobile slaves was fairly obvious, their relationship to freedom and ownership was not. Travel documents had to be carried at all times to make such distinctions clear. Well before visas, passports, and drivers' licenses, documentation granting slaves limited forms of mobility were necessary to govern blacks' mobility within and outside the United States. This documentation was a form of both verification and surveillance. It verified that mobile African Americans, although traversing slavery's spatial territories outside the direct purview of their owners, were still legitimately bound to the social, economic, and legal institution of slavery. In other words, these documents sanctioned black mobility, but only through a differential form of surveillance, that of the document. It also created a means of surveillance via identification—a precursor in many ways to later forms of travel documentation more often formulated in terms of citizenship and international travel.[36] The extent of this surveillance in the South was such that any white person was obligated to monitor and intervene when a black wasn't under obvious supervision. More specific to the driver's license, it was in many states demanded that potential drivers indicate their race on the application for such a license, thereby allowing discriminating practices in the very access to the document that "granted" automobility and aiding in the collection of race-specific data regarding mobility. This was a point of contention by African American senators from the state of New York, who successfully called for a ban of such verification in 1955.[37]

This long tradition of monitoring space via race is still with us in many ways. As mentioned above, Nadel argues that in the United States public space is coded white. Space is racialized, and blacks in white space are made conspicuous. It is in this sense that I want to more generally situate DWB. The origination and continuation of the term *driving while black* in African American culture and communities points out the fact that race does matter when traversing public space by automobile. Furthermore, like the more popularly known acronyms in white culture and communities DUI (driving under the influence) or DWI (driving while intoxicated), which all imply criminality, DWB does so ironically. African Americans recognize that by virtue of their race their mobility is a criminal act. It is a crime against white space.

The maintenance of white space is complicated by the automobile. As discussed in earlier chapters, it is not so easy to monitor automotive traffic. Police efforts to do so are aided by all sorts of technologies of identification and the social technology of panopticism. Race-based monitoring operates somewhat differently. First, the knowledge component—or recognition— must be accounted for. How does one know when and where blacks are driving? Cultural practices, economic imperatives, and criminal profiles are called upon to fill in this knowledge gap. Two, panopticism, when it comes to race, works differently in two crucial ways for blacks than for whites. First, police presence operates differently in black communities than in predominantly white areas. Second, the stated goal of the police—traffic safety—is, even more than in some of the cases outlined in other chapters, a pretext for other, more nefarious purposes. The mere recognition of police presence is said to insure safe driving in a white population through panopticism. In other words, the presence or always potential presence is said to produce a will to safety, a self-disciplining of the driving subject. It seems, however, at least as evidenced by police conduct, that mere presence is not enough when it comes to black drivers.

Steve Herbert, in his book *Policing Space*, marks this difference of approach according to not simply race, but how race is interpreted through other categories that organize the police's understanding of the territories they police. "Racial considerations," he writes, "shape which normative order(s) officers mobilize to interpret and enact a situation. For example, officers are more likely to see minority-dominated areas as unsafe and morally unclean, as places where they can find dangerous foes against which they can act with masculine aggressiveness. The result is a more confrontational and less nuanced policing that creates tension between residents and officers."[38] This helps us understand how police relate to minorities in "their own" communities, but it doesn't fully allow for an understanding of the further element of transgression of those boundaries. When black drivers enter white space, police have long felt the need to pull them over and inspect them face to face. They check insurance forms, driver's licenses, criminal records, and behavior that might further indicate (beyond the mere fact of their race) present, rather than merely latent, criminality. The surveillance and interrogation measures are far more intrusive and thorough.

Before moving forward, an important point needs to be made regarding the specific criminal-system context in which many black drivers, especially males, operate. When in some U.S. cities close to 50 percent of black men between the ages of eighteen and thirty-five are on parole or probation, every time the police pull over a car whose driver or passengers are young black men, there is a bounty of potential criminal activity. From a certain perspective, parole and probation are means of monitoring and limiting the mobility of criminality. And when the criminal system in the United States is so ridiculously skewed against young black men, is not parole just one more means by which to surveil and regulate the mobility of black men; to keep them "in their place"? These policing tactics operate as a self-serving means for the maintenance of white social space. As such, safe driving behavior is not enough to shield black drivers from intrusive police tactics. They may be pulled over regardless of their conduct for any number of traffic offenses. In the same way the assumed normal user of the roads is an automobile driver as opposed to a motorcyclist, the assumed automotive driver is white—in white social space—thereby making the black driver conspicuous regardless of his specific driving behavior. This leaves several questions unanswered. One, can the police simply pull over black motorists with no probable cause, and if so, under what conditions and on what pretenses? Two, it is fairly easy to tell the difference between automobiles and motorcycles, but might it not be hard to tell the difference between black and white drivers on congested urban streets or highways? Last, are there any tactics to combat such spatial segregation?

The answer to the first question is fairly easy. Yes, the police can and do (in)discriminately pull over black motorists. Nearly all the legal scholarship on racial profiling makes this case. It is not simply the case that police forces use racial profiling, which they do, but that courts have continually upheld the use of race as a means of determining criminality. As Randall Kennedy, in his book *Race Crime and the Law*, explains, "Most courts that have confronted issues have authorized police to use race in making decisions to question, stop, or detain persons so long as doing so is reasonably related to efficient law enforcement and not deployed for purposes of racial harassment."[39] Yet, this doesn't necessarily mean it doesn't lead to harassment, which, according to the various accounts Kennedy provides, it clearly does, but rather that if there is law enforcement justification for using race as one among other factors, it is acceptable to do so. However, many of these other factors are themselves cultural markers of race. That is, the other indicators of criminality are cultural characteristics that are for the most part relegated to particular ethnic groups. The Cadillac, especially in its pimped-out form, is an example of one such marker. So are certain styles of dress, hair, or even forms of language. In a sense, culture becomes criminalized or at least used to mark potential criminality or what we might call dangerousness.[40] Dangerousness is an assumed potentiality that may erupt into criminality at any moment, and it is used to guide police practices through surveillance, interrogation, record keeping, statistics, and racial/cultural profiling.[41] Particular corridors are notorious as racial profiling hot spots. These areas, for example, I95 running north to south from eastern New Jersey, a particularly notorious state for racial profiling, all the way to southern Florida, are known for ridiculously unfair ratios of traffic stops.[42] This "drug corridor" logic, feeds on any number of racist assumptions regarding the police and the public's profile of the typical drug dealer. For instance, the Florida State Police use such possible signifiers as "large, late-model cars with tinted windows, radar detectors and lots of radio antennas" as well as "drivers wearing lots of gold" or "who throw things out the window" to spot a drug courier.[43] Being black, male, young, and in the wrong model car on this highway is a criminal offense, at least as far as local and state police forces are concerned. This is felt daily and is inescapable, according to a number of black authors who write from personal experience. As Don Jackson, himself a former police officer, made evident in his essay "Police Embody Racism to My People," "There are cars we are not supposed to drive, streets we are not supposed to walk. We may still be stopped and asked 'Where are you going, boy' whether we're in a Mercedes or a Volkswagen."[44] Actually, Jackson might even be pulled over on a Huffy, Schwinn, or Trek. The first such legal case of "biking while black" appeared in 1998 after several years of harassment in suburban Detroit, where the chief of police in very simple language explained, "My instructions to the officers were to investigate *any* black youths riding through *our* subdivisions (emphasis added)."[45]

Jackson's remark deserves further attention, as it points toward two contradictory logics that organize spatial and social mobility. On the one hand, there is a class logic infused with a notion of deserved privilege. This is to say, if one drives a Mercedes, access to all social spaces should necessarily open up owing to an assumption of class privilege. Furthermore, it is the automobile that marks this privilege. The all-too-common sight of a new Porsche parked in a No Parking zone that fronts a trendy restaurant is a rather mild example. I'm not criticizing Jackson simply for his bad class politics, but rather I am pointing out a particular logic of privilege that seems to infuse even much of the critical legal scholarship, which has been and continues to be profoundly important in struggles to overturn racial profiling. Yet it almost exclusively focuses upon the harassment of middle-class African American drivers in nicely appointed vehicles.[46] This tendency is self-selectively biased because of a reliance on case history and the general lack of access to the legal system of the financially disenfranchised. These two forces work in conjunction to leave out the more prevalent and insidious practices of monitoring existent in police-targeted urban areas or in those cases in which the car might be an old Volkswagen crossing over into white space. Worse yet, the critical legal scholarship often provides a very limited notion of the costs of DWB, often described in terms of police-citizen relations without acknowledging that the reason for the poor relations is that the police have historically existed to enforce a societal order of white privilege, partially through the maintenance of white space. The role of the police in this sense is precisely to operate as roving border patrol agents, treating black youth in particular as illegal immigrants sneaking into white America. When the ultimate hope for solving the DWB problem is simplified by the legal scholarship to this type of statement, "racial minorities may finally be able to trust a legal system," red flags should be waved.[47] Yet the point needs to be addressed in at least two more ways.

First, the U.S. legal system does not recognize culture as a marker or category of affiliation. Given this fact, the cultural attributes of a population's automotive forms, which are used as signs of potential criminality, are not acceptable forms of evidence to prove discrimination. In other words, if pimped-out cars are used as a profiling trait, and this type of automobile is a prominent element of African American culture, it is not considered to be racial in nature, and thus no violation of civil rights is said to exist. Second, going back to *Ebony*'s discussion of the debate over whether the Negro should drive a Cadillac, we see that it has been signified as a marker of class status and even considered a weapon in the war against oppression. Yet the Caddy's failure to bestow special status upon the driver when he or she is black is what very often seems to infuriate middle- and upper-class African Americans, as evidenced by their quotes in newspaper stories and critical legal scholarship. There is a sense that class should trump race and that somehow class privilege, distinction, and segregation are acceptable, while that of race is not. Clearly I am not arguing that it should be; rather, I want to point out that class distinctions are also used to limit mobility, possibly in a less stringent and spectacular fashion, but it happens nonetheless in very real ways. Neither mode of segregation should be acceptable, yet the one is seemingly written over in our haste to point out the atrocities of the other. In an age of increasingly segregated neighborhoods and public spaces class is very often used, sometimes in accordance with race, to mark space as not only white, but wealthy.[48]

In this final section the case will be made that greater attention to culture needs to be maintained if we are to fully understand how black mobility is policed. The cultural dimension to be addressed has to do with a few obvious markers of African American automobility, the low-riding pimpmobile and the recent trend, most spectacularly witnessed within hip hop, toward flash automotive accoutrements best exemplified by Dubs. Two less spectacular, though more specifically criminalized forms of African American automotive culture, tinted windows and ground-shaking stereo systems, will also be analyzed. In all four cases, the tension first addressed through Ellison's *Cadillac Flambé* and his insights regarding visibility and invisibility orient this concluding section.

There is a clear line to be drawn between the pimpmobile most spectacularly evidenced during the 1970s in the blaxploitation films that often gave a positive spin to the black gangster lifestyle and more general and popular displays of flamboyant automotive display. To be pimped-out most specifically references the flamboyant style of the street pimp: he is the male aesthetic equivalent of the street-walking prostitute and her often malicious "daddy." In these films the pimp was violent, sexually potent, ostentatious, and in some cases the antiestablishment protagonist. My investment is in both the positive aspects this image provided for a form of black masculinity, recognizing its obvious sexist, violent, and homophobic foibles, in often disempowered communities and the obvious negative connotations this image continues to incite in a white audience and in the law enforcement establishment. It is hard to imagine a more street-level embodiment of Ellison's explanation of the compelling need for visibility. Yet, it is also precisely this flaunting of criminality that strengthens the articulation between black success and an underlying suspicion that all black successes are potentially tainted. All black displays of this nature get drawn into a series of articulations that negate or at least reorient the vectors of interpretation. This isn't exactly new, as I attempted to show through the Ruth Brown example. But by the early 1970s even Cambridge sociologists were interested in the business of pimping, where the Cadillac served as both a symbol of economic achievement and a motor for it. The Cadillac was "used to conduct business, usually illegal," as it provided a "private, mobile, office."[49] Could we then suggest that the pimp conducting business from his "mobile office" was something of a precursor to the contemporary auto-mobile corporate workforce conducting business from their suvs, so fetishized in media accounts? Whether that line can be drawn from city to suburb, the blaxploitation movies clearly brought a mythic urban street figure to the suburbs and made it clear that if white suburbia wasn't already afraid of black masculinity, black mobility, and supposed criminality, they had certainly better be now.

Eithne Quinn argues that the 1970s infatuation with the pimp begins in 1969 with the publication of Iceberg Slim's autobiography *Pimp*.[50] The book became known among young men in many black communities as simply "the book." According to Quinn, the pimp became a different form of black power for a public slowly losing its taste for the mass political movements of civil rights. *Ebony's* thesis that the Cadillac was a weapon in the war for racial equality is grandly supported in the ethos of Iceberg Slim, the pimp protagonist of *The Mack* and, in a slightly different way, the drug-dealing antihero of *Superfly*. What stands out in all three accounts is the overwhelming desire to drive a flash car, most notably a Cadillac, and the felt sense that it was the ticket to notoriety and further success. For the pimp, the Cadillac wasn't simply a sign of success: it was one of the very means to achieve it. It was an essential element in proving one's capability to potential "whores" for one's stable. Slim receives this bit of advice during a conversation with an experienced pimp:

> "What kind of wheels you got?"
> "Temporarily I got a Ford."
> He threw his head back and started laughing. I thought he had flipped his cork. He died laughing for a full minute. The tears were rolling down his cheeks when he stopped. . . .
> "You ain't no pimp. These slick Niggers will steal that young bitch [his lone prostitute at the time] as soon as you down her . . ."
> "You ain't got no front and flash. Some of these bootblacks [shoe-

shiners] got 'Hogs [Cadillacs] . . .' Get out of town and be a good pimp in a chump town."[51]

The very possibility of Slim's success is governed by his ability to flash, most specifically through the most ubiquitous and prominent signifier in *Pimp*, a "hog." Slim's Ford wasn't just a sign of failure, it perpetuated it. Furthermore, in a land (Chicago) where mere bootblacks could flash more brightly, what were Slim's chances to prove he was and could make it as a pimp? As he came to understand, "A pimp's wardrobe has to be spectacular. His wheels must be expensive and new."[52] His only recourse was to out-flash the hog. He needed a Duesenberg. As would be later witnessed in 1990s hip hop, the one-upmanship of automobile flash has endured. As Cadillac fell to Mercedes Benz, and Mercedes to Bentley, a virtual arms race was begun in which the markers of race were still maintained, but by other means.

Hip hop, as it culled the musical past for mixable beats, also dipped into the styles of the past, and one of the richest periods for poaching was the early 1970s. While movies like *Boyz n the Hood* and *Do the Right Thing* were acclaimed for their veracity and explication of the effects of violent street life, another set of films were being criticized for their glorification of urban gangsterism. The thread that holds these two discourses together is that of keeping it real. It is the call to be true to street life, whatever that might mean, which has continued to be used by film critics, journalists, hip hop artists, fans, promoters, and even academics;[53] such attention legitimates a form of representation that must dwell in the realm of street-cred and hence the gangster life. The politics of truth are always fraught with political pitfalls, and as in so many cases it isn't just what truth is being told, but, equally important, who gets to tell that truth and according to what rules. For the present analysis the most important question regards the will to truth, the establishment of truth in representation as the defining criteria for judging a work of artistic expression. The world presented to news audiences of violent, drug-infested urban neighborhoods became the measuring stick by which films, novels, and hip hop songs were judged beginning in the early 1990s. Jimmie Reeves's and Richard Campbell's seminal analysis of the news media coverage throughout Reagan's and George H. W. Bush's war on drugs provides us with an understanding of how an "us vs. them" mentality was fixed in the American mind along the fault lines of black/white, inner-city/suburb, and violent, drug-dealing criminal/endangered citizen. This "cocaine narrative" which the news media told not only lent legitimacy to the street-cred claims of 1990s films and hip hop, but set the very parameters of what was a believable, and thereby acceptable, representation of black life. All roads led to the 'hood and on those roads we found a newly restored, though differently customized, pimpmobile.

Lest this will to truth thesis be seen as overstated or outdated, I'll jump to 2004 and an already-in-operation historicizing and cooptation of the 1990s period of pimpmobile customizing. Two excerpts from a *New York Times* feature article will help situate the following discussion. The first example details the rise of a new automotive subculture magazine, *Dub*. It is just one of many such magazines devoted to a specific group of gearheads who are themselves devoted to a particular style of customizing, form of automotive racing, or brand of automobile. The *Times* explains, "In the four years since *Dub* began publishing in Los Angeles, what might be called the *Dub* lifestyle of eye-popping jewelry, ear-splitting hip-hop and, of course, traffic-stopping cars customized to the hilt has moved from the streets of East Los Angeles to the boardrooms of Hollywood, Madison Avenue and even the Big Three automakers. What *Slam* is to basketball or *Playboy* was to a certain type of 1970's man, *Dub* is to drivers who like their cars loud, flashy and tricked out with clunky chrome wheels."[54] Here we begin to see a number of juxtapositions and historical articulations.

This new lifestyle came from where? The streets of East Los Angeles. Thus it's legitimated through its roots in the 'hood. But, now it is not just the life or the thug life, but rather an equivalent to the *Playboy* lifestyle, a mix of sexual, consumption, and leisure stylizations that can easily be branded and broadened to a wide audience. It takes only a few sentences for the editor of *Dub* to legitimate its roots through gangsterism and the thug life, reiterate assumptions regarding the criminality of the pimpmobile, and distance this new lifestyle from those articulations. The *Times* continues, "'Back in the 1990's, if you had chrome rims on your car, you were either a thug or a drug dealer,' said Myles Kovacs, 30, *Dub's* editor. Nowadays, custom wheels are showing up on TV, in General Motors showrooms and at suburban grocery stores. 'They have become socially acceptable,' he added. Does the magazine glorify the thug life? 'It's not so much about selling the gangster lifestyle, it's about showing the reality of their lives,' said Mr. Kovacs."[55] Like all coverage of hip hop and the urban gangster movies, the parameters of debate here are, does this glorify gangsterism? or is it just representing reality? The defense and the glorification are both bound to the same representational logic, that it is real. And it is this reality which is called upon by the criminal injustice system to validate racial profiling and criminalize particular African American forms of automotive culture.

Yet this form of customization, even within the realm of social acceptance, is also used to validate and demarcate race and hip hop subcultural associations for those within the culture. A telling example of this is evidenced by the following excerpt: "'If your Bentley is customized with 24 rims, you know the guy sitting in the back isn't just Donald Trump,' said Avon Bellamy, who owns Real Wheelz, an auto customization shop in Baltimore. 'Otherwise, you're just another C.E.O.'"[56] Isn't *just* Donald Trump? Does this "just" refer to Trump's lack of wealth; as if the driver of a Bentley (with a starting cost of $169,000 for a 2007 Continental) might be mistaken for some mythical underpaid CEO? Almost assuredly not. So being just another CEO must imply a different sort of difference. In fact, the difference that seemingly matters, a cultural difference, is a claim to legitimacy and belonging within a raced subcultural style. This style seemingly matters more, trumps, one might say, the need to simply signify social mobility. It also, however, may hark back to the 1990s, when it was understood that driving a pimped-out car indicated gangster connections. Might some want to be mistaken for gangsters? Could it be that the association hasn't been replaced but laid alongside of, denoting, while also denying?

A decade before their upscale market infiltration, dubs had been assumed to give a very different message. "Drive a car with flashy wheels and you are waving a red flag that says: 'Come get me,' said Los Angeles Police Detective Pete Razanskas."[57] The statistics cited by the *Los Angeles Times* indicated that at least ten drivers a year were killed for their flash rims (in 1994 at the time of this rim scare, the term *dubs* had yet to pass into journalistic vernacular). In this period of car-jack concern nearly any automotive activity could seemingly get you jacked and killed. The automobile once again became a trap. Simply driving, and particularly in "sketchy" neighborhoods, was seen as an invitation to violence. A flash vehicle was akin to a shiny fishing lure, it attracted bigger, more dangerous fish. The driver of such a vehicle was unsuspecting bait. One figure who had reformed his attention-attracting ways was Freeway Rick: "'It's like an elite class: To have rims means you are a successful person,' said Ricky Donnell Ross, known as Freeway Rick, once one of South-Central Los Angeles' most notorious drug lords, who used his illicit proceeds to purchase a now-defunct wheel shop. Ross, who completed a prison sentence recently, drove a car with rims until he felt that he needed to maintain a lower profile on the streets."[58] The road from drug dealer to ex-con to failed entrepreneur, it seems, had taught Rick some important lessons regarding the dangers posed by flashy rims. It must have been hoped Freeway Rick's education would help steer your average reader of the *Times* away from such dangerous and unnecessary a display of elite status. Why else feature such a fear-mongering portrait of black automotive culture? Readers were assured that safety was the only reason Rick might choose a lower *profile* on the streets? Other than car jackers and rim thieves, who else might be interested in the profile of "notorious drug lords"? Letting our imaginations run wild for a moment, if someone was interested, what other automotive characteristics might be used to fill out this profile?

Maybe the story of Ricky Martinez will begin to answer one of these questions and allow for a further understanding of how some of the decades-old assumptions about race and the flashy car continue to animate public discourse. "Martinez works seven days a week to support his car," says an article in the *Los Angeles Times*, "earning $5 an hour at a Whittier automobile tint shop. He purchased the 1978 Cadillac Coupe de Ville from its previous owner, who was heartbroken when it was stolen and recovered completely stripped. Using his savings, Martinez set about refurbishing it: a brandy-wine paint job, stereo, and, of course, $2,000 rims."[59] The *Times*'s telling of Martinez's story reconfirms the long-standing notion that minority car owners give in to their desire for flashiness at the expense of frugality. As "sensible middle class readers whose economic rationality is never in doubt" "we" are supposed to understand the absurdity of such commodity fetishism prevalent in "them." Yet can we imagine a story something like this?

John Smith works 70 hours a week at his downtown job in a prominent law firm. His salary, however, is just enough to keep his convertible Twin Turbo Porsche Carrera on the road. With monthly payments running into the 5th digit, insurance costs greater than the average American's mortgage, and a $600 price tag for a simple oil change (not to mention the cost of his recreational cocaine habit), it's hard to imagine why Mr. Smith would devote so much of his hard-earned pay to a car that he "barely has time to drive." Yet, for Mr. Smith, the prestige, not to mention dates, he garners from driving the Porsche far outweigh the costs, as it allows him to show off his wavy blonde hair and surfer-boy good looks while catching a tan with the top down. And as he sensibly asks, "What other car goes 0–60 in under 5 seconds and has enough space to store my golf clubs? Besides, if it's stolen I've got Lojack and insurance."

Mr. Smith would never be featured in such a story because Mr. Smith's commodity fetishism and workaholic desire to be flashy wouldn't be problematized according to race or the safety of driving such an automobile. There is no profile Mr. Smith would fit into that would be used by the police either, unless we count him as one of the general us against the them that Martinez seems to be a part of, as the *Times* somewhat surprisingly pointed out. "Rimjackers are not the only hazard. Martinez is frequently pulled over by police who are suspicious of the baby-faced youth piloting a set of expensive wheels. He does not care. 'It's just something I always wanted. I will some day get rid of them, but right now I'm having fun,' he said. 'It's not worth dying for, but I love driving my car.'"[60] What is odd here is that the *Times* treats this as *his* problem. They don't ask if this sort of profiling and unjust harassment are part of a racist policing regime. In other words, it is to be understood that racial profiling is simply part of the driving terrain, something to take into account when deciding what kind of car to drive. And in the end, the *Times* claims Martinez "does not care." About what? The fact that he knows he is under constant police surveillance because he drives a flashy Cadillac? Maybe Martinez knows it is simply a matter of degree. If one is under surveillance in white space anyway, maybe the relative costs are not so great. Maybe, as Ellison so long ago pointed out, the dual imperative/curse of visibility and invisibility is a game that can never exactly be won, but in which stalemate is the best one can hope for.

Two other popular forms of automotive customizing, window tinting and loud stereos, have been articulated not only to black and other minority drivers, but also to safety, criminality, and gangsterism. Both these forms have been criminalized across much of the United States through a network of local and state ordinances. What follows is an overview of the logics used to justify the illegality of both practices and an analysis of how these practices were connected to the drug war and the monitoring of mobility. The concern regarding safety, left dormant for much of this chapter, becomes the means by which such legislation is passed. Clearly the logic of safety, as has been pointed out in other chapters, is neither infallible nor value free in its application. So the question here is, How are tinted windows and loud stereos made to seem dangerous? It will be argued that a long-standing logic of automotive communication is the basis for both antitinting and antinoise ordinances. Of equal importance, the fallibilities immanent in such safety claims will be offered as a counterpoint to the ubiquity of safety's legitimacy. Following upon the themes built throughout this chapter, it should be of little surprise that these automotive practices have been racialized. Through a brief examination of some of the news coverage and legislative debate during the period when these practices were criminalized, it should become evident how these practices were either directly articulated to gang-related criminality or to the danger such activities posed not just for drivers, but to the police officers said to be on the front lines of the drug war.

Automobile window tinting has been widely used in southern areas of the United States for several decades. The reason for its popularity is quite simple. It reduces the unbearable solar heat generated in automobiles driven in sun-drenched states. Air conditioning in automobiles was still fairly uncommon throughout the 1970s and didn't begin to climb until its widespread inclusion in packaged groupings of features that took off in the 1980s. California and Florida were the first states to seriously examine the issue of window tinting as a safety concern. By the early 1980s, coinciding with the first rumblings of the drug war, the concern was spreading northward. The early concern in California during the late 1960s died off within a few years. Many safety concerns, in the absence of constant public exposure, fall away, like any other social problem du jour. So why does the safety concern start to blossom outside the South in the early 1980s? A brief excerpt from a *Chicago Tribune* article that reiterated the importance of antitinting laws makes clear the logic: "The drivers were between 22 and 34 years of age, state police said. It's illegal in Illinois to tint front windshields and the windows by the driver's and front passenger's seats in cars manufactured since 1982, when the law went into effect. The law was designed to improve traffic safety and cut down on crime, such as drug deals, taking place under the cloak of tinted car windows."[61] Two immediate and complementary objectives are said to be realized. Both have to do with safety. On the one hand, there is said to be an improvement in general traffic safety. On the other, a blow will be struck against the public health crisis caused by epidemic drug use.

A possible third safety benefit started to arise later in the 1980s and early 1990s and began to organize a renewed public and legislative discussion, as witnessed in the innocuously titled *New Orleans Times-Picayune* article "Driving with Dracula": "State law specifies how dark the tinting can be, and there's a good public safety reason for setting a limit. The same tinting that keeps out sunlight can also make it impossible to see what's happening inside a vehicle, including criminal activity. Police officers take a big enough risk when they approach a vehicle without having to wonder whether an armed driver or passenger is concealed behind darkened glass. Capt. Anthony Cannatella, commander of the 6th District, said he had noticed a correlation between drug dealers in the area and dark windows in expensive suvs and luxury cars."[62] Captain Cannatella clearly articulates the assumed relationship, the anecdotal correlation, between drug dealers, dark windows, and luxury cars.

Clearly, these are the same luxury cars witnessed in other representations and descriptions of the pimpmobile and the wheels of the drug-dealing gangster. Not atypically, these tinted-windowed luxury cars and suvs, especially in particular areas, automatically signify criminality. It is this ability to signify which I will once again turn toward. It is what I've called elsewhere the discourse of lack and excess, which is used to organize safety discussions pertaining to the use of automotive communications devices, such as car radios, horns, cbs, mobile phones, and even traffic signs.[63] In all of these cases, the ability to drive safely is said to be made problematic either by a lack of communicative ability or by an excess of communication. In the case of window tinting at least two forms of lack are said to be produced. The following excerpt from the *Los Angeles Times sums* up the public presentation of these dangers as well as the tautological justification for such laws: "'You know that they can't pass laws like this unless there's a good reason,' Daily says. The most important, he says, is that tinting 'reduces the driver's ability to see. It's difficult, if not impossible, for a driver wearing shades to see even during the brightest daylight. And it eliminates eye contact between drivers, and between drivers and pedestrians. That increases the chance of accidents.'"[64] This lack of vision and communicative eye contact function as one form of lack. The other, already partially discussed, is the police's inability to look into cars, which places them in danger. What isn't acknowledged in the first scenario is the lack of vision which an abundance of light might produce through a nontinted window. More interestingly, the standard-issue sunglasses so long a part of police officer and secret service gear seem to never impair *their* vision, especially in situations when misidentifying a wallet for a gun could lead to an innocent's death. But I digress and will turn toward my more substantial argument regarding a lack of vision.

The real issue of signification and recognition here, it seems, is that of race. On the one hand, window tinting produces privacy of the type enjoyed by every limousine passenger on the road. There is a sense that what goes on behind those closed car doors should be kept private, as if along with all the other privileges of wealth the ability to *not signify* who one is should also be granted. The case of the limousine raises several issues. First, who is able to maintain privacy on the road? Second, why might someone want to maintain privacy? Third, to what degree is tinting itself a means of signifying social status via the preexistent assumptions regarding the limousine? Last, how else might tinting come to signify?

These questions will be answered by reframing the discussion of tinting within the context of racial profiling and the maintenance of white public space. In this context, window tinting is a means not specifically of personal privacy, but of racial privacy. Tinting is a weapon in the fight against racial profiling, as it makes it impossible for police to determine the race of the driver without pulling them over and checking up close and personal. What tinting silences is the communication of race. The danger, insofar as the maintenance of white space is concerned, is that racial profiling can't be carried out if cars have tinted windows; the police no longer know who is properly in their place. Yet this weapon, through its articulation to drug dealing, gangsterism, and low-riding, becomes a de facto signifier of race, and like so many weapons in these struggles, it is criminalized. So in a sense it was both a crackdown against African American cultural forms and a crackdown that allowed for racial profiling to continue — all in the name of safety.

Antinoise ordinances work in reverse. Multiblock-booming bass-thumps oversignify, marking out one's presence in advance and retreat. The tricked-out, hopped-up car stereo system boom of the 1980s opened a new terrain for surveillance and display, a fairly simple one to criminalize. Here too we can raise the issue of to what effect and according to what logics were these ordinances passed. Again, safety is the culprit. Whereas tinting was said to produce a lack of vision, loud stereos via an excess of noise ultimately produced a lack of noise or, rather, a lack of hearing. That is, it was argued that drivers were unable to hear important aural signifiers of impending doom or rescue. In fact, outfitted with a booming stereo and darkly tinted windows, our hypothetical young African American driver might not even realize there is a police officer behind him attempting to pull him over. And to think said officer is merely attempting to serve and protect this wayward youth. But such a scenario doesn't exhaust the dangers of these menacing stereos, as one newspaper made ridiculously clear, "According to police, gang members often compete with each others' sound systems by raising the decibels and bass. Some amplifiers for car stereos measure up to 1,000 watts."[65] Thus if they weren't considered enough of a nuisance by themselves, they were worthy of further police scrutiny, as such stereos were not only a sign of criminality, but also a weapon in gang-related turf wars. The use of "1,000 watts" as a means of denoting the severity of the problem is reminiscent of news descriptions of gang members' arsenal, said to be filled with Glocks and .44 Magnums. The *Denver Post* featured a headline that so patently connected such stereos to the drive-by shootings associated with gang violence that it would be laughable if such rhetoric was not so prevalent. The article described a recent law as combating "ear assaults by 'drive-by stereos.'"[66] This interlinking of criminality, black automotive culture, and safety works to present an increasing number of reasons to pull over black drivers, harass them, or, as Chicago police officers hoped to do, confiscate their cars for such infractions.[67] One last example will show that even the most widely accepted and lauded safety practices can be used with discriminatory effects.

Debate in numerous states in the late 1990s, as the federal government was coercing states into passing legislation that would allow police to stop drivers for noncompliance of mandatory safety belt legislation, made clear how safety legislation can be used as a means of maintaining the discriminatory access to free mobility. It was argued, most often by black legislators and activist groups, that mandatory safety belt laws would allow for free-floating surveillance via the traffic stop. These individuals and groups made clear that such legislation afforded police a convenient procedural loophole allowing them to carry out racial profiling and harassment tactics. This is extremely significant. This stance made eminently clear that whether in theory or in its effects, safety-oriented legislation is not only about saving the population. Even in the most statistically obvious case of beneficial safety practice, wearing a seat belt, the obvious "goodness" of mandatory safety belt legislation is still up for debate. The reason is that the goals for which such legislation is used have nothing necessarily in common with the goals of such legislation. This is not to say that such legislation won't be successful in convincing drivers and passengers to wear safety belts. Nor is it to say, as some do, that safety belts in fact don't save lives. Rather, the policing of such use, as is often the case with the policing of almost all traffic violations, may fundamentally or at least secondarily be executed for drastically different ends than safety. In this case, as the Urban League makes clear, legislation which allows police to pull over the noncompliant is a means of monitoring the mobility of African Americans. It grants the police another excuse to discriminatorily monitor, interrogate, and harass mobile African Americans. What makes this practice even more problematic is the low compliance by young African American men. In fact, the rhetoric of crisis has been used to describe the lack of compliance as a public health concern. Whether as a way to flaunt a disrespect for the law, a sign of machismo, a statement regarding one's civil liberties, or a general disbelief in safety, the relatively low compliance rate opens young African American men up to even further police discrimination. Thus, the claimed reason for such legislation (low compliance) is also that which makes such police stops seem legitimate. In other words, if statistics show that young African American men have low compliance, then one should expect they will be pulled over more frequently. This double bind makes the passage of such legislation particularly troubling, especially in cases in which African American leadership changes its position to support such laws.

Situating Ellison's argument regarding the African American duality of visibility and invisibility in the United States in terms of surveillance and mobility will be the starting point for some concluding remarks on the troubled problematic of the automobile as cause and solution of contemporary practices of freedom. Clearly, it is not only African Americans who have been interested in the signifying characteristics of their automobiles. Automotive excess flourished among wealthy white Americans ever since the advent of the automobile over a hundred years ago. During their infancy, automobiles were built individually for prospective owners and very often featured exotic flourishes specific to both individual customers and their specially hired designers. Often called the Golden Age of Motoring, this period featured production and ownership practices that served almost exclusively the ultrarich. Jack Johnson's flamboyant automobiles were not so out of character in terms of automotive style, but clearly they were in terms of race. As automobiles became increasingly homogenous through mass production, even luxury cars eventually looked much the same and lacked the characteristic flourishes that once distinguished one robber baron's car from another's. As noted earlier, this lack of individuality could be seen as problematic for the corporate set trying to announce that they aren't just any CEO. But it's not clear that "just any CEO" or even African American CEOs are compelled to make sure their automobile signifies their affiliation with a specific community other than that of the wealthy. In other words, class may be all that one cares to signify. Yet the most prevalently seen black celebrities, primarily from the realms of sports and hip hop, do signify according to a lexicon of raced signification; a mode of signification, as argued above, that has been distinctly linked, furthermore, to gangsterism and criminality. In many ways it is through the very celebrity of the gangsta rapper that the identification between hip hop, low-riding, pimping, and criminality was so easily popularized. Thus, the spectacular rise in popularity of hip hop beginning in the 1990s, the increased crossover between it and sports, and the reemergence of gangsta masculinity all helped to make spectacular a form of culture with roots deep in the poorer Latino and black neighborhoods of the Southwest.

As has been the case when earlier emanations of black and Latino popular culture spreads to the suburbs, it is criminalized and provided all sorts of destructive capacities. Just as earlier forms passed through their purified spokespersons, such as Elvis with rock and roll, pimping is now purified by MTV's *Pimp My Ride*. This show, begun in 2004, features an array of multicultural young men and women whose "hoopty"—"an old car in poor condition"[68]—is "pimped out" by one of a number of professional automotive shops who specialize in this southern California cultural form. This democratization, or suburbanization, of pimping is perfectly in line with the general dominance of hip hop style over youth culture of the past decade. Fittingly, rapper Xzibit hosts. But this can't be the entire story. It isn't as if such subcultural co-optation, the bread and butter of youth-focused media industries for the past fifty years, marks the end of the racial profiling addressed above. Just because white suburban kids have pimped their Honda Civics won't necessarily lead to an end to police surveillance tactics. Nor does it necessarily end the racial recognition of such practices, as "impure" as they might have always been. Rather, it's equally possible that this democratization will deflect attention from such racially motivated policing practices, as they won't be seen to be as racially specific.

More important, the primary argument of this chapter has been that the automobile figures into a complex web of articulations when it comes to African American mobility and social mobility. The line between publicity and surveillance is difficult to distinguish in this instance. Just as the Cadillac can be argued to be a weapon in the war for racial justice by publicizing black entry into the wealthy classes, it can as easily be used as the panoptic element of the cage by allowing continual surveillance in space. It is in this metaphorical sense that I want to more broadly address the binarism that too often is used to describe differences between safety and mobility as well as freedom and bondage. It may often be that through one's practice of one form of freedom, say, economic display, that the potentiality for bondage is created, via debt and the loss of anonymity. But this certainly doesn't apply only to African Americans. Rather, the double bind that Ellison describes may become increasingly important for all who hope to maintain mobility while maintaining privacy or, what Jack Bratich calls, the right to secrecy.[69] That is, under circumstances of undemocratic policing and surveillance, we should call not just for privacy, which is grounded in liberal and neoliberal conceptions of property rights and faith in publicity as the preeminent means of exposing unfair power relations. Rather, there should be a right to secrecy as a means of combating intrusions into political thought and actions that are designed to destroy the very possibility of resistance. As automobiles increasingly become signifiers of one's identity through a host of surveillance, identification, and recognition technologies which are said to promise greater freedom, we may be witnessing a period in which everyone loses their ability to avoid profiling and tracking. It is still abundantly clear that the dangerousness attributed to black mobility in white public space remains a hugely discriminatory practice. Yet new racial profiles have become increasingly popular in relation to transportation and mobility, owing, once again, to the perceived dangerousness of such populations in the post-9/11 world. More insidiously, the tactics of racial profiling are, in effect, experiments for governing mobility writ large, and there are signs, as I discuss at length in chapter 7, that future forms of governance will draw heavily upon the lessons learned by policing agencies in the governance of minority mobility. Such plans may be more democratic in that all citizens will be equally governed as a threat, but they don't provide a vision driven by creating democratic forms of mobility. As new automotive technologies promise greater freedom, increased safety, and added national security, primarily in luxury cars featuring a plethora of interconnected communications devices like GPS, will LeeWillie's insight regarding the facade of his supposed Cadillac-induced freedom be forgotten? Blackness is not the only racial signifier of danger in the United States, nor is the Cadillac the only means for tracking the movement of such danger. Even so, might it take the fear mongering and racist ramblings of a southern politician to make the sham of this new automotive freedom manifest?

# CHAPTER 6

# RAGING WITH A MACHINE

*Neoliberalism Meets the Automobile*

### Introduction: Death Race and the Race Toward Death

Over thirty years ago a low-budget Roger Corman movie offered a prophetic vision of proliferating aggressive and violent driving for the year 2000. In the film, the U.S. highways were the battleground on which the annual Death Race took place. This transcontinental race lasted three days and pitted a group of racers against each other, the clock, and unfortunate bystanders. Victory depended upon two factors—speed and points. As in most races, crossing the finish line first was the ultimate goal, but in *Death Race 2000* the competitors also scored points by murdering and maiming random pedestrians, Death Race spectators, and fellow racers with their customized cars. Adorned with giant knives, oversized steer horns, machine guns, and gargantuan teeth, these cars were mobile killing machines, built for speed and slaughter. The Death Race was the new millennium's most popular entertainment event, and much like Roman gladiator battles, these government-sponsored races satiated their public. The public didn't take part in the highway slaughter, except as unsuspecting victims and ravenous fans. Movies like *Death Race 2000*, however, are said to have not only prefigured the future but helped to bring it about. According to current traffic safety experts, nearly all drivers exhibit the aggressive driving behaviors that a generation ago provided movie audiences with B-grade laughs and thrills. The experts warn this is no laugh-

**FIGURE 28. Death Race Poster**
The blood being splattered in this movie poster is the result not of an accident, but of sport. *Death Race 2000* was a huge hit for the low-budget film producer Roger Corman during its theater run in 1975. *DEATH RACE 2000* POSTER (1975). FROM HTTP://WWW.MOVIEGOODS.COM. RETRIEVED MAY 15, 2006.

ing matter. In fact, media representations which make light of this violent road behavior are one of the many factors, experts caution, that produce our current highway races toward death. Its most violent form they call road rage. The American people are no longer simply spectators, but rather are said to exhibit road rage everyday and in increasing numbers. After all, as many recent reports have noted, all you have to do is watch the nightly news to recognize the magnitude of the problem.

Road rage burst onto the scene in 1995. Media of every sort intensified efforts to warn viewers of the dangers drivers and their emotions posed to people's personal safety and to social cohesion. Previous chapters have dealt with social problems related to mobility and efforts to solve such problems. Road rage is the most recent example of this type of social problem to en-thrall auto-mobile America.[1] Unlike the other problems, though, this one has no specific problem population to pin the blame on. U.S. highways are not littered with randomly scattered bad seeds: where road rage is concerned anyone and everyone poses a potential threat. The modes of governing and eradicating road rage thus differ from previous attempts to restore safety. Whereas governmental surveillance and monitoring have played a large part in governing past problems, it is self-monitoring which is largely called for with road rage. This shift corresponds to a more general shift toward neo-liberal governing in general. It also casts a broader net over the problem. Whereas previous attempts to reduce highway carnage have worked through actuarial, demographic, and stereotyping practices, this campaign has instead been geared toward all drivers, not simply those who statistically or metaphorically pose a threat to safety and the status quo. From the most successful business commuters to drive-by gang-bangers, rage is said to percolate and erupt on the roads of all social sectors.

### Defining Rage and Declining to Engage:
### Causing and Solving the Problem

It's a jungle out there. Well not really: it's worse than a jungle. It's a stretch of roadway anywhere in America, and in place of the ravenous tigers and stampeding rhinos and slithery anacondas are your friends and neighbors and co-workers, that nice lady from the church-choir and the cheerful kid who bags your food at the local Winn Dixie—even Mom and Dad and Buddy and Sis. They're in a hurry. And you're in their way. So step on it! That light is not going to get any greener! Move it or park it! Tarzan had it easy. Tarzan didn't have to drive to work.

ANDREW FERGUSON, "ROAD RAGE"[2]

The initial interest in road rage appears to have occurred in the late 1980s, when violent criminal behavior, specifically the shooting of fellow drivers, received attention first in scattered local news reports and then eventually in the national media outlets. The term *road rage* was coined at the time, but it didn't gain extensive usage until shortly after the completion and dissemination of a AAA-funded study titled "Aggressive Driving." The insurance agency hired a criminologist to determine the extent and the causes of and solutions to the perceived increase in aggressive driving incidents, particularly on the metropolitan-area Beltway around Washington, D.C. This concern arose following extensive coverage in D.C., and to a lesser degree in the national media, of a high-speed civilian chase that ended in a crash that killed two innocent bystanders. The study's data were culled from available police reports in which criminal violence had been inflicted with, in, or around automobiles. AAA released this study to news agencies along with a press release explaining the devastating effect and widespread occurrence of road rage and aggressive driving. In fact, it became the media problem du jour. As Michael Fumento noted in 1998 in an *Atlantic Monthly* article, "'Road Rage' Versus Reality," the number of news stories in printed media rose from zero to three per year from 1988 to 1993. In 1994 there were twenty-seven, in 1995 almost five hundred, in 1996 over eighteen hundred, and in 1997 more than four thousand.[3] To a degree this represents the use of a specific term, *road rage*, when describing news events that were already being reported, like local automobile accidents. The death of Princess Diana also sparked intense media coverage of the supposed road rage epidemic, as it was first blamed on speeding, soon after on motorcycle-riding paparazzi, then on road rage in general, later on drunk/drugged driving, then on the lack of safety belt use, and last on some combination thereof. Any number of traffic safety explanations can be applied in many fatal automobile accidents. More important, the "epic tragedy" of Diana's accident solidified and intensified the road rage discourse by escalating it out of the banality of commuting and into the realm of international celebrity. But the story is far more complex than this. The vast media coverage did play a significant role in bringing road rage to national prominence. This media coverage, though, did not in and of itself produce any significant changes in how mobility is governed, or even necessarily conceptualized. Furthermore, the media coverage, in many ways, was responding to and appropriating descriptions of road rage from governmental agencies and self-proclaimed road rage experts. Behind these obvious participants lurks the insurance industry, which first provided "scientific" evidence that road rage and aggressive driving (RR/AD) were on the rise. The ability of the insurance industry to initiate and orient traffic safety discussions has been discussed in earlier chapters. Needless to say, it has the most to gain financially by making as many forms of driving conduct criminal, thereby decreasing liability and in theory the actual practices that lead to accidents. What makes the media coverage of RR/AD most interesting is the degree to which it responded to the insurance industry's press releases and created a discursive vortex in which the growing media concern became the ultimate sign of RR/AD's seriousness. By the summer of 1997, a congressional hearing before the Subcommittee on Surface Transportation was held. As expected, this further legitimated the importance of the

**U.S.News** & WORLD REPORT

JUNE 2, 1997 / $2.95

**Road Rage**

Why American
drivers are ruder,
meaner, and
more dangerous
than ever

**FIGURE 29. Road Rage Cover**
This magazine cover was typical of the highly charged and
overwrought rhetoric that prevailed during the road rage scare of
the mid- to late 1990s. The driver has been morphed into a car with
metallic paint, headlights for eyes, and tire tread eyebrows. U.S. NEWS
AND WORLD REPORT, COVER, JUNE 2, 1997.

issue and spurred more national news coverage. For instance, the day after
the hearing, July 18, the *New York Times* ran a story with the title "Temper
cited as cause of 28,000 road deaths a year."[4] The media coverage has yet
to diminish a full ten years after the first news blitz. A Google news search
for the term "road rage" for a one-week period in late October 2007 located
1,465 different new stories. The earliest coverage quoted extensively from the
same small group of RR/AD experts, government agencies, and police. This
uniformity of sources and limited number of experts has produced a fairly
uniform discourse, the primary concerns and orientations of which are described below. These experts and invested parties are certain to explain that

their concern is simply an addendum to intense citizen concern. As if they were responding to, rather than creating, the public concern. In the press release that accompanied AAA's first American report of RR they had this to say: "The Foundation [AAA] realized that although the topic of aggressive driving seemed of great concern to motorists, there was little real knowledge of the extent of the problem or of any trends in the phenomenon. Thus the Foundation set out to determine a true picture of the extent of aggressive driving behavior."[5]

And an ugly picture it was, according to the experts.

## Definitions

When one critically approaches any social problem, a number of potential questions need to be answered. For instance: What is the problem? How do we know it exists? Who is telling us it exists? Who is trying to solve the problem and in what ways? The question at hand essentially concerns power/knowledge relationships. A circularity of coreinforcing effect tends to play itself out in such situations. On the one hand are numerous invested parties, or moral entrepreneurs,[6] who to a greater or lesser degree are not only invested in claiming jurisdiction over the problem, but are in fact quite often already granted jurisdiction because of their governmental or economic positioning. It should come as no surprise that insurance industry agents, high-placed National Highway Traffic Safety Administration (NHTSA) officials, and university-funded psychologists were the primary speakers at the subcommittee hearing on RR/AD in 1997 (well before the media hype peaked). These are the same experts who have guided safety policy since the first Crusade for Traffic Safety. However, this is not to say the outcome of such an investigation was predetermined; it is to a large degree still undecided. On the other hand are typical knowledge formations which have been granted legitimacy within specific contexts. As has been shown in previous chapters, psychology, quantitative social science, criminology, actuarial demography, and economics are all culturally validated forms of knowledge production when it comes to auto-mobility. Thus one would expect, when it comes to road rage, that these are the discourses that would be encountered. Largely this is the case. These forms of knowledge production are valorized by the organizations and institutions that have been granted jurisdiction over traffic safety. These specific types of knowledge also validate and are accompanied by particular sorts of solutions, owing to the theoretical underpinnings which drive their inquiry. Most specifically, it is their theory of the subject, as either the rational subject of economy, the discipline-demanding subject of criminology, or the always potentially pathological subject of psychology, which drives the types of solutions and corresponds to the types of causes manifest in safety discussions in general and road rage in particular.

This said, How is the issue to be defined? In other words, just what is road rage or aggressive driving? This is not such an easy question to answer. Not in that it is difficult to relay the operative definitions of road rage used in the literature, but insofar as there are numerous discursive locales that demand differing definitions. In fact, an inability to legally define road rage was the primary impediment faced by state legislators around the nation as they quickly attempted to follow the public uproar with punitive fury. Insurance agencies, however obviously, had an investment in defining road rage as a criminal activity, as this could potentially free them from economic responsibility in acccidents induced by road rage. Causal blame, legal responsibility, and destructive capacity were all important matters to insurance industries. Psychologists, on the other hand, were invested in the production of a new pathology. There was in fact a veritable race to pathologize road rage in order to lay claim to its inclusion in *The Diagnostic and Statistical Manual of Mental Disorders* (DSM4) by various driving psychology experts (my personal favorite, Dr. Leon James of the University of Hawaii, calls himself Dr. Driving).[7] The definition of a problem, then, is not a disinvested attempt to most accurately and objectively describe a condition. Definitions structure and organize thought about an event in a particular fashion, legitimate authority, and, by implication, authorize certain solutions while invalidating others. Last, insurance companies most often demand that official DSM prognosis accompany any insurance payout. Unless road rage was provided official status, psychologists would not be able to profit from this newfound pathology.

The first major hurdle for all parties involved was how to respond to the journalistic tag, road rage, which had gained currency in popular discourse, while maintaining some sense of scientific decorum. Journalistic accounts had been first on the scene, and one must acknowledge the part they played. It was this very fact which opened up a new arena for governance, but also set the stage on which the aforementioned invested parties had to act. Their first action was to attempt to rearticulate the very actions which constituted the problem. The initial media reports focused on dramatic, criminal actions that often led to mass destruction, mayhem, and death. This included, though was not limited to, drivers shooting at each other, forcing each other off the road, and racing at high speeds in contests that went awry. The safety establishment—fixated on creating perpetual traffic safety anxiety, making the roadways safe, and maintaining their role in the establishment—was interested in connecting this criminal activity with what came to be called aggressive driving. This would extend the scope of the problem, link it to more mundane forms of driving, and ultimately make all drivers accountable. One key to making the articulation stick was to make it seem natural, to make a "not necessarily" into a necessity. In order to firmly link aggressive driving with road rage, the safety establishment created structuring logics of progression and association. These logics asserted that aggressive driving could induce road rage in others, and a series of steps that ended in road rage all stemmed from aggressive driving.

There are several types of definitions, and by explicating them we can begin to see the productive capacity they have for orienting thought on the governance of mobility. The first study of RR/AD conducted in the United States was sponsored by the AAA and carried out by Louis Mizell, the "owner of a corporation that maintains databases of crime reports."[8] The study was circulated to media channels and structured much of the media reports and further studies. Mizell's study was based on police reports and thus covered only the incidents that were "so extreme that they resulted in a police crime report or a published newspaper article. They undoubtedly represent a small fraction of the total number of such incidents."[9] Mizell, and by extension the AAA, defined aggressive driving as "an incident in which an angry or impatient motorist or passenger intentionally injures or kills another motorist, passenger, or pedestrian, or attempts to injure or kill another motorist, passenger, or pedestrian, in response to a traffic dispute, altercation, or grievance. It is also considered 'aggressive driving' when an angry or vengeful motorist intentionally drives his or her vehicle into a building or other structure or property."[10]

Mizell's definition is important in several key ways. First, it rejects the term *road rage*, thus altering the psychological makeup of the driver from one who is enraged to one who is merely aggressive. Rage is a temporary state, something which can't be controlled and, sometimes even in the case of murder, reduces the legal consequences of one's actions. Being aggressive describes, as most of this literature informs us, the contemporary American's outlook on life. Aggressiveness can be held accountable as a motive, controlled, altered, regulated, and triumphantly overcome. Second, we can see from Mizell's definition the limits of his database and, to a degree, the investments of his clients. Only actual disputes or reportable events make it into his definition. In other words, aggressive driving is an activity that results in damage to persons or property, a primary concern of insurance agencies. It is not, at least at this point in the formation of the discourse, a way of being. Instead, it is seen as an isolated event, although one that is, according to his statistics, on the rise.

Mizell's definition depends upon a rupture—"the cumulative result of a series of stressors in a motorist's life." They make the driver crack. "As with most human behavior, there is a stated and unstated, a conscious and unconscious motivation."[11] The focus was upon the driver, not the environment, most specifically on the logic of causality and motivation. This double movement, toward cause and motive, mirrors legal and psychological frameworks, which are the two main players in later discussions regarding RR/AD. The first is set upon defining the legal criteria by which the activity can be criminalized, legislated against, monitored, and eradicated. The second is invested in determining the internal workings of the mind that at first cause the malady but can later be reprogramed to purge it. This framework of locating road rage's cause in the driver was countered by social scientific experts and to a degree by the Department of Transportation (DOT), which is invested in how highway engineering can be utilized to increase safety. Therefore, if a structural problem was creating road rage, for instance, traffic congestion, the government's role could be increased as the agent of change (e.g., by building more highways).

The legal definition of road rage took on a different inflection. Following the initial 1997 subcommittee hearing which articulated the media coverage to governmental concern, there was an outbreak of legislative action to actively deal with RR/AD on the state level, where driving policy is enacted. At this legislative level, the most difficult problem was not determining the causes or even necessarily the solutions to RR/AD. Rather, the major difficulty was defining it in a manner that was legally applicable and enforceable by police. The legal issues were complicated by the fact that most actions that were typically defined as road rage, that is, violent actions directed at another motorist, were already covered by nontraffic misdemeanors and felonies. If you shoot and kill someone, it is considered murder of some variety, whether it occurs in a Corvette, on a street corner, or in your courtyard. Furthermore, in many instances of murder, attempted murder, or assault, an automobile can be considered as deadly a weapon as a gun. Therefore, some doubt existed as to whether in these extreme cases it was even necessary to create new legislation. In fact, as late as 1999 no legal scholars, lawyers, judges, or police officials contacted by the AAA for their study "Controlling Road Rage" believed specific legislation was necessary to combat RR/AD. This didn't stop legislators in nine states from introducing laws that specified RR/AD as a separate charge from other driving offenses.[12] However, there was a formulation of RR/AD driving which defined the activity in much broader terms.

The subcommittee hearings, which helped spur legislative activity, provided numerous definitions of RR/AD which included all sorts of driving behavior under the umbrella of RR/AD. David K. Willis, the president of the AAA Foundation for Traffic Safety, specifically responded to the problems associated with Mizell's definition provided above. He claimed it was important to keep the limits of Mizell's definition in mind because it "can exclude some truly horrific incidents."[13] Dr. Ricardo Martinez, administrator of the NHTSA, defined RR/AD as "driving behavior that endangers or is likely to endanger people or property. This definition includes a broad spectrum of driving behaviors, ranging from risky driving and escalating to dueling and violence on the road."[14] The next logical question is what driving behavior is considered risky. But this isn't the question that is answered next. Rather, skipping over at least two argumentative steps, he says that aggressive drivers are more likely to "speed, tailgate, fail to yield, weave in-and-out of traffic, pass on the right, make improper and unsafe lane changes, run stop signs and red lights, make hand and facial gestures, scream, honk and flash their lights."[15] This sleight of hand makes two assumptions. First, that the forms of behavior described are the result of aggression. Second, it assumes there is such a thing as an aggressive driver from which we can establish a list of specific characteristics. In one fell swoop the NHTSA had created (1) a new form of subjectivity, the aggressive driver; (2) a list of this population's characteristics; and (3) a set of identifying actions not simply illegal unto themselves (like speeding), but specifically illegal as forms of RR/AD. This definition provided legislators with a list of signifying practices which could be legislated against, monitored, and acted upon by police in their attempt to uphold their duty as part of the safety apparatus, not after the fact of violence, but before the more extreme types of behavior would supposedly be committed.

The very language of aggressive driving diminishes the role of the accident. In other words, there are no longer accidents, or at least not as many as in the past. Instead, there are now aggressive driving incidents. There are avoidable motivated incidents in which aggressive driving leads not to an accident, but to an act of road rage. So the speeding driver who rear-ends the rapidly decelerating truck in front of him or her is not involved in an accident but instead committed a crime. The potential possibilities of extending these legal definitions are seemingly endless. If speeding, for instance, is considered an act of aggressive driving, as it is in many states, then if one crashes while speeding, has one committed an act of road rage? Or is one simply involved in an accident, as it was defined in the past?

This expansion of the definition of RR/AD had a far more important effect though; it made it possible to consider nearly everyone an aggressive driver and thus potentially dangerous. The third major figures in the RR/AD discourse are those who specialize in "driving psychology." For the most part they are affiliated with research universities, and at least one of them appeared in nearly every newspaper, magazine, radio, or television story on RR/AD. Two of them spoke before the initial subcommittee hearing: Dr. Leon James (Dr. Driving) of the University of Hawaii and Dr. John A. Larson, the director of the Institute of Stress Medicine. Larson explains that the "headlines [of violent RR incidents] tell only part of the story; the assaults are the tip of an iceberg of increased aggressive driving practices, manifested by speeding, tailgating, failure to yield right of way, lane changes without signaling, weaving, cutting in, and rude, provocative behavior including facial rage, obscene gestures, and swearing. In my view 'Road Rage' represents the culmination of an escalating sequence of punitive behaviors meted out from one driver to another."[16]

For Larson, these particular forms of AD lead from things like cursing to harassing other drivers to ultimately intentionally injuring other drivers.

But all of these AD behaviors are a part of, and in fact induce, RR. Thus, as with the legal expansion of the definition, a vast array of driving behaviors is called RR/AD. James doesn't even bother with a basic definition of RR. He claims that "nearly every driver has feelings of rage and thoughts of retaliation."[17] These have increased and rather than simple RR/AD occurring under certain circumstances, he claims that "what's on the increase is the sheer amount of habitual road rage . . . a persistent state of hostility behind the wheel, demonstrated by acts of aggression on a continuum of violence, and justified by righteous indignation. Driving and habitual road rage have become virtually inseparable."[18] Thus for James, RR/AD is not about specific traffic safety breakdowns. Instead, the entire system has broken down, and this in turn causes the specific instances to occur. This is where the psychologist's conception of the matter veers in a different direction from that of much the rest of the safety establishment. The difference depends on causality.

The most telling and inclusive of all the psychological explanations comes from Arnold Nerenberg, a California psychologist and media-savvy RR/AD expert. He is "America's [self-proclaimed] Road Rage Therapist." He states that there is a need for an official DSM category: "road rage disorder." In his formulation "cutting in front of other drivers, slamming on the brakes to surprise a tailgater, obscene gestures and yelling, honking the horn, and flashing headlights repeatedly are considered pathological if exhibited twice within a one-year period."[19] This definition, combined with the general case study data from nearly all of the reports, would produce a fully pathological driving population consisting of 75–90 percent of drivers. My issue, again, is not with the specifics of the definition or with the RR/AD data, but with the fact that the definitions create a grid of interpretation in which nearly everyone is either pathological or potentially pathological. This inclusive logic legitimates an all-encompassing response that targets everyone and demands that each driver be concerned not just about a social problem, but, more important, *about themselves.*

The definition of a problem sets the stage for how it is addressed as policy. As has been shown, institutional and discursive contexts figure heavily in determining the shape and scope of these definitions. These definitions also tend to link a type of population—with a corresponding subjectivity—to the problem. These forms of subjectivity and definitions are employed to inform and legitimate one another. It is not the "fact" of this population's existence which affirms the category: rather, the research uses the corresponding category in a way that automatically affirms the existence of the group, and the data retrieved can then be used to describe and validate the definition. For instance, in an NHTSA study, a series of questions derived by Dr. Driving and correlated to the definition of aggressive driving were used to separate aggressive drivers from general drivers: "The most aggressive third of the general population drivers had scores of six or more on the screening questions. Accordingly, six was established as the threshold for qualifying participants in the aggressive driver groups."[20] Thus, an abstract definition was applied to a series of supposedly corresponding characteristics, which were then used to produce the aggressive driver groups by arbitrarily deciding that 30 percent of drivers are aggressive. From these typologies, important "facts" about aggressive drivers are "discovered" and used to verify the extent and severity of the RR/AD problem. They also are used to provide a description of what aggressive drivers are like, a description that researchers knew from the beginning because the questionnaire determined the very makeup of the category. The importance of this point is not so much to put in question the validity of government statistics and claims. It is instead to make apparent the logic, both methodological and governmental, by which such problems are approached. This approach produces a very different array of policy effects than do the psychologists or the legal experts.

## Causes

A plethora of causes were provided by experts and journalists to explain the presence of and increase in RR/AD. By organizing them according to type, the forms of investigation and the assumptions regarding how to govern mobility will be made clear. Much like the varying definitions, the demand for causal explanations is a by-product of any social problems discourse. The stated causes fit within generally acceptable forms. In this instance they can be loosely organized according to the structures which are assumed to animate the causes. In varying instances these productive structures are said to be social, cultural, psychological, historical, or institutional. One way to think about these issues is to compare them to more general concerns regarding lack of civility and the collapse of the public sphere, the general decline in education, or the difficulties of multiculturalism. So the general anxieties that plague social scientists and political theorists reappear as explanations for why there is trouble on the road.

Many immediate situations are said to cause incidents of road rage: among them are getting cut off, being tailgated, having to slow down for another driver, people passing in the wrong lane, slow driving in the passing lane, feeling endangered by another driver's mistake, being detained, being forced to listen to another driver's radio playing too loudly, involvement in a fender bender, battling for a parking space, getting honked at, oncoming high beams, traffic blockages, failure to accelerate at a green light, "debating" over the right of way at stop signs, crossing lanes without signaling, getting "dissed," agitation with those driving or the feeling of power in driving "BMWs, pick-up trucks, sports cars, or off road vehicles," and other miscommunications.[21] For instance, mistaking a friendly wave of appreciation for being "flipped off." Hidden in each of these scenarios is the potential for a RR/AD event. In fact, you never know when you might incur someone else's rage or aggression by committing one of these potentially fatal errors. This always-looming threat reorients the road as a place demanding extreme caution, a place where civil conduct is not simply a nicety or a necessary means of survival, but might itself be the very cause of incivility. The RR/AD discussions are full of such advice. It is drivers' responsibility not only to conduct themselves properly, but to constantly monitor others in order to stay clear of the factors that might cause RR/AD. These are generally seen as the "straw that broke the camel's back" or the "spark that ignited the explosion." In other words, they are only causal to the extent that drivers were already predisposed to take action. But it's not enough that you concern yourself with driving behavior. There are also immediate environmental causes which are said to increase your chances of raging or being raged at. Heat and congestion are the two environmental hazards that are particularly dangerous. So the next time you're driving in your BMW or, worse yet, in your new BMW X-5 SUV, in the summer and you're stopped at a particularly lengthy stoplight, and you wave over a merging "Ford Tough" pickup, the odds are high that you may be raged at. You should use extreme caution and prepare for the worst. In fact, it is probably best to avoid the situation altogether by not allowing the Ford to merge. But this too is dangerous, as the driver may feel "dissed." Maybe it's best if you simply don't drive at all.

The psychological evaluations of drivers in the 1950s were oriented around gender and maturity. The question they answered was, why is it that particular populations are safer drivers than others? Contemporary driving psychologists are more invested in explaining the particularities of individual driving behavior and the psychological responses within a specific cultural context. These responses are dependent upon genetic hardwiring in many explanations. In these ways, the psychologists lay claim to both the internal workings of the mind and the external cultural context. This best-of-both-worlds approach creates a form of explanation that can seemingly account for anything, and in this case seems to account for nearly everything. Thus the genetic predisposition to get anxious in crowded environments, as studies on rat behavior in confined spaces confirm, and the generally violent society that we live in can seamlessly be brought together to account for RR/AD.[22] What follows is a broad discussion of these various causes that will help explain the specific solutions that are addressed later. As in most problem/solution discourses, attempts are made to correlate solutions to causes. This is particularly the case within the psychological and sociological strains of the discourse. There is a tendency to try to get at the root cause so that the solution won't provide simply a Band-Aid that addresses the aftereffects. Instead, social scientists advocate the elimination of the causal agent. This often fails to manifest itself in the actual governmental solutions provided. Rather, governmental attempts tend to follow established means of controlling a situation by directing already existing agencies to intensify and expand efforts used to solve other problems.

The first set of causes might be considered the unfortunate hardwiring of our brains that predisposes us to react in an uncivil manner to uncomfortable situations. For instance, it is said that the design of the brain doesn't allow for control over emotions.[23] In fact, anger is not only unavoidable, but seductive as well. It is said to draw one in and create a "rage rush."[24] RR/AD within this discourse offers drivers a very uncivil and immoral pleasure. Much like the addictive and seductive characteristics of other rushes, for example, those derived from sex, cocaine, or shopping, the RR/AD rush must be tamed. But this can be difficult; not only do humans get a rush from it, but the car has become an extension of our territory and "human beings are territorial."[25] Thus we react to invasions of our territory by defending it and attempting to reestablish it. This is particularly sticky when someone cuts a driver off, and the driver feels the need to take back their space and assert dominance. Might there be a space for safe road rage rushes? Does this explain the existence of the county fair crash derby? For now, we'll have to wait for answers. It is possible, though, to assert that the feeling of power behind the wheel leads to RR/AD.

This particularly compelling argument raises a series of disturbing questions for commercial airline pilots and cruise ship captains. We are told in the literature that the automobile produces a feeling of immense power. In fact, this power is said to be magnified in the case of the ubiquitous SUV. The power to control one's destination and the speed with which one gets there are of paramount importance to the SUV driver. When something impedes this progress, a feeling of powerlessness or a sense that one's power is diminished sets in. This lack or loss triggers a response for the need to reestablish power and often entails retaliation. Power diminished offers an opportunity to prove one's power. The multi-ton SUV provides much power, and it is in fact a "car designed for war."[26] Furthermore, an owner's choice of automobile is said to correspond to his or her sense of self. Given the large numbers of SUVs on the road, it is quite apparent that more aggressive and power-hungry people are on the road.

This psychological explanation depends upon a series of articulations and assertions that are not as apparent as psychologists may desire. The explosion of SUVs was one of the most visible changes in the American driving environment during the 1990s. Historically, larger vehicles and particularly vehicles that provided the opportunity to seat more passengers and to be used for travel have been articulated to notions of an idealized family. Earlier incarnations include the station wagon (see chapter 1), and the minivan. There is, then, no necessary correspondence between large, multipassenger vehicles and a desire for power. If there were, wouldn't the drivers of garbage or dump trucks and semitrailers be the most aggressive drivers of all? Television commercials have described the SUV as the ultimate vehicle to help deal with congestion, but it was its capability to go off-road and circumvent traffic jams, not its destructive capability, that was tapped. The ideology of freedom was signified more than power. Power was simply the means to an end, not an end itself. But, more important, it is the obviousness of the articulation which largely makes it possible. If we assume that RR/AD was not actually on the rise in the 1990s, as was made clear earlier, the question is how discourses describe reality. They operate largely through simple articulations following given structures. Suppose sales of sports cars had tripled during the 1990s. The supposed psychological makeup of the sports car driver as aggressive, interested in getting someplace fast, self-centered, and someone who likes to show off would have been used to explain the rise in RR/AD. If RR/AD had been an issue during the 1980s, it would have been attributed by left scholars as the outcome of Rambo/Reagan-era hypermasculinity.[27] My point is this: the causal explanatory structures seem largely determinative, rather than attributable to SUVs, cranial hardwiring, or right-wing-inspired aggression.[28]

I want to mention a number of the causes that appear in the RR/AD discussion in order to paint a general picture of what kind of driving environment conceptualizes experts' explanations and responses. They see cars as a private realm of complete control, at least in the minds of drivers. There is also a feeling of anonymity. Unlike other social situations, driving largely allows for anonymity. This would seem to contradict the notion that driving and one's car are forms of self-expression: after all, who wants to express something if they will remain anonymous? There is also a sense of invulnerability. This is ironic in that it is said to be the outcome of safety devices, which make people seem safe. Yet we are constantly told by safety advocates and automobile advertisements that there is a desire for more safety devices, which implies a notion of lack. If we already feel invincible, why would we need or desire more devices? This snapshot of the contemporary American driver would shape up something like this: an anonymous, self-centered, power-hungry, defensive, invincible, determined to "educate," SUV driver, like a moth drawn to fire, desires the thrill of "rage rush" and is continually defending her territory.[29]

RR/AD experts don't stop at describing the inner workings of the mind: they go to great lengths to explain how the "culture of rage" breeds this undesirable conduct and creates a "reservoir of anger."[30] The United States is said to be a violent society. Violence on the road is thus considered acceptable, or at least understandable.[31] Americans are also described as being incredibly competitive in all facets of life, even where they shouldn't be, like on the road. This is a particularly troubling cause because, as we'll see, eliminating this American trait strikes at the core of conservative conceptions of American individuality and economic success. Dr. Driving explains that immigrant drivers bring different driving styles to American roads, and this produces differing expectations and behavior that tends to cause friction.[32] There has also been a decline in traditional driver's education, from 90 percent of all new U.S. drivers in the 1970s to as few as 30 percent in the 1990s who complete an official driver's education course.[33] And those that still exist have been dumbed down, just like the rest of the curriculum. When driver's education is in effect it produces problems nonetheless and isn't exempt from the same issues of RR/AD experienced by other drivers. In North Carolina, a driver's education instructor ordered his student to speed up to catch a driver who cut them off in order to punch the offender.[34] More generally, Dr. Driving blames defensive driving for RR/AD, although that is the type of driving taught in most driver's education courses. He claims that it creates a driving environment in which we assume the worst of other drivers, which keeps us on the lookout for offensive behavior. Busy schedules, typified by the business commuter and soccer mom, are mentioned in nearly every report. Reduced levels of police enforcement are also blamed. Because drivers feel they aren't being watched or given citations, they think they can get away with RR/AD. In addition, increased speed limits are said to lead to more aggressive drivers and raise expectations for shorter drives. But the media have been identified as one of the most prevalent causes of RR/AD. This takes two very different courses.

In the first line of reasoning, the media are blamed as being the cause of RR/AD. In the second, the media are blamed for exaggerating or even fabricating the extent of RR/AD. In both cases, the media are described too loosely and are granted hypodermic capacity. In his testimony before the House Transportation Committee, Larson, misrepresenting Marshall McLuhan, claimed that the media are the message and that the message is clear: violent driving is an acceptable and even glorified activity. He claimed that all we had to do to see the origins of the problem was to take a look at automobile commercials, televised racing, movies that feature car chases, and, most blatantly, "Road Warrior type movies of the 1980s. In this movie, Mel Gibson, leading a group of vehicles across Australia, becomes a 'Road Warrior,' fighting vehicle to vehicle with a gang of villains."[35] Furthermore, "they teach a distrust of usual police methods, and the heroic identification figures are vigilante types, working outside the law."[36] Thus, the road rager who punishes other drivers to teach them a lesson is in fact a vigilante. Dr. Driving is not as specific about the television shows or movies that cause RR/AD, but he is quite sure the media play an integral role: "The culture of road rage has deep roots. We inherit aggressive and dangerous driving patterns as children, watching our parents and other adults behind the wheel, and by watching and absorbing bad driving behaviors depicted in movies and television commercials."[37] It makes one wonder why RR/AD became a serious problem only in the 1990s. The decade that is best known for violent road movies and massive car chases is certainly the 1970s. *The Getaway, The Duel, The French Connection, Gone in Sixty Seconds,* and all the cross-country road movies discussed in chapter 4 very specifically deal with such themes, and in some cases the entire movie is simply an extended car chase. *Death Race 2000* is the most auto-violent movie made to date (with the possible exception of *Mad Max* (1980) or *Crash* (1997). All of these movies are artifacts of the 1970s, yet RR/AD doesn't even make a blip on the social problems radar during that decade. Nonetheless, these arguments are fairly rudimentary. As with any other social problem, the culture can always be blamed, and more often than not this means popular culture representations of whatever conduct is considered a problem.

The most interesting explanation of what caused RR/AD is primarily the work of *Atlantic* contributor Fumento. In "'Road Rage' Versus Reality," he argues that the media have blown the extent of RR/AD way out of proportion by overcovering it, misconstruing the statistics, and failing to seriously examine the experts' findings.[38] Fumento's article is a strong critique of the media's tendency to exaggerate particular social problems. His position is basically that of a better journalist. He simply dug further. More specifically, he turned journalistic practices back upon the journalistic apparatus. To a degree, this is precisely what I am doing in this chapter. I turn methods of critical investigation against competing methods of investigation. As one would expect and possibly hope for, Fumento has what Michael Schudson called the naïve empiricism of journalistic objectivity, in which there is still faith in the apparatus as a tool for exposing the truth of a given situation.[39] This chapter is instead an attempt to reorient the terrain of investigation, which depends on how the categories of investigation are theorized. Fumento ends by glorifying other safety campaigns and concerns, without giving them the same critical attention he levels against RR/AD. This incongruity reestablishes the credibility of safety campaigns by positing a positive other against which RR/AD can be measured and deemed insignificant, in this case, running red lights and driving drunk.

## Solutions

Given all these causes, it should be obvious that the potential for governmental solutions is vast. In fact, the solutions proposed were many and fell into five categories. The first sort is rather straightforward and is based upon technological determinism. These are traffic engineering solutions. The second depends upon police intervention. The third is educational/propagandistic. The fourth is aimed at the driver, in which therapeutic tools are provided for producing new forms of self-regulation, self-mastery, and self-creation. The fifth is the most interesting for this book, as its aim and tools are culture. More specifically, it initiates new modes of community as a means of altering and monitoring driving conduct. These types, of course, cross over. Certainly part of the educational campaign is an attempt to alter how one views one's own driving conduct. Police surveillance is said to do the same, and the classic model of disciplinarity works on just that principle. Taken as a whole, the solutions represent but a small part of the larger driving-control apparatus. The solutions are typical of past attempts to deal with safety concerns, but the specific application of therapeutic self-creation mechanisms and the use of community reorient the focus of most safety campaigns. This marks an increased investment in neoliberal strategies for governing mobility.

The technological solutions are primarily of a traffic engineering sort. Engineering of all varieties, especially when working in the interest of capital, is fundamentally enthralled by efficiency. In this instance, efficiency is blocked by congestion, and most traffic engineers and government agencies involved in road construction and planning see congestion as the primary cause of RR/AD. Their solution is simple in theory, though far more difficult in application. The most common response of this group is to simply construct more roads. This, it is said, will decrease congestion and therefore increase efficiency. The counterargument to this claim is almost as ubiquitous: "If you build it they will come." Another, cheaper method of keeping traffic flowing is the use of closely monitored traffic lights, particularly on highway entrances and at busy intersections. The ultimate engineering solution is to simply eliminate the human factor altogether. This has been a public dream of traffic engineers ever since the 1939 World's Fair in New York, where the first "intelligent highway system" was on display. This solution is the meta-solution of traffic safety. In this scenario, drivers no longer control their cars.

Instead, cars are remotely guided by an elaborate road-to-automobile communication/monitoring system. This will apparently solve all human error safety concerns, basically those dealt with in these chapters. No longer will the public have to concern itself with the tedium of controlling its own mobility. As in so many engineered dreams, the mechanical will free the human. A few side concerns have arisen, the most obvious being the tremendous public and private costs of implementing such a system. But certain types of vehicles, motorcycles, for instance, by necessity of their control dynamics, would be eliminated from the roads altogether. As reminiscent of Flash Gordon as this scheme may seem, initiatives begun in the early 1990s earmarked over half a billion dollars to begin preliminary research into just such a project, as is discussed further in the following chapter.[40]

If you can't eliminate the human element, at least you can more closely police it. Policing has been offered as a solution to nearly every traffic safety concern. For RR/AD it involved a few new wrinkles. Stricter licensing practices were demanded by numerous organizations and agencies. Although RR/AD was not considered exclusively or even primarily a problem caused by youth, many were calling for curtailed youth driving hours and curfews on their night driving. A call went out to crack down on such offenses. This demanded two steps. First, legislation was needed to define what to look for. This extended typical police surveillance of monitoring infractions to searching the souls of drivers in order to locate motive. Traffic infractions are fairly clear-cut, and with the help of cameras, radar detection, and speed traps, they can easily be recognized. Motive or emotion is not so easily monitored, especially when someone is inside a speeding car. Thus internal psychological mechanisms had to be articulated to external signifiers. For instance, passing on the right side, changing lanes without signaling, and flashing lights when approaching a slower car in the passing lane all became signifiers of RR/AD. It was these newly created or newly articulated signifiers, speeding, for instance, which were brought to the attention of police. They were told to monitor such signifiers more vigilantly and increase their quotas for issuing citations. Ricardo Martinez claimed, "People tend to respect what the police inspect."[41] Police crackdowns were often an integral part of such anti-RR/AD campaigns as "Smooth Operator," initiated in California. Supposedly catchy phrases and acronyms were invented. Some especially clever examples are Aggressive Drivers Are Public Threats (ADAPT) in Colorado, 3D (Drunk, Drugged, and Dangerous) in Massachusetts, "Take it Easy" in Delaware, and Targeting Reckless and Intimidating Aggressive Drivers (TRIAD) in Ohio. Other than being named for pop songs and the Chinese mafia, these campaigns are notable for their commitment to linking public education, roadside signage, and a highly visible police presence. More generally, increased police monitoring was said to be a great deterrent to other forms of criminal activity. If anyone was unconvinced, the then-recent apprehension of Timothy McVeigh was offered up by the NHTSA in its presentation before Congress as the clearest proof of the effectiveness of increased policing.[42]

The anti–drunk driving campaign was cited in nearly every call to implement anti-RR/AD educational and propaganda campaigns. The statistics of how many lives have supposedly been saved by decreasing drunk driving incidents since 1980, when Mothers Against Drunk Driving (MADD) first began its crusade were presented as unquestionable proof that this was indeed the best way to deal with RR/AD. In fact, two such organizations, Children Against Road Rage (CARR) and Citizens Against Speeding and Aggressive Driving (CASAD), were formed by the time the initial congressional hearing took place in July 1997, less than a year after the initial AAA study was released. CARR was begun by Dr. Driving and CASAD by Lisa Sheikh, who spoke at the hearing and at the time worked for the Child Welfare League of America on children's safety. Although this is a sort of citizen involvement, it is fairly clear that neither of the founders can be described simply as concerned citizens. More important, the means of educating the public is assumed to be the responsibility of special interest groups, not the state. As part of their anti-RR/AD campaigns mentioned above, states put up billboards and flashing traffic signs that warned against the dangers of RR/AD and ordered drivers to "take it easy." Over twenty million anti-RR/AD pamphlets were sent out to cellular phone service customers along with their monthly bill. Why this particular segment of the population was given special treatment is not exactly clear, though studies do claim that talking on the phone while driving is more dangerous than driving with a .10 blood-alcohol level (a common level used by police to determine a drunk driving offense). But there were few formal plans to, for instance, radically alter driver's education. Dr. Driving did argue passionately that because RR/AD is learned at an early age, CARR needed to include children. Furthermore, driver's education should involve "training in emotional intelligence" and be taught in K-12 in order to combat all of the "insidious generational imprinting" received in all other sectors of society.[43] His educational plan was also to combat defensive driving and the problems associated with it mentioned above. The ultimate goal of this driver's education was an "attitude of latitude."[44] The new attitude would diminish the likelihood of an aggressive response to potentially inflammatory situations. This new form of driver's education, though, would work only on the young drivers-to-be. For the current driver, therapeutic self-help regimes were constructed.

By far the most common solutions offered were not top down. Instead, much of the expert advice and nearly all of the popular media advice was personal in nature. Rather than demanding government intervention or calling for citizens' action committees, newspaper story after talk show after nightly news report asked drivers to keep themselves in check. Citizen drivers were able to combat RR/AD in three ways. The easiest was to avoid provoking other drivers. Otherwise, we are told, "you are playing Russian Roulette."[45] Drivers should "keep their cool in traffic."[46] After all, "you can't control traffic, but you can control your reaction to it."[47] Drivers should be capable of controlling themselves at least to the same degree as an animal: "Never assume that an apparently aggressive act was intended as such. We all make mistakes. So don't bite back. If we take an example from studies of animal behavior in the wild, the dominant animal in the group will rarely get involved in petty fights and disagreements. Although confident in his ability to defeat any opponent, there is always the risk of injury."[48] Statements like this reify the hardwired psychological explanations of RR/AD while also reassuring the audience they are like the "dominant animal" when they turn away. Engagement in restraint is thus not an act of the weak, which overturns the typical macho associations of automobile competition. This sort of basic advice assumed that for the most part the audience was not comprised of those afflicted with RR/AD. But they could potentially invoke a driver who was. The flip side of this dichotomy is the sense in all of the literature that everyone has the potential to be an RR/ADer every time they get into their automobile. Thus the advice about not provoking others is also advice to stop drivers from raging themselves. This advice also takes a more therapeutic turn.

The three psychologists cited here all provide more clinical diagnostic devices. Mostly in the form of personality tests, these diagnostic question-naires list a number of potentially inflammatory situations or reactions and ask respondents to rank themselves according to the rules established by the test.[49] After tallying the results, the driver fits himself/herself into a statistical grid that explains the severity of the pathology and the steps which should be taken to reeducate oneself. Dr. Driving's program calls this a "driving personality makeover project."[50] In his version drivers make a "self witnessing tape." These are recordings of actual driving behavior used to self-realize the extent of one's aggression and rage. Drivers share their tapes with others in group therapy that he calls Quality Driving Circles (see below). Other psychologists, like Dr. Nerenberg, give one-on-one therapy to those who need it. By driving in congested conditions, your therapist in the passenger seat informing you of your wrongdoings, you can overcome your RR/AD problem. This sort of back-seat-driver therapy is aimed at the truly pathological, but the more mundane forms of therapy are supposed to be aimed at all drivers. The problem is, of course, that most drivers assume it is other drivers who are the problem. Nearly all the experts acknowledge that the first step must be self-recognition. This mirrors nearly all such self-help/group-therapy programs, in which acknowledging that one has a problem comes first and that one has the desire to overcome it is second. But what is to be done when everyone is said to have the same problem?

One solution came from a *Seattle Times* journalist in an article published on July 22, 1997.[51] She claimed that all citizens should be made to read "Rules of Civility: The 110 Precepts that Guided our First President in War and Peace" by Richard Brookhiser. Her solution is summed up by this quotation: "For men and motorists who aspire to something higher than boorishness, the 'Rules of Civility' serve as clear and fundamental rules of the road without the psychobabble. Simple good manners, Washington taught, are the first step to greatness—and they may even save lives."[52] I present this solution for two reasons. First, it displays a commonsense approach that journalism tended to provide in its description of the problem. It is still a form of self-help, much like Benjamin Franklin's diary was meant not only to be a history, but also a useful guide for those who might aspire to such greatness. These guides, and those who propose that we use them, are invoking a public sphere sense of civility, the crumbling of which is said to cause many ills of the nation, including RR/AD. These neoconservative responses are not that far removed from the "psychobabble." Each demands and promises a form of self-evaluation, self-control, and self-creation, which will be good primarily for self and secondarily for society.

### Grass-Rooting Out the Problem

The last solution to be discussed is based upon neoliberal uses of community, as described by Nicholas Rose. He sees community as being synonymous with the third way of governing. Community is the compromise that forms the third space of governing between the state and the individual. It is an active zone of governance that has occupied social theorists' fancy for two hundred years. But in its current formulation, community "is a moral field binding persons into durable relationships."[53] It depends upon affective emotional relationships, identities, and microcultures of value and meaning. This web of investment can be utilized through a multiform focus upon self-management in the name of local moral standards and affiliations. Rose calls this "government through community."[54] Dr. Driving has formulated and instituted just such a plan for governing RR/AD. Quality Driving Circles (QDC), the name for his driving therapy session groups, and grassroots lobbying organizations like CARR, which he instituted, and Youth Against Road Rage (YARR), are presented as the only means to truly solve the RR/AD problem. They are said to produce a shared set of group-enforced moral attitudes. The QDC bears further elaboration, as it provides an example of how this specific form of governing operates.

Leon James writes, "The dynamic power of groups to influence individual behavior is well known to social scientists."[55] It is exactly this technology of power that Dr. Driving orients his QDCs around. The QDCs are composed of groups of drivers who regularly meet to discuss their driving. Members bring their self-witnessing tapes and share them as well as make them available to a larger library of tapes accessible to other QDCs, which together form "a sort of community grassroots organization."[56] QDCs are also useful to the state: "They are principally cultural motivators for a value change. But they also are the best source of continuous data for tracking the level and intensity of aggressive driving."[57] This is because members participate as stationary and mobile witnesses to record and track RR/AD incidents as well as other traffic violations. The QDC will also provide a ready-made solution for drivers' reeducation mandated by the courts. In fact, the courts have increasingly been turning to anger-management therapy for violent offenders. The ultimate goal of the QDC, however, is to create "emotionally intelligent" driver-citizens. Of particular importance is "learning to satisfy the sense of personal freedom through smart driving."[58] QDCs work to articulate freedom to a differing ethic, one which isn't purely focused upon a reduction in impediments, but a mind-set that isn't determined to struggle against impediments beyond one's control. This reorientation of the self is dependent upon having a commitment to a community-held set of ideals. But community is not a natural aggregate of similar individuals holding similar ideals. Instead, as Rose and others have suggested, community must be manufactured.

This is the goal not only of Dr. Driving's QDCs, but also of such lobbying groups as CASAD. It involves a twofold practice. First, there is an attempt to reproduce a type of community sensibility which is said to have been lost in contemporary America. Numerous articles present this as one of the main causes of road rage. In fact, it is a paramount part of the discussion in driver's education manuals beginning in the 1930s and carrying through to the 1950s. If *Man and the Motorcar* (see chapter 1) is correct, maybe it is this very fact which accounts for the loss of community, seeing as learning to drive a car was synonymous with learning to be a good citizen. However, by re-creating a grassroots type of community organization that is specifically geared to alleviate road rage, traffic safety advocates are attempting to create a very different type of community. Typically, citizens' action groups, particularly those of a crime-watch nature, are local and fairly immobile. Their direct concern is spatially limited according to neighborhood boundaries (themselves fairly arbitrary). But with QDCs there is no spatially or temporally cultural binding similarity or form of affiliation used to create community. Instead, common perceptions of risk are said to be the glue that holds these groups together. As Lisa Sheikh, the founder of CASAD states, "I have met many residents who feel exactly the same as I do—that the risk we're encountering daily on our roads is unacceptable. I've met drivers who speak of frightening commutes to work every day, pedestrians who say they feel unnerved when trying to cross the street, and victims whose stories confirm our most dreaded fear: that deadly driving behavior is going largely unpunished in our society at the present time."[59] This association by fear is bound into a moral code in which retribution should be focused upon the cause of such fear, the deadly RR/ADers. But they are also the common enemy. Thus the community must work against an other, but also on itself.

This directive is the demand that these community groups operate as peer pressure or moral arbiters in that self-monitoring and surveillance are tied into and made public through a process of community confession. This adherence to community standards and moral surveillance reenergizes earlier modes of disciplining drivers by demanding adherence to community standards. The reinvigoration of such a discourse ties together more general desires to create and abide by so-called community standards and raises the question of whose standards are synonymous with those of the community.

The second part of the process is the negotiation of the relationship between these standards and one's self-relation. The interplay between the self-monitoring tapes and their public display and filing[60] brings one into the fold, so to speak. It does so by making one's in-car behavior a public, as opposed to private, activity. The privacy of the automobile is claimed to be another cause of road rage. Thus making behavior that was private public demands a different formation of the driving-self: a self that will, by necessity of the maintenance of face, be increasingly decorous, at least if Erving Goffman's assessment of social pressure holds true.[61] This reorientation makes public every action taken on the highway. Thus by establishing driving as a public activity, a public driving-self is demanded, replacing the private driving-self.

The manifestation of different motivations is called upon to fill the gap between desire and conduct. Rather than focusing on one's own goals, like getting somewhere on time, displaying driving skill, or punishing others for impeding one's progress, the new driving-self is asked to be both decorous and zenlike, by giving up selfish personal drives for more communal and spiritual ones. These include getting rid of the "belief and virtue of setting rigid and fastest possible travel times."[62] Instead of "making good time," drivers should "make time good" by enjoying the time spent driving, through conversation, music, food, and other "creative ideas." This new orientation also entails not gaining self-esteem from automotive competition. Instead, drivers should gain self-esteem through treating themselves and others "royally." As Dr. Larson states, "Life needs to be lived, truly lived while driving, not put on hold as a series of competitions unfolds."[63] Furthermore, drivers should not attach value to stopping other hurried drivers but instead should recognize that they are probably running late. After all, a display of courtesy quickly melts the combative attitude of both drivers. Last, we should welcome diversity on the roads and not look to ridicule those who are different.

This seemingly un-American type of reorientation, Larson assured the House subcommittee, will not seriously affect the American competitive spirit: "Again, there's nothing wrong with competition per se; it is an attitude that constantly propels individuals within a culture to come up with something better. A competitive and democratic culture appears to be better than culture based on religious, authoritarian, socialistic, or communistic designs. We are evolving from cultural values derived from God, kings, dictators, or doles, to one derived from man-made law, and market forces."[64] Thus the establishment of a community on the road creates a special place where "typical American behavior" can be put aside. The establishment of community, we are assured, does not correspond to communism or even the dole. Instead, for *one's own benefit* we are told to be a part of a community. The orientation is not for establishing a commonality among individuals who then work together to reach a shared goal. Instead, community becomes another means to activate self-motivation: in this case a motivation based on one's personal safety. As with so many other neoliberal strategies for social improvement, market forces are said to provide the ultimate solution. This appeal intensifies the sense that everyone is ultimately responsible for their own safety. This mirrors the neoliberal attempt to shift the focus of health from the state to the individual. Samantha King explains how this is done in relation to philanthropy. The similarity of the two modes of governing is that both community and philanthropy have an automatic positive connotation, yet in each case, the Race for the Cure in King's example and the QDCs, the brunt of responsibility shifts from the state to individuals for insuring one's own well-being.

### The Woman Driver Revisited

Interestingly, the community type of noncompetitive driving was called for as an answer to 1950s hot-rodding. With road rage, at least as it is defined in the general sense, the competition is not specific to formalized or even ritualized circumstances. A road rage race can break out at any time, anywhere, and between anyone. There are no specific rules for winning, and there are no cheering spectators. Instead, there are only dangerous and deadly possibilities. But two differences demand explanation. The first has already been noted. Road rage is said to infect everyone. Hot-rodding was seen as a specifically male and youth activity and was dealt with as such. Of great concern, in fact, is the sense that road rage is not a specifically male activity. There is great anxiety that women are catching up to men when it comes to aggressive driving. Whereas women have historically been the beacon of hope for safe driving advocates and the benefactors of actuarial goodwill, insurance rates and driving citations are rising for women of all ages. Numerous attempts have been made to explain this behavior. The explanations vary from technological determinism ("the SUV made me do it"), changing demands (the increase in family plus work stress), and male-female competition (If men can drive fast, then why can't women?). What is never offered as an explanation is that the essentialized categories that have always dictated what type of driving behavior is "naturally male" and "naturally female" were both socially manufactured and socially productive. There is, then, no necessary correspondence between gender and driving.

Just as other activities and arenas have opened up to women, so too have driving and the road. In fact, there has recently been a significant increase in female-auto-mobile-travel-literature. A few books that deal explicitly with women's desire for and relationship to auto-mobility are *Driving to Detroit*, *Flaming Iguanas*, and *The Perfect Vehicle*.[65] *Passionfruit*, a magazine written by women primarily for women, deals with women traveling both domestically and abroad. Many of the stories link automobiles and the specific relationship women have to them. One of the specific issues dealt with in all of these narratives is the struggle to overcome the fear they are "naturally" supposed to have regarding cars, travel, and especially motorcycles. In both *The Perfect Vehicle* and *Flaming Iguanas*, as well as in the ethnography *Motorcycle Gangs* by Suzanne McDonald-Walker, an academic, it is incredibly obvious that fear is one of the major reasons women do not ride motorcycles.[66] It is an inhibiting factor for most, but it is even more so for women, who are "naturally" predisposed to fear them and not coincidentally the men who drive them. But if it is definitely the case with motorcycles as the most extreme example, so too is it the case when it comes to automobiles. Women are taught repeatedly by magazine articles, by parents, and in women's safety campaigns to fear them. They are a cause of fear for the parents of daughters, both for what they represent sexually and their potentially destructive capability. Daughters are far more likely to receive cellular phones from their parents as a safety measure for driving purposes than their male counterparts, and they cite automobile safety as a reason for buying cellular phones more often than men. All of this is to say that one problem safety advocates have always had is convincing women to self-monitor their driving more. It was assumed women were obsessed with safety out of fear and docility. What the new road rage campaign has allowed is a new way to bring women into the discussion. This allows for the conceptual framework that includes all drivers, not just men or a specific group of men. For instance, a story in *Time* magazine opens with a lengthy description of a woman driving a Suburban recklessly and aggressively while trying to get herself and her children to her daughter's soccer match. The anecdote ends with this articulation between women, aggression, and "our" place in the universe: "'I don't think I'm an aggressive driver,' Anne says. 'But there are a lot of bad drivers out there.' Too true, too true. But the example of Anne—prosperous, well-adjusted Anne, loving wife and mother—raises the overarching question of road anarchy. Residents of late twentieth-century America are arguably the luckiest human beings in history: the most technologically pampered, the richest, the freest things on two legs the world has ever seen. Then why do we drive like such jerks?"[67] Anne sits in as the ultimate expression of the female who shouldn't be raging on the road. As a middle-class mother, wife, and American, she, of all people, should be a docile driver; a safe driver, "By God, a good mother." The article later states that 53 percent of aggressive drivers are in fact female.[68] We have, then, in many ways come full circle regarding gender and driving. The RR/AD discourse has renewed the 1950s concern about women drivers dealt with in chapter 1, and this rearticulation involves the same stereotypical suburban mothers. Instead of taking Bobby to Boy Scouts she is now taking Meagan to soccer practice, and rather than driving a station wagon/"grocery-getter," she drives an SUV, a "glorified-grocery-getter." But, most important, rather than being the epitome of the good driver, she is now, once again, able to strike fear into the hearts of other drivers.

## Conclusion

Efforts to solve the RR/AD problem are not exactly new. They do mark an intensification of previous efforts to diminish and redirect traffic safety concerns. The most far-reaching aspect of this intensification remains to be seen. The most troubling, though, is the ease with which the RR/AD discussions came to situate all drivers as potentially problematic and therefore worthy of scrutiny. Previous chapters have largely dealt with very narrowly defined forms of conduct or very specific problem populations. RR/AD breaks with both of those patterns, and for these reasons the modes of governance are also different. The question remains as to whether these changes simply correspond to more extensive political and cultural changes, as would be suggested by neoliberal governmentality scholars like Rose, Graham Burchell, and Colin Gordon, or whether there is something unique about governing mobility that does not necessarily follow from general formulations of governance. As I suggested in the opening chapter, the creation of a disciplined mobility is nothing new. It is integral to the modern liberal state and has been a concern of governmentality from the outset. To suggest that just because much of the governance is not state-initiated or even state-funded and organized misses one of the most important points made in Foucault's lecture on governmentality. The real concern is not whether the state has become more governmental, but rather how governmental thought has come to be the operative logic for all institutions that are concerned with human conduct.

The establishment of an anti-RR/AD community may very well fit into Rose's conceptualization of how neoliberal government works. Rose goes much further in his argument. He sees community as a part of an entirely new diagram of power, one which replaces, so to speak, disciplinary power and biopower. He calls this ethico-politics. This is a reorientation of the relation between governed and governor, and rather than individualizing and normalizing disciplinarity or collectivizing and socializing biopower, ethico-politics "concerns itself with the self-techniques necessary for responsible self-government and the relations between one's obligation to oneself and one's obligation to others."[69] As shown in the discussion of QDCS, this is precisely what occurs in these self-forming, in both senses of the word, groups. They are said to come together because of commonality, though this is shown to be misleading, and they are supposed to be an aid in each member's "personality makeover project."[70] This makeover is itself the most important aspect of this new diagram. In it lies the essence of the conception of self; a safety-motivated self that must come to know "the truth of oneself" through the normalizing logic of psychology via the public confessional. It is, then, ultimately a pathology that unifies or produces an identity for this community: a pathology of fear or aggression. On the one hand is a desire to create a fear-free world, on the other a kinder-gentler driver. In either instance, established experts have validated the existence of the pathologies and prescribed community, disciplinary, and self-help solutions.

A somewhat modified version of the moral imperatives of community and driving is echoed in the What Would Jesus Drive? campaign (WWJD). The campaign garnered much fanfare upon the release of commercials in 2001–02 arguing that Jesus would not drive an SUV. What he would drive is something small and fuel-efficient. The moral imperative in operation is an extension of the New Testament Golden Rule according to the Baptist minister Rev. Jim Ball, the executive director of the Evangelical Environmental Network. "When you look at the impact of transportation on human health and on global warming and Jesus was the great physician of body and soul," Ball told *Good Morning America*. "the most basic teaching of Jesus is to love your neighbor like yourself. How can you do that when you are filling your neighbor's lungs with pollution?"[71]

Like the QDCs, the WWJD campaign depends upon a channeled form of self-reflection via a moral imperative generated through community; what one pastor calls in the campaign, "communities of faith."[72] These communities try to draw across denominations to produce an eco-auto-morality, which, like the Crusade for Traffic Safety's pledge in the 1950s, calls upon specialists and laymen alike to help in any way they can. Lawyers, doctors, professors, engineers, politicians, and especially clergy are requested to spread and validate the word. Christian drivers are asked to take the What Would Jesus Drive Pledge, which includes recognizing Christ as "the Lord of my transportation choices."[73] The pledge asks that one attempt to take alternative forms of transportation, and if that is impossible to make eco-friendly automobile decisions. In what seems like a direct response to such anti-SUV religious moral sentiment, GM sponsored the sixteen-city "Come Together and Worship Tour" in 2002 as a means of bridging any potential moral gap between Evangelical Christians and GM's automotive product. GM's sponsorship of Christian pop bands was touted as a breakthrough marketing strategy and marked a joining of religious, media, and corporate forces. This was in some ways a new form of political-economic venture criticized roundly by Christians, who saw it as selling out to the forces of Satan, and by the left, who saw it as just another usurpation of the life-world by economic forces.

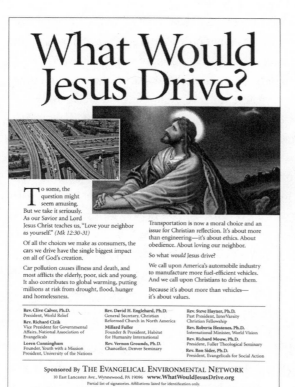

## What Would Jesus Drive?

To some, the question might seem amusing. But we take it seriously. As our Savior and Lord Jesus Christ teaches us, "Love your neighbor as yourself." (Mk 12:30-31)

Of all the choices we make as consumers, the cars we drive have the single biggest impact on all of God's creation.

Car pollution causes illness and death, and most afflicts the elderly, poor, sick and young. It also contributes to global warming, putting millions at risk from drought, flood, hunger and homelessness.

Transportation is now a moral choice and an issue for Christian reflection. It's about more than engineering—it's about ethics. About obedience. About loving our neighbor.

So what *would* Jesus drive?

We call upon America's automobile industry to manufacture more fuel-efficient vehicles. And we call upon Christians to drive them.

Because it's about more than vehicles— it's about values.

Rev. Clive Calver, Ph.D.
President, World Relief
Rev. Richard Cizik
Vice President for Governmental Affairs, National Association of Evangelicals
Loren Cunningham
Founder, Youth with a Mission President, University of the Nations

Rev. David H. Englehard, Ph.D.
General Secretary, Christian Reformed Church in North America
Millard Fuller
Founder & President, Habitat for Humanity International
Rev. Vernon Grounds, Ph.D.
Chancellor, Denver Seminary

Rev. Steve Hayner, Ph.D.
Past President, InterVarsity Christian Fellowship
Rev. Roberta Hestenes, Ph.D.
International Minister, World Vision
Rev. Richard Mouw, Ph.D.
President, Fuller Theological Seminary
Rev. Ron Sider, Ph.D.
President, Evangelicals for Social Action

Sponsored By THE EVANGELICAL ENVIRONMENTAL NETWORK
10 East Lancaster Ave., Wynnewood, PA 19096   www.WhatWouldJesusDrive.org
Partial list of signatories. Affiliations listed for identification only.

**FIGURE 30. What Would Jesus Drive?** This advertisement represents an attempt to articulate Christian values with those of environmentalists by using a play on the popular What Would Jesus Do? form of ethical reflection. "WHAT WOULD JESUS DRIVE?" PRINT AD. FROM HTTP:// WHATWOULDJESUSDRIVE .ORG/TOUR/PUBLICITY .PHP. RETRIEVED JUNE 12, 2006.

In both the religious and civic cases, a moral imperative is linked to a form of self-regulation and governance legitimated by nontraditional notions of community. Furthermore, the SUV is specifically seen as the locus of critique. As they gained in popularity during the 1980s and 1990s they have organized various moral responses, including a pro-SUV response, not simply led by their producers, but by their owners as well; a sort of SUV il Rights campaign. In 2003 the SUV Owners of America (SUVOA) led a counterattack against the What Would Jesus Drive? campaign with an ad of their own. This ad asked, "What Does Jesús Drive?" The answer, not surprisingly was an SUV, and why?, you might ask: because "For millions of people like Jesús Rivera, it's all about safety, utility and versatility. Maybe that's why they call them SUVs." The S has historically stood for Sports, but as far as how they are touted, the makers might as well have called them Safety Utility Vehicles. It is, after all, much easier to make moral claims through appeals to safety than to sport. Yet, much like CARR and CASAD, SUVOA is not exactly a grassroots organization. Jason Vines, the president of SUVOA, was not only once a vice president of communications at Ford, but the company he consults for, Stratacomm, has a client list that includes each of the big three, Ford, GM, and Daimler Chrysler, not to mention the Alliance of Automobile Manufacturers, American Highway Users Alliance, Automotive Retailing Today, *Car and Driver Magazine*, Future Truck, and the National Automobile Dealers Association. What we see, again, is an attempt to create a grassroots community that supports the ends of a specific organization or industry. Furthermore, the activation of community implies a kinship among SUV owners. SUVOA presents it as if these owners are all in some struggle together as an active membership of concerned citizens and not as a vastly dispersed group of individualistic conspicuous consumers, who, given the expense of SUV ownership, are hardly a downtrodden group struggling for their civil right to freely consume.

The fact that morality and safety have come to organize validations for and criticisms of the SUV can be viewed as either entirely obvious or somewhat surprising. As I argued earlier, safety has become a mode of morality. It is not simply a term to describe a relative relationship to risk or harm. Instead, people consider the lack of safety as immoral and a truth. To be unsafe is to be wrong, stupid, and potentially immoral. It is a damning condemnation to call someone unsafe. When we compare the pro-SUV and anti-SUV campaigns, it should come as no surprise that they both depend upon the same matrix of statements to defend their respective positions. They both depend on the discourses of morality, safety, and freedom. The antis see SUVs as an immoral choice that is destructive of the environment and humankind, at the individual and societal level. The rhetoric of freedom is couched in terms of civic responsibility and the enunciation of a freedom from formulation (harm, smog, pollution, Middle East oil dependency). The pros use morality by invoking family, civil rights, and choice, while claiming they are safer and that they produce the freedom to access points otherwise inaccessible by auto. The calculus needed to determine whether SUVs as a whole cause more deaths or save more lives than economy cars and sedans is not only beyond this author, but seems to be beyond the reach of contemporary statistics. All the variables can't be taken into account. Certainly, in a collision between an SUV and a Prius (Toyota's first hybrid-powered car touted by the WWJD movement's leader as the car Jesus would drive) my money is on the SUV,

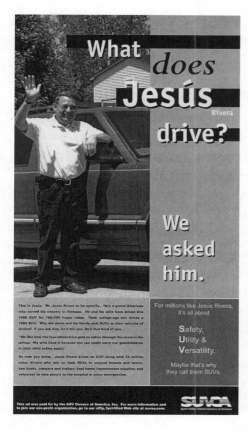

**FIGURE 31.**
**What Does Jesús Drive?**
The What Does Jesús Drive?
campaign of 2003 was an attempt
by the automotive industry public
relations front group Sport Utility
Vehicle Owners of America, to
counter the What Would Jesus
Do? campaign. "WHAT DOES JESÚS
DRIVE?" SUV OWNERS OF AMERICA.
PRINT AD. FROM HTTP://WWW.SUVOA
.COM/MEDIA/ADS.CFM. RETRIEVED
JUNE 12, 2006.

yet an SUV-free world of Priuses would almost certainly be a safer world in terms of the crash, the environment, and a lack of an oil-driven maintenance of empire. Even so, such an argument fails to address all the other considerations taken into account when individual drivers consider the benefits and costs of the SUV. Safety, as I've been arguing, is not the only measure by which we might or should weigh in on concerns of mobility.

Gender would appear to be a nearly constant organizing thematic in the discourses of safety and mobility. The reemergence of the dangerous woman driver is important for more than a few reasons. By establishing that women are equally, if not more, inclined to be RR/ADers, the experts reinvigorated debate over who is the better driver, represented women in a new suburban-stereotyped fashion, and, most important, disrupted the easy articulation between women and safety. This comes at a time when motherhood was both the focus of Volvo-like car advertisements and the moral backbone of the MADD campaign. The typical response of the media is shocked disbelief. The news stories follow a narrative path that begins with "Isn't it great that women are catching up with men in all areas of society?" and ends with "Unfortunately, they've also taken on some bad characteristics of men." This both reinforces the stereotypes regarding docility and aggression and establishes moral criteria by which to judge allegedly natural feminine and masculine behavior. The seemingly inescapable gender comparisons are thus a means of governing mobility while mobility further becomes a means of governing gender.

Finally, RR/AD provides an example of radical articulation at its most inventive. A whole gamut of driving offenses, violations, and inconsiderations are brought under the umbrella of RR/AD. Furthermore, the process provides a morality, a motive, and a pathology to the visible practices said to signify states of rage and aggression. Thus nearly all driving conduct can be framed within a dichotomy of aggressive or emotionally intelligent driving. Speeding is no longer a traffic violation but a sign of aggressive tendencies that are at any minute likely to escalate into rage and, ultimately, violence. Moreover, speeding is also a sign of an unintelligent or immature disregard for community standards and one's own life. It is not the informed decision of a driver who has assessed the balance of one's skill, the mechanical prowess of one's vehicle, and the prevailing driving conditions. This act of closure has to a degree prevailed for decades, but it has rarely if ever been pathologized and moralized. By closing off the potential to rearticulate personal or even communal codes of conduct, Rose argues, ethico-political modes of governance may prove most alarming and destructive.

# CHAPTER 7

# SAFETY TO SECURITY
*Future Orientations of Automobility*

This concluding chapter is an attempt to understand an emergent formulation for the governance of automobility. As the title makes evident, concern for security, national security specifically, is replacing traffic safety as the problem to be solved through the governance of automobility. Dangers arise when attempting to characterize the emergent, to, in essence, predict the future. But it is dangerous to make no attempt to understand how unacceptable futures could come to pass. And the future described below should be regarded as unacceptable. It is a future in which automobiles will be made to drive themselves. Drivers will be free to conduct all forms of business and leisure from the seat of their automobile, not having to concern themselves with the tedium of paying attention to stop signs, highway exits, and the always present danger of other drivers' errors or ire. The dream of such a future has been part of the American popular imaginary for three-quarters of a century. Yet such a future is entirely dependent upon a network of communication, control, and command technologies (c3) that will create a degree of surveillance and control over the automobile population historically only imagined in science fiction visions of horrific futures. The aforementioned freedom it will provide drivers and the immense gains in traffic safety such a system would create have historically been the reasons such technologies were deemed desirable. Under the guidance of the Department of Homeland Security

(DHS) the reasons have changed. National security is now used to legitimate such a future. And as will be shown, such a future is being experimented with in national security battles in the United States and in war theaters abroad. Automobility figures as an integral element in these wars on terror. As evidenced in previous chapters, this is not the first time the rhetoric of war has been used as a means of explaining how to govern automobility. I will begin with two war metaphors as a starting point for examining the shift from safety to security.

For President Truman and, shortly thereafter, President Eisenhower the still-recent success of military and civilian operations and organization during World War II was a model for approaching the perceived danger posed by automobility. The first war metaphor is clearly witnessed in a photo and caption from the driver's education manual *Man and the Motorcar* (1949) (see figure 32).[1] The photo on the top features a group of soldiers marching in perfectly synchronized order; the caption reads, "In wartime we practice self-discipline for the common good. Driving also calls for self-discipline for everyone's safety."[2] If it's not yet apparent, the preceding chapters in part outlined a series of attempts to do just that; create forms of "self-discipline for everyone's safety." The project of government agencies and other agents of governance, such as the insurance industry, attempted to discipline the population and individuals alike in order to reduce traffic fatalities. The preceding chapters also tell the story of how automobility and safety have been used as a means of maintaining the unequal relations of power that have worked against women, youth, the working class, and people of color. In these ways, disciplined mobility, in the name of safety, has been a mechanism for social control.

*Man and the Motorcar* presented a second war-infused metaphor for understanding the importance of automotive safety: the atomic bomb. It appeared in a photo facing the marching soldiers and featured a mushroom cloud rising above the waves of what can only be imagined by an American audience as a far-off tropical land. The accompanying caption reads, "Today's great problem is modern man's control of power." This second metaphor was both timely, in that the atomic bomb was newly configuring global relations of power, and prescient. As I explain below, this war metaphor is more apt than might at first be imagined given the political changes in the United States that have followed the attacks of 9/11/2001. The automobile's imag-

**FIGURES 32A and 32B. Marching Soldiers and Mushroom Cloud**
These two images from the driver's education manual *Man and the Motorcar*
metaphorically represent a shift in how automobility has been governed over the
past half century: from disciplinarity to control. ALBERT WHITNEY, *MAN AND THE
MOTORCAR* (NEW YORK: NEW JERSEY DEPARTMENT OF LAW AND PUBLIC SAFETY, 1949),
4–5.

ined destructive potential is newly organizing attempts to govern automobility, not according to a logic of safety but in terms of national security. As Whitney explained over fifty years ago, *"intelligent control"* was the means for dealing with power, whether it be "obtained from atomic fission, or from the combustion of a gasoline-air mixture."[3] The shift in emphasis from "self-discipline" to *"intelligent control"* mirrors the broad shift described as that from a disciplinary society to a control society. Not only is automobility a useful example for understanding how such a shift has been occurring, but, as I will argue, recently formulated means for controlling automobility are experiments in exerting more general control of the population. What follows is an examination of the shift from safety to security and the accompanying shift from disciplinarity to control. Strange as it may seem, the automobile's power is no longer simply metaphorically related to war. In the war on terror and homeland security, the automobile needs to be controlled precisely because it has come to be problematized as a bomb.

I have been careful to ground previous chapters in a historical archive in order to avoid generalizations about the all-encompassing nature of automobility and to emphasize that not all forms of automobility are equal in their effects and political importance. So even as in this chapter I explain how safety is being replaced by security as the primary means for problematizing the governance of automobility, I do not mean to suggest that such a change negates the importance of class or race. Altering driving behavior through scare tactics, traffic rules, education programs, and surveillance has been a massive undertaking by a cluster of invested governing agencies. Previous chapters have shown how a series of safety crises have created different problematic mobile populations which have been the target of disciplining campaigns. Women, youth, motorcyclists, truckers, and minorities have all been claimed to be a threat to themselves and to others. As groups who historically have been lacking in political, economic, and cultural capital gained access to automobility or created different forms of automobility, their mobile behavior was described as a threat. These supposed threats were almost exclusively responded to in terms of traffic safety and police surveillance. If the danger they posed is instead understood in terms of how increased mobility disrupts social order, then safety, at least partially, needs to be understood in political terms. One question that follows is, How has safety been used to alter or maintain asymmetric relations of power? This is not just a question of who gets to drive and with how much latitude as if the equation is simply car=freedom=equality. As noted previously, automobility and the freedom it promises need to be understood as an obligation as well. The system of automobility in the United States in many ways demands that one must drive a car. The disciplining of mobility organized through traffic safety is thus a means of keeping the system running smoothly, even as it often works as a means of keeping systems of social inequality intact.

This said, the relationship between the state and citizen under a rubric of safety could be described as a sort of paternalism, or what Michel Foucault has described as pastoralism. In this conception, each paternal subject of the state, the "safe citizen," is looked after as an individual subject worthy of care and protection and as an integral part of the population as a whole. There is an assumed symbiotic relationship between individual and populace in which what is good for the individual subject benefits the population more generally. Health, or the maintenance and creation of the productive capacity of the body—biopower—is a good example. The general health of the society, the "public health," depends upon the relative health of the individuals of which it is comprised. Healthy individuals, for instance, minimize the spread of communicable disease and decrease the overall strain placed on the health care system, which allows for the better allocation of medical resources, which leads to healthier individuals, and so on. Traffic safety has been similarly imagined and in fact is in some governmental quarters treated as a public health issue. In order to create a safe driving environment, every individual's driving behavior is targeted for alteration both for his or her own benefit and for the benefit of other drivers. Thus a safe driving environment depends upon safe individual drivers, and the safer the environment, the safer the individual. Two coalescing changes in the political formulation of citizen to state are altering this formulation for the governance of automobility. The first will be characterized as a shift in how automobility, and mobility generally, is problematized. This shift is characterized as that from safety to security. The second alteration has been gaining force since the 1960s, when technological solutions to traffic safety were beginning to be imagined as more effective than driving behavior modification.[4] Increasingly, the technological solutions work through c3 networks, the military leading the way in their development.

The most notable attacks against U.S. hegemony have been carried out with or on transportation technologies. The 9/11 attacks on the World Trade Center and the Pentagon are the most spectacular examples of a transportation technology being turned into a weapon—becoming a bomb—but it is only one among numerous cases in which transportation technologies have been used as weapons against U.S. interests, for example, in Beirut in 1982, at the Twin Towers in 1994, in Oklahoma City in 1995, on the USS *Cole* in 2000, etc. The car bomb has been a weapon of choice of the IRA and of liberation forces in Palestine and elsewhere. Various forms of mobility, as points of reaching the mass, as signifiers of the global reach of capital, have also been the object of attack (most notably the airplane and train), and under section 801 of the first PATRIOT Act (Providing Appropriate Tools to Intercept and Obstruct Terrorism) attacks on mass transportation systems were newly criminalized as acts of terrorism, not simply as crimes unto themselves. At border crossings, airport terminals, roadside police interrogations, ports, and security checks at government buildings what is often referred to as freedom of movement has become one site where the homeland's security is seen to be at risk. Conceptions of who has such freedom and of how, when, where, and with what velocity it can be enacted have all changed. As the DHS Website states, "The increasing mobility and destructive potential of modern terrorism has [*sic*] required the United States to rethink and rearrange fundamentally its systems for border and transportation security."[5] Yet mobility is also imagined as a productive force for ensuring homeland security, as a number of programs call upon the auto-mobile citizen to expand the capacities of state surveillance. For instance, the Terrorism Information and Prevention System called for citizens to keep on eye out for potential terrorist activity. The three hundred thousand transportation industry workers were called upon by the American Trucking Association and the DHS to take part in Highway Watch, which would conscript truckers as part of a mobile surveillance system, an effort we've seen previously (see the discussion of truckers and CBs in chapter 4). This isn't to say we are simply facing a more repressive form of power in which we are constantly being told, "No. You can not enter [or leave] here," though for many this has been the case.[6] Rather, how mobility is governed has changed. It is in essence a question of how mobility has been differently problematized. For one thing, the space of governance has changed significantly. The advent of the DHS and of the global war on terror, as much as the first attacks on the U.S. mainland in nearly two centuries, has turned all of global space, all terrain, into a war zone. Under this new dispensation, we must ask to what degree the logic of national security now organizes policing mechanisms in the United States and abroad. But the secrecy of terrorists creates a situation in which combatants cannot be known in any field of battle, which means everyone will be policed as if they are potential terrorists. At the same time, all citizens are asked to join in the war on terror as part of DHS initiatives. This alteration and bifurcation in the relationship between the state and citizenry is particularly telling in terms of automobility.

One of the problematic elements of such attacks for a military operating under the Revolution in Military Affairs (RMA) and biopolitical formations of empire is that the suicide bomber makes apparent "the ontological limit of biopower in its most tragic and revolting form."[7] Whereas RMA military strategy minimizes its own military casualties in acknowledgment of the productive capacity of life, the suicide bomber inverts this notion to acknowledge and exploit the destructive (resistant) capacity of life. As a problematic of governance, the suicide bomber exposes the limits of disciplinarity as a means of governing at a distance, that is, organizing, regulating, and making productive the mobility of individuals and the population alike without direct governmental control.[8] If all automobiles are potential bombs, then in a time when the U.S. government is operating under a state of perpetual warfare, governing at a distance cannot merely depend upon panopticism and disciplinarity to create docile citizens. In a biopolitical order the pastoral relation of state and subject makes life the end-goal of and motor for creating a productive population and, thereby, a productive nation. When life is not invested as a desired end equally by state and citizen, life is treated not only as that which must be groomed and cared for, but also as a constant, immanent threat which needs diffusing or extinguishing.[9]

The governance of automobility, then, needs to be understood in terms of this new problematic, mobility as immanent threat. As I have shown, over the past fifty or sixty years automobility has been imagined as an arena fraught with danger to the citizen subject. The question was, How can we keep citizens from endangering themselves as well as others? The problem posed by transportation technologies and their attendant citizen subjects was not only their mobility per se, but rather whether it would create a problem in ensuring safe travel. In what has been described as the new normal, a state of perpetual war,[10] the subject is no longer treated as a becoming accident, but a becoming bomb. The accident is a formulation through which a set of internalized modes of safe conduct and safe technologies can be activated and initiated in order to save mobile subjects from themselves. For the regime of homeland security in the United States, it is not the safety of citizens that is at stake, but rather the stability of empire's social order generally and more the security of the state form specifically.[11] It is a war in which the state form fears, all that may become problematic, become bomb. So the new mode of problematization treats all mobilities as potential bombs. Technologies of control are being developed and applied to the automobile as a means of addressing such perceived threats.

**Auto-control Society**

Control society is an emergent formation of power that according to Gilles Deleuze corresponds to a "particular kind of machine . . . cybernetic machines and computers."[12] Their modus operandi is not, as this quote might seem to imply, technologically determined. In order to understand the complexities and contours of this new formation "you must analyze the collective arrangements of which the machines are just one component."[13] As I've argued throughout, disciplinarity in many ways structured earlier forms of automobility. Even though the space of automobility is not limited by clearly demarcated spaces of confinement, the processes of surveillance, testing, knowledge production, repetition, self-reflection, internalization of the gaze, and the partitioning and regularity of space worked in an attempt to produce docile mobile subjects. During the period discussed in previous chapters, the use of cybernetic and computer technologies, as they apply to automobility and safety, began to take root. This application of c3 technologies, as witnessed through the integration of two-way radio in fleet scenarios, allowed for the coordination of movement from a distance while increasing the range of surveillance. In this sense, the desire to control specific fleets of vehicles, like those of the police or taxis companies, has been in operation since the late 1920s. For the most part, however, the application of cybernetic and computer technologies has been seen as the ultimate tool for fixing an unsafe automobility system. In this imagined future, driver error would be eliminated from the equation through the creation of fully auto-controlled automobiles. The imagined future of the automobile system answered to the dreams of a perfectly efficient and perfectly safe driving environment. Under the truth regime of DHS, auto-control imagines itself as the ultimate sapper. Space is not a minefield; mobility is a mine.

One element of the model of the control society is the management of access to space. That is, the ability to be mobile, to move from one place to another, can be governed at the level of the individual. Within a disciplinary regime such access took place in terms of the precept, particular forms of mobility operated according to the rules of conduct in that space which couldn't necessarily disallow access to mobility in general or to particular spaces according to who but rather only according to how. For instance, driving might be governed according to population (only those aged sixteen and older) and by the rules of conduct of the road (at certain speeds, in certain directions, in particular types of vehicles). Automobility and the spaces open to it were controlled according to a set of precepts which, as we've seen, were surveilled and in theory internalized. It was only at particular checkpoints (with the exception of some of the discriminatory practices discussed in previous chapters), most notably borders, though secondarily antidrunk driving roadblocks, and in cases of witnessed rule infractions that the *who* of mobility came into being through technologies of verification, most often the driver's license, but also through technologies such as proof of insurance, automobile registration, and license plates.[14] As is explained further below, these forms of verification can be made mobile and not just activated by the checkpoint. However, through the integration of various communications, insurantial, verification, and information technologies the precept/surveillance couplet can be replaced by the password.

As Deleuze argues, we need to see into the future before the dawning of this control society in order to prepare modes of resistance. He looks to Felix Guattari's imagined future in which everyone must use an electronic card to move into and out of particular spaces. The card can be made to work one day at one time, valid one day but not the next. It is not the precept, the rule for conduct, that determines access, but rather the constantly modulatable password, actualized via the pass-card. If we take this future as our starting point, we can move in time in two directions. Forward, we can imagine not simply specific sites through which one must pass or cards which stand in as a sign of one's identity. Rather, as the recent science fiction movies *Gatacca* and *Minority Report* make clear, the body, in conjunction with biometric recognition technologies, becomes its own technology of verification. But in both of these movies there are still checkpoints or mobile surveillance forces that must surveil and search space for individuals. In simple terms it is still the space that is the site of control, not the very mobility of any given individual or population. For this second possibility to come into being, all of space would be a perpetual checkpoint. In Deleuzean terms this space would be neither striated nor smooth, but smoothly striated. Striated space is that which has been organized according to a set of rules and patterns for how the space can be used, traversed, and even imagined. Smooth space has no such rules. There would not be a grid covering space according to a set of coordinates, as if on a map with boundaries, but rather each and every point in space would always be the center of spatial organization for the individual at that point. Forces of control would always be focused on every occupied point, but only on those points occupied. Mobility, not space, would become that which is the imagined "site" of control. Furthermore, the trace of movement would become the predictor for what might happen in the future. For this to happen, all mobilities would have to be fully monitored, a database of recorded movement would need to be generated, an algorithm would make predictable sense of such movement, and all mobilities would need to be potentially remotely controlled. That is the dystopic vision of a control society future: all individuals remotely controllable. And in fact, *Minority Report* provides just such a vision when the automobile that John Anderton, the movie's protagonist played by Tom Cruise, is using to escape an unjustified police arrest is remotely controlled in an attempt to bring Anderton to the police station and to justice. The automobile, so long envisioned as a mode of escape, is turned into a mobile jail cell.

### Historical Homelands and Future Combat Zones

It is in the past and the past future that we can see the beginnings (for technological, military, economic, and political reasons) of this future auto-control society. The automobile, particularly in the United States, where, as previously noted, it currently is used for over 90 percent of travel,[15] became the primary mode of transport over the past century. Even given the various nightmare scenarios regarding its ultimate demise, this astounding saturation of use continues to increase. Given the enormity and ubiquity of automobile use and its continued growth, an obvious point of investigation of the technologies and machinic arrangements of the (be)coming control society is automobility. The automobile has been a site of remote control innovations for years, and such control has primarily been achieved via a network of communications technologies. As noted above, it was most often done at the behest of safety and economic efficiency.[16] What follows is a brief history of some of the developments and imagined plans for creating a fully controlled automobile/highway system. More important, through an examination of these imagined futures we can discern just how deeply rooted and widely spread the desire for an auto-control society has been over the past century. Furthermore, contemporary imaginings regarding the automobile are taking place in two distinct arenas. First, there were a number of pre-9/11 initiatives for what have variously been called Automated Highway Systems (AHS), Intelligent Transportation Systems (ITS), and the Intelligent Vehicle Highway System (IVHS); research and development began in the early 1990s when Congress allocated a billion dollars of start-up capital. Second, the U.S. military is currently developing a program called Combat Zones That See (CTS), touted for initial use as part of the U.S. military's operations in Baghdad. These two historically and technologically overlapping initiatives need to be thought of in tandem as a set of theaters for experimenting with implementations of control society. It is not simply that there is a desire to control automotive conduct, but increasingly, under the logic of perpetual war, the more far-reaching consequences are that the automobile acts as the site for experimentation on the control of all bodily mobility.

The history of the imagined future of the automobile tells us much about not simply the future, but the underlying cultural, political, and economic logics that continue to animate dreams of technological and social mastery over everyday life. Central to nearly all these envisioned futures is the fully automatic automobile, or what is often called the driverless car. In these visions, the driver becomes passenger in his technologically chauffeured, streamlined mobile "rocket ship" (I employ gender specificity here for historical accuracy). As recently as 1997, the year 2005 was predicted as the year of commercial viability of an AHS.[17] This is not too surprising. Ever since the World's Fair in 1939, predicting the driverless automobile has been an integral part of envisioning and marketing the future.

As one of the earliest and certainly the most widely cited and recognized of such futuristic visions, GM's exhibit Highways and Horizons (often called

Futurama), designed by Norman Bel Geddes, provided what would become a fairly common sensibility of what this future world might look like. In this vision cars were controlled by radio—a feat accomplished in 1924, in which the car was said to be driven "as if a phantom were at the wheel." Somehow the frightening, otherworldly nature of these technological feats would soon disappear.[18] The set of six enormous dioramas was viewed by fair visitors from moving seats, which ran on a track surrounding the exhibit. Futurama envisioned a highway system that seamlessly drifted into, through, and back out of the rapidly expanding "Midwestern City of 1960." The driverless automobile and its attendant highway system were not only the engine for suburban expansion, but also an individuated coach to the furthest reaches of the United States, where mountains, the monotony of the plains, and vast bodies of water all would easily be surmounted in a mere twenty years. Thus the automobile would motor commerce and family adventure; free markets aligned with the freedom of movement that was said to be part of the natural makeup of everyday Americans' frontier spirit. It is vitally important to note that this is a vision of the automobile as a vision of *the* future. The automobile was conceived of as the key to both understanding and implementing a supposed better life, a freer, yet controllable future.

GM would revisit the future numerous times over the next six decades, most notably with their 1964 update of Futurama, again at a New York World's Fair. During the 1950s the future popped up everywhere for GM. In particular, their Firebird series of cars (the "laboratory on wheels") with its turbine engine was presented as "an amazing experience in automatic car control." In addition to being displayed at promotional events and GM's various Motorama exhibits, the car appeared in 1956 in GM's short targeted at women "Design for Dreaming," in which the driver proclaims, "Firebird II to control tower, we are about to take off on the highway of tomorrow," at which point the happily middle-class couple drive into the future. The Firebird's electronic guidance system was said to be ready for the "electronic highway of the future," which GM, along with General Electric and others, flirted with throughout the decade. Given the postwar and cold war intermingling of scientific exuberance and anxiety, GM's auto-future is no great surprise, as it offers up a vision of social progress through better science and personal satisfaction through the consumption of the fruits of that science. But at a time when the Interstate Highway System was really taking off in its already-

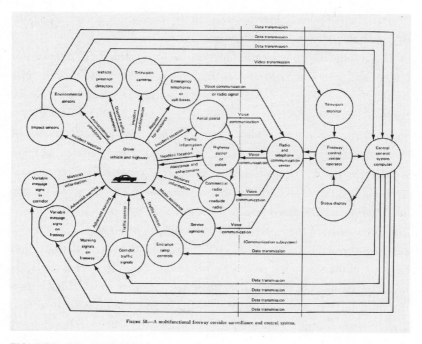

FIGURE 58.—A multifunctional freeway corridor surveillance and control system.

**FIGURE 33. Control Diagram**
U.S. Department of Transportation's *Urban Freeway Surveillance and Control: State of the Art.*

antiquated, nonelectronic form, the notion that what America needed was a new highway system, prior to the implementation of the original one, seems in retrospect more than a bit far-fetched. What does become clear is the long-standing desire for a truly free, yet electronically controlled, freeway system. The freedom derived from the task of driving is, however, always dependent upon an obligation to an electronic system. This electronic highway would pass from designer's dream to traffic engineer's Holy Grail.

The diagram above, from the U.S. Department of Transportation's *Urban Freeway Surveillance and Control: State of the Art* (or, more accurately, *art of the state*), makes apparent the auto-centric nature of auto-control (see figure 33). This particular vision of control appeared in 1972, before a number of events, including the OPEC oil crisis, extensive emissions controls, and safety standards, radically changed the driving environment. Onboard computers, GPS systems, black boxes, and other communications devices had not yet arrived. In other words, many of the regulatory and technological forces currently at play didn't exist then or had yet to be integrated into the automobile.

This diagram of power nevertheless points to some of the underlying methods and goals of such "surveillance and control."

The automobile quite clearly functions as the central focus of such initiatives and in essence operates as the sender, message, and receiver in a communicative network encompassing the automobile driver and "central control." Notice in the diagram the single circle titled "Vehicle presence detectors." Three important points can be gleaned from a closer analysis of this single node in the diagram. First, "presence" is primary, as it is the space which is imagined to both preexist the vehicle and supersede its importance. After all, it is the "freeway" (I withhold irony for the moment) being surveilled and controlled, while the vehicle is treated as a potential problem, a disrupting force in that spatial system through its potential to create inefficiencies—breakdowns, accidents, collective congestion. Second, this singular point in the diagram represents nine specific groupings of technologies, including though not limited to photoelectric, infrared, sonic, radar, inductive loop, magnetic, pneumatic, hydraulic, chemical, and smoke detectors. Thus various communicative forms are made conspicuous to the freeway monitoring systems. (Can we think of the exhaust system as a medium and $CO_2$ emissions as a message or sign? We must if we are to understand how these elements "speak" to each other.) The freeway is not only imagined as a track on which cars are guided and moved along, but also turned into a surveillant recognition machine in a control network. This recognition is just one element in what is imagined as a circulatory system akin to that in the human body, in which various other systems recognize and respond to potential blockages, inadequacies of flow, the movement of contaminated elements, or even full-blown rupture. The system, then, is what is at stake, and in many ways it is a closed system. Individual mobilities are merely an element to be managed for the relative health of the whole.

In many ways this was the operative logic for AHS right up to 9/11. Government research money and the promised profits of a new market fueled extensive research, development, and public relations hype. News stories told of a not-too-distant future in which highway deaths would be radically diminished by eliminating human error from the system. Furthermore, the cost benefits of developing a far more efficient automated system as compared to those of building more highway lanes were said to make undeniable sense. Within the economic sector AHS was described as a boom industry worthy of capital investment and was said to represent a quantum leap in efficiency and the minimization of productivity losses. On the consumer level it was sold as a way to expand freedom and ensure greater safety. AHS would turn the car into an efficient, networked mobile office and a safe media-savvy family room. These networked capabilities were not only a consumer-driven option, but also the means by which this newly automated highway could be made to function. As in early models of highway management, a C3 system was envisioned as the synaptic trigger for such dreams.

The history of the convergence or synergy of communications and automobiles goes back much further than is often imagined.[19] GPS units, satellite radio, and even GM's OnStar system are merely three of the recent combinations of communications and automotive technologies. But, as explained in regard to 1970s "art of the state," the automobile has been understood as primarily a mobile communicative actor in a larger system. Yet the automobile wasn't exactly a networked actor, but rather a sign emitter. In the newer version of AHS/IVHS adjacent automobiles speak to each other while also speaking, more broadly, to the system. Networking capability is what has made and will continue to make the expansion of surveillance and ultimately control possible. The system doesn't just depend on the networking capability. Rather, the networking is the system. As a result, the theory of how a workable AHS/IVHS system should be created has changed radically over the past thirty years. Rather than a ground-up central control system, recent attempts have envisioned the networking and integration of already existent technologies, including mobile telephony, GPS, light-emitting diodes (LED), satellite radio, black boxes, digital video recorders, computer processors as well as a host of internal engine, tire, weather, and performance monitors. These technologies and others have been used most extensively in private sphere fleet applications and by the military (more on this later). Integrated Communications and Navigation is the industry catch-all for such so-called services. "Every new wireless location tool that has appeared in the marketplace has been used in fleet tracking systems of one variety or another," claims one industry Website.[20] The economic gains associated with employee and asset surveillance and control have pushed trucking firms and rental car companies to the forefront of such applications. The network is altered by and integrative of existent technologies and adaptable to new ones as they come on board. Of equal importance, each car is no longer imagined as a problem to be overcome (how to avoid congestion, breakdown, the accident), but rather as the very means by which the system comes into being. Each automobile is a mobile intelligence-collecting machine, data processing unit, and capable communicator that passes along information to other cars, all of which is then further collected, made predictive, and acted upon by a smart highway.

In control society, the stability and maintenance of a system are not necessarily what are at stake. In fact, it is precisely adaptability and mutability that signify and fuel its health and success. It is a constantly unfolding set of assemblages in response to changing scenarios, goals, and speeds. Yet the rhetoric used by DHS's first leader, Tom Ridge, was that of systems maintenance: "The Department of Homeland Security is committed to further securing our nation's highways, mass transit systems, railways, waterways and pipelines, each of which is critical to ensuring the freedom of mobility and economic growth."[21] In Ridge's words, rhetoric diverges from tactic, while maintaining the ironic stance on freedom of mobility. Securing here is seen as stasis; in Texas they might say, "to hold down the fort." But what happens when the state form shifts from the fortification of a position to fortifying a means of control? How can we think of security not in terms of homeland defense, but in terms of offensive (in both senses of the term) mobilizations? Can automobility become a means for an extension of control, not simply a threat to a fortified position?

If, as I argue, the earlier auto-mobile individual was subject to the normalizing power of safety, what animates the subject of security? Deleuze suggests that in a society of control the individual is replaced by the dividual; a modulating subject adjustable (able to adjust?) to differing expectations for productivity, consumption, and political conduct. The vision of a control society which Deleuze describes is one that demands flexible agents, while the rhetoric of free market neoliberal apologists equates flexibility with freedom and choice. This disconnect marks a point of seeming contradiction in discussions between the freedom-inducing potential of auto-controlled mobility and its network-dependent formation. As outlined in the introduction and exemplified in this book as a whole, power has been treated in a Foucauldian/Deleuzean sense, in which the freedom of movement in control society is not simply a break with the repressive confinement of disciplinarity. In this formulation, freedom is not counterposed to power, as if power is only that which limits freedom. Rather, freedom of movement is both the problematic for control and the motor that powers its expansion; in Foucauldian terms, power is always productive. It is through the mobile subject that expanded and flexible forms of productivity, consumption, and control are made possible. Yet, as the DHS has made so abundantly clear, mobility is also seen as a threat to the very infrastructural networks by which the mobility of U.S. capital and military expansion/excursion is enacted. It thus should come as no surprise that the most autonomous, adaptable, and modulatable form of mobility, automobile travel, is a preeminent battlefield in the war on terror domestically and abroad.

In July 2003, the Defense Advanced Research Projects Agency (DARPA) announced it planned to create CTS and recruit private industry to do the research and development work necessary for such creation. The Department of Defense's "high risk," "high payoff"[22] research arm wanted to "produce video understanding algorithms embedded in surveillance systems for automatically monitoring video feeds to generate for the first time, the reconnaissance, surveillance, and targeting information needed to provide close-in, continuous, always-on support for military operations in urban terrain."[23] DARPA claimed these objectives were technologically feasible[24] and, more important, militarily necessary where "Military Operations in Urban Terrain (MOUT) are fraught with danger."[25] What DARPA called for, in essence, was the full surveillance of mobility in a circumscribed zone. What would seem to be a monumental administrative and technological task was, according to DARPA, not simply possible, but accomplishable with fairly simple and readily available technologies, items they call COTS (Commercial Off The Shelf). CTS is an appeal to existing private industry surveillance specialists to create an all-seeing and all-knowing surveillance apparatus. Such an apparatus, DARPA hoped, would provide the exact sort of intelligence needed in RMA-inspired wars, which are built around intelligence collection and the minimization of loss of American lives. The specific way CTS will operate and the means by which it will do so provide evidence for clarifying three integral logics of the terror war.

First, as numerous civil liberties watchdogs and military specialists have made clear, CTS could easily be transferred not only from a war zone to the homeland, but from urban centers to expansive spaces. As one Pentagon researcher claims, the program "seems to have more to do with domestic surveillance than a foreign battlefield and more to do with the Department of Homeland Security than the Department of Defense."[26] If we believe this sort of military intelligence regarding CTS, then we must treat the war in Iraq as in part an experimental theater in which tactics for future modes of homeland governance are being invented, tested, honed, and advertised. That is, the use of such technologies and their attendant media spectacularization make ready not only the technologies, but the American media audience, which is being primed for their eventual use at home. As I argue above, in this new state of war, the state of exception, all terrain has become a battlefield. The war on terror is being conducted not simply on enemies abroad, but upon citizens in the homeland. After CTS is battle-tested abroad, it very well could be implemented in the United States.

Second, the operation of CTS is built upon existing technologies and is easily transferable to the U.S. context. As is true of IVHS, the strength and affordability of these technologies is their networkability. Simple technologies can be made complex through their integration. CTS combines digital surveillance cameras directly linked to a processing unit, which can transmit already analyzed and compressed data, thereby significantly reducing the amount of bandwidth needed if all the data captured by camera were transmitted to a central processor. Via a network of video cameras the entirety of a spatial field of governance could, in theory, be surveilled in real time. This alone is not groundbreaking. What is new is the recognition software under development for automobiles and movement. Even this is simply an extension of facial recognition technology. However, with facial recognition technology the face or identity of a conspicuous subject comes from an existent database. Some process of identifying a particular individual or population as dangerous is used to create a compendium of risky identities, and facial recognition technologies comb the data looking for matches. With CTS, however, identity is replaced by mobility; the past (an accretion of the past) is replaced by the future (that which probably will come to pass).

Last, mobility itself has now been given an identity. Not simply the individual who is mobile, but in this instance the automobile (not necessarily the driver) is provided an "intelligence" or is made into an acting being. The activity of the being is used to predict the future actions (movements and targets) of each particular vehicle. This tracking and predictive element could be viewed as an additive form of intelligence collection to be placed into the mix with other forms of dataveillance to more fully construct knowledge about the subject. Or, as I'm arguing, this mobility could be replacing the individual as the means by which dangerous identities are formulated. The production of a predictive mode of mobility assessment creates a risk identity for that mobility which in no way depends upon the individual driver. The identity of the driver is of no consequence; traditional identity categories do not matter, only movement. As DARPA states, "Predictive modeling, plan recognition, and behavior modeling should alert operators to potential force protection risks and threat situations. Forensic information (where did a vehicle come from, how did it get here?) should be combined and contrasted with more powerful 'forward-tracking' capabilities (where could the vehicle go, where is the vehicle going?) to provide operators with real-time capabilities to assess potential force protection threats. MPA (Motion Pattern Analysis) should assist operators in correlating and identifying links between seemingly unrelated events."[27] Recognition is dependent entirely upon pattern recognition based on movements in space and time. Through a series of ever-modulating algorithms, themselves based upon the movements within the system, the imaginary future is created. In essence, the identity of a threat is the prognostication of future "force protection threats," not in terms of a terrorist, but rather "vehicles." Identities are produced through assessment algorithms of mobilities. It is not a matter of who is a threat, but of what vehicular movement can be used to predict a threat. This is not to say that traditional identity categories used in profiling will disappear. But, given the state of perpetual war-mindedness, in which it is unclear who may next threaten U.S. hegemony, ever-modulating hybrid threat-identities are likely to be produced. Other factors, such as the vehicle itself, as has happened with truckers, have become threat-identities. In the case of the trucker as a specific bomb, a program to track and control access to potentially dangerous spaces has been initiated.

We can see some of the earliest uses of such identities closer to the homeland, and other emanations of c3 hybrids are beginning to appear in an as-yet networked fashion. Some of these are taking place in relation to crime control, another via insurance companies' offer to decrease rates for safe drivers, and at least one by Homeland Security itself. In a related way the militarization of the driving population itself might be seen as a part of this process. None of these events in and of itself marks the instantiation of a control society, nor does it guarantee that homeland security will necessarily be the primary motivation for its implementation. And certainly it could be argued that when one is looking for signs of such an event, our findings may be more than slightly overdetermined. But one of the goals of criticism, at least as envisioned by scholars from Marx and Weber to Foucault and Deleuze and, more recently, Hardt and Negri, is to describe not only the past, but also the trends that continue to animate the future. When Marx was writing about the nature of industrial capitalism in the mid- to late nineteenth century, most production still existed outside capitalistic structures and most of western Europe's population, let alone that of nonindustrial nations, worked in agriculture. The bureaucratic state described by Weber was similarly a potentiality only. When Foucault wrote his histories of the present—of disciplinarity and sexuality—he too was writing "fictions," not only of the past or present, but, I would argue, of the future, as he considered them to be experiments with the real. That is, experiments with the future insofar as thought is an engagement with how things will come to be. Deleuze succinctly points to such a conception when he describes the goal of philosophical thought as being engaged not only with description, but with imagining resistant futures that must in a sense respond to that which has yet come to be. Or, as Hardt and Negri point out, the forms of labor, political organization, and resistance forming under the rubric of empire may not yet have fully come to fruition, but the object is to draw out the tendencies which seem to be catapulting the past and present into the future. We must keep such sentiments in mind, for any attempt to "predict" the future is not only fraught with danger but guaranteed in some ways to fail. More important, the goal of prediction is not to simply "get it right": it is to point out why such a future should not come to be.

One of the prime organizing forces of automobile conduct, as I have reiterated throughout, has been and continues to be the insurance industry. Two current examples will show that just as they were at the forefront of earlier safety campaigns, so they are now using risk analysis to imagine a future world in which c3 can control their financial future and our automobile future. One such push by the insurance industry is the expanded use of what they call bait cars. These automobiles, which can be fully tracked and controlled from afar by the police, are placed in crime-susceptible areas for the sole purpose of baiting citizens into stealing them. As of early 2005 over one hundred police departments around the United States were using such bait as a means to reduce automotive thefts. Insurance companies provide bait cars for police departments in many instances, and the National Insurance Crime Bureau's spokesperson made clear that "everyone—me, you, even President Bush"—saves money as a result of such a program. This does raise the question of whether someone who doesn't own an automobile or someone fortunate enough to live in New Hampshire, the only state whose citizens are not legally bound to "own" automobile insurance, benefits. It also makes one wonder if President Bush has to pay the insurance for his Secret Service limousines. In any event, the supposed economic benefits are said to support the use of entrapment techniques and, more insidiously, legitimate the use of police tracking and control devices in fighting crime. This sort of technology can already be purchased as a crime-prevention option on some cars and is part of the package of services provided by GM's OnStar system, which allows for remote tracking and some elements of control, such as turning the engine on and off or locking and unlocking its doors.

Another measure in experimental use is most succinctly described by the Website "Why Not," which offers up ethically challenging technology scenarios for the Internet citizenry to debate and vote upon. Here is the scenario:

> Create a combination of technologies (GPS, radar or sonar, automotive system monitoring, video cameras, weather devices) to monitor everything your car does and its environment. Monitor location, speed, brake application, use of turn signals, seatbelts, radio, road conditions, etc. Use this information to apportion liability in the event of an accident or as evidence in court for defense or prosecution.
>
> Insurance companies would offer lower premiums to drivers who choose to have these technologies (collectively called "black box") installed. They would be paid for by insurance companies out of greater profits or drivers out of lower premiums. Safe drivers would choose to install the black box to be rewarded for their safe driving. Drivers with black boxes would presumably drive more safely.
>
> Eventually, insurance companies might only insure drivers with black boxes. Then every driver would have to have one and every driver would drive more safely, saving billions in property damage, litigation and medical expenses, not to mention addressing a leading cause of death among healthy young people.[28]

The logic of economic self-analysis, coupled with the eventual pricing out of the market of the "unsafe" (or the poor), is seen as the ultimate means by which to save lives. The insurance industry has in fact begun to institute just such incentives-based programs on a limited scale. One major concern with such technologies is their obvious potential to be integrated into a command and control scenario in which all automobiles on the road could be monitored and controlled. This neoliberal solution to traffic safety places the onus on the market and on consumers to "freely" choose whether the system will come into being. As of early 2007, the yes votes outnumbered the no votes four to one on whynot.net.

Lest all the blame be placed upon the insurance industry, consider the automotive industry and a group of Hummer owners, both of whom see their SUVs as an integral element in homeland (or auto-home) security. At the North American International Automotive Show in 2005, Ford debuted the SYNUS, said to be "Vaulting Into the Automotive Future." Ford describes this dangerous future world and how the SYNUS will combat such dangers in its promotional copy:

> As the population shifts back to the big cities, you'll need a rolling urban command center. Enter the SYNUS concept vehicle, a mobile techno sanctuary sculpted in urban armor and inspired by the popular B-cars of congested international hotspots. Short and slim for easy city maneuvering, it looks bank-vault tough on the outside—with intimidating and outrageous styling that even features a vault-style spinner handle in back with deadbolt door latching. When parked and placed in secure mode, SYNUS deploys protective shutters over the windshield and side glass. Small windows on the flanks and roof are non-opening and bullet-resistant. The SYNUS concept also signals security through its use of a driver-side dial operated combination lock on the B-pillar. Flat glass in a slightly raked windshield furthers the armored-car look of this concept.[29]

Ford's description of a "rolling urban command center" will enable drivers to "secure" themselves in "international hotspots." The SYNUS is not alone in preparing citizen drivers to play a part in this new militarized driving environment. Volunteer Hummer owners are creating a nationwide network known as Hummer Owners Prepared for Emergencies (HOPE), whose members will act to reach disaster areas unreachable by vehicles not built for mili-

**FIGURE 34. SYNUS**
Ford's SYNUS is just one example of the many vehicles being created or modified with armor and bulletproof windows in order to outfit the American civilian population for the supposedly warlike driving terrain of U.S. city streets. "SYNUS CONCEPT FOR SECURE URBAN PARKING AND DRIVING." FROM HTTP://WWW.GIZMAG.COM/GO/3592/. RETRIEVED MAY 27, 2006.

tary theaters (Hummers are the civilian version of the military's Humvee, made infamous in the second war in Iraq by its lack of protective shielding against mines). If "all terrain" is now a potential hot spot in the war on terror, then not only does the war open itself up to civilians being regarded as a potential threat, but, under neoliberal military strategy, civilians can offer themselves up as auto-citizen soldiers in the war.[30]

Like the rest of the chapters that analyzed the various and multiple forces—economic, cultural, and other—which have come to organize and regulate automobility through a concern with safety, this chapter has begun to point out how many of the same forces are in play but, in the so-called new normal, have come under the rubric of national security. The new normal is both a historical period, hence new, and one that predicts its own longevity, that is, it is now normal. The question remains to what degree safety as the animating logic for governing automobility will be replaced by concerns over national security. Regardless of the extent to which security comes to define how automobility is governed and the longevity of its application, a number of key concerns need to be reiterated in terms of what the effects of such a transformation might be. Most generally, as I have continually argued, safety has been used to legitimate a number of restrictive measures on the mobility of subjugated populations for the past fifty years and more. As I noted, this by no means undermines the relative gains made in the survival rate in traffic accidents or the number of fatalities per million miles driven (the most widely used statistical measure). It does, however, seriously call into question the legitimacy of safety as the only benchmark for determining policy initiatives regarding automobility. Furthermore, I have taken care to expand the debate beyond a simple binary opposition between freedom and rights versus regulation and public good. As has been amply shown, automobility provides a perfect example of freedom and regulation operating in a symbiotic relationship, not simply in opposition to each other. Of far greater importance, debate regarding safety and automobility needs to acknowledge how different populations are adversely affected and unfairly targeted by many safety crises and subsequent crackdowns.

We saw, for instance, that hitchhiking enabled youth to organize and build community across vast spaces and in specific locales. It also afforded cheap transportation to a population who lacked the economic capital to maintain such networks via more acceptable means of travel. In addition, it aided in the amassing of radical protests throughout the United States during a period often glorified for just such political engagement. Last, it constituted a crucial form of mobility where none existed in the everyday lives of young people making their way through a period generally characterized by relative economic disenfranchisement. More generally, the example of hitchhiking points out the limitations of thinking about mobility purely in terms of individual rights. When particular forms of mobility are a means of constructing and maintaining community and cultural affiliation as well as a possible catalyst activating political participation, the simple discourse of rights fails to acknowledge the complexities of culture and power. It is a violation of civil rights to unduly profile any given segment of the population for harassment, citation, and possible arrest (the three are intricately linked, as one often leads to the other). But, as has been shown in regard to African Americans, Latinos, hitchhikers, and motorcyclists, profiling is not simply a violation of individuals' rights, but an attack on the very mechanism through which these groups build, perform, and negotiate their cultural identities and their place in the larger society. When examining the effects of post-9/11 racial profiling, we need to ask about the economic, cultural, and political effects that practice has on its subjects in terms of their ability to maintain the international community ties that so often mark the space of their already liminal existence.

Though these various safety crises have often led to seemingly oppressive restrictions and surveillance, they may yet pale in significance to the forms of surveillance and control that seem to be arising through new C3 technologies coordinated and animated by national security considerations. The preceding examples of a few of the ways these technologies are currently being implemented offer insight into where the governance of highly mobile populations is headed. Particularly frightening to U.S. citizens is the prospect that what currently passes for a strategic response to the danger posed by insurgents in Iraq could come to be used as a means of controlling the population of the homeland as well. But it is important not to miss the insight regarding how the economic logic of neoliberal governance, coupled with risk analysis, may be equally insidious in the creation of a remote control automobile society. Automotive design and production, the free market logic of consumer desire, and a belief in market efficiency all feed off the rhetoric of personal control and freedom. Yet these purported freedoms and personal control are entirely dependent upon GPS, vast networks of communications devices, an ever-widening and more integrated surveillance apparatus, and an increasingly intelligent command center. In other words, just as the rhetoric of freedom is being used to justify a war in Iraq, it is also being used to produce consumer desire for new dependencies upon control mechanisms. The technologies employed abroad to do battle in the name of freedom may soon come home to be used upon a citizenry that already seems to be happily buying into such rhetoric. In a time characterized by globalization and the supposed end of the nation-state, the U.S. State (of War) has emerged stronger than ever, flexing its muscle abroad while it has also recoiled, tightening its grip on the homeland.

## NOTES

### Introduction

1. Jean Baudrillard, *America*, trans. Chris Turner (London and New York: Verso, 1998), 54.

2. Albert Whitney, *Man and the Motorcar* (New York: New Jersey Department of Law and Public Safety, 1949), 59.

3. Alexis de Tocqueville, *Democracy in America* (Colonial Press, 1835/1900).

4. Automobility has come to mean many things for many people. Here are a few of the more significant ways it has been understood. First, automobility refers to the increased mobility that automobiles and other forms of personal motorized transportation allow. This is something of an individual centered approach and typical of what we might characterize as the American vernacular understanding. Second, it refers to the increasingly automatic nature of mobility. Through new technologies, driving continues to be divorced from physicality. This is a characteristic that I will deal with explicitly in the final chapter. Third, the auto in automobility suggests the increased singularity and insularity that automobiles allowed for. The individual, partially because of increases in mobility, was seen as being less dependent upon others, locale, or even time. These aspects of automobility emphasize a type of freedom, which in turn is both the means for and a site of governance particularly important for neoliberalism and a point emphasized by James Hay ("Unaided Virtues: The (Neo)Liberalization of the Domestic Sphere," in *Television and New Media*: 1:1, Feb. 2000: 53–73). Most all-encompassing, the British sociologist John Urry suggests that we cannot look only at the automobile itself, but what he calls an automobility system. He states, "Sociology has ignored the key significance of automobility, which reconfigures civil society, involving distinct ways of dwelling, travelling and socializing in, and through, an automobilised time-space. Civil societies of the west are

societies of automobility. This is neither simply a system of production nor of consumption, although it is of course both of these" ("Automotility, Car Culture and Weightless Travel" [1999, draft] [Department of Sociology, Lancaster University]: http://www.comp.lancaster.ac.uk/sociology/soc008ju.html, and later published in *Sociology beyond Societies: Mobilities for the Twenty-First Century* [New York: Routledge, 2000]).

5. These critical histories first began to appear in the early 1970s and, taken as a whole, constituted a backlash against what had become by then an intransigent system of social organization. Helen Leavitt's *Superhighway-Superhoax* (New York: Doubleday, 1970) sums up the sentiment best in this blurb from the dust jacket: "From Sea to Shining Sea: we are strangling in a concrete straitjacket that pollutes the environment and makes driving a nightmare." Other books from this period worked the same terrain (Ben Kelley, *The Pavers and the Paved* [New York: Donald W. Brown, 1971] and A. Q. Mowbray, *Road to Ruin* [New York: J. B. Lippincott Company, 1969]) and the movement gained momentum during the 1973 OPEC oil embargo. The art collective Ant Farm critically dealt with the topic of automobility throughout the early 1970s in a number of art installations and performances. The most well known is the "Cadillac Ranch" in Texas, which features a series of Cadillacs half-protruding from the Texas ground, and the most bizarre was an event called "Media Burn," in which a futurized Cadillac coined the "Phantom Dream Car" crashed through a twenty-foot wall of burning television sets. The book, *Automerica: A Trip Down U.S. Highways from World War II to the Future* (New York: E. P. Dutton, 1976), documents much of Ant Farm's work from this period.

6. Though now dismissed by most historians, Turner's frontier thesis exerted a certain hegemonic clout well beyond the academy in terms of describing an American restless spirit. See Frederick Jackson Turner, "The Significance of the Frontier in American History."

7. Books that have celebrated the history of the automobile and American roads far outnumber those that are critical. In one form or another they began appearing as early as the 1940s and were often devoted to a singular highway (see, for instance, Roger Stephens, *Down That Pan American Highway* [Roger Stephens, Publisher, 1946], and George Stewart, *U.S. 40: A Cross Section of the United States* [Houghton Mifflin, 1953], R. George, *N. A. 1: Looking North and Looking South* [Houghton Mifflin, 1957]). Later, the broader consequences of not just an individual road, but automobility more generally would be celebrated. The clearest expressions of such an approach can be found in Phil Patton's *Open Road: A Celebration of the American Highway* (New York: Simon and Schuster, 1986) and Christopher Finch's *Highways to Heaven: The AUTO Biography of America* (New York: Harper Collins, 1992).

8. Baudrillard, *America*, 23.

9. In *Discipline and Punish* (Pantheon, 1978) the French historian Michel Foucault first outlined his explanation of disciplinarity. The disciplining of individuals was accomplished through "correct training," which, among other elements, included education, surveillance, and the organization of movement through time and space. One aim of my book is to outline how individuals' automobility has come to be disciplined or governed. Whereas Foucault, as Virilio points out (Speed and Politics, 1986), has often been considered a "theorist of confinement," I would argue along with the French philosopher Gilles Deleuze (see Foucault, 1984) that Foucault's work helps provide a number of useful means of understanding mobility. Disciplinarity is one such means and, as will become obvious in successive chapters, so does his explanation of power/knowledge (see in particular, Michel Foucault, *Power/Knowledge: Selected Interviews and Other Writings, 1972–1977* [1980]).

10. Herbert J. Stack, "Introduction," in Whitney, *Man and the Motorcar*.

11. Whitney, *Man and the Motorcar*, 23.

12. American Federation of Labor president George Meany in 1953 used Wilson's statement as the rhetorical centerpiece of labor's critique of the strikebreaking tactics used by companies such as GM following passage of the Taft Hartley Bill. "'We don't take the position of Charlie Wilson,' he asserted. 'He says what's good for General Motors is good for America. The A.F.L. takes the opposite position. We say what's good for America is good for us." *New York Times*, September 18, 1953, 14.

13. Whitney, *Man and the Motorcar*, 294.

14. Ibid, 298.

15. Ibid, 294.

16. Ibid.

17. Ibid.

18. Ibid, 295.

19. Ibid, 296.

20. Ibid, 297.

21. Ibid.

22. Ibid.

23. Ibid.

24. Ibid.

25. Ibid.

26. Beginning in the early 1960s the focus on the motorist began to change. Safety measures in automobile engineering began to receive greater attention and scrutiny. This culminated in 1966 in the implementation of the National Highway Safety Act following the highly publicized Senate hearings in which Ralph

Nader, among others, brought intense scrutiny upon the Big Three's poor safety record.

27. Whitney, *Man and the Motorcar*, 224.

28. The work of Mary Douglas on the cross-cultural evaluation of risk has been an ongoing project for the past thirty-odd years. Her major insight is that all cultures' understandings of risk are largely culturally determined, and, furthermore, they are inextricably bound up in political struggles over the control of behavior and resources.

29. *Risk Society: Towards a New Modernity*, trans. Mark Ritter (London: Sage Publications, 1992/1986).

30. From the moment of its English language publication and the reviews that quickly followed, *Risk Society* and Beck's work generally have been situated in relation to the work of Mary Douglas partially owing to the fact that Douglas's *Risk and Blame: Essays in Cultural Theory* (New York: Routledge) was also published in 1992. However, more than one reviewer tended to focus on the degree to which Beck's vision of risk was as a social construct (in line with Douglas's account) or as an increasingly (and thereby measurable) threatening presence in contemporary life (see Elaine Draper, "Risk Society and Social Theory," *Contemporary Sociology* 22:5 (1993): 641–44.

31. Beck, as cited in Cabe Mythen, *Ulrich Beck: A Critical Introduction* (London: Pluto Press, 2004), 15.

32. Beck's term used to distinguish human-created risks from natural disasters.

33. The car has often functioned as an opening for psychologizing drivers and as a metaphor for personality types or society as a whole. See, for instance, Peter Marsh and Peter Collett's *Driving Passion: The Psychology of the Car* (Boston: Faber and Faber, 1987), which elaborates the psychological ramifications and associations of automobiles with costume, fashion, jewelry, uniform, fantasy, icons, weapons, and thrills.

34. Baudrillard, *America*, 54.

35. John Urry, "Automotility, Car Culture and Weightless Travel" (1999, draft), (Department of Sociology, Lancaster University): http://www.comp.lancaster.ac.uk/sociology/soc008ju.html.

36. Urry, "Automotility, Car Culture and Weightless Travel," 1999.

37. Jeremy Packer, "Disciplining Mobility: Governing and Safety." In *Foucault, Cultural Studies and Governmentality*.

38. Jorg Beckmann, 81–100.

39. Ibid., 95.

40. Ibid.

41. The most extensive account and analysis of these films can be found in the documentary *Hell's Highway: The True Story of Highway Safety Films* (2003), Dir. Brett Wood. Kino International.

42. *Car Crash Culture* (New York: Palgrave, 2001), edited by Mikita Brottman, collects twenty-eight essays that attempt to investigate the cultural significance of Americans' fascination with automobile accidents. Brottman also invokes Virilio's famous quote as a means of discussing the perverse way in which even such safety devices as the airbag produce their own accidents. The point of referencing such a collection is to argue that whether the "accident" is imagined to be overlooked or obsessed over is truly a question of perspective and not one that can be empirically proven.

43. James Carey, "Technology and Ideology: The Case of the Telegraph," in *Communication as Culture* (New York: Unwin Press, 1988), 201–30.

44. Virilio argues that the difference between the accident and an attack is not easily distinguishable, and I would add that increasingly the accident provides lessons in how to attack. For a further discussion, see chapter 7.

45. Urry, "Automotility, Car Culture and Weightless Travel," 1999.

46. Studies have, in fact, shown that although alcohol affects everyone, it does so in different ways. Furthermore, rarely do studies acknowledge the preexisting differences in driving ability across test subjects.

47. Numerous studies have applied the same risk analysis experiments to test subjects driving while talking on a cellphone as those used to test alcohol-impaired drivers. The studies are nearly unanimous in their findings. More than driving under the most commonly criminalized blood alcohol limit of .08 percent, driving while talking on a cellphone decreases response times, impairs drivers' ability to stay in their lanes, and reduces the ability to maintain proper following distances.

## 1. The Crusade for Traffic Safety

1. President Dwight D. Eisenhower, *President's Action Committee for Traffic Safety: Crusade for Traffic Safety* (Washington D.C.: U.S. Government Printing Office, 1954).

2. Harry R. DeSilva, *Why We Have Automobile Accidents* (New York: John Wiley, 1942), 3.

3. There was a sharp increase in safety concerns during the mid- to late 1930s. Various organizations, mostly nongovernmental, either studied or advocated for traffic safety. These organizations were made up of members of the automotive industry, insurance companies, academic scholars (with Northwestern's Traffic Research Laboratory and Yale's ENO Institute being the most prominent), petroleum companies, the highway construction, steel, and transportation industries, tire manufacturers, and other economically invested interests. They had names like the Highway Traffic Safety Organization and published safe-driving manuals and journals on the subject.

4. *President's Action Committee for Traffic Safety*, front cover.

5. Ibid., 1.

6. Ibid., 2.

7. Ibid.

8. Ibid., 3.

9. Ibid., 5.

10. Ibid., 6.

11. Ibid., 9.

12. Ibid.

13. Ibid., 10.

14. Ibid.

15. Ibid., 13.

16. Ibid.

17. Ibid.

18. Ibid.

19. Ibid., 3.

20. "Ad Council Notes Success in Year," *New York Times*, July 13, 1955, 34.

21. *President's Action Committee for Traffic Safety*, 3.

22. Ibid.

23. This form of reference was common during the 1930s as well. "In the brief span since Armistice Day, 1918, 250,000 have paid for the ignorance of drivers with their lives" (Richard Alexander Douglas. *Common Sense in Driving Your Car* [New York: Longmans, Green, 1936], 5). "During the eighteen months that we were in the World War our losses were 50,475 killed and 234,300 wounded in combat; while in the eighteen months including the year 1936 and the first six months of 1937, 55,000 Americans were killed on our streets and highways and nearly 1,450,000 were injured" (John L. Floherty, *Youth at the Wheel: A Reference Book on Safety* [Philadelphia: J. B. Lippincott, 1937], 10.). What is peculiar or at least unique about the comparison is that war is considered the comparable activity. One might suggest that the number of deaths accorded to disease, malnourishment, or economic hardship could also be used. After all, war demands mass destruction and killing; while the automobile accident is a side effect, rather than the means to accomplishing its ends.

24. *President's Action Committee for Traffic Safety*, 2.

25. I owe the title of this section to Lynn Spigel; I am grateful to her for providing a method of approaching the issue of social anxiety concerning women and new technology, both of which were borrowed from her book *Make Room for TV: Television and the Family Ideal in Postwar America* (Chicago: University of Chicago Press, 1992).

26. Ronald Schiller and Guy Henle, "America Discovers the Station Wagon: All-Purpose Car For Your Family," *Woman's Home Companion*, February 1954, 117–. 28. Quotations on 117.

27. Articles in women's magazines were calling for and explaining the necessity of the two-car family. In "Coming Up—The Two-Car Family" (*Woman's Home Companion*, June 1955, 62–63), Guy Henle describes various "typical families" in ways that verified the necessity, particularly for women, of the second car. These stressed the different commute shifts of wife and husband, the necessity of a car for the suburban wife at home while the husband has the car at work, and the desire of teenage children to drive (62).

28. Again, see Lynn Spigel's general summary of this historical regularity and the particular shape it took with the introduction of television into women's lives in *Make Room for TV*.

29. Kathleen McHugh, "Women in Traffic: L.A. Autobiography," *The South Atlantic Quarterly* 97:2 (Spring 1998): 391–412.

30. John Hartley, *Uses of Television* (London: Routledge, 1999).

31. *Highway Design and Construction*, revised in 1950, 5.

32. Arthur W. Baum, "All-American Automobile," *Saturday Evening Post*, May 26, 1956, 112–15.

33. Schiller and Henle, "America Discovers the Station Wagon," 126.

34. "Gypsies But Neat," *Woman's Home Companion*, August 1952, 73.

35. "We Took the Kitchen With Us," *Woman's Home Companion*, July 1952, 71.

36. *Life* magazine ran a feature story in the issue for November 17, 1952, entitled "Trailer Life" describing this growing trend along with the extravagances such a life might entail; such as a sixty-five-foot trailer that featured a full service bar, a built in TV, movie screen, and even a radio telephone. The cost for such luxury? $75,000.

37. Dick Reddy, "The Hazards of Summer Driving," *Cosmopolitan*, August 1954, 43.

38. Kay Lane, "How to Travel With a Boyfriend," *American Magazine*, October 1955, 20–21, 107–09.

39. Hazel Rawson Cades, "Good Looks On the Road," *Woman's Home Companion*, 30 June 1954, 30–31.

40. "The Easy Way to Wash the Car," *Woman's Home Companion*, August 1953, 103.

41. "Like a New Car," *Better Homes and Gardens*, May 1947, 33–37.

42. Baum, "All-American Automobile," 113.

43. Behling "'The Woman at the Wheel': Marketing Ideal Womanhood, 1915—1934," *Journal of American Culture* 20:3 (Fall 1997): 13–30.

44. Sam Boal, "Woman Driver: A Myth Exploded," *New York Times Magazine*, November 4, 1951, 18, 46–47.

45. Albert Whitney, *Man and the Motorcar* (New York: J. L. Little, 1936), 67.

46. "Woman Driver Signals A 'Civil Rights' Protest," *New York Times*, February 1, 1952, 10.

47. "Women Disregard Rules in Buffalo," *New York Times*, July 1, 1934, E6.

48. "Woman Driver Tested," *New York Times*, March 8, 1936, XX12.

49. Milton Lehman, "The First Woman Driver," *Life*, September 8, 1952, 83–84.

50. Howard Becker, *Outsiders: Studies in the Sociology of Deviance* (New York: Free Press, 1963).

51. Eisenhower, *President's Action Committee for Traffic Safety*, fig. 1.

52. "Sudden Death for the Second Million," *Ladies' Home Journal*, January 1952, 6.

53. For an excellent account of how this occurs in the case of the drug war, see Jimmie Reeves and Richard Campbell, *Cracked Coverage: Television News, the Anti-Cocaine Crusade, and the Reagan Legacy* (Durham: Duke University Press, 1994).

54. Becker, *Outsiders*, 148.

55. As automobile insurance became mandatory in states throughout the United States, this became a less pressing need.

56. Francois Ewald, "Insurance and Risk," in *The Foucault Effect: Studies in Governmentatlity*, ed. Graham Burchell, Thomas Gordon, and Peter Miller (Chicago: University of Chicago Press, 1991).

57. Ibid., 198.

58. Ibid., 199.

59. Ibid.

60. Ibid., 200.

61. Maurice Zolotow, "Your Emotions Can Kill You," *Cosmopolitan*, January 1955, 14–19.

62. Berton Braley, "Who's the Better Driver?" *American Mercury*, March 1956, 24–27.

63. Ibid., 24.

64. Ibid.

65. "You Can Be an Expert Driver," *Better Homes and Gardens*, September 1951, 168.

66. "Are *You* Really a Safe Driver?" *Better Homes and Gardens*, November 1952, 179.

67. Ibid.

68. Margo Fischer, "So You Think Women Can't Drive!" *Saturday Evening Post*, April 14, 1951, 34.

69. Ibid., 143.

70. Max Gunther, "Who Are America's Worst Drivers?" *Popular Science*, January 1957, 133–35.

71. Zolotow, "Your Emotions Can Kill You," 14.

72. Ibid., 17.

73. Ibid., 15.

74. The most obvious example is David Reisman's *The Lonely Crowd* (New Haven: Yale University Press, 1950).

75. "He has a happy-go-lucky attitude toward sex and family responsibility. He has

a spotty employment record. He hates authority. He likes adventure and excitement. His irresponsibility may be the expression of deep-rooted conflicts having their origin in his childhood" (Zolotow, "Your Emotions Can Kill You," 18). This deep-rootedness speaks volumes regarding the essentialization of a character that was provided by such accounts. Bad driving was a sign of much more than a mere lack of concentration. A similar checklist is provided by A. R. Lauer, in the *Popular Science* article "Portrait of a Problem Driver": "1. He is resentful of authority, doesn't like to take orders from anyone—at home, at school, or on the job. 2. He is a poor sport—won't follow the rules of the game. 3. He is an exhibitionist—watch out for squirrel tails. 4. He is irresponsible, undependable—flits from one job or task to another. 5. He is likely to be on the delinquent side. There is a close parallel between the ages at which youths get into trouble generally, and when they commit traffic violations. 6. At the wheel, he is given to speeding, tailgating, unnecessary passing. 7. He is overconfident about his driving—thinks he is more skillful than he actually is" (Gunther, "Who Are America's Worst Drivers?" 135). The links between good driving and good behavior are strikingly obvious in this quote. What is apparent also is the extent to which one's entire moral being could be read off of one's driving.

76. Zolotow, "Your Emotions Can Kill You," 18.

77. Ibid., 19.

78. Ibid., 16.

79. Ibid.

80. Ibid., 19.

81. Ibid., 20.

82. Eddie Abbot, "Don't Tell Me Women Are Helpless," *Woman's Home Companion*, July 1954, 32–34.

83. Gunther, "Who Are America's Worst Drivers?" 134.

84. Ibid., 135.

85. Early books focused on youth driver's education in the 1930s were often part informational, part scare literature, and part educational. They were almost all concerned with youth immaturity. *Drive and Live* is dedicated "to the young driver: may he realize his responsibility and attain sanity in driving his automobile on the highways of our country" (vii) (Fitzgerald Bayston, *Drive and Live* [Richmond, Va.: Johnson, 1937]). Other books abounded, for example, *Youth at the Wheel* and *Common Sense in Driving Your Car*, which were written for a youth audience.

86. Lawrence Grossberg, "The Political Status of Youth and Youth Culture," *Adolescents and Their Music: If It's Too Loud, You're Too Old*, ed. Jonathan S. Epstein (New York: Garland, 1994), 25–46; Dick Hebdige, *Hiding in the Light* (New York: Routledge, 1988); Jon Lewis, *The Road to Romance and Ruin: Teen Films and Youth Culture* (New York: Routledge, 1992); and Deena Weinstein, "Expendable

Youth: The Rise and Fall of Youth Culture," in *Adolescents and Their Music: If It's Too Loud, You're Too Old*, ed. Jonathon S. Epstein (New York: Garland, 1994), 67–86.

87. "#1 Dating Menace — The Automobile," *Ladies' Home Journal*, November 1955, 54.

88. Margaret Hickey, "Young Drivers Learn Good Road Habits . . . at School Safety Institute," *Ladies' Home Journal*, May 1954, 29.

89. See John Cusack in *Better Off Dead* for an example of the emasculated boy losing numerous traffic light drags while being taunted by the opposing driver over a loudspeaker.

90. Keefer Sutherland is the quintessence of this type in *Stand By Me*.

91. *Daily Variety*, January 22, 1947, as cited in the AFI Catalog website.

92. Advertisement for "Street Rod," *New York Times*, August 16, 1953, BR16.

93. "New Books for the Younger Readers' Library," *New York Times*, November 16, 1958, BR54.

94. Hunter Thompson provides a similar account of the origins of motorcycle gangs in California in *Hell's Angels* (New York: Ballantine, 1966).

95. *Driving Ambitions: An Analysis of the American Hot Rod Enthusiasm* provides a sociological account of hot-rodding over the past sixty years. Moorhouse argues that the uses of automobiles have been overlooked in sociology mainly because of an overemphasis on the processes of production as opposed to those of consumption, leisure, and use. H. F. Moorhouse, *Driving Ambitions: An Analysis of the American Hot Rod Enthusiasm* (Manchester: Manchester University Press).

96. Ibid., 40.

97. Hickey, "Young Drivers Learn Good Road Habits," 29.

98. E. W. James, "Should Schools Teach Safety?" *Safety Digest, Automotive Safety Foundation* 1:1, 1952, 17.

99. Ibid.

100. Ibid., 19.

101. Whitney, *Man and the Motorcar*, 59.

102. Ibid., 17.

103. Hickey, "Young Drivers Learn Good Road Habits," 189.

104. Ibid.

105. See Miller and Reeves, *Cracked Coverage*.

106. Hickey, "Young Drivers Learn Good Road Habits," 89.

107. Cameron McCarthy and Greg Demetriadis explain recent attempts in education to formulate a similar apparatus of surveillance. See "Creating a New Panopticon: Columbine, Cultural Studies, and the Uses of Foucault," in *Foucault, Cultural Studies, and Governmentality*, ed. Jack Bratich, Jeremy Packer, and Cameron McCarthy (Albany: SUNY Press, 2003).

## 2. Hitching the Highway to Hell

1. *Daily Variety*, April 1953, 8.
2. *New York Times*, April 27, 1953, 42.
3. Chapman J. Milling, "Hitchhike Passports," *Forum*, August 1938, 78.
4. Ibid.
5. Ibid., 80.
6. Dick Hebdige. *Hiding in the Light* (New York: Routledge, 1988), 27.
7. Ibid.
8. Foucault's conception of biopolitics along with Deleuze's notion of articulation is useful here. Foucault notes that in order to organize and direct the conduct of citizens, they must be understood in terms of a unified body, or population. It is that conspicuous mark of coherence, in this instance, age or activity (hitchhiking), which actualizes treatment. That is to say, the difference which distinguishes becomes the difference that demands eradication or integration (Deleuze, *Foucault*; Foucault, *Politics Philosophy Culture*).
9. Samuel D. Zeidman, "Thumb Fun!" *Review of Reviews*, April 1937, 55–56.
10. Ibid., 56
11. "Girls' Experience Shows Hitch-Hiking Reasonably Safe," *Science News Letter*, July 2, 1941, 22.
12. Booth Jameson, "Hitchhikers by Night Light," *Saturday Evening Post*, May 5, 1928, 22–23, 130–39, and "A Hitchhiking Reformer," *Saturday Evening Post*, September 22, 1928, 22–23, 141–48.
13. "Of late the ranks of the hitchhikers have been augmented by an increasing proportion of women, chiefly girls from industrial towns and independent unmarried women of an adventurous nature." This quote from a 1938 *Forum* article (cited above) is typical of the claims made during Phase I.
14. Paul Dimaggio, *The Hitchhiker's Field Manual* (New York: Macmillan, 1973).
15. Lee Grieveson, "Fighting Films: Race, Morality, and the Governing of Cinema," *Cinema Journal* 38 (1998): 40–61.
16. Dimaggio, *Hitchhiker's Field Manual*, 10.
17. As Virginia Scharff argues in *Taking the Wheel: Women and the Coming of the Motor Age* (New York: Fee Press, 1991), the Mann Act further assumed that women would be the passengers in automobiles that crossed state lines.
18. Milling "Hitchhike Passports," 78–81.
19. "Thousands of fingerprints would thus be obtained, some of which would undoubtedly prove useful later on. But what of drifters and criminals who would, for the most part, remain unregistered and whose fingerprints are the ones really wanted? These dangerous and irresponsible vagrants would, by the very nature of the law, remain outside the pale, and there would no longer be any excuse for their presence on the roads. If ever arrested for attempting to secure a ride with-

out a license, they could then be fingerprinted as violators of a State law. I believe that such a statute would all but abolish hitchhiking crimes" (Milling, "Hitchhike Passports," 81).

20. Ibid., 57.

21. "Driver's Downfall," *Newsweek*, September 14, 1953, 86.

22. Frank Krutnick, *In a Lonely Street: Film Noir, Genre, Masculinity* (New York: Routledge, 1991); Ann E. Kaplan, ed., *Women in Film Noir* (London: British Film Institute, 1978); James Maxfield, *The Fatal Woman: Sources of Male Anxiety in American Film Noir, 1941–1991* (London: Associated University, 1996).

23. Graham Burchell, "Liberal Government and Techniques of the Self," in *Foucault and Political Reason: Liberalism, Neo-Liberalism and Rationalities of Government*, ed. Andrew Barry, Thomas Osborne, and Nikolas Rose (Chicago: University of Chicago Press, 1996).

24. Gwyneth Cravens, "Hitching Nowhere: The Aging Young on the Endless Road," *Harper's*, September 1972, 66–70.

25. Lawrence Grossberg, *We Gotta Get Outta This Place: Popular Conservatism and Postmodern Culture* (New York: Routledge, 1992), 27.

26. For instance, in *The Making of a Counterculture* (New York: Doubleday, 1969). Theodore Roszak acknowledges that "roadmen" make up one contingency of those attempting to "float the Pentagon" in 1967.

27. J. Edgar Hoover, *J. Edgar Hoover on Communism* (New York: Paperback Library, 1970), 133.

28. Ibid., 139.

29. Hoover, as cited in "Thumbs Down on Hitchhiking," *Reader's Digest*, January 1970, 128–31.

30. Tom Grimm, "The Thumb as Travel Agent: Pleasure and Perils," *New York Times*, December 13, 1970, 384.

31. William Wolf, "Hitchhiker to Stardom," *Boston Sunday Globe*, November 1, 1970, 22–24.

32. Janet Graham, "Rule of Thumb for the Open Road," *Sports Illustrated*, June 6, 1966, 76–90.

33. "A New Rule of Thumb," *Newsweek*, June 16, 1969, 63.

34. Ibid.

35. Ibid.

36. Ibid.

37. Douglas Anderson, "Meditations on a Hitchhiking Ticket," *National Review*, September 24, 1971, 1069.

38. Ken Hicks, *The Complete Hitchhiker: A Handbook for Bumming Around America* (New York: Tobey, 1973), 63.

39. Ibid., 9.

40. Ibid., 50.

41. DiMaggio, *Hitchhiker's Field Manual*, acknowledgments page.

42. Ibid., 7.

43. Hicks, *The Complete Hitchhiker*, 10.

44. Ibid., 50.

45. Tom Grimm, *Hitchhiker's Handbook* (New York: Plume Book, 1972), 26.

46. Ibid., 80.

47. Ibid., 82.

48. Ibid.

49. "A New Rule of Thumb," 63.

50. Maitland Zane, "The Hardy Hitchhikers," July 20, 1970, *New York Times*, 4.

51. Lester David, "Hitchhiking: The Deadly New Odds," *Good Housekeeping*, July 1973, 38–46.

52. Katherine Dunn, *Truck* (New York: Harper and Row, 1971).

53. Tom Robbins, *Even Cowgirls Get the Blues* (New York: Bantam Books, 1976).

54. "A New Rule of Thumb," 63.

55. Grimm, "The Thumb as Travel Agent," 384.

56. Ibid.

57. Robert Reinhold, "Hitchhiking Curb Aimed at Drivers," *New York Times*, June 20, 1971, 50.

58. "Hitchhiker Controls Spread," *San Jose Mercury News*, August 13, 1970, 27.

59. "Ban on Hitchhiking Due Some Study by Panel at Santa Cruz," *San Jose Mercury News*, August 27, 1970, 37–4.

60. "Hippies Protest LA hitchhiking Ban," *Los Angeles Times*, October 15, 1970, 6.

61. "Hitchhikers Held in Berkeley Raids," *New York Times*, August 9, 1970, 37.

62. John Kifner, "They Use the Thumb to Roam the Land," *New York Times*, August 8, 1971, 33.

63. Ibid.

64. "A Major Yippie Theorist Seized on Drug Charges," *New York Times*, July 26, 1971, 16.

65. "Hitchhikers Held in Berkeley Raids," *New York Times*, August 9, 1970, 37.

66. Walter F. Weiss, *America's Wandering Youth: A Sociological Study of Young Hitchhikers in the United States* (New York: Exposition Press, 1974).

67. Ibid., 48

68. See such classic examples as *Subculture: The Meaning of Style* (1979), *Resistance through Rituals* (1993), and *Learning to Labor* (1981). For an insightful understanding of how existentialism worked for youth, see Paul Willis's chapter, "The Cultural Meaning of Drug Use," in *Resistance through Rituals*.

69. See *Feminism and Youth Culture* (1990) for a critique of this masculine bias in the study of youth.

70. "Rules of Thumb," *Newsweek*, February 19, 1973, 38.

71. Susan Gordon, "Hitchhiking Really Isn't Cool," 210.

72. "Rules of Thumb," 38.

73. Edwin T. Dahlberg, *I Pick Up Hitchhikers* (Valley Forge: Judson Press, 1978).

74. Ibid., 9.

75. See, for instance, any of the following three books published between 1969 and 1971: Helen Leavitt, *Superhighway-Superhoax* (New York: Doubleday, 1970); Ben Kelley, *The Pavers and the Paved* (New York: Donald W. Brown, 1971); and A. Q. Mowbray, *The Road to Ruin* (New York: J. B. Lippincott, 1969). This genre might best be summed up by this jacket blurb from *Superhighway Hoax*: "From sea to shining sea we are strangling in a concrete straightjacket that pollutes the environment and makes driving a nightmare."

76. William Endicott, "Hitchhikers Seeking State ID Cards—With Small Thumb Tax," *Los Angeles Times*, June 6, 1973, 4.

77. Ann B. Silverman, "Car-Pooling to the School on Time," *New York Times*, October 12, 1980, WC 28.

78. Susan J. Gordon, "Car Pools: Rules of the Road for a Suburban Ritual," *New York Times*, October 10, 1982, WC 30.

79. Georgia Dullea, "The Suburban Car Pool: Even More Vital Today," *New York Times*, January 4, 1974, 16.

80. The continuation of hitchhiking youth has been maintained primarily through the small community of ex-hippies and neo-hippies who followed the Grateful Dead until Jerry Garcia's death and then followed Phish or who gather for such hippie fests as the Rainbow Gathering or the Further Festival.

81. The artist David Wojnarowicz described such encounters and practices in two autobiographic books, *Memories That Smell Like Gasoline* (1992) and *Close to the Knives: A Memoir of Disintegration* (1991).

82. William Least Heat Moon's *Blue Highways: A Journey Into America* (1983) echoed the sentiment described earlier by Robert M. Pirsig in *Zen and the Art of Motorcycle Maintenance* (1974) that "on the old highway maps of America, the main routes were red and the back roads blue. Now even the colors are changing. But in those brevities just before dawn and a little after dusk—times neither day nor night—the old roads return to the sky some of its color. Then, in truth, they carry a mysterious cast of blue, and it's that time when the pull of the blue highway is strongest, when the open road is beckoning, a strangeness, a place where a man can lose himself" (frontispiece).

## 3. Motorcycle Madness

1. Patricia Zonker, *Murdercycles: The Facts About America's Number One Blood Sport* (Chicago: Nelson-Hall, 1978).

2. Hunter S. Thompson, *Hell's Angels: A Strange and Terrible Saga* (New York: Ballantine, 1966), 6.

3. Melissa Holbrook Pierson, *The Perfect Vehicle: What It Is About Motorcycles* (New York: W. W. Norton, 1997), 70.

4. "Cyclist's Holiday," *Life*, July 21, 1947, 31.

5. A motorcycle run is a gathering of motorcyclists that usually involves a fairly lengthy ride (run) in order to get to the gathering spot. These were traditionally planned around motorcycle races, but as the police began to crack down and prohibit any large gathering of motorcyclists following the Hollister incident, bikers would stage more spontaneous runs. Such currently massive events as the annual Sturgis South Dakota rally have their roots in such runs.

6. Paul Willis, *Profane Culture* (New York: Routledge, 1978).

7. Tom Wolfe, *Electric Kool-Aid Acid Test* (New York: Bantam, 1969).

8. Thompson, *Hell's Angels*, 81.

9. Mark Williams, *Road Movies: The Complete Guide to Cinema on Wheels* (New York: Proteus Books, 1982), 58.

10. Barbara Klinger, "The Road to Dystopia: Landscaping the Nation in *Easy Rider*" in *The Road Movie Book*, ed. Steven Cohan and Ira Hark (London: Routledge, 1997), 179.

11. In fact, one member of my dissertation committee, who advised an earlier version of this research, admitted to having been inspired to take a cross-country journey of his own after viewing *Easy Rider*.

12. Lawrence Grossberg. *We Gotta Get Outta This Place: Popular Conservatism and Postmodern Culture* (New York: Routledge, 1992), 177.

13. Ibid.

14. See, for instance, the already mentioned *We Gotta Get Out of This Place*, the much-discussed work of Dick Hebdige, particularly *Subculture: The Meaning of Style* (1979), or the work of Deena Weinstein, particularly chapter 7, "Maligning the Music," in *Heavy Metal: A Cultural Sociology* (1991).

15. *Motorcycles in the United States: Popularity, Accidents, Injury Control*. U.S. Department of Health, Education, and Welfare (Public Health Service Publication No. 999-UIH-7, Washington, D.C., 1967), 2.

16. One of my high school teachers told me the story of an assailant in a pickup truck who deliberately drove him off the road while he was riding on his motorcycle. After pulling himself out of the ditch, he followed the driver to his home, where he asked the man for an explanation. The driver simply stated, "I hate motorcyclists." Warren La Coste (*Holy Rider: The Priest and the Gang* [Far Hills, N.J.: New Horizon Press, 1992]) relates a similar experience: "I noticed a car quickly moving toward me. Instinctively, I moved over, giving the driver more latitude, and was about to dismiss the incident as mere carelessness by this driver. But

the car kept coming until I was almost forced off the road. I turned to face the driver and was shocked to see a man with fiery red face and clenched teeth. He had a death grip on the steering wheel. He acted as if he were an avenging angel intent on ridding the world of scum" (120). La Coste was a priest at the time of this incident.

17. *Motorcycles in the United States*, 2–4.

18. Ralph Nader, *Unsafe at Any Speed* (New York: Grossman, 1965).

19. James O'Connell and Allen Myers, *Safety Last* (New York: Avon, 1966).

20. It is not until the mid-1970s that this begins to change. In December 1975, Nori-yoski Uno, Director, Engineering Division, Road Transport Bureau, Ministry of Transport, Government of Japan, had this to say in his opening remarks to the International Motorcycle Safety Conference: "The development of safer hard-ware is also indispensable, however, because motorcycle safety depends on many factors—not only the human driver, but also the condition of the road and the vehicle. Furthermore, we cannot say that the development of safer motorcycle hardware is sufficient at the present time. In fact, until now such emphasis has been applied mainly to cars" (4). This opening speech was followed over the next two days by twenty presentations, of which only two dealt with rider safety, while eighteen focused on technological improvements. One way to understand this is that the industry was making a concerted effort to appear more interested in safety, following the suit of automobile manufacturers, in a public relations effort to appease the outrage of some safety advocates who claimed, that "motorcycles are so dangerous [they] should be banned from the streets and highways" (319). *Proceedings: International Motorcycle Safety Conference, December 16 & 17, 1975* (Washington, D.C.: Department of Transportation, National Highways Traffic Safety Association, 1977).

21. La Coste, *Holy Rider*.

22. Ibid., 23.

23. Pierson, *The Perfect Vehicle*.

24. *Motorcycle Driver Education Workshop*, held at the University of Illinois, August 4 and 5, 1967 (Proceedings. 388.3475 m85p, 1967), 11.

25. Ibid, 7.

26. Ibid., 23

27. The first of these laws made it illegal for anyone under the age of nineteen to ride a motorcycle over 150cc. An engine of this size was generally limited to off-road bikes and scooters, which were considered much more acceptable, par-tially owing to ad campaigns that portrayed them as good clean fun for men and women, thus emasculating them. Thus young men, the major threat, were limited to riding off-road, where they were supposedly less likely to hurt them-selves. Of course they also couldn't go anywhere, or they could ride an emas-

culated scooter which outside Europe, especially Great Britain, had no macho value. The second law forbade motorcycles 150cc or less from the highway system, supposedly based on their inadequate speed, which was not nearly always the case. These two laws in conjunction outlawed sixteen to eighteen year olds from riding on the highway, thus seriously curtailing their mobility, especially if they lived on the outskirts of suburbia and were thus connected to the world only through the new highway systems.

28. *Motorcycle Driver Education Workshop*, 23–34.

29. "In traffic safety campaigns, scare techniques are common. So are claims for their effectiveness. But there is no evidence for those claims. In fact, psychological studies in related fields show that scare campaigns as now conceived may do more harm that good." Malfetti, from *Traffic Safety*, quoted in O'Connell and Allen Myers' *Safety Last*, 57.

30. Motorcycle riders do, however, benefit from added warmth as well. But even this gain belies an inability to "tough it out." Thus, the constant tension is almost always open for invocation.

31. Norman Denzin, *Interpretive Interactionism* (Newbury Park, Calif.: Sage Publications, 1989), 15.

32. Kevin Cameron, "New Riders," *Cycle World*, June 1996, 16.

33. "Survival 1995: *Motorcyclist* Editors' Greatest Hits," *Motorcyclist*, September 1995, 43–58.

34. Based on a 1968 study published as *Motorcycle Safety Final Report*, all of these "countermeasures" were called for: mandatory helmet and goggle use, windshields on all motorcycles, mandatory glove use, mandatory protective jacket and pants, high visibility vest, uniform control locations, mandatory fairings, boots, crash bars, electric starter, motorcycle lane on highway, lights on at all times, and yearly motorcycle inspections.

35. Friedman, "What to Look for in Crash Protection," *Motorcyclist*, September 1995, 56.

36. "Survival 1995: *Motorcyclist* Editors' Greatest Hits," *Motorcyclist*, September 1995, 43.

37. Ibid.

38. Here and below I'm making liberal use of Kenneth Burke's five key terms that inform his *Grammar of Motives*. They are act, scene, agent, agency, purpose.

39. "Survival Section," 43.

40. Ibid., 46.

41. Ibid., 48.

42. Ibid., 50.

43. Ibid., 55.

44. Ibid., 46.

45. Thompson, *Hell's Angels*, 109.

46. Ibid., 110.

47. Snell is an organization devoted to testing and furthering helmet safety technology.

48. Thompson, *Hell's Angels*, 124.

49. For some motorcyclists, it is nearly impossible to afford insurance, and it is certainly cost-prohibitive to purchase any coverage, let alone the medical insurance that for so many young riders is needed, as they have no other medical coverage. In *Murdercycles*, Zonker sees this as a good thing, as it reduces the number of riders and signals how terribly dangerous riding is. As stated in other chapters, the insurance industry not only has a vested interest in exploiting fears and stereotypes, but is often the major source that promotes them.

50. The Motorcycle Safety Foundation is an organization that provides motorcycle education and training for free to anyone who wants it. It is a quasi-governmental organization in that the MSF course is accepted in lieu of taking the riding exam at state-run licensing facilities. The course is widely praised by other safety organizations and is mentioned often in motorcycle magazines.

51. Michel Foucault, *Politics Philosophy Culture: Interviews and Other Writings 1977–1984*, ed. Lawrence Kritzman (New York: Routledge, 1990), 124.

52. La Coste, *Holy Rider*, 120.

53. Suzanne McDonald-Walker, *Bikers: Culture, Politics, and Power* (London: Berg, 2000), 23.

54. Thompson, *Hell's Angels*, 345.

55. Tony Bennett, *The Birth of the Museum* (New York: Routledge, 1995).

56. Rick Woodward, "The Art of the Motorcycle," *ARTnews* 97:8 (1998): 167.

57. Paul Schjeldahl. "Gehry in Gear," *Village Voice*, September 1, 1998, 125.

58. "The Art of the Motorcycle," *In the Field* 69:6, 1998, 1.

59. R. Kennedy, "Engines Roaring, Pagers Beeping: Middle Class Leads a Renewed Romance with Biker Culture," *New York Times*, July 12, 1998, 23–27.

60. Ali Subotnick, "Look Ma, No Hands," *ARTnews* 97:9, 1998.

## 4. Communications Convoy

1. John Schlossberg and Edwin Brockman, *The All New Fact-Packed 1977/78 CB Guide* (New York: Bantam, 1977), 6.

2. FCC, *Report to Congress*, October 14, 1975, 3.

3. "Nuisance or a Boon? The Spread of Citizens' Radios," *U.S. News and World Report*, September 29, 1975, 26–28.

4. Armand Mattelart, *The Invention of Communication* (Minneapolis: University of Minnesota Press, 1994/1996), xvii.

5. Barry Smart, "The Politics of Truth and the Problem of Hegemony," in *Foucault: A Critical Reader*, ed. David Couzens Hoy (London: Basil Blackwell, 1986).

6. Toby Miller, *Technologies of Truth: Cultural Citizenship and the Popular Media* (Minneapolis: University of Minnesota Press, 1998), 18.

7. Ibid.

8. "How was this continental union to be held together? . . . the answer was sought in the word and the wheel, in transportation and transmission, in the power of printing and civil engineering to bind a vast distance and a large population into cultural unity or, as the less optimistic would have it, into cultural hegemony" ("Introduction," *Communication as Culture* [New York: Routledge, 1989], 55). "It was the cable and telegraph, backed, of course, by sea power, that turned colonialism into imperialism: a system in which the center of an empire could dictate rather than merely respond to the margin" ("Technology and Ideology," *Communication as Culture* [New York: Routledge, 1989], 212). See also "Space, Time, and Communications: A Tribute to Harold Innis," *Communication as Culture*, 142–72.

9. As Andrew Barry notes, "The communications infrastructures came to function as perfect embodiments of the liberal political imagination: maximizing the density, intensity, and spatial extension of interactions within the social body itself while, at the same time, minimizing the direct demands made by the state on the people" ("Lines of Communication and Spaces of Rule," in *Foucault and Political Reason: Liberalism, Neo-liberalism and Rationalities of Government*, ed. Andrew Barry, Thomas Osborne, and Nikolas Rose [Chicago: University of Chicago Press, 1996]).

10. As discussed below, CB use was growing faster than any communications device since the television. The most popular sets were for automobiles, but home devices as well as watercraft units were also prominent.

11. This channel may not be used for private conversations. It is to be used, instead, for "emergency communications involving the immediate safety of life of individuals or the immediate protection of property" or "communications necessary to render assistance to a motorist." (Part 95, Section 41[2] FCC Code of Regulations).

12. A small number of scholarly articles did appear in 1978–81. These dealt with one of three themes: CB as a replacement for face-to-face sociability (Ramsey, Dannefer, Poushinsky et al.), CB culture (Thomas, Kerbo et al.), and CB linguistics (Smith and Ramsey).

13. Susan Douglas details the vital role the navy played in the formation of two-way radio communications. Her work shows the need to take into account state uses of and influences on communication technologies, which often orient and guide citizen use (Susan J. Douglas, *Inventing American Broadcasting, 1899–1922* [Baltimore: Johns Hopkins University Press, 1987]).

14. Lynn Spigel provides a fine overview of these competing rhetorics and the pitfalls of technological determinism when approaching new communication tech-

nologies (*Make Room for TV: Television and the Family Ideal in Postwar America* [Chicago: University of Chicago Press, 1992]).

15. Schlossberg and Brockman, *1977/78 CB Guide*, 71.

16. FCC guidelines demanded that owners keep a set of written rules alongside all CB transmitters. The CB guides all contained a full set of rules and thus operated as a necessary accompaniment.

17. Schlossberg and Brockman, *1977/78 CB Guide*, 72.

18. *Network*, directed by Sidney Lumet, 1976.

19. Schlossberg and Brockman, *1977/78 CB Guide*, 73–74.

20. Alan Burton, *Police Telecommunications* (Springfield, Ill.: Charles C. Thomas, 1973).

21. Andrew Barry, "Lines of Communication and Spaces of Rule," 138.

22. See, for instance, *Foucault and Political Reason*, ed. Barry, Osborne, and Rose.

23. Gilles Deleuze, *Foucault* (Minneapolis: University of Minnesota Press, 1988).

24. In its most concrete form we have what officers call "off-the-street-patrol," essentially police cars parked looking for speeders and other offenders. But the real issue here is to what extent observation is internalized. To what extent are drivers always unaware of how thoroughly the streets are being monitored and the possibility that at any particular moment they may be under surveillance? *The Police Traffic Supervision Manual* from this era states, "This reminder of the police presence will linger after the police vehicle is no longer in sight" (105). Yet the duration is said to depend upon two things. First, the symbol of enforcement authority is paramount. This is said to be ensured by a vigorous and focused enforcement policy. In other words, officers must hand out violations continuously. Second, motorists must see the symbols frequently. Hence, off-the-street patrol cars must station themselves along highly traveled routes. This observation plan is summarized as follows: "A long-range, comprehensive traffic enforcement program seeks to generate voluntary compliance. When enforcement practices are uniformly and extensively conducted over a long period of time, drivers become aware of the risks and no longer depend on seeing a police officer to be reminded of enforcement practices or his own driving behavior" (105). Charles G. Vanderborsch, International Association of Chiefs of Police, *The Police Traffic Supervision Manual* (Washington, D.C: Library of Congress, 1969).

25. William Jeans, "Tuning in Justice on Your CB Radio Dial, *Car and Driver*, 10.

26. Brock Yates, "One Lap of America," *Car and Driver*, February 1975, 27–30.

27. Ibid., 30.

28. For a historical discussion of the significance of aural surveillance, see Dorte Zbikowski. "The Listening Ear: Phenomena of Acoustic Surveillance," in *ctrl[space]: Rhetorics of Surveillance from Bentham to Big Brother*, ed. Levin, Frohne, and Weibel (Cambridge, Mass.: MIT Press, 2002), 33–49.

29. FCC, *To Permit Aliens to Operate Radio Stations*, Subcommittee on Communications Hearing, October 8, 1970.

30. Jane Stern, *Trucker: A Portrait of the Last American Cowboy* (New York: McGraw Hill, 1975).

31. The fact that Peckinpah was famous for such westerns and neowesterns as *The Wild Bunch, Bring Me the Head of Alfredo Garcia,* and *The Getaway* deserves mention. In the 1970s, when the classic Hollywood system was a thing of the past, new genre hybrids appeared that often borrowed heavily in both narrative form and iconography from established genres of the past. The movies of Peckinpah are a perfect example of this, and *Convoy* is the most exemplary of these trucker-westerns.

32. Film critics unanimously panned these movies, and *Convoy* was considered to be one of the worst. See, for instance, *New York Times*, August 16, 1978.

33. Red Sovine, *Truck Driver's Prayer.*

34. Ibid.

35. See James H. Thomas, *The Long Haul: Truckers, Truck Stops, and Trucking* (Memphis: Memphis State University Press, 1979).

36. Miller, *Technologies of Truth*, 14–22.

37. Robert Sherrill, "Raising Hell on the Highways," *Reader's Digest*, July 1978, 121–25.

38. "Nuisance or a Boon?" 26.

39. Ibid., 28.

40. "Even during their first few trial months with CB, Missouri's Highway Patrol received reports of 27 wrong-way drivers, and arrested 11 of them, booked 101 of 112 apparently drunken motorists, arrested 22 of 31 reported speeders" (Leo Sands, "Radio on Wheels: The CB Communications Freeway," *Popular Mechanics*, December 1975, 81). Magazine articles were full of such stories and statistics during the height of CB's newsworthiness.

41. "The Drivers' Network," *Time*, September 22, 1975, 48–49.

42. FCC, *Report to Congress.*

43. Robert Lindsay, "The Angry Truck Driver: 'We've Got to Show 'Em,'" *New York Times*, December 4, 1973, 6.

44. Ibid.

45. "The Great Truck Blockade," *U.S. News and World Report*, December 17, 1973, 14.

46. Dan La Botz, *Rank and File Rebellion: Teamsters for a Democratic Union* (New York: Verso, 1990).

47. Hearings before the Committee on Interstate and Foreign Commerce on February 6, 1974, 93rd Congress, 2nd Session, Serial 93–58.

48. Ibid.

49. Ibid.

50. Ibid.

51. Phillip Shabecoft, "Truck Drivers Plan National Stoppage," *New York Times*, December 8, 1973, 1.

52. See Gilles Deleuze and Félix Guattari, *A Thousand Plateaus: Capitalism and Schizophrenia* (Minneapolis: University of Minnesota Press, 1987), 26–38.

## 5. Of Cadillacs and "Coon Cages"

1. "Why the Negro Drives a Cadillac," *Ebony*, September 1949, 34.

2. Ralph Ellison, "Cadillac Flambé," *American Review: The Magazine of New Writing*, February 1973, 249–69.

3. Ibid.

4. See, for instance, *Baadasssss Cinema* (2002) (V). Directed by Isaac Julien.

5. Clearly there is a very obvious political economic reason that the Bond producers attempted to take advantage of the massive popularity of the blaxploitation fad. Yet, as has been made eminently clear by numerous scholars (most notably Bennett and Woollacott in *Bond and Beyond*), Bond villains are highly charged ideological signifiers that figure prominently in the political contexts from which they emanate. It is, then, significant that Mr. Big, as a threat to Western political hegemony, appears to be on a par with such previous threats as "mutually assured destruction" (*Dr. No* [1962], *You Only Live Twice* [1967], and *Thunderball* [1965]) or the collapse of capitalism owing to the destruction of the gold upon which it was thought to be grounded (*Goldfinger* [1964]) before the gold standard was abandoned.

6. Paul Gilroy, "Driving While Black," in *Car Cultures*, ed. Daniel Miller (New York: Oxford Books, 2001).

7. This argument is made convincingly in Lee Grieveson, "Fighting Films: Race, Morality, and the Governing of Cinema," *Cinema Journal* 38:1 (1998): 40–61.

8. Ralph Ellison, *The Collected Essays of Ralph Ellison* (New York: Modern Library, 1995), 397.

9. Alan Nadel, "Black Bodies in White Space," unpublished lecture.

10. "Why the Negro Drives a Cadillac," 34.

11. Roger I. Yoshino, "The Stereotype of the Negro and His High-Priced Car," *Sociology and Social Research* 44:2 (November–December 1959): 112–18.

12. Gilroy, "Driving While Black."

13. *Ebony*, November 1945, 1.

14. "Why the Negro Drives a Cadillac," 34.

15. Ibid.

16. Ibid.

17. Ibid.

18. Gilroy ("Driving While Black") points out the problems of such a position, sug-

gesting that too often struggles against racial oppression envision freedom as the ability to shop on the same terms as those more privileged.

19. "Why the Negro Drives a Cadillac," 34.

20. Sabe Bruton, "Critic Says Cadillac Holds Up Our Wheels of Progress by Not Hiring Negro Salesmen," *New York Age*, April 1959, 19.

21. Corey T. Lessig. *Automobility: Social Changes in the American South, 1909–1939: American Popular History and Culture* (New York: Routledge, 2001), viii, 142.

22. Ibid. But all was not that simple. As Lessig makes clear, the automobile also aided in the ability of lynchings, which reached their highest levels during the first two decades after the automobile was introduced. He summarizes this duality via Jack Temple Kirby, who wrote, "Autos probably worsened and improved racial relations at once" ("Black and White in the Rural South, 1915–1954," *Agricultural History* 58 [July 1984]: 420).

23. Gilroy, "Driving While Black," 97.

24. "Time to Stop Crying Wolf," *Ebony*, June 1952, 116.

25. Ibid.

26. "High Powered Cars a Tradition in Negro Community," *Ebony*, July 1951, 18.

27. *Ebony*, February 1954, 47.

28. Roland Marchand. *Advertising the American Dream: Making Way for Modernity, 1920–1940* (Berkeley: University of California Press, 1985).

29. Pamela Walker Laird, "The Car Without a Single Weakness: Early Automobile Advertising," *Technology and Culture* 37 (October 1996): 796–812.

30. Ibid.

31. Walter Lowe, "Negroes Buy 5,000,000 Cars a Year, But Get No Dealerships!" *Chicago Defender*, September 13, 1963, 4.

32. "Nation's Top Negro Car Dealer," *Ebony*, April 1958, 85.

33. Yoshino, "The Stereotype of the Negro and His High-Priced Car."

34. "Ruth's Cadillacs Cause Unpleasantness in the South," *Ebony*, May 1952, 56.

35. Dick Gregory, *From the Back of the Bus* (New York: Avon, 1962), 36.

36. For a thorough and insightful analysis of the relationship between verification documents, mobility, and the state, see the work of Craig Robertson, especially *"Passport Please": The United States Passport and the Documentation of Individual Identity* (Ann Arbor, Mich.: UMI dissertations, 2003) and "The Ritual of Verification? The Nation, the State, and the U.S. Passport," in *Thinking With James Carey: Essays on Communications, Transportation, History*, ed. Jeremy Packer and Craig Robertson (New York: Peter Lang, 2005).

37. "Harriman orders dropping of the word 'color' on applications for driver's license." *New York Amsterdam News*, December 17, 1955, 1.

38. Steve Herbert, *Policing Space: Territoriality and the Los Angeles Police Department* (Minneapolis: University of Minnesota Press, 1997), 6.

39. Randall Kennedy, *Race Crime and the Law* (New York: Pantheon, 1997), 141.

40. It is the potential of criminal activity, not a visible act itself, which is being targeted. As Foucault has pointed out, it is through the operation of normalization, that others come to be treated as abnormal and dangerous. Foucault calls this "dangerousness," which means that the individual "must be considered by society at the level of his potentialities and not at the level of his acts" (as quoted by Arnold I. Davidson, in his introduction to *Abnormal: Lectures at the Collège de France 1974–1975*, xxiii).

41. Richard Ericson and Kevin Haggerty, in *Policing the Risk Society* (Toronto: University of Toronto Press, 1997), argue that the primary role of the police is that of collecting, filing, and organizing evidence on the population. Far more of their time is spent on this task than any other.

42. Ibid. See, for instance, Kenneth Meeks, *Driving While Black* (New York: Broadway Books, 2000), in which he describes in detail New Jersey's notoriety.

43. "Drug-Courier Profile," *Miami Herald*, June 6, 1985, 24A.

44. Randall Kennedy, *Race Crime and the Law*, 152.

45. Elizabeth Rusch, "Biking While Black," *Mother Jones*, September–October 2002, 25.

46. David A. Harris acknowledges that he deliberately chose to focus on the middle class in order to point out that it happens to "all blacks." "The Stories, the Statistics, and the Law: Why 'Driving While Black' Matters," *Minnesota Law Review* 84 (1999): 265–326.

47. Kathleen M. O'Day, "Pretextual Traffic Stops: Protecting Our Streets or Racist Police Tactics?" *University of Dayton Law Review* 23:2 (Winter 1998): 313–36.

48. See in particular Mike Davis's *City of Quartz* (1989) and *Ecology of Fear* (1999) for a thorough description of this phenomenon in Los Angeles over the past two decades.

49. David Dodd, "Swing Low, Sweet Cadillac," *New Society* October 25, 1973, 199–201, 199.

50. "'Pimpin' Ain't Easy': Work, Play, and 'Lifestylization' of the Black Pimp Figure in Early 1970s America." In *Media, Culture, and the Modern African American Freedom Struggle*, ed. Brian Word (Gainesville: University Press of Florida, 2001), 211–32.

51. Iceberg Slim, *Pimp* (Los Angeles: Holloway House, 1969), 102–3.

52. Ibid., 250.

53. See Todd Boyd, *Am I Black Enough for You?: Popular Culture from the 'Hood and Beyond* (Bloomington: Indiana University Press, 2002).

54. Danny Lee, "Driving; The Dub Generation: Gearheads Go Hip-Hop," *New York Times*, April 23, 2004.

55. Ibid.

56. Ibid.

57. Nora Zamichow, "Wheel Rims Add Glitter, But Increasingly Lure Deadly Violence Crime," *Los Angeles Times*, October 8, 1994.

58. Ibid.

59. Ibid.

60. Ibid.

61. "Something shady about all those tinted car windows," *Chicago Tribune*, July 8, 1992.

62. "Driving with Dracula," *New Orleans Times-Picayune*, July 24, 2003.

63. See, for instance, "Crossing the Media(-n): Auto-mobility, the Transported Self, and Technologies of Freedom," with James Hay, in *MediaSpace: Scale and Culture in a Media Age*, ed. Nick Couldry, and Anna McCarthy (New York: Routledge, 2004), 209–32; and "Rethinking Dependency: New Relations of Communications and Transportation," in *Thinking with James Carey*, ed. Jeremy Packer, and Craig Robertson (New York: Peter Lang, 2006).

64. "Too Many Drivers Are in the Dark About Window-Tinting Laws," *Los Angeles Times*, December 22, 1988.

65. "City Council Lowers Boom on Boom Boxes," *Los Angeles Times*, October 17, 1989.

66. "Pueblo Law Hits 'Drive-by Stereos,'" *Denver Post*, February 15, 1995.

67. Ironically this bill was supported in an op-ed article in the *Chicago Defender*. "Let's hear it for the bill to quiet boom boxes," *Chicago Defender*, June 4, 1996.

68. It is telling that one source for up-to-date definitions of such slang comes from police departments. This particular one comes from the Berkeley, California, police department, but any number of other "crime" websites and databases feature a glossary of such "gang-related" terminology. http://crime.about.com/od/efg/g/gl_p_hoopty.htm, visited on January 24, 2005.

69. Jack Bratich, "Public Secrecy and Immanent Security: A Strategic Analysis," *Cultural Studies* 20:4–5 (2006): 493–511.

## 6. Raging with a Machine

1. The even more recent Ford/Firestone tire debacle follows a different structure. As it relates to automobiles, this sort of event's narrative and explanation follow the script of Ralph Nader's *Unsafe at Any Speed*. What we get is a general explanation of the automobile industry's lack of investment in safety and then a specific example of how this lack produces Corvairesque carnage. The story was retold in the 1970s with the infamous exploding Ford Pinto. The basic tenets of this story are that corporate greed will overshadow an implicit contract with citizens to offer them safe products. It is, then, a structural problem, built into capitalism, which must be fixed through government initiative, citizen watchdogs, and a liti-

gious public. The battleground is more economic and technological than social and governmental. The issue is not so much how to alter individual conduct, but rather how to deal with structural problems between the competing interests of capital and civil society.

2. Andrew Ferguson, "Road Rage," *Time*, January 12, 1998, 64.

3. Michael Fumento, "'Road Rage' vs. Reality," *Atlantic Monthly*, August 1998, 12–17.

4. Matthew L. Wald, "Temper Cited as Cause of 28,000 Road Deaths a Year," *New York Times*, July 18, 1997: A14.

5. "AAA Foundation's Road Rage News Release and Press Report Summary," *American Automobile Association Foundation for Traffic Safety* (August 29, 2000): 3, http://www.aaafts.org/text/research/RoadRage.html, 3.

6. See chapter 1 for a lengthier discussion of this.

7. *The Diagnostic and Statistical Manual of Mental Disorders* is used by medical professionals as a guide for diagnosing depression and other mental disorders.

8. "AAA Foundation's Road Rage News Release and Press Report Summary," 3.

9. Ibid.

10. Ibid., 5.

11. Ibid., 3.

12. Daniel B. Rathbone and Jorg C. Huckabee, "Controlling Road Rage: A Literature Review and Pilot Study," *American Automobile Association Foundation for Traffic Safety* (August 29, 2000): 6, http://www.aaafts.org/text/research/RoadRage Final.html.

13. David K. Willis, "Testimony to House Transportation and Infrastructure Committee; Surface Transportation Subcommittee, Road Rage: Causes and Dangers of Aggressive Driving" (July 17, 1997).

14. Ricardo Martinez, "Testimony to House Transportation and Infrastructure Committee; Surface Transportation Subcommittee, Road Rage: Causes and Dangers of Aggressive Driving" (July 17, 1997).

15. Ibid.

16. John Larson, "Testimony to House Transportation and Infrastructure Committee; Surface Transportation Subcommittee, Road Rage: Causes and Dangers of Aggressive Driving" (July 17, 1997).

17. Leon James, "Testimony to House Transportation and Infrastructure Committee; Surface Transportation Subcommittee, Road Rage: Causes and Dangers of Aggressive Driving" (July 17, 1997).

18. Ibid.

19. "Aggressive Driving." *NCSL Transportation Review* (August 29, 2000): 2, http://www.ncsl.org/programs/esnr/498rage.htm.

20. Mathew Joint, "Road Rage," *American Automobile Association Foundation*

*for Traffic Safety* (August 29, 2000): 4, http://www.aaafts.org/text/research/agdrtext.html.

21. Larson, "Testimony," 4.

22. Joint, "Road Rage," 18.

23. Ibid., 28.

24. Ibid., 29.

25. Ibid., 18.

26. Ferguson, "Road Rage," 5.

27. See Douglas Kellner, *Media Culture* (1995) for an example of how this articulatory logic operates.

28. In fact, Dr. Driving, with Rush Limbaugh obviously in mind, warns against listening to "inflammatory talk radio" while driving.

29. Why "she" is driving and not "he" will later be explained.

30. "AAA Foundation's Road Rage News Release and Press Report Summary," 7.

31. Ibid., 29

32. James, "Testimony," 4.

33. Larson, "Testimony," 4.

34. James, "Testimony," 4.

35. Larson, "Testimony," 5.

36. Ibid.

37. James, "Testimony," 7.

38. Fumento, "'Road Rage' vs. Reality."

39. Michael Schudson. *Discovering the News: A Social History of American Newspapers* (New York: Basic Books, 1978).

40. For further elaboration of these systems, see James Hay and Jeremy Packer. "Crossing the Media(-n): Auto-mobility, the Transported Self, and Technologies of Freedom," in *Media/Space: Scale and Culture in a Media Age*, ed. Nick Cauldry and Anna McCarthy (Routledge, New York, 2004).

41. Martinez, "Testimony," 3.

42. Ibid.

43. James, "Testimony," 3.

44. Ibid., 8.

45. "AAA Foundation's Road Rage News Release and Press Report Summary," *American Automobile Association Foundation for Traffic Safety* (August 29, 2000), http://www.aaafts.org/text/research/RoadRage.html.

46. Ibid., 14.

47. Ibid., 16.

48. Joint, "Road Rage," 20.

49. The Dr. Driving test includes twenty questions that correspond to escalating acts of aggression. For instance, the first question has to do with mentally con-

demning other drivers, the sixth, with preventing someone from passing because you're mad, the thirteenth, with getting out of the car and engaging in a verbal dispute, the sixteenth with trying to run another car off the road, and the twentieth with killing someone. He claims that over half the respondents have escalated to at least the thirteenth level. James, "Testimony."

50. Ibid, 11.
51. Michelle Malkin, "A Founding Father's Rules Might Cure Raging Drivers," *Seattle Times*, July 22, 1997, 24.
52. Ibid., 2.
53. Nicholas Rose, *Powers of Freedom: Reframing Political Thought* (New York: Cambridge University Press, 1999), 172.
54. Ibid., 176.
55. James, "Testimony," 12.
56. Ibid.
57. Ibid.
58. Ibid., 13.
59. Lisa Sheikh, "Testimony to House Transportation and Infrastructure Committee; Surface Transportation Subcommittee, Road Rage: Causes and Dangers of Aggressive Driving" (July 17, 1997).
60. These tapes are put on as part of a vast data collection enterprise which is said to be vital to gauging progress and trends in aggressive driving. See Dr. Driving.
61. Erving Goffman, *The Presentation of Self in Everyday Life* (New York: Doubleday, 1959).
62. Larson, "Testimony," 6.
63. Ibid., 6.
64. Ibid., 4.
65. *Driving to Detroit, Flaming Iguanas*, and *The Perfect Vehicle*.
66. Suzanne McDonald-Walker, *Bikers: Culture, Politics, and Power* (London: Berg, 2000).
67. Ferguson, "Road Rage," 2.
68. Ibid., 4.
69. Rose, *Powers of Freedom*, 188.
70. James, "Testimony," 11.
71. "A Divine Driver: Commercials Say Jesus Wouldn't Drive an SUV," http://abcnews.go.com/sections/GMA/GoodMorningAmerica/GMA021121Jesus_drive.html June 25, 2004.
72. Marilyn Gardner, "Anti-SUV Query: "What Would Jesus Drive?" *Christian Science Monitor*, June 4, 2001.
73. See http://www.whatwouldjesusdrive.org/action/pledge.php, June 25, 2004.

## 7. Safety to Security

1. Albert Whitney. *Man and the Motorcar* (New York: New Jersey Department of Law and Public Safety, 1949).

2. Ibid.

3. Ibid., 4.

4. The publication of Ralph Nader's *Unsafe at Any Speed: The Designed-In Dangers of the American Automobile* (New York: Grossman, 1965), the congressional hearings that led from the publication, and the resultant creation of the National Highway Traffic Safety Agency mark this shift.

5. Department of Homeland Security website, http://www.dhs.gov/dhspublic/.

6. In some cases, Guantanamo for instance, in terms that Foucault called domination rather than power in the last interview he gave before his death (*The Final Foucault*), access to mobility and the legal-juridical apparatus is completely denied. Prisoners essentially cannot act through any acceptable channels to resist, effect, or reformulate their situation. In absolute terms they may, depending upon how complete their confinement, have the power to take their own life, thus usurping the state's sovereign potential to do the same, but for all intents and purposes they are powerless. Deleuze suggests this return of sovereign forms may be an integral part of the changes coinciding with the dawning of the control society: "It may be that older means of control, borrowed from the old sovereign societies, will come back in to play, adapted as necessary" ("Postscript on the Control Society," in *Negotiations* [New York: Columbia University Press, 1990, 1995], 182).

7. M. Hardt and A. Negri, *Multitude* (New York: Penguin, 2004), 54.

8. For a historical explanation of how the articulation of transportation and communication technologies operates as the activating mechanism for such transformations, see Jeremy Packer, "Rethinking Dependency."

9. Even the notion of grooming and "caring for" gets inverted as part of the preparatory program of the suicide bomber in cutting one's hair, shaving, shining ones shoes, and generally perfecting the presentation of self for the afterlife.

10. Jack Bratich, "Spies Like Us: Popular Secrecy, Immanent Security, and Citizen-subjects," and Mark Andrejevic, "Offloading Homeland Defense in an Interactive Era: The Participatory Promise of Ready.Gov," in *Cultural Studies* 20:4–5 (2006): 441–58.

11. Hardt and Negri, *Multitude.*12. "Control and Becoming," in *Negations* (New York: Columbia University Press, 1990, 1995), 175.

13. Ibid.

14. Craig Robertson, "The Ritual of Verification? The Nation, the State, and the U.S. Passport," in *Communications, Transportation, History: Rethinking the Legacy*

*of James Carey*, ed. Jeremy Packer and Craig Robertson (New York: Peter Lang, 2005).

15. The number of miles driven per capita rose over 50 percent between 1970 and 2000 (U.S. Department of Transportation, *Our Nations Highways 2000* [2000]), http://www.fhwa.dot.gov/ohim/onh00/onh2p1.htm.

16. A more thorough examination of the coupling of communications and transportation technologies can be found in Packer, "Rethinking Dependency."

17. "But could it do a handbrake turn?" *Electronics Weekly*, August 20, 1997. See www.electronicsweekly.com/Article8767.htm.

18. Packer, "Rethinking Dependency."

19. These notions of synergy and convergence, specifically in relation to communications and automobiles, is critiqued for the simplistic notion of what comprises a technology in J. Hay and J. Packer, "Crossing the Median." We argue that the automobile, GPS, or even the car radio are themselves an amalgam. The automobile in this sense is an ever-changing arrangement of technologies, cultural forms, and governmental programs. It is an always-in-process imaginary potential that is altered through its attachment and integration with other technologies. GPS is not simply added to the automobile, but rather it makes the automobile a new technology (J. Packer and J. Hay, "Crossing the Media(-n): Auto-mobility, the Transported Self, and Technologies of Freedom," in *Media-Space: Scale and Culture in a Media Age*, ed. Nick Couldry and Anna McCarthy (New York: Routledge, 2004), 209–32.

20. Fall Creek Consultants, "Creating the Convergence," www.comm-nav/commnav.htm, visited February 7, 2005.

21. Department of Homeland Security Press Release, "Department of Homeland Security announces $179 million in grants to secure America's Ports," http://www.dhs.gov/dhspublic/display?content=3031.

22. Defense Advanced Research Projects Agency (DARPA), "Home Page," www.darpa.mil/.

23. DARPA, "Proposer Information Pamphlet (PIP): Combat Zones That See (CTS)": www.darpa.mil/ixo/solicitations/CTS/file/BAA_03–15_CTS_PIP.pdf, visited February 7, 2005.

24. "'There's almost 100 percent chance that it will work,' said Jim Lewis, who heads the Technology and Public Policy Program at the Center for Strategic and International Studies, 'because it's just connecting things that already exist.'" Noah Schachtman, "Big Brother Gets a Brain," *Village Voice*, July 9–15, 2003: 2, www.villagevoice.com/issues/0328/schachtman.php.

25. DARPA, "Combat Zones That See."

26. Schachtman, "Big Brother Gets a Brain," 2.

27. DARPA, "Combat Zones That See."

28. "Black Box for Cars?" *Why Not?* http://www.whynot.net/view_idea.php?id=1380, visited February 7, 2005.

29. Ford, "SynUS," http://www.fordvehicles.com/autoshow/concept/synus/.

30. See Mark Andrejevich, "Offloading Homeland Defense in an Interactive Era: The Participatory Promise of Ready.Gov," *Cultural Studies* 20:4–5 (2006): 441–58, for a discussion of the involvement of citizens as part of a neoliberal strategy in homeland security.

# WORKS CITED

"#1 Dating Menace, the Automobile." 1955. *Ladies' Home Journal.* November.

"AAA Foundation's Road Rage News Release and Press Report Summary." 2000. *American Automobile Association Foundation for Traffic Safety.* August 29. http://www.aaafts.org/text/research/RoadRage.html.

Abbot, Eddie. 1954. "Don't Tell Me Women Are Helpless." *Woman's Home Companion.* July.

Adams, Nathan M. 1973. "Hitchhiking—Too Often the Last Ride." *Reader's Digest.* July.

"Ad Council Notes Success in Year." 1955. *New York Times.* July 13.

A.F.L. "Chief Asserts Eisenhower Yields." 1953. *New York Times.* September 18.

"Aggressive Driving." 2000. *NCSL Transportation Reviews.* August 29. http://www.ncsl.org/programs/esnr/498rage.htm.

Anderson, Douglas. 1970. "Meditations on a Hitchhiking Ticket." *National Review.* September 24.

Andrejevic, Mark. 2006. "Interactive (In)security: The Participatory Promise of Ready.gov." *Cultural Studies* 20:4–5: 441–58.

*Angels as Hard as They Come.* 1971. Dir. Joe Viola. New World Pictures.

*Angels Die Hard.* 1970. Dir. Richard Compton. New World Pictures.

*Angels from Hell.* 1968. Dir. Bruce Kessler. Fanfare Film.

Ant Farm. 1976. *Automerica: A Trip Down U.S. Highways from World War II to the Future.* New York: E. P. Dutton.

"Are *You* Really a Safe Driver?" 1952. *Better Homes and Gardens.* November.

Arnold, Peter. 1974. *Lady Beware.* New York: Doubleday.

———. 1974. "What You Should Know Before Hitchhiking." *Seventeen.* February.

"The Art of the Motorcycle." 1998. *In the Field* 69:0.6, 1.

*Baadasssss Cinema.* 2002. Dir. Isaac Julien. New Video Group.

"Ban on Hitchhiking Due Some Study By Panel at Santa Cruz." 1970. *San Jose Mercury News*. August 27.

Barrett, Michele. 1991. *The Politics of Truth: From Marx to Foucault*. Stanford: Stanford University Press.

Barry, Andrew. 1996. "Lines of Communication and Spaces of Rule. In *Foucault and Political Reason: Liberalism, Neo-liberalism and Rationalities of Government*, ed. Andrew Barry, Thomas Osborne, and Nikolas Rose. University of Chicago Press.

Baudrillard, Jean. 1988. *America*. New York: Verso.

Baum, Arthur W. 1956. "All-American Automobile." *Saturday Evening Post*. May 26.

Bayston, Fitzgerald. 1937. *Drive and Live*. Richmond, Va.: Johnson Publishing.

Beck, Ulrich. 1986/1992. *Risk Society: Towards a New Modernity*, trans. Mark Ritter. London: Sage Publications.

Becker, Howard. 1963. *Outsiders: Studies in the Sociology of Deviance*. New York: Free Press.

———. 1966. *Social Problems: A Modern Approach*. New York: Wiley.

Beckman, Jorg. 2004. "Mobility and Safety." *Theory Culture and Society* 21:4–5: 81–100.

Behling, Laura L. 1997. "'The Woman at the Wheel': Marketing Ideal Womanhood, 1915–1934." *Journal of American Culture* 20:3: 13–30.

Belt, Forest H. 1973. *Easi-Guide to Citizens Band Radio*. Indianapolis: Howard W. Sams.

Bennett, Tony. 1992. "Putting Policy into Cultural Studies." In *Cultural Studies*, ed. Lawrence Grossberg, Carey Nelson, and Paula Treichler. New York: Routledge.

———. *The Birth of the Museum*. New York: Routledge, 1995.

Bennett, Tony, and Janet Woolacott. 1987. *Bond and Beyond: The Political Career of a Popular Hero*. London: Methuen.

Bernaur, James, and David Rasmussin, eds. *The Final Foucault*. Boston: MIT Press, 1988.

Bernstein, Walter. 1948. "A Trip by Thumb." *New Yorker*. October 2.

*Better Off Dead*. 1985. Dir. Steve Savage. Paramount Studios.

Birmingham, John, et al. 1970. *Our Time Is Now: Notes from the High School Underground*. New York: Bantam.

*B.J. and the Bear*. NBC, 1979–82.

"Black Box for Cars?" 2004. *Why Not?* June 2. http://www.whynot.net/ideas/1380.

Boal, Sam. 1951. "Woman Driver: A Myth Exploded." *New York Times Magazine*. November 4.

Boroughs, Bob. 1974. "America by Thumb." *Senior Scholastic*. April 24.

Boyd, Todd. 2002. *Am I Black Enough for You?: Popular Culture from the 'Hood and Beyond*. Bloomington: Indiana University Press.

Braley, Berton. 1956. "Who's the Better Driver?" *American Mercury*. March 24–27.

Brand Names Foundation Advertisement. 1954. *Ebony*. February.

Bratich, Jack Z. 2006. "Public Secrecy and Immanent Security: A Strategic Analysis." *Cultural Studies* 20:4–5: 493–511.

Bratich, Jack Z., Jeremy Packer, and Cameron McCarthy, eds. 2003. *Foucault, Cultural Studies, and Governmentality*. Albany: SUNY Press.

*Bring Me the Head of Alfredo Garcia*. 1974. Dir. Sam Peckinpah. MGM.

Brottman, Mikita. 2001. *Car Crash Culture*. New York: Palgrave.

Bruce, Arthur Garfield. 1950. *Highway Design and Construction*. New York: International Textbook.

Bruton, Sabe. 1959. "Critic Says Cadillac Holds Up Our Wheels of Progress by Not Hiring Negro Salesmen." *New York Age*. April.

Buckwalter, Len. 1976. CB *Radio: A Complete Guide*. New York: Tempo Books.

Burchell, Graham. 1996. "Liberal Government and Techniques of the Self." In *Foucault and Political Reason: Liberalism, Neo-Liberalism and Rationalities of Government*, ed. Andrew Barry, Thomas Osborne, and Nikolas Rose. Chicago: University of Chicago Press.

Burchell, Graham, Colin Gordon, and Peter Miller. 1991. *The Foucault Effect: Studies in Governmentatlity*. Chicago: University of Chicago Press.

Burke, Kenneth. 1969. *A Rhetoric of Motives*. Berkeley: University of California Press.

Burton, Alan. 1973. *Police Telecommunications*. Springfield, Ill.: Charles C. Thomas.

"But could it do a handbrake turn?" 1997. *Electronics Weekly*. August 20.

Cades, Hazel Rawson. 1954. "Good Looks on the Road." *Woman's Home Companion*. June 30.

Cameron, Kevin. 1996. "New Riders." *Cycle World*. June.

Canby, Vincent. 1978. "Peckinpah's 'Convoy,' Open-Road Machismo," *New York Times*. June 28.

"Capital Beltway Update: Beltway User Focus Group." 2000. *National Highway Traffic Safety Administration*. 29 August 2000. http://www.nhtsa.dot.gov/people/injury/research/aggressive/final.rpt.html.

Carey, James. 1988. *Communication as Culture*. New York: Unwin Press.

*C.C. and Company*. 1970. Dir. Seymour Robbie. Rogallan, Inc.

"City Council Lowers Boom on Boom Boxes." 1989. *Los Angeles Times*. October 17.

Cohan, Steven, and Ina Rae Hark. 1997. *The Road Movie Book*. Routledge: London.

Collett, Peter. 1987. *Driving Passion: The Psychology of the Car*. Boston: Faber and Faber.

Connell, Dominick. 1998. "Driver Aggression." *American Automobile Association Foundation for Traffic Safety*. August 29, 2000. http://www.aaafts.org/text/research/agdrtext.html.

*Convoy*. 1978. Dir. Sam Peckinpah. EMI/United Artists.

Cravens, Gwyneth. 1972. "Hitching Nowhere: The Aging Young on the Endless Road." *Harper's*. September.

*Crash*. 1997. Dir. David Cronenberg. New Line Cinema.

"Cyclist's Holiday." 1947. *Life*. July 21.

Dahlberg, Edwin T. 1978. *I Pick Up Hitchhikers*. Valley Forge, Pa.: Judson Press.

Dannefer, Dale, and Nicholas Poushinsky. 1978. "The C.B. Phenomenon, A Sociological Appraisal." *Journal of Popular Culture* 6: 42–56.

DARPA. 2003. "Proposer Information Pamphlet (PIP): Combat Zones That See (CTS)." www.darpa.mil/ixo/solicitations/CTS/file/BAA_03–15_CTS_PIP.pdf.

David, Lester. 1973. "Hitchhiking: The Deadly New Odds." *Good Housekeeping*. July.

Davis, John P. 1959. "A Stranger in the Car." *Reader's Digest*. August.

Davis, Mike. 1991. *City of Quartz: Excavating the Future in Los Angeles*. New York: Verso.

———. 1998. *Ecology of Fear: Los Angeles and the Imagination of Disaster*. New York: Metropolitan.

*Deathrace 2000*. 1975. Dir. Paul Bartel. New World Pictures.

Deferet, Daniel. 1991. "'Popular Life' and Insurance Technology." In *The Foucault Effect: Studies in Governmentality*, ed. Graham Burchell, Colin Gordon, and Peter Miller. Chicago: University of Chicago Press.

Deleuze, Gilles. 1988. *Foucault*. Minneapolis: University of Minnesota Press.

———. 1995. *Negotiations: 1972–1990*. New York: Columbia University Press.

Deleuze, Gilles, and Félix Guattari. 1987. *A Thousand Plateaus: Capitalism and Schizophrenia*. Minneapolis: University of Minnesota Press.

Denzin, Norman. 1989. *Interpretive Interactionism*. Newbury Park, Calif.: Sage Publications.

Department of Homeland Security. 2003. "Department of Homeland Security announces $179 million in grants to secure America's Ports." December 10. http://www.dhs.gov/dhspublic/display?content=3031.

DeSilva, Harry R. 1942. *Why We Have Automobile Accidents*. New York: John Wiley.

de Tocqueville, Alexis. 1835/1900. *Democracy in America*. New York: Colonial Press.

*Devil's Angels*. 1967. Dir. Dan Haller. New World Pictures.

Dimaggio, Paul. 1973. *The Hitchhiker's Field Manual*. New York: Macmillan.

"A Divine Driver: Commercials Say Jesus Wouldn't Drive an SUV." 2004. *ABC News .com*. June 25. http://abcnews.go.com/sections/GMA/GoodMorningAmerica/GMA021121Jesus_drive.html.

*Dr. No*. 1962. Dir. Terence Young. MGM.

Dodd, David. 1973. "Swing Low, Sweet Cadillac." *New Society*. October 25.

Douglas, Mary. 1992. *Risk and Blame: Essays in Cultural Theory*. New York: Routledge.

Douglas, Mary, and Aaron Wildavsky. 1982. *Risk and Culture: An Essay on the Selec-*

*tion of Technical and Environmental Dangers*. Berkeley: University of California Press.

Douglas, Richard Alexander. 1936. *Common Sense in Driving Your Car*. New York: Longmans, Green.

Douglas, Susan J. 1987. *Inventing American Broadcasting, 1899–1922*. Baltimore: Johns Hopkins University Press.

Draper, Elaine. 1993. "Risk Society and Social Theory." *Contemporary Sociology* 22:5: 641–44.

"Driver's Downfall." 1953. *Newsweek*. September 14.

"The Drivers' Network." 1975. *Time*. September 22.

"Driving with Dracula." 2003. *New Orleans Times-Picayune*. July 24.

"Drug-Courier Profile." 1985. *Miami Herald*. June 6.

*The Duel*. 1972. Dir. Steven Spielberg. Universal.

*The Dukes of Hazzard*. 1979–84. CBS.

Dullea, Georgia. 1974. "The Suburban Car Pool: Even More Vital Today." *New York Times*. January 4.

Dunn, Katherine. 1971. *Truck*. New York: Harper and Row.

*Easy Rider*. 1969. Dir. Dennis Hopper. Pando Productions.

"The Easy Way to Wash the Car." 1953. *Woman's Home Companion*. August.

Ellison, Ralph. 1995. *The Collected Essays of Ralph Ellison*. New York: Modern Library.

Endicott, William. 1973. "Hitchhikers Seeking State ID Cards—With Small Thumb Tax." *Los Angeles Times*. June 6.

Ericson, Richard, and Kevin Haggerty. 1997. *Policing the Risk Society*. Toronto: University of Toronto Press.

Ewald, Francois. 1991. "Insurance and Risk." In *The Foucault Effect: Studies in Governmentality*, ed. Graham Burchell, Thomas Gordon, and Peter Miller. Chicago: University of Chicago Press.

FCC. 1970. "To Permit Aliens to Operate Radio Stations." *Subcommittee on Communications Hearing*. October 8.

———. 1975. "Actions Taken or Needed to Curb Widespread Abuse of the Citizens Band Radio Service." *Report to Congress*. October 14.

Fall Creek Consultants. 2005. "Creating the Convergence." www.comm-nav/comm nav.htm.

Ferguson, Andrew. 1998. "Road Rage." *Time*. January 12.

Finch, Christopher. 1992. *Highways to Heaven: The AUTO Biography of America*. New York: Harper Collins.

Fischer, Margo. 1950. "So You Think Women Can't Drive!" *Saturday Evening Post*. April 14.

Floherty, John L. 1937. *Youth at the Wheel: A Reference Book on Safety*. Philadelphia: J. B. Lippincott.

Ford. 2004. *SynUS*. http://www.fordvehicles.com/autoshow/concept/synus/.

Foucault, Michel. *Madness and Civilization: A History of Insanity in the Age of Reason*. New York: Random House, 1965.

———. 1978. *Discipline and Punish: The Birth of the Prison*. New York: Vintage.

———. 1980a. *The History of Sexuality: An Introduction*. New York: Vintage Books.

———. 1980b. *Power/Knowledge: Selected Interviews and Other Writings 1972–1977*. New York: Pantheon Books.

———. 1983. "The Subject and Power." In *Michel Foucault: Beyond Structuralism and Hermeneutics*, ed. Paul Rabinow and Hubert Dreyfus. Chicago: University of Chicago Press.

———. 1988. "The Ethic of Care for the Self as a Practice of Freedom." In *The Final Foucault*, ed. James Bernauer and David Rasmussen. Boston: MIT Press.

———. 1989. *Foucault Live*. New York: Semiotext(e), 1989.

———. 1990. *Politics Philosophy Culture: Interviews and Other Writings 1977–1984*, ed. Lawrence Kritzman. New York: Routledge.

———. 1991. "Governmentality." In *The Foucault Effect: Studies in Governmentality*, ed. Graham Burchell, Colin Gordon, and Peter Miller. Chicago: University of Chicago Press.

———. 1999. "Pastoral Power and Political Reason." In *Religion and Culture*, ed. Jeremy Carrette. New York: Routledge.

———. 2003. *Abnormal: Lectures at the Collège de France 1974–1975*. New York: Picador.

*The French Connection*. 1971. Dir. William Friedkin. Twentieth Century Fox.

Friedman, Martin. 1995. "What to Look for in Crash Protection." *Motorcyclist*. September.

Fumento, Michael. 1998. "'Road Rage' vs. Reality." *Atlantic Monthly*. August.

Gardner, Marilyn. 2001. "Anti-SUV Query: 'What Would Jesus Drive?'" *Christian Science Monitor*. June 4.

Gates, Kelly. 2005. "Advocating Alternative Futures: Screening Biometrics and Related Technologies in Science Fiction Cinema." *Social Text*. July.

*The Getaway*. 1972. Dir. Sam Peckinpah. First Artists.

Gilroy, Paul. 2001. "Driving While Black." In *Car Cultures*, ed. Daniel Miller. New York: Oxford Books.

"Girls' Experience Shows Hitch-Hiking Reasonably Safe." 1941. *Science News Letter*. July 2.

Glassner, Barry. 1999. *The Culture of Fear: Why Americans Are Afraid of the Wrong Things*. New York: Basic Books.

Goffman, Erving. 1959. *The Presentation of Self in Everyday Life*. New York: Doubleday.

*Goldfinger*. 1965. Dir. Guy Hamilton. MGM.

*Gone in 60 Seconds*. 1974. Dir. H. B. Halicki. Media Home Entertainment.

Gordon, Marsha. 1972. "Hitchhiking Really Isn't Cool." *Seventeen*. October.

Gordon, Susan J. 1982. "Car Pools: Rules of the Road for a Suburban Ritual." *New York Times*. October 10.

Gottlieb, Robert. 1966. "Cars and the Law." *Motor Trend*. December.

Graham, Janet. 1966. "Rule of Thumb for the Open Road." *Sports Illustrated*. June 6.

"The Great Truck Blockade." 1973. *U.S. News and World Report*. December 17.

Gregory, Dick. 1962. *From the Back of the Bus*. New York: Avon.

Grieveson, Lee. 1998. "Fighting Films: Race, Morality, and the Governing of Cinema." *Cinema Journal* 38: 40–61.

Grimm, Tom. 1970. "The Thumb as Travel Agent: Pleasure and Perils." *New York Times*. December 13.

———. 1972. *Hitchhiker's Handbook*. New York: Plume Books.

Grossberg, Lawrence. 1992. *We Gotta Get Outta This Place: Popular Conservatism and Postmodern Culture*. New York: Routledge.

———. 1994. "The Political Status of Youth and Youth Culture." In *Adolescents and Their Music: If It's Too Loud, You're Too Old*, ed. Jonathan S. Epstein. New York: Garland.

*The Gumball Rally*. 1976. Dir. Chuck Bail. First Artists/Warner Brothers.

Gunther, Max. 1957. "Who Are America's Worst Drivers?" *Popular Science*. January.

"Gypsies But Neat." 1952. *Woman's Home Companion*. August.

Hall, Stuart, and Tony Jefferson. 1976. *Resistance through Rituals: Youth Subculture in Post-war Britain*. London: Harper Collins Academic.

Hardt, Michael, and Antonio Negri. 2000. *Empire*. Cambridge, Mass.: Harvard University Press.

———. 2004. *Multitude*. New York: Penguin.

Hardyman, Hugh. 1931. "The Art of Hitchhiking." *New Republic*. July 29.

"Harriman orders dropping of the word 'color' on applications for driver's license." 1955. *New York Amsterdam News*. December 17.

Harris, David A. 1999. "The Stories, the Statistics, and the Law: Why 'Driving While Black' Matters." *Minnesota Law Review* 84: 265–326.

Hartley, John. 1999. *Uses of Television*. London: Routledge.

Hay, James. 2000. "Unaided Virtues: The (Neo-)liberalization of the Domestic Sphere." *Television and New Media* 1:1: 53–73.

Hay, James, and Jeremy Packer. 2004. "Crossing the Media(-n): Auto-mobility, the Transported Self, and Technologies of Freedom." In *MediaSpace: Scale and Culture in a Media Age*, ed. Nick Couldry and Anna McCarthy. New York: Routledge.

Hazleton, Leslie. 1998. *Driving to Detroit: An Automotive Odyssey*. New York: Free Press.

"Hearings before the Committee on Interstate and Foreign Commerce." 1974. 93rd Congress, 2nd Session, February 6, Serial 93–58.

Hebdige, Dick. 1979. *Subculture: The Meaning of Style*. New York: Routledge.

———. 1988. *Hiding in the Light*. New York: Routledge.

*Hell's Angels 1969*. 1969. Dir. Lee Madden. Tracom.

*Hell's Angels on Wheels*. 1967. Dir. Richard Rush. U.S. Films.

*Hell's Highway: The True Story of Highway Safety Films*. 2003. Dir. Brett Wood. Kino International.

Henle, Guy. 1955. "Coming Up—The Two-Car Family." *Woman's Home Companion*. June.

Herbert, Steve. 1997. *Policing Space: Territoriality and the Los Angeles Police Department*. Minneapolis: University of Minnesota Press.

Hickey, Margaret. 1954. "Young Drivers Learn Good Road Habits . . . at School Safety Institute." *Ladies' Home Journal*. May.

Hicks, Ken. 1973. *The Complete Hitchhiker: A Handbook for Bumming Around America*. New York: Tobey.

"High-Powered Cars a Tradition in Negro Community." 1951. *Ebony*. July.

"Hippies Protest LA hitchhiking Ban." 1970. *Los Angeles Times*. October 15.

"History of AAA-Chicago Motor Club." 2000. *Chicago Motorclub Online*. August 29. http://www.aaa.com/aaa/020/corphist.htm.

*Hitchhiker*. 1953. Dir. Ida Lupino. Kino.

"Hitchhiker Controls Spread." 1970. *San Jose Mercury News*. August 13.

"Hitchhikers Held in Berkeley Raids." 1970. *New York Times*. August 9.

"The Hitchhiker You Pick Up May Be a Dangerous Criminal!" 1957. *Saturday Evening Post*. December 14.

"Hitching a Ride Across America." 1971. *Life*. August 27.

Holbrook Pierson, Melissa. 1997. *The Perfect Vehicle: What It Is About Motorcycles*. New York: W. W. Norton.

Hoover, J. Edgar. 1970. *J. Edgar Hoover on Communism*. New York: Paperback Library.

Houston, Jourdan. 1974. "Rules of Thumb." *Saturday Review World*. May 4.

James, E. W. 1952. "Should Schools Teach Safety?" *Safety Digest, Automotive Safety Foundation*, 1:1: 17.

Jameson, Booth. 1928. "Hitchhikers by Night Light." *Saturday Evening Post*. May 5.

———. 1928. "A Hitchhiking Reformer." *Saturday Evening Post*. September 22.

Jeanes, William. 1975. "Tuning in Justice on Your CB Radio Dial." *Car and Driver*. July.

Joint, Mathew. 1996. "Road Rage." *American Automobile Association Foundation for Traffic Safety*. August 29, 2000. http://www.aaafts.org/text/research/agdrtext .html.

Kaplan, E. Ann, ed. 1978. *Women in Film Noir*. London: British Film Institute.

Kelley, Ben. 1971. *The Pavers and the Paved*. New York: Donald W. Brown.

Kelner, Douglas. 1995. *Media Culture: Cultural Studies, Identity, and Politics between the Modern and the Postmodern*. New York: Routledge.

Kennedy, R. 1998. "Engines Roaring, Pagers Beeping: Middle Class Leads a Renewed Romance with Biker Culture." *New York Times*. July 12.

Kennedy, Randall. 1997. *Race Crime and the Law*. New York: Pantheon.

Kerbo, Harold, Karrie Marshall, and Phillip Holley. 1978. "Reestablishing "Gemeinschaft? An Examination of the CB Radio Fad." *Urban Life* 7:3: 337–58.

Kerouac, Jack. 1959. *On the Road*. New York: Viking.

Kifner, Jon. 1971. "They Use the Thumb to Roam the Land." *New York Times*. August 8.

King, Samantha. 2003. "Civic Fitness: Breast Cancer, the Race for the Cure, and New Technologies of Ethical Citizenship." In *Foucault, Cultural Studies, and Governmentality*, ed. Jack Z. Bratich, Jeremy Packer, and Cameron McCarthy. Albany: SUNY Press, 2003.

Klinger, Barbara. 1997. "The Road to Dystopia: Landscaping the Nation in *Easy Rider*." In *The Road Movie Book*, ed. Steven Cohan and Ira Hark. London: Routledge.

Krutnick, Frank. 1991. *In a Lonely Street: Film Noir, Genre, Masculinity*. New York: Routledge.

Kundera, Milan. 1974. "The Hitchhiking Game." *Esquire*. April.

La Botz, Dan. 1990. *Rank and File Rebellion: Teamsters for a Democratic Union*. New York: Verso.

La Coste, Warren. 1992. *Holy Rider: The Priest and the Gang*. Far Hills, N.J.: New Horizon Press.

Lane, Kay. 1955. "How to Travel with a Boyfriend." *American Magazine*. October.

Larson, John. 1997. "Testimony to House Transportation and Infrastructure Committee." *Surface Transportation Subcommittee*. July 17.

Lavigne, Yves. 1987. *Hell's Angels*. New York: Lyle Stuart.

Leavitt, Helen. 1970. *Superhighway-Superhoax*. New York: Doubleday.

Lee, Danny. 2004. "Driving; The Dub Generation: Gearheads Go Hip-Hop." *New York Times*. April 23.

Lehman, Milton. 1951. "The First Woman Driver." *Better Homes and Gardens*. July.

Lessig, Corey T. 2001. *Automobility: Social Changes in the American South, 1909–1939. American Popular History and Culture*. New York: Routledge.

"Let's hear it for the bill to quiet boom boxes." 1996. *Chicago Defender*. June 4.

Lewis, Jon. 1992. *The Road to Romance and Ruin: Teen Films and Youth Culture*. New York: Routledge.

Lieberman, Jethro, and Brian Rhodes. 1976. *The Complete CB Handbook*. New York: Avon.

"Like a New Car." 1947. *Better Homes and Gardens*. May.

Lindsay, Robert. 1973. "The Angry Truck Driver: 'We've Got to Show 'Em.'" *New York Times*. December 4.

*Live and Let Die*. 1973. Dir. Guy Hamilton. MGM.

Lopez, Erika. 1997. *Flaming Iguanas: An Illustrated All Girl Road Novel Thing*. New York: Scribner.

*Lost Highway*. 1996. Dir. David Lynch. Paramount.

Lowe, Walter. 1963. "Negroes Buy 5,000,000 Cars a Year, But Get No Dealerships!" *Chicago Defender*. September 13.

*Mad Max*. 1980. Dir. George Miller. Warner Brothers.

"A Major Yippie Theorist Seized on Drug Charges." 1971. *New York Times*. July 26.

Malfetti, James. 1958. "Human Behavior-Factor X." *The Annals of the American Academy of Political and Social Science*. November.

Malkin, Michelle. 1997. "A Founding Father's Rules Might Cure Raging Drivers." *Seattle Times*. July 22.

*A Man Escaped*. 1956. Dir. Robert Bresson. New Yorker Video.

Marchand, Roland. 1985. *Advertising the American Dream: Making Way for Modernity, 1920–1940*. Berkeley: University of California Press.

Marsh, Peter, and Peter Collet. 1986. *Driving Passion: The Psychology of the Car*. Boston: Faber and Faber.

Marshall, El Trains. 1973. "Truckers' Revolt." *New Republic*. December 22.

Matson, Robert. 1974. "On the Road." *Harper's*. November.

Mattelart, Armand. 1996. *The Invention of Communication*. Minneapolis: University of Minnesota Press.

Maxfield, James. 1996. *The Fatal Woman: Sources of Male Anxiety in American Film Noir, 1941–1991*. London: Associated University.

Mayer, Milton. 1982. "Sore Thumbs." *The Progressive*. August.

McDonald-Walker, Suzanne. 2000. *Bikers: Culture, Politics, and Power*. London: Berg.

McHugh, Kathleen. 1998. "Women in Traffic: L.A. Autobiography." *South Atlantic Quarterly* 97:2: 391–412.

McRobbie, Angela. 1991. *Feminism and Youth Culture: From 'Jackie' to 'Just Seventeen.'* New York: Unwin.

Meeks, Kenneth. 2000. *Driving While Black*. New York: Broadway Books.

Miller, Abraham. 1973. "On the Road: Hitchhiking on the Highway." *Society*. July/August.

Miller, Daniel. 2001. *Car Cultures*. New York: Oxford Books.

Miller, Toby. 1998. *Technologies of Truth: Cultural Citizenship and the Popular Media*. Minneapolis: University of Minnesota Press.

Milling, Chapman J. 1938. "Hitchhike Passports." *Forum*. August.

Mizell, Louis. "Aggressive Driving." *American Automobile Association Foundation*

*for Traffic Safety*. August 29, 2000. http://www.aaafts.org/text/research/agdrtext
.html.

Moon, William Least Heat. 1982. *Blue Highways: A Journey into America*. New York:
Fawcet Crest.

Moorhouse, H. F. 1991. *Driving Ambitions: An Analysis of the American Hot Rod Enthusiasm*. Manchester: Manchester University Press.

*Motorcycle Driver Education Workshop*. 1967. Held at the University of Illinois Aug 4
and 5, 1967. Proceedings. 388.3475 m85p.

*Motorcycles in the United States: Popularity, Accidents, Injury Control*. U.S. Department of Health, Education, and Welfare. 1967. Public Health Service Publication
No. 999-UIH-7. Washington, D.C.

*Movin' On*. 1974–76. NBC.

Mowbray, A. Q. 1969. *Road to Ruin*. New York: J. B. Lippincott.

Mythen, Cabe. 2004. *Ulrich Beck: A Critical Introduction*. London: Pluto Press.

Nadel, Alan. 2005. *Television in Black-and-White America: Race and National Identity*. Lawrence: University of Kansas Press.

Nader, Ralph. 1965. *Unsafe at Any Speed*. New York: Grossman.

*National Velvet*. 1944. Dir. Clarence Brown. MGM.

"Nation's Top Negro Car Dealer." 1958. *Ebony*. April.

*Network*. 1976. Dir. Sidney Lumet. Warner Brothers.

"A New Rule of Thumb." 1969. *Newsweek*. June 16.

"Nuisance or a Boon? The Spread of Citizens' Radios." 1975. *U.S. News and World
Report*. September 29.

O'Connell, James, and Allen Myers. 1966. *Safety Last*. New York: Avon.

O'Malley, Patrick. 1996. "Risk and Responsibility." In *Foucault and Political Reason:
Liberalism, Neo-liberalism and Rationalities of Government*, ed. Andrew Barry,
Thomas Osborne, and Nikolas Rose. Chicago: University of Chicago Press, 1996.

Packer, Jeremy, and Craig Robertson. 2006. *Thinking With James Carey: Essays on
Communications, Transportation, History*. New York: Peter Lang.

Patton, Phil. 1986. *Open Road: A Celebration of the American Highway*. New York:
Touchstone.

Peteren, Alan, and Robin Bunton. 1997. *Foucault, Health and Medicine*. New York:
Routledge.

Pirsig, Robert M. 1975. *Zen and the Art of Motorcycle Maintenance*. New York: Bantam.

President's Action Committee for Traffic Safety. 1954. *Crusade for Traffic Safety*.
Washington D.C.: U.S. Government Printing Office.

*Proceedings: International Motorcycle Safety Conference*. Washington D.C.: U.S. Department of Transportation, 1975.

"Pueblo Law Hits 'Drive-by Stereos.'" 1995. *Denver Post*. February 15.

Quinn, Eithne. 2001. "'Pimpin' Ain't Easy': Work, Play, and 'Lifestylization' of the

Black Pimp Figure in Early 1970s America." In *Media, Culture, and the Modern African American Freedom Struggle*, ed. Brian Word. Gainesville: University Press of Florida.

Rae, John B. 1971. *The Road and the Car in American Life*. Cambridge, Mass.: MIT Press.

Ramsey, Richard. 1978. "The People versus Smokey Bear: Metaphor, Argot, and CB Radio." *Journal of Popular Culture* 8: 79–84.

Rathbone, Daniel B., and Jorg C. Huckabee. 1998. "Controlling Road Rage: A Literature Review and Pilot Study." *American Automobile Association Foundation for Traffic Safety*. August 29, 2000. http://www.aaafts.org/text/research/RoadRage Final.html.

*The Rebel Rousers*. 1969. Dir. Marin Cohen. Paragon International.

Reddy, Dick. 1954. "The Hazards of Summer Driving." *Cosmopolitan*. August.

Reeves, Jimmie, and Campbell Richard. 1994. *Cracked Coverage: Television News, the Anti-Cocaine Crusade, and the Reagan Legacy*. Durham: Duke University Press.

Reinhold, Robert. 1971. "Hitchhiking Curb Aimed at Drivers." *New York Times*. June 20.

Reisman, David. 1950. *The Lonely Crowd*. New Haven: Yale University Press.

Reiss M., and J. Haley. 1968. *Motorcycle Safety Final Report*. Washington, D.C.: National Highway Safety Bureau, 1968.

Rheingold Beer Advertisement. 1953. *New York Times*. April 27.

Robbins, Tom. 1976. *Even Cowgirls Get the Blues*. New York: Bantam Books.

Robertson, Craig. 2003. *"Passport Please": The United States Passport and the Documentation of Individual Identity*. Ann Arbor, Mich.: UMI Dissertations.

———. 2006. "The Ritual of Verification? The Nation, the State, and the U.S. Passport." In *Thinking With James Carey: Essays on Communications, Transportation, History*, ed. Jeremy Packer and Craig Robertson. New York: Peter Lang.

Roszak, Theodore. 1969. *The Making of a Counter Culture: Reflections on the Technocratic Society and Its Youthful Opposition*. Garden City: Anchor Books.

"Rules of Thumb." 1973. *Newsweek*. February 19.

"Rumors of the Road." 1979. *Human Behavior*. January.

*Run, Angel, Run*. 1969. Dir. Jack Starret. Fanfare.

Rusch, Elizabeth. 2002. "Biking While Black." *Mother Jones*. September–October.

"Ruth's Cadillacs Cause Unpleasantness in the South." 1952. *Ebony*. May.

Sands, Leo. 1975. "Radio on Wheels: The CB Communications Freeway. *Popular Mechanics*. December.

Schachtman, Noah. 2003. "Big Brother Gets a Brain." *Village Voice*. July 9–15.

Scharff, Virginia. 1991. *Taking the Wheel: Women and the Coming of the Motor Age*. New York: Free Press.

Schiller, Ronald, and Guy Henle. 1954. "America Discovers the Station Wagon: All-Purpose Car for Your Family. *Woman's Home Companion*. February.

Schjeldahl, Paul. 1998. "Gehry in Gear." *Village Voice*. September 1.

Schlossberg, John, and Edwin Brockman. 1977. *The All New Fact-Packed 1977/78 CB Guide*. New York: Bantam.

Schudson, Michael. 1978. *Discovering the News: A Social History of American Newspapers*. New York: Basic Books.

Sherril, Robert. 1977. "Raising Hell on the Highways." *New York Times Magazine*. November 27.

Silverman, Ann B. 1980. "Car-Pooling to the School on Time." *New York Times*. October 12.

Slim, Iceberg. 1969. *Pimp*. Los Angeles: Holloway House.

Smart, Barry. 1986. "The Politics of Truth and the Problem of Hegemony." In *Foucault: A Critical Reader*, ed. David Couzens Hoy. London: Basil Blackwell.

Smith, Jerome. 1981. "Gender Marking on Citizens Band Radio: Self-Identity in a Limited-Channel Speech Community." *Sex Roles* 7:6: 599–606.

*Smokey and the Bandit*. 1977. Dir. Hal Needham. Universal.

*Smokey and the Bandit II*. 1980. Dir. Hal Needham. Universal.

"Something Shady About All Those Tinted Car Windows." 1992. *Chicago Tribune*. July 8.

Sovine, Red. 1969. *Truck Driver's Prayer*. Starday.

Spigel, Lynn. 1992. *Make Room for TV: Television and the Family Ideal in Postwar America*. Chicago: University of Chicago Press.

*Stand By Me*. Dir. Rob Reiner. Sony Pictures.

"Statement of Purpose." 1945. *Ebony*. November.

Steinbeck, John. 1939. *The Grapes of Wrath*. New York: Viking.

———. 1967. *Travels With Charley*. New York: Penguin.

Stephens, Roger. 1946. *Down That Pan American Highway*. New York: Roger Stephens.

Stern, Jane. 1975. *Trucker: A Portrait of the Last American Cowboy*. New York: McGraw Hill.

Stewart, George R. 1953. *U.S. 40: A Cross Section of the United States*. New York: Houghton Mifflin.

———. 1957. *N. A. 1: Looking North and Looking South*. New York: Houghton Mifflin.

Subotnick, Ali. 1998. "Look Ma, No Hands." *ARTnews* 97:9.

"Sudden Death for the Second Million." 1952. *Ladies' Home Journal*. January.

Surface, Bill. 1969. *Family Safety*. New York: Doubleday.

"Survival 1995: *Motorcyclist* Editors' Greatest Hits." *Motorcyclist*. September.

Thistle, Frank. 1974. "Hitchhiking: There's No Better Way to Meet a Crazy." *PTA Magazine*. September.

Thomas, James. 1976. "Truck Stops, Truckers and Trucks." 1976. *Journal of Popular Culture* 3: 221–28.

Thomas, James H. 1979. *The Long Haul: Truckers, Truck Stops, and Trucking*. Memphis: Memphis State University Press.

Thompson, Hunter S. 1966. *Hell's Angels: A Strange and Terrible Saga*. New York: Ballantine.

"Thumbs Down on Hitchhiking." 1970. *Reader's Digest*. January.

*Thunderball*. 1965. Dir. Terence Young. MGM.

"Time to Stop Crying Wolf." 1952. *Ebony*. June.

"Too Many Drivers Are in the Dark About Window-Tinting Laws." 1988. *Los Angeles Times*. December 22.

Traffic Institute. 1964. *Instructor's Manual for Training Motorcycle Riders*. Evanston, Ill.: Northwestern University.

Turner, Frederick Jackson. 1894. "The Significance of the Frontier in American History." *Report of the American Historical Association for 1893*. Washington, D.C.

U.S. Department of Health, Education, and Welfare. 1967. *Motorcycles in the United States: Popularity, Accidents, Injury Control*. Washington, D.C.: Public Health Service Publication No. 999-UIH-7.

U.S. Department of Transportation. 2000. *Our Nation's Highways 2000*. http://www.fhwa.dot.gov/ohim/onh00/onh2p1.htm.

Urry, John. 1999. "Automotility, Car Culture and Weightless Travel." Department of Sociology, Lancaster University.

———. 2000. *Sociology Beyond Societies: Mobilities for the Twenty-First Century*. New York: Routledge.

Vanderborsch, Charles G. 1969. "The International Association of Chiefs of Police." *Traffic Supervision*. Washington, D.C: Library of Congress.

Vest, Jason, Warren Cohen, and Mike Tharp. 1997. "Road Rage." *U.S. News and World Report*. June 2.

Virilio, Paul. 1986. *Speed and Politics: An Essay on Dromology*. New York: Semiotext(e).

"Vogue's Tip Sheet on the New Cars." 1954. *Vogue*. February 5.

Wald, Matthew L. 1997. "Temper Cited as Cause of 28,000 Road Deaths a Year." *New York Times*. July 18.

Walker Laird, Pamela. 1996. "The Car Without a Single Weakness: Early Automobile Advertising." *Technology and Culture* 37.

Weinstein, Deena. 1991. *Heavy Metal: A Cultural Sociology*. Lanham, Md.: Lexington Books.

———. 1994. "Expendable Youth: The Rise and Fall of Youth Culture." In *Adolescents and Their Music: If It's Too Loud, You're Too Old*, ed. Jonathon S. Epstein. New York: Garland.

Weiss, Walter F. 1974. *America's Wandering Youth: A Sociological Study of Young Hitchhikers in the United States*. New York: Exposition Press.

"We Took the Kitchen With Us." 1952. *Woman's Home Companion*. July.

Wharton, Don. 1955. "Thumbs Down on Thumbs Up." *Reader's Digest*. June.

"What Causes Accidents?" 2001. MSNBC Special Report. April 14.

Whitney, Albert. 1949. *Man and the Motorcar*. New York: J. L. Little.

"Why the Negro Drives a Cadillac." 1949. *Ebony*. September.

*The Wild Bunch*. 1969. Dir. Sam Peckinpah. Warner Brothers.

*The Wild One*. 1954. Dir. Laslo Benedek. Kramer/Columbia.

Williams, Mark. *Road Movies: The Complete Guide to Cinema on Wheels*. New York: Proteus Books.

Willis, Paul. 1976. "The Cultural Meaning of Drug Use." In *Resistance through Ritual: Youth Subcultures in Post-war Britain*, ed. Stuart Hall and John Jefferson. London: Harper Collins Academic, 1976.

———. 1978. *Profane Culture*. New York: Routledge.

———. 1981. *Learning to Labor: How Working Class Kids Get Working Class Jobs*. New York: Columbia University Press.

Wojnarowicz, David. 1992. *Close to the Knives: A Memoir of Disintegration*. New York: Vintage Books.

———. 1991. *Memories that Smell Like Gasoline*. San Francisco: Artspace Books.

Wolf, William. 1970. "Hitchhiker to Stardom." *Boston Sunday Globe*. November 1.

Wolfe, Tom. 1969. *Electric Kool-Aid Acid Test*. New York: Bantam.

"Woman Driver Signals a 'Civil Rights' Protest." 1952. *New York Times*. February 1.

"Woman Driver Tested." 1936. *New York Times*. March 8.

"Women Disregard Rules in Buffalo." 1934. *New York Times*. July 1.

Woodbury, Clarence. 1948. "You and the New Car." *Ladies Home Companion*. August.

Woodward, Rick. 1998. "The Art of the Motorcycle." *ARTnews* 97:8: 167.

Yates, Brock. 1975. "One Lap of America." *Car and Driver*. February.

"You Can Be an Expert Driver." 1951. *Better Homes and Gardens*. September.

*You Only Live Twice*. 1967. Dir. Lewis Gilbert. MGM.

Youth Liberation of Ann Arbor. 1972. *Youth Liberation: News, Politics, and Survival Information*. Washington D.C.: Times Change Press.

Zamichow, Nora. 1994. "Wheel Rims Add Glitter, But Increasingly Lure Deadly Violence Crime." *Los Angeles Times*. October 8.

Zane, Maitland. 1970. "The Hardy Hitchhikers." *New York Times*. July 20.

Zbikowski, Dorte. 2002. "The Listening Ear: Phenomena of Acoustic Surveillance." In *ctrl[space]: Rhetorics of Surveillance from Bentham to Big Brother*, ed. Thomas Levin, Ursala Frohne, and Peter Weibel. Cambridge, Mass.: MIT Press.

Zeidman, Samuel D. 1937. "Thumb Fun!" *Review of Reviews*. April.

Zolotow, Maurice. 1955. "Your Emotions Can Kill You." *Cosmopolitan*. January.

Zonker, Patricia. 1978. *Murdercycles: The Facts About America's Number One Blood Sport*. Chicago: Nelson-Hall.

# INDEX

Federal Bureau of Investigation (FBI), 18, 78, 84–85, 88–89, 184

Federal Communications Commission (FCC), 21, 161–63, 165, 174, 175, 181–82, 184, 312 n. 16

Felson, Henry Gregor, 63–65

Fifty-five-mile-per-hour speed limit, 21, 172–73, 178, 182

Finch, Christopher, 294 n. 7

*Flaming Iguanas*, 158, 259

Fonda, Peter, 120–21

Ford, Harrison, 62

Ford Motor Company, 17, 264, 288–89; advertisements for, 36–39, 44, 289; Firestone tire design flaw and, 317–18 n. 1; Pinto design flaw and, 10

Foucault, Michel, 286; biopower/bio-politics and, 122, 124–25, 303 n. 8; dangerousness and, 214, 316 n. 40; discipline and, 124–25, 295 n. 9; on domination, 321 n. 6; governing at a distance and, 162–63, 170–71; normalization and, 316 n. 40; pastoral power and, 172, 271; power and knowledge and, 53, 295 n. 9; on power as productive, 282–83; on radical thought and politics, 146–47; on state and governmentality, 261; surveillance and, 171–73, 295 n. 9; truth claims and, 103

Freedom: as American trait, 2, 8, 28; from danger, 84; control vs., 186–87, 290; from driving, 267; as means of governance, 109–10, 163–64, 170–71, 256, 270–71, 282–83, 291; of mobility, 11, 25, 28, 185, 272; motorcycling and, 113; in opposition to safety, 18, 20, 27–28, 71; race and, 189–90, 199, 210–11, 227, 229–30; rhetoric of, 25, 36–38, 176, 264, 291; of the road, 82–83, 89–92, 102–4, 120–21; running away and, 100–102; of speech and communication, 163, 169–70; for women 39–40, 95–96

Frontier thesis, 2, 92, 294 n. 6

Fumento, 234, 249

Futurama, 278. *See also* Highways and Horizons

*Gatacca*, 275

General Motors, 5, 17, 22, 43–44, 72–73, 198–99, 201, 203, 208–9, 219, 277–78, 287, 295 n. 12

Gilroy, Paul, 196, 314–15 n. 18

Giuliani, Rudolph, 210

Global positioning system (GPS), 25, 230, 279, 281, 291. *See also* Communication, command, and control systems

Goffman, Erving, 257

*Good Housekeeping*, 33, 95, 97

Good Samaritanism, 18, 80–81, 84, 104

Governing, governance: of automobility 3, 23–24, 73–74, 261, 289–90; through community, 255–58; through culture, 154–57; at a distance, 162–63, 273; via epiphany, 134–46; governmentality and, 146, 261; hitchhiking and, 107; responsibilization and, 87; safety and, 11, 13–14, 52–53

Gregory, Dick, 208–9

Grossberg, Lawrence, 88, 122

Guantanamo Naval Base, 321 n. 6

*Hardcore*, 101–2

Hardt, Michael, 286

Harley Davidson Motorcycle Company, 20, 110, 114, 116, 117, 120, 127, 153–54

*Harpers Magazine*, 19, 91

Hartley, John, 34

Hay, James, 293 n. 4

Hell's Angels (motorcycle gang), 119–20, 122, 141–42

Hell's Angels (novel), 20, 111, 119–20, 127, 141–42, 151, 302 n. 94

Hell's Highway: The True Story of High-way Safety Films, 296 n. 41

Helmet law, 10, 136–37, 140–41

Highway Safety Foundation, 15

Highways and Horizons, 277–78

Highway system, 2, 5–6, 7, 35, 38, 73, 242, 250–51. See also Automated Highway System; Intelligent Vehicle Highway System, Intelligent Highway System

Hitch-Hiker, The, 19, 77–78, 86

Hitchhiking, 11, 18–19, 74–75, 77–110; economics and, 80, 90, 105–9, 290; gender and, 81–83, 86, 94–98, 303 n. 13; guides, 91–94; laws against, 83–84, 93–94, 98–100; overseas, 91

Holbrook Pierson, Melissa, 116, 128–29

Hollister incident, 19, 117–19

Honda Motor Company, 123, 130, 229

Hoover, J. Edgar, 84, 88–89

Hopper, Dennis, 122

Horse Whisperer, The, 114

Hot-rodding, 60–69, 258–59; drag clubs and, 67–69; film and, 60–63

Hummer, 288–89

Hummer Owners Prepared for Emergencies (HOPE), 288–89

Iceberg Slim's Pimp, 217–18

Indian Motorcycles, 116, 120, 127, 136

Innis, Harold, 163

Insurance industry, 286–88; creation of fear by, 18, 84–85, 310 n. 49; economic interests of, 10, 51–54, 130, 132, 287–88, 300 n. 55

Insurantial logic, 9–10, 35, 52–53, 275

Intelligent Vehicle Highway System, Intelligent Highway System (IVHS), 24–25, 250, 276–82, 284. See also Automated Highway System

Interstate highway system, 73, 94, 183, 278–79, 294 n. 7

Iraq, war in, 284, 291

James, Leon (Dr. Driving), 237, 241–43, 247–48, 252–58, 319 n. 28, 319–20 n. 49

Johnson, Jack, 193–94

Kerouac, Jack, 19, 87–88, 90–91

Kesey, Ken, 92

La Coste, Warren, 128, 308 n. 16

Ladies' Home Journal, 33, 60–61

Larson, John, 241–42

Leavitt, Helen, 294 n. 5

Life Magazine, 19, 117–18, 299 n. 36

Limbaugh, Rush, 319 n. 28

Long, Long Trailer, The, 40–41

Los Angeles Times, 220–22

Lost Highway, 114

Lupino, Ida, 78

Man and the Motorcar, 1, 3–7, 45, 256, 268–70

Mandatory seat belt laws, 226–27

Mann Act: gender and, 83, 303 n. 17; race and, 193

Martinez, Ricardo, 240, 251

Marx, Karl, 286

Masculinity and driving, 54–55, 61–63, 209, 259, 300–301 n. 75, 302 n. 89

McCall, C. W., 21, 177, 180

McCarthy, Cameron, 302 n. 107

McHugh, Kathleen, 34

McLuhan, Marshall, 248

and, 239–41, 248, 250–52; role of, in
traffic safety, 8–9, 49–51, 251–52, 312
n. 24. *See also* Racial profiling

Politics of mobility, 88–90, 98–101, 103,
105–6

Popular truth, 31–32, 49, 82, 84, 89, 97,
109

Power, knowledge, 3, 53, 236–37

Problem(atic) population, 10, 53–54,
73–74; hitchhiking and, 81, 83–84,
93–94; road rage and, 232–33, 260–
61; youth as, 35

Problematization, 31–32, 50–51, 57–58,
79, 81, 83, 272–74

Profiling, 285–86, 290–91. *See also*
Racial profiling

Psychology: of driving, 24, 47, 49–50,
54–60, 73–74, 243–48, 300–301 n. 75;
of the car, 296 n. 33

Quality Driving Circles (QDC), 254–58

Race: African American mobility and,
22–23; automotive culture and,
209–30; "new race" and, 6–8; racial
recognition and, 210–11, 225

Racial profiling, 225, 211–16, 229–30

Reagan, Ronald, 207, 210, 218

Reeves, Christopher, 113–14

Revolution in Military Affairs (RMA),
273, 283

Ridge, Tom, 282

Risk, risk analysis, 9, 52–54, 297 n. 47; as
positive experience, 141–42, 149–50;
risk(y) identity and, 284–85; statistics
and, 9, 16, 23–24, 49

Road rage, 23–24, 72, 74, 231–62

*Road Runners*, 68–69

Robbins, Tom, 96

Robertson, Craig, 315 n. 36

Rose, Nicholas, 67–68, 255–56, 261–62,
266

Roszak, Theodore, 304 n. 26

*Route 66*, 90

Safety: automobility vs., 13–17; crises
of, 8–9; morality and, 59–60, 62;
replacement of, by national security,
271–74; resistance to, 146–52; safety
conscious society and, 4–7; scare
tactics and, 136–42; technological
solutions and, 27–28, 125–27

*Safety Last*, 126

Scharff, Virginia, 303 n. 17

*Scholastic*, 91

Schrader, Paul, 101

Schudson, Michael, 249

Self-discipline, 115, 148–49, 268

Self-monitor, 74, 149, 172, 233, 257, 260

Senate hearings, 295–96 n. 26. *See also*
Congressional hearings

Sheikh, Lisa, 252, 256

*Smokey and the Bandit*, 21, 175

Sociology: automobility and, 1, 12; of
Chicago School and gangs, 119;
hitchhiking and, 102–3

Sovine, Red, 176–78

Space: as field of governance, 284;
gendered, 34–35, 39–44, 75, 95–96;
raced, 22, 193–95, 208, 210–15, 222;
smooth and striated, 276; territorialized and deterritorialized, 121

Speed, speeding, 5–6, 65, 66–69, 71,
155; motorcycling and, 116–17, 127,
130, 131, 133, 158; as sign of road rage,
240–43, 266; speed limit and, 8, 10,
16–17, 21, 46, 67, 72, 164, 171, 248,
251–52; trucking and, 165, 171–87. *See
also* Fifty-five-mile-per-hour speed
limit

World War I, 298 n. 23

World War II, 7, 32–33, 115–17, 268

Xzibit, 228

Youth: motorcycling and, 20, 117–19, 121–25, 129–32; as problem, 17–18, 60–73, 88–89, 251; radical youth movement and, 18–19, 88–89, 98–100, 110; Youth Liberation and, 101

*Zen and the Art of Motorcycle Maintenance*, 122, 306 n. 82

Jeremy Packer is an associate professor of communications at North Carolina State University. He is a coeditor of *Foucault, Cultural Studies, and Governmentality* (2003) and *Thinking with James Carey: Essays on Communications, Transportation, History* (2006).

Library of Congress Cataloging-in-Publication Data
Packer, Jeremy, 1970–
Mobility without mayhem : safety, cars, and citizenship / Jeremy Packer.
p. cm.
Includes bibliographical references and index.
ISBN-13: 978-0-8223-3952-6 (cloth : alk. paper)
ISBN-13: 978-0-8223-3963-2 (pbk. : alk. paper)
1. Automobiles—Social aspects—United States—History. 2. Motor vehicles—Social aspects—United States—History. I. Title.
HE5623.P295 2008
303.48′320973—dc22    2007038462